FOUR HUNDRED SOULS

A

COMMUNITY

HISTORY OF

AFRICAN AMERICA,

1619-2019

FOUR HUNDRED SOULS

EDITED BY

IBRAM X. KENDI
AND KEISHA N. BLAIN

THE BODLEY HEAD
LONDON

1 3 5 7 9 10 8 6 4 2

The Bodley Head, an imprint of Vintage, is part of the Penguin Random House group
of companies whose addresses can be found at global.penguinrandomhouse.com.

Penguin
Random House
UK

Copyright © Ibram X. Kendi and Keisha N. Blain 2021

Ibram X. Kendi and Keisha N. Blain have asserted their right to be identified as the
author of this Work in accordance with the Copyright, Designs and Patents Act 1988

Copyright to each contribution is owned by its author.
A list of copyright credits begins on page 471.

First published by The Bodley Head in 2021

www.penguin.co.uk/vintage

A CIP catalogue record for this book is available from the British Library

Hardback ISBN 9781847926869

Text design by Barbara M. Bachman

Printed and bound in Great Britain by Clays Ltd., Elcograf S.p.A.

The authorised representative in the EEA is Penguin Random House Ireland,
Morrison Chambers, 32 Nassau Street, Dublin, DO2 YH68.

Penguin Random House is committed to a sustainable future for
our business, our readers and our planet. This book is made from
Forest Stewardship Council® certified paper.

To all the souls

taken by COVID-19

CONTENTS

———

PART THREE

PART FOUR

PART FIVE

PART SIX

PART SEVEN

PART EIGHT

A COMMUNITY OF SOULS

—

An Introduction

IBRAM X. KENDI

IN AUGUST 1619, WHEN THE TWENTY "NEGROES" STEPPED OFF the ship *White Lion* and saw the British faces, they didn't know.

As their feet touched Jamestown, Virginia, they didn't know their lives would never be the same. They didn't know they would never see their community again.

Maybe they did remember the waters on the other side of the Atlantic Ocean surging into the Cuanza River that flowed into their West African homeland. Maybe they did not, too weary from the Middle Passage to picture Ndongo.

The West African nation of Angola derives its name from *ngola*, the royal title of Ndongo's head of state. The twenty Ndongo people who arrived in Jamestown in August 1619 had likely been seized in a slave raid earlier that year in modern-day Angola and brought to the Portuguese port colony of Luanda unaware that they were pregnant with a new community.

In Luanda, they joined about 350 other captured Ndongo people, all now herded like chattel onto the *São João Bautista*. The Portuguese slave traders set sail for Spain's plantation colony of Vera Cruz, Mexico. But they never arrived. The *White Lion*, an English privateer captained by John Jope, and another English privateer, the *Treasurer*, attacked in the glistening Caribbean waters. Not as abolitionists. As warriors against Europe's declining superpower at the time: Spain.

The men-of-war kidnapped from the kidnappers a community of sixty or so enslaved people, probably the healthiest and youngest aboard. They divided the human bounty between the *Treasurer* and the *White Lion* and headed north to the British colonies.

The twenty or so Ndongo people went into labor as the *White Lion* sailed up the Atlantic. Historical forces were shaping this community—and the community was shaping historical forces. The community delivered—and was delivered—on Virginia's shores on August 20, 1619, the symbolic birthdate of African America.

The Ndongo people were not the first people of African descent to land in the Americas. The first arrived before Christopher Columbus. Some people from Africa may have joined Spanish explorers on expeditions to the present-day United States during the sixteenth century. A revolt of enslaved Africans prevented Spanish slaveholders from establishing plantations in current-day South Carolina in 1526. "A muster roll for March 1619 shows that there were already thirty-two African slaves" in Virginia, historian Thomas C. Holt explained. But no one knows how or when they arrived. No one knows the *precise* birthdate of African America.

Perhaps no one is supposed to know. African America is like the enslaved woman who tragically never knew exactly when she was born. African America is like the enslaved man who chose his own birthday—August 20, 1619—based on the first record of a day when people of African descent arrived in one of the thirteen British colonies that later became the United States. Since 1619, the people of African descent arriving or born in these colonies and then the United States have comprised a community self-actualizing and sometimes self-identifying as African America or Black America. *African* speaks to a people of African descent. *Black* speaks to a people racialized as Black.

BLACK AMERICA CAN BE defined as individuals of African descent in solidarity, whether involuntarily or voluntarily, whether politically or culturally, whether for survival or resistance. Solidarity is the womb of community. The history of African America is the variegated story of this more-than-400-year-old diverse community. Ever since abolitionist James W. C. Pennington wrote *The Origin and History of the Colored People*, the inaugural history of Black America published in 1841, histories of Black America have almost always been written by a single individual, usually a man. But why not have a community of women and men chronicling the history of a community? Why not a Black choir singing the spiritual into the heavens of history? *Four Hundred Souls: A Community History of African America, 1619–2019* is that community choir for this historic moment.

Award-winning historian and editor Keisha N. Blain and I assembled a community of eighty Black writers and ten Black poets who represent some of the best recorders of Black America at its four-hundred-year mark. The community is a remarkable sampling of historians, journalists, activists, philosophers, novelists, political analysts, lawyers, anthropologists, curators, theologians, sociologists, essayists, economists, educators, poets, and cultural critics. The writing community includes Black people who identify (or are identified) as women and men, cisgender and transgender, younger and older, straight and queer, dark-skinned and light-skinned. The writers are immigrants or descendants of immigrants from Africa and the African diaspora. The writers are descendants of enslaved people in the United States.

Most of the pieces in this volume were written in 2019. We wanted the community to be writing during the four-hundredth year. We wanted *Four Hundred Souls* to write history and *be* history. Readers of this communal diary will forever know what Black Americans were thinking about the past and present when African America symbolically turned four hundred years old.

Each of the eighty writers here chronicles a five-year span of Black America's history to cover the four hundred years. The volume's first writer, the Pulitzer Prize–winning creator of *The 1619 Project*, journalist Nikole Hannah-Jones, covers from August 20, 1619, to August 19, 1624. The volume's final writer, Black Lives Matter cofounder Alicia Garza, covers from August 20, 2014, to August 20, 2019. Each piece has been written distinctively while being relatively equal in length to the others, making for a cohesive and connected narrative with strikingly different—yet unified—voices. A choir.

And collectively this choir sings the chords of survival, of struggle, of success, of death, of life, of joy, of racism, of antiracism, of creation, of destruction—of America's clearest chords, year after year, of liberty, justice, and democracy for all. Four hundred chords.

Each piece revolves around a person, place, thing, idea, or event. This cabinet of curiosities of eighty different topics from eighty different minds, reflecting eighty different perspectives, is essential to understanding this community of difference that has always defined Black America.

Four Hundred Souls is further divided into ten parts, each covering forty years. Each part concludes with a poem that recaptures its span of history in verse. These ten poets are like lyrical soloists for the choir, singing historical interludes. Sometimes history is best captured by poets—as these ten poets show. Indeed, the first verses sprang from those original twenty Ndongo people.

VIRGINIA'S RECORDER GENERAL John Rolfe, known as Pocahontas's husband, produced Black America's birth certificate in 1619. He notified Sir Edwin Sandys, treasurer of the Virginia Company of London, that "a Dutch man of Warr . . . brought not any thing but 20 and odd Negroes" and traded them for food.

Not anything?

Life was not promised for this newborn in 1619. Joy was not promised. Peace was not promised. Freedom was not promised. Only slavery, only racism, only the mighty Atlantic blocking the way back home seemed to be promised. But the community started to sing long before anyone heard that old spiritual:

We shall overcome,
we shall overcome someday.

There is no better word than *we*. Even when it is involuntary—meaning to be Black in America is to almost never be treated like an individual. The individual of African descent is not seen. The Black race is seen in the individual. All Black women are seen in the woman. All Black men are seen in the man.

Racist power constructed the Black race—and all the Black groups. *Them*. Racist power kept constructing Black America over four hundred years. *Them* constructed, again and again. But the antiracist power within the souls of Black folk reconstructed Black America all the while, in the same way we are reconstructing ourselves in this book. *We* reconstructed, again and again. *Them* into *we*, defending the Black American community to defend all the individuals in the community. *Them* became *we* to allow *I* to become *me*.

Individuals of African descent came to know that they would not become free until Black America became free. Individuals bonded into community to overcome.

And we—the community—did manage to overcome at times. The community managed to secure moments of joy and peace amid sorrow and war. The community managed to invent and reinvent cultures and subjects and objects again and again. The community managed to free itself again and again. But someday has not yet arrived. The community is still striving to overcome four hundred years later.

There may be no better word to encapsulate Black American history than *community*. For better or worse, ever since the twenty Ndongo people arrived, individuals of African descent have, for the most part, been made into a community, functioned as a community, departed the community, lived through so much as a community.

I don't know how the community has survived—and at times thrived—as much as it has been deprived for four hundred years. The history of Black America has been almost spiritual. Striving to survive the death that is racism. Living through death like spirits. Forging a soulful history. A history full of souls. A soul for each year of history.

Four Hundred Souls.

PART ONE

1619–1624

ARRIVAL

NIKOLE HANNAH-JONES

———

FOUR HUNDRED YEARS AGO, IN 1620, A CARGO SHIP LOWERED its anchor on the eastern shore of North America. It had spent sixty-six grueling days on the perilous Atlantic Ocean, and its 102 passengers fell into praise as they spotted land for the first time in more than two months.

These Puritans had fled England in search of religious freedom. We know all their names, names such as James Chilton, Frances Cook, and Mary Brewster. Their descendants proudly trace their lineage back to the group that established self-governance in the "New World" (that is, among the white population—Indigenous people were already governing themselves).

They arrived on the *Mayflower*, a vessel that has been called "one of the most important ships in American history." Every fall, regaled by stories of the courageous Pilgrims, elementary school children whose skin is peach, tan, and chestnut fashion black captain hats from paper to dress up like the passengers on the *Mayflower*. Our country has wrapped a national holiday around the Pilgrims' story, ensuring the *Mayflower*'s mythical place in the American narrative.

But a year before the *Mayflower*, in 1619, another ship dropped anchor on the eastern shore of North America. Its name was the *White Lion*, and it, too, would become one of the most important ships in American history. And yet there is no ship manifest inscribed with the names of its passengers and no descendants' society. These people's arrival was deemed so insignificant, their humanity so inconsequential, that we do not know even how many of those packed into the *White Lion*'s hull came ashore, just that some "20 and odd Negroes" disembarked and joined the British colonists in Virginia. But in his sweeping history *Before the Mayflower*, first published in 1962, scholar Lerone Bennett, Jr., said of the *White Lion*, "No one sensed how extraordinary she really was . . . [but] few ships, before or since, have unloaded a more momentous cargo."

This "cargo," this group of twenty to thirty Angolans, sold from the deck of the *White Lion* by criminal English marauders in exchange for food and supplies, was also foundational to the American story. But while every American child learns about the *Mayflower*, virtually no American child learns about the *White Lion*.

And yet the story of the *White Lion* is classically American. It is a harrowing tale—one filled with all the things that this country would rather not remember, a taint on a nation that believes above all else in its exceptionality.

The Adams and Eves of Black America did not arrive here in search of freedom or a better life. They had been captured and stolen, forced onto a ship, shackled, writhing in filth as they suffered and starved. Some 40 percent of the Angolans who boarded that ghastly vessel did not make it across the Middle Passage. They embarked not as people but as property, sold to white colonists who just were beginning to birth democracy for themselves, commencing a four-hundred-year struggle between the two opposing ideas foundational to America.

And so the *White Lion* has been relegated to what Bennett called the "back alley of American history." There are no annual classroom commemorations of that moment in August 1619. No children dress up as its occupants or perform classroom skits. No holiday honors it. The *White Lion* and the people on that ship have been expunged from our collective memory. This omission is intentional: when we are creating a shared history, what we remember is just as revelatory as what we forget. If the *Mayflower* was the advent of American freedom, then the *White Lion* was the advent of American slavery. And so while arriving just a year apart, one ship and its people have been immortalized, the other completely erased.

W.E.B. Du Bois called such erasure the propaganda of history. "It is propaganda like this that has led men in the past to insist that history is 'lies agreed upon'; and to point out the danger in such misinformation," he wrote in his influential treatise *Black Reconstruction* (1935). Du Bois argued that America had falsified the fact of its history "because the nation was ashamed." But he warned, "It is indeed extremely doubtful if any permanent benefit comes to the world through such action."

Because what is clear is that while we can erase the memory of the *White Lion*, we cannot erase its impact. Together these two ships, the *White Lion* and the *Mayflower*, bridging the three continents that made America, would constitute this nation's most quintessential and perplexing elements, underpinning the grave contradictions that we have failed to overcome.

These elemental contradictions led founder Thomas Jefferson, some 150 years later, to draft the majestic words declaring the inalienable and universal rights of men for a new country that would hold one-fifth of its population—the literal and figurative descendants of the *White Lion*—in absolute bondage. They would lead Frederick Douglass—one of the founders of American democracy—to issue in 1852 these fiery words commemorating an American Revolution that liberated white people while ensuring another century of subjugation for Black people:

This, for the purpose of this celebration, is the 4th of July. It is the birthday of your National Independence, and of your political freedom.

What have I, or those I represent, to do with your national independence? Are the great principles of political freedom and of natural justice, embodied in that Declaration of Independence, extended to us? Fellow-citizens; above your national, tumultuous joy, I hear the mournful wail of millions! whose chains, heavy and grievous yesterday, are, to-day, rendered more intolerable by the jubilee shouts that reach them. If I do forget, if I do not faithfully remember those bleeding children of sorrow this day, "may my right hand forget her cunning, and may my tongue cleave to the roof of my mouth!" To forget them, to pass lightly over their wrongs, and to chime in with the popular theme, would be treason most scandalous and shocking, and would make me a reproach before God and the world. My subject, then fellow-citizens, is AMERICAN SLAVERY. I shall see, this day, and its popular characteristics, from the slave's point of view. Standing there, identified with the American bondman, making his wrongs mine, I do not hesitate to declare, with all my soul, that the character and conduct of this nation never looked blacker to me than on this 4th of July! Whether we turn to the declarations of the past, or to the professions of the present, the conduct of the nation seems equally hideous and revolting. America is false to the past, false to the present, and solemnly binds herself to be false to the future.

The contradictions between these two founding arrivals—the *Mayflower* and the *White Lion*—would lead to the deadliest war in American history, fought over how much of our nation would be enslaved and how much would be free. They would lead us to spend a century seeking to expand democracy abroad, beckoning other lands to "Give me your tired, your poor, Your huddled masses yearning to breathe free," while violently suppressing democracy at home for the descendants of those involuntary immigrants who arrived on ships like the *White Lion*. They would lead to the elections—back-to-back—of the first Black president and then of a white nationalist one.

The erasure of August 1619 has served as part of a centuries-long effort to hide the crime. But it has also, as Du Bois explained in *The Souls of Black Folk*, robbed Black Americans of our lineage.

Your country? How came it yours? Before the Pilgrims landed we were here. . . . Actively we have woven ourselves with the very warp and woof of this nation,—we fought their battles, shared their sorrow, mingled our blood with theirs, and generation after generation have pleaded with a headstrong, careless people to despise not Justice, Mercy, and Truth, lest the nation be smitten with a curse. Our song, our toil, our cheer, and warning have been given to this nation in blood-brotherhood. Are not these gifts worth the giving? Is not this work and striving?

Would America have been America without her Negro people?

We cannot fathom it. Black Americans, by definition, are an amalgamated people. Our bodies form the genetic code—we are African, Native, and European—that made America and Americans. We are the living manifestation of the physical, cultural, and ideological merger of the peoples who landed on those ships but a year apart, and of those people who were already here at arrival. Despite the way we have been taught these histories, these stories do not march side by side or in parallel but are inherently intertwined, inseparable. The time for subordinating one of these histories to another has long passed. We must remember the *White Lion* along with the *Mayflower*, and the Powhatan along with the English at Jamestown. As Du Bois implores, "Nations reel and stagger on their way; they make hideous mistakes; they commit frightful wrongs; they do great and beautiful things. And shall we not best guide humanity by telling the truth about all this, so far as the truth is ascertainable?"

The true story of America begins here, in 1619. This is our story. We must not flinch.

AFRICA

MOLEFI KETE ASANTE

—

NO ONE KNOWS THE PRECISE DATE OF THE ARRIVAL OF Africans in North America. Africans could have arrived centuries before the historical record indicates. We know they arrived in what is now South Carolina with Lucas Vázquez de Ayllón in 1526. In 1565 a marriage was recorded between Luisa de Abrego, a free African woman, and Miguel Rodríguez, a Segovian conquistador, in Spanish Florida. This is the first known Christian marriage in what is now the continental United States. Those Africans in Spanish Florida eventually fought against the colonists and found refuge among Native Americans. The ones who did not escape into the forest eventually made their way to Haiti.

By the time the first British North American colony was established in 1607, Africans had already been in the Caribbean region for over one hundred years. Africans entered the Jamestown colony at Point Comfort in Virginia in 1619. By 1624, a tapestry of ethnic convergence in North America was already being woven. Yoruba, Wolof, and Mandinka people had already been taken from their coasts and brought to the Americas. It is this mixture of cultures that constitutes the quintessential African presence in the British North American colony.

Throughout these years, Africans back on the continent fought off the threat of political dismemberment as the European powers, including the English, Portuguese, Spanish, Dutch, and French, attacked the continent's people and resources in a constant barrage of murder, theft, and brutality. In 1626, on the eastern side of Africa, Emperor Susenyos I of Ethiopia agreed to allow Patriarch Afonso Mendes the primacy of the Roman See over the Ethiopian Orthodox Tewahedo Church. The Roman See quickly renamed the Ethiopian Church the Catholic Church of Ethiopia; this arrangement would not be permanent because the Ethiopians would later advance their autonomy.

In other developments taking place in Africa, Muchino a Muhatu Nzingha of the kingdoms of Ndongo and Matamba of the Mbundu people met with the Portuguese governor in 1622. By 1624, war was on the horizon. João Correia de Sousa, the Portuguese governor, offered Nzingha a floor mat, instead of a chair, to sit on during the negotiations—an act that in Mbundu custom was appropriate only for subordinates. Unwilling to accept this degradation, Nzingha ordered one of her servants to get down on the ground, and she sat on their back during negotiations. She agreed to become a Catholic in 1622, but by 1626 she knew she had made a mistake in her fight against Portuguese slave traders. Whatever negative traits the Portuguese saw in Africans, the English Puritans came to Massachusetts in the late 1620s with an attitude just as horrible. They believed that Africans were similar to the devil and practiced an evil and superstitious religion.

Back in West Africa, the remnants of the Ghana, Mali, and Songhay kingdoms were losing their people to the encroaching European merchants who kidnapped Africans in what became the largest movement of one population by another in world history. Mandinka, Peul, Wolof, Yoruba, Hausa, and other ethnic groups would be uprooted on one side of the ocean and planted on the other.

Since no *African slaves* were brought to the Americas, but only *Africans who were enslaved*, it is safe to assume that among the arrivals in the 1620s were the usual human variety of personalities with an equally impressive number of character traits. Out of the cauldron that was developing under the hegemony of Europeans emerged several recognized types: the recorder of events, the interpreter of events, the creator of events, the advancer of events, the maintainer of events, and the memorializer of events.

Each of these archetypes was rooted in African cultures and stretched back in time long before 1624. The *recorder* (whom the Wolof and Mandinka referred to as the *djeli* and whom the Serer, Asante, Yoruba, and Bakongo called by other names) functioned as the one who listened to everything, saw everything, and remembered the secrets of all, so that he or she could later recall patterns of the past. The *interpreter* was a seer, whose purpose was to make sense out of the familiar and the unfamiliar, so that the African population would be sustained by the integration of African motifs, icons, and values into the rifts of the new place. The *creator* of events emerged in the 1620s as the African person who farmed, cleared the forests, and confronted the difficulties of living in a world made by Europeans, whose assaults on African dignity and Native Americans' inheritance were constant. The *advancer* of events was the person who sought to adjust African cultures and values to the newly forming American society. To advance events is to expose the nature of American activities in the early frontiers of the colonies and to encourage a form of governance that would secure the rights of Africans. The *maintainer* of events exhibited a clear conception of the society in order to service the polity with integrity, harmony, and preparedness for any eventuality. The *memorializer* of events assumed a spiritual role in the community, suggesting to other Africans in the colonies the need for African people to take account of and remember the events that created community. Many times these individuals would bring out the spiritual characteristics inherited from their African origins.

All these roles were played by women and men in the early period of African socialization in the Americas; they would become the archetypes through which the African community would tell its own story, establishing its heroic nature and distinguishing its epochal struggle for liberation from that of other peoples over the generations.

WHIPPED FOR LYING WITH A BLACK WOMAN

IJEOMA OLUO

—

MY MOTHER IS WHITE, AND I AM BLACK. SHE IS MY BIO-logical mother. Half of my genetic makeup came from her. My skin is not the rich deep brown of my father's, having been lightened to a deep tan by my mother. I have my mother's eyes, my mother's face—and yet she will always be white, and I will always be Black. When people want to know why my skin is the color it is, or why my features are racially vague, I will say, "I am half Nigerian," or "I am mixed-race Black," or "my mother is white." But I am not white—I'm not even half-white. My mother is white. I am Black.

My mother is white and I am Black because in 1630 a Virginia colonial court ordered the whipping of Hugh Davis, a white man, as a punishment for sleeping with a Black woman. He was whipped in front of an assembled audience of Black and white Virginians, to show everyone what the punishment would be for "abusing himself to the dishonor of God and shame of Christians, by defiling his body in lying with a negro."

Prior to the whipping of Hugh Davis, anti-Black racism already existed in the colonies. At the time, when there were scarcely one hundred Africans in Virginia, anti-Black racist ideas operated mostly in religious terms—whites referred to themselves as Christians and Africans as heathens.

Anti-Black racism did not arrive on the shores of the New World fully formed. Step by step, anti-Blackness and slavery justified, strengthened, and expanded each other, building a vast network of systemic inequity that dictates large amounts of Black and white American life to this day.

But in 1630 the whipping of Hugh Davis wrote one important concept of race in America into law: the exclusivity of whiteness.

Davis was not whipped because he had polluted a Black woman. There was no record of the Black woman in question being punished for polluting herself with whiteness. Davis was whipped for polluting whiteness—his own and that of his community. This was the first recorded case of its kind in the United States, establishing that whiteness was susceptible to pollution from sexual contact with Blackness, and that "pure" whiteness must be protected through law.

I remember my mother asking me a few years ago why I did not call myself half-white. I explained to her: "You cannot become part-white."

Whiteness is a ledge you can only fall from.

The fact that whiteness was something that could exist only in purity, not in percentages, was something reinforced throughout my entire life. Some of my earliest childhood memories are of other children asking me if I was adopted. After answering that no, I was not adopted, the white lady they saw with me was my mother, they would still stare at me confused, unable to comprehend how I came to be. As I grew older, teachers, bosses, and police officers would see only my Blackness. When people met my mother, they would look at her with pity, imagining the story of a white woman lost—lured and abandoned by Blackness and left with two Black children to forever remind her of her fall.

To many, my mother represented the fears of those white colonial Virginians who had ordered Hugh Davis whipped brought to life. Purity forever tainted, bloodlines lost. Establishing whiteness as a race of purity meant it was not something that could be mixed, it could only be turned into something else—removing it from whiteness altogether. The idea that racial mixing would not spread whiteness or even alter it but would destroy it would become a primary motivation for many racist laws and attitudes.

With the whipping of Hugh Davis, we saw the first separation of Black from white in the North American colonies as an issue of white survival instead of racial preference. This fear would lead to violence far beyond the whipping of a white man for lying with a Black woman. Shortly after establishing the legal need to protect whiteness from contamination, the consequences for such contamination were shifted from the white participant to the Black person who dared pollute whiteness. By 1640, when another white man was brought before Virginia law for impregnating a Black woman, it was the Black woman who was whipped, while the white man was sentenced to church service.

By the 1800s, this fear and anger over the possible destruction of whiteness justified the segregation of cities and towns, workplaces and schools, that would consign Black Americans to substandard living, working, and educational conditions. It justified the arrests, beatings, and lynching of Black Americans. Even today the fear of racial destruction heard in warnings of "white genocide" made by white hate groups rationalizes violence against Black Americans.

The idea of white purity not only served to narrowly define whiteness for over four hundred years, it also ensured that Blackness could hardly benefit socially, politically, or financially from proximity to whiteness in any meaningful way. If a white parent's offspring ceased to be white because the other parent was Black, then those offspring were cut off from all opportunities that whiteness afforded, and so were their offspring for generations to come. If we cannot always recognize Blackness in skin tone, we can recognize Blackness in unemployment rates, poverty rates, school suspension rates, arrest rates, and life expectancy.

And so today I am Black, and my mother is white. I am Black because I have no choice but to be, and I am Black because I choose to be. While I may always be Black to the cop who pulls me over, and to the manager evaluating my work performance, I also choose to be Black with my friends and family. I choose to look in the mirror and see Black.

I have been accused of allowing white supremacist notions of race to dictate how I see myself. I have been told that in this day and age, over fifty years since antimiscegenation laws were deemed unconstitutional, I have the freedom to claim the whiteness of my mother.

Every time I was told that my hair was too kinky, it was my Black hair that was disparaged. Every time I was told that my nose was too wide, it was my Black nose that was rejected. Every time I was called a monkey or a gorilla, it was my Blackness that was hated. Every time I was called loud or angry, it was my Blackness that was feared.

And it is my Blackness that has fought back. My Blackness that has survived. The vast majority of Black Americans, often through the rape of Black ancestors by white enslavers, have the ancestry of white Americans running through them. But when the privileges of whiteness were kept from us, it was our Blackness that persevered. I am so very proud of that.

I love my mother. I see her face when I look in the mirror. But whiteness, as a political and social construct, exists because of the fear of my very existence, and it functions to this day to aid in my oppression and exploitation.

Until the systemic functions of whiteness that began with the whipping of Hugh Davis are dismantled, I cannot claim whiteness. And as long as my survival is tied to my ability to resist the oppression of white supremacy, I'll be damned if I'll let whiteness claim me.

1634–1639

TOBACCO

DaMaris B. Hill

——

BEFORE HE BECAME A PLANTER, ROLFE TOLD GO-GO THAT stalagmite was a diamond. He had never seen any actual diamonds but couldn't admit it.

Diamonds in the colonies were travelers' lies, like the streets of gold and the mercy of missionaries. The only real thing in his life was an African girl he plucked from Bermuda, the one twin who wasn't traded for Spanish tobacco seeds on the high seas off the legal coast of what used to be called Virginola. That girl was carried into Jamestown and appeared as a speck of wonder to the eye of a young Indian princess called Pocahontas. This girl's skin with its brush of indigo was a lush wonder among the pale settlers the Indian princess witnessed.

And now Rolfe loved her. He showed her how to find the veins in each tobacco leaf, showed her how to crawl between the rows and look for parasites. Ever since the enslaved African and tobacco appeared in Jamestown, English colonists found ways to trade for food and plant tobacco after the last frost. Pocahontas was young and sure that this little girl was a Jogahoh, a trickster who knew the secrets of the earth. And that became the name they started calling her, Go-Go. What power did Rolfe have to make the magic people do his bidding?

No one was left to tell the record keepers about Go-Go's sister, the one Rolfe traded for the sweetest tobacco seeds a Spanish conquistador could smuggle. He quickly pacified his anxiety about leaving the other twin with the conquistadors sailing back to Portugal, because they were on their way to their wives. Why worry about the girl? Where was the room for worry in the New World? The anxiety about a lost twin? Where was space to remember any of them?

It is August 1635. Rolfe is long dead, and the indigo girl Go-Go is an old woman who has made generations in the marshes of Virginia, while the English cycle in on sponsored passage to the Americas, dreaming about a better life than London had to offer. In the squalor of London, they were nursed at poverty's breasts, especially the women. Even with the odds of three men to one woman, none of them found fortune on the passage. No man had a penny to pay. After a few weeks at sea and as the rations got low, few of the men honored English law or cared how some hoity man lost his head for raping his rich wife, as was the punishment. The men were tired of taking turns on one another and began to reason about raping women. This was not the only abuse these English women would come to know. Their bodies would come to know how a snake is wicked only if it is under your foot and how a leech can become an anchor. They came to know that either could drown you in a few inches of water and that the lush leaves of tobacco did not provide shade. They came to know the work without boundaries.

Before and after 1636, ships come from Angola and the Caribbean carrying Africans who add life to the scourge of death in the colonies. When they arrive, the Indians and indentured whites who speak to them tell them about the ten colonists who became two in the first year. Then they tell them about the packs of English who creep up like wild crops in the forest and always with a woman running away. Then they say that everything was new when the Rolfe showed up with seeds and the indigo girl, the Jogahoh, who grew up without sickness and became the woman Go-Go. Then they count her children and grandchildren aloud. They explain how to know her. Her hands and skin stained blue with other-world Godliness. The Indians tell the Africans that Go-Go was the one who made this tobacco spring from the earth. The Indians tell the Africans that the English have proven to be liars since the first lot, and that the latest lie is: "Only the African can keep the Spanish tobacco alive." The lie is that the Africans are the only ones who can cut tobacco at the base and survive the stalk.

The truth is that King Charles can't get enough of taxes. By 1639, he divides Virginia into shires, and everyone needs to count every body to calculate the assessment owed to the king for his armies. It is in this year that Go-Go calls out her sister's sacred name as she watches her pale-eyed granddaughter sold across the river to cover the tax on tobacco.

BLACK WOMEN'S LABOR

Brenda E. Stevenson

———

ENSLAVEMENT IN THE AMERICAS WROUGHT MULTIPLE, complex horrors in the lives, families, communities, and cultures of the millions of Africans who fell captive to the inhumane system of the Atlantic slave trade. Those who arrived in British North America were hardly immune to these brutalities. Not the least of these abuses was the persistent assault on gendered identities as part of the effort to erase captives' humanity, self-worth, and traditional roles within their Indigenous cultures and communities.

One of the first attempts to codify these practices took place in March 1643, when Virginia's General Assembly passed the following measure:

> Be it also enacted and confirmed that there be four pounds of tobacco . . . and a bushel of corn . . . paid to the Ministers within the several parishes of the colony for all titheable persons, that is to say as well for all youths of sixteen years of age as [upwards?] and also for all negro women at the age of sixteen year.

These few words designated a Black female of sixteen years or older as a "tithable"—meaning that taxes paid to the church would be assessed on these women. Neither white nor Indigenous women had that distinction. In that way, Virginia's earliest leaders legally equated

African women with men, erasing these women's public claim to feminine equality with other women. These elite white men did so through British colonial society's most important legal institution, their elected governance body. Their justification was that taxing Black women was a necessary part of the financial support structure for the colony's most important sociocultural establishment, the Church of England.

The impact on the lives of African women in the colony, whether they were indentured, enslaved, or free, was immediate. Enslavers passed the pressure of having to provide the taxes assessed for their Black bonded women directly onto these women. The legal designation of Black women as fundamentally different, in body and character, from other women in colonial society directly influenced African women's workloads and the punishments they endured if they could not meet these expectations. These enhanced labor assignments, in turn, damaged women's health, prenatal care, and the amount of attention that they could give their dependent kin. Single, free Black women struggled to make their own tax payments, a financial obligation that contributed to the likelihood of their impoverishment and dependency. They also suffered the consequences of being viewed as less desirable spouses in the eyes of other free Blacks who were reluctant to take on their additional financial responsibilities. This "othering" of Black women in colonial American society was foundational in the assault on Black femininity, masculinity, the Black family, and the sociocultural roles of Black adults.

From this initial effort, and from many more that were rapidly legalized or customarily practiced in the seventeenth century, an image of Black womanhood emerged that adhered to female gender prescriptions neither of Africans nor of Europeans. It was a womanhood synonymous with market productivity, not motherhood; with physical prowess instead of feminine vulnerability; and with promiscuity rather than modesty or a heightened moral sensibility. Such a distortion of Black women's physical, emotional, cultural, gendered, and spiritual selves led to the broad public's imagining of Black women as workhorses, whores, and emasculating matriarchs. Today this historical misrepresentation remains a common "justification" for the theft of our children; our physical, medical, political, and sexual exploitation; and our broad criminalization.

The timing of the 1643 legislation was neither accidental nor incidental. It occurred once it was clear that the colony would survive and could turn a profit with sufficient labor resources. By the third decade of British residence, African female workers were a part of the formula for colonial settler success. The fledgling British mainland colony's 1620 census counted fifteen such female workers that year, all thought to have arrived on the *White Lion* and the *Treasurer* in 1619. While more than a few perished in the Anglo-Powhatan War of 1622 or other military hostilities, as well as from disease, exposure, malnutrition, random acts of violence, poor medical attention, and accidents, the cargoes of bound Black female workers continued to arrive. Although no population enumerations have been recovered for 1640, ten years later Virginia was home to three hundred Africans, many female laborers among them.

The skills that the first arrivals brought with them prepared them to be productive farmers and livestock keepers. Many who arrived from Angola, for example—like many of the earliest captives in British North America—were skilled farmers. In their home communities, they had cultivated a variety of crops, some for many generations. The crops included various types of corn and grains such as millet and sorghum, as well as bananas, plantains, beans, peanuts, pineapples, rice, pepper, yams, sweet potatoes, sugarcane, palm oil, and citrus fruits. They were accustomed to clearing land by using slash-and-burn methods, and they used hoes to prepare soil and to remove weeds. They practiced crop rotation. Many also had raised, butchered, traded, and prepared for the table cattle, goats, chickens, sheep, pigs, and other livestock.

Labor in their West-Central African homes was gender distinct, unlike their experiences in early-seventeenth-century Virginia and other British settler colonies. Among farming peoples, men cleared the brush and cultivated tree crops such as those that produced palm oil and wine and from which they made medicines and sculpted. Women planted, weeded, and harvested other crops. Men were responsible for building houses, making cloth, sculpting, working iron, and long-distance trading and hunting. Women cooked, cared for their children, and performed other domestic tasks. Women in seaside communities also dived for marketable seashells and boiled salt water in order to produce salt, another highly sought-after market item.

It did not take long before their skills as livestock keepers, domestics, and especially agriculturalists were recognized, prompting one mid-seventeenth-century Virginia governor to note that the planting of crops would occur "on the advice of our Negroes." Settlers, however, demanded that Black women perform the same tasks as Black men. These women, like Black and white indentured men, had to clear their owners' heavily wooded frontier lands, carry wood, and help construct dwellings, outhouses, and fences. Archaeological records from the seventeenth-century Chesapeake, for example, document the kinds of upper skeletal damage that young Black women sustained, probably by carrying heavy loads of wood on their heads or shoulders. They routinely planted, nurtured, weeded, and harvested corn and other plants, in addition to caring for tobacco—the most important cash crop of the era, and a very labor-intensive one. As early as five years after the first known captive arrivals, one planter could boast that his Black and white laborers produced a tobacco crop valued at ten thousand English pounds.

When not working outside under the supervision of men, African women worked for their mistresses. Their assigned domestic tasks included barnyard labor, tending to livestock, cooking, butchering, salting and preserving meat, making soap and candles, housecleaning, laundry, sewing, carding, spinning, weaving, bathing, dressing and dressing the hair of their mistresses, and caring for children—their owners' and their own. Many also had to perform sexual labor.

Between 1639 and 1644, work defined Black women's lives, and the law of 1643 codified their differentiation from other women. This law led to a host of inhumane, defeminizing consequences for African and African-descended women. The endorsement by British North America's first permanent colony's two essential bodies of influence, the General Assembly and the Church of England, proved unshakable.

ANTHONY JOHNSON, COLONY OF VIRGINIA

Maurice Carlos Ruffin

———

ICOME DOWN TO MY WATER ON MORNINGS SUCH AS THESE. Sunrise breaks through fog and tree limb like skin beneath skin, the smell of another's fire. This is what the memory of my own death and rebirth has done. Killed my sleep and woke my spirit so that rest is not possible. So many mornings, I wander as a sick bear cub does. It's fog, a dream to my mind. But clear as this gnarled branch under my boot.

In the hold of the small ship that stole me from my home. Tall but not yet strong I crouched in the dark with others like me, six men and two women between barrels of red palm oil and what bolts of Europe wool and silk went unsold. We shared skin, but not tongue. One woman's eye never blinked during her hand motions that showed when she was taken three children of her flesh became orphans.

Lashed to the underdeck in chains, we gaped like mud fish when water pooled in the hull not well sealed by pitch. I never left the green hills of my homeland, which the Portuguese men had taken to hunting as their own. But we were on the vast water, and I knew our pomegranate husk would sink if sea came. After starving on rope-tough meat and sitting in my own leavings for endless days, I liked to dive deep and never rise. But not so. We landed ashore. My rebirth and years of forced work followed.

But that was before. How my life has bloomed like a strange flower. Since I met my Mary. Skin of my skin. Soul of my soul. I was told of steel horses. But that is less pleasing to me than this: once my freedom earned, my term of service done, my freedom fee collected— no more lashes to drive me to the field before the cockerel's crow— I bought Mary's freedom and the contracts of five men to work my will. And in the way of the good laws of this land—King Charles's laws—gathered a fifty-acre plot for each manservant. I claim this stretch of God's land as my own. And I work as I please.

Rising the path from the riverbank, I find a small bush. Not a bush but a deer melting back to earth. Feasted on. Nature's way. But I gather a few leafy branches, cover the critter, and cross myself. My hand comes to the right side of the cross, where Jesus's palm hung bleeding, when I freeze for leaves crunching behind. I don't have my musket or my scythe. But I have hands. I clinch my fist.

"Pap!" the voice says. My youngest, Walter, runs in the bramble, his knees bouncing in the dew. "Quick! Come see."

"Such a call!" I say, rubbing Walter's head. "Respect your old father." His mouth moves. His eyes dart. But he does not bend his head. I squeeze his shoulder in pride of him. His nerves ride him. That is his spirit. But his body is coming on strong, less bedeviled by bad humors in his lungs. The ones that took his older brothers when they were cubs.

"That white man, one of the brothers Parker. He walking in the patch." Walter leads along the creek trail, the beery nose scent of sassafras everywhere. Turtle climbs a log. Reeds and rushes brush my legs. Many acres. God's land. My land. To be Walter's land.

My tobacco field with a ghost mist on it. The man stoops here and again. He touches my leaves as if they are born of his labor. Robert Parker. Some of these fields were his father's. But today the Parkers have only one man under contract and a few hay acres upriver.

John Casor, my third man, holds the rein of the Parker horse and holds a roped calf. John fears his old master, Robert. John stands on the path by the field, his look goes everywhere except to Robert.

"You let a fox in my patch," I say. I send Walter to the cornfield to give word.

John dips his head. "He wouldn't listen to the likes of Poor John." We have the same outside color, but his insides are smoke to me. He shows dumb, but I know he is cunning. He shows weak, but he has a lion inside. He works less well than he can, so I task him to my fields longer.

My hands on my sides, I say, "You come out from there."

"Look ye here," Robert says, his sweaty hair dripping onto his shoulders, a long dagger in his belt. He has a false manner of speaking, a squire's manner. They call Robert a freeboot who betrayed the crown during his journeys. Other men would be in stocks if not in servitude. But here he stands. Free as clover. "It's my old mate, Antonio."

I step into my patch. When he came before, he did not smile as I picked at his body for flea beetles that eat tobacco. But that plague is gone, or I would pick again. "You know my chosen name is Anthony, after the saint."

"So it is," he says.

Colin, my best field man, gallops to the field's edge and dismounts. White-skinned. A big man, a head above us.

"I came as soon as I heard, Mr. Johnson. Now, this one wouldn't be bothering you today, would he? I'll toss him in the shuck if that's the matter."

"If you would have your head cleaved from your shoulders, papist." Robert spits in the dirt. Touches his dagger.

"No," I say. "I have need of an animal." My oldest daughter, Eliza, is to be married to a freeman like myself called Wiltwyck of New Sweden. I chose a fatted calf as her gift. A fat calf would mean a strong union and hardy children. But disease spread among the many beasts of the colony last spring. Robert has the last ones.

"I assure you this is finest of my stock, valiant Moor."

A fine calf announces itself the same as people, by temper. I run my hand across the babe's glossy coat. I place my finger at its teeth, and the creature suckles, its ears moving. A fine calf. I give Robert a leather pouch of forty shillings. He counts each one.

Colin passes to me a legal paper that I unroll. The village justice made this. I am not learned in the work of scribes, but my Mary, who has eyes of stars, is and smiled at it. My daughter Eliza, who is as learned of work of scribes, will also smile when she has her calf. I show the paper to Robert, who does not look at it.

"I need not sign a deed for the likes of you!" Robert pushes the paper away. "Take the animal as he stands. That is your proof of possession."

"The Lord covers me and mine in eternity, and the king's law covers me and mine here. I keep my papers."

Robert spits again. Part of it hits his own boot. He mounts his horse and pulls the calf behind. Down the path, he dismounts. His dagger flashes in the sun and disappears by the animal's neck. The calf falls to dirt. Robert rides off. Colin shakes his head. John Casor shows his teeth. Colin says Robert has my shillings, and he is right. The calf's tail twitches in the dirt.

"What now, sir?" Colin says.

I am back on the ship in the hold. But my sons and daughters and their sons and daughters are with me in the dark. Chains clink on their legs. We are on the shore. We are in the woods. A girl in the mist of tomorrows watches me from a coach tied to one of the steel horses I was told of. She laughs like she is happy to meet me. And behind her in the coach are her sons and daughters and their sons and daughters.

"The calf dies," I say, "but the law will always hold me. And my Eliza will have her calf."

THE BLACK FAMILY

HEATHER ANDREA WILLIAMS

———

I N 1649 THREE HUNDRED BLACK PEOPLE LIVED IN THE ENGLISH colony of Virginia. Even fewer Black people lived in the more northern Dutch town of New Amsterdam that later, under British rule, would become New York City.

Slavery had not yet evolved into the pervasive institution that would devour the labor and lives of millions of people of African descent. Still, during these early years, among the small numbers of Black people who were free, enslaved, or lingering in some degree of unfreedom, it is possible to glimpse evidence of family formations and priorities that would become far more visible as slavery expanded.

By the time they reached an American colony, most captives had already experienced forced separation from their families and communities, some of them more than once. They had been taken from families and communities in West and Central Africa and may have lost contact with a close shipmate after the Middle Passage journey. Some lost the family and community they created while they sojourned in the Caribbean or South America before being taken to North America.

Once in America, some of these people created families through marriage, childbirth, and informal adoptions. They remained vulnerable to being sold or given away. Many of them struggled to keep their families intact, to provide protection for their loved ones, and to take advantage of loopholes that might extricate them and their family members from enslavement.

Some Black people also responded to the era's high mortality rates by taking responsibility for children who were not their own. In New Amsterdam, Emmanuel Pietersen and his wife, Dorothe Angola, raised a child of their deceased friends, and when the child reached the age of eighteen, Pietersen sought to gain legal protection for him. In his petition to officials of the colony, Pietersen asserted that his wife had stood as "godmother or witness at the Christian baptism" of Anthony, whose parents had died shortly thereafter. The petition asserted that Dorothe, "out of Christian affection, immediately on the death of his parents, hath adopted and reared him as her own child, without asking assistance from anyone in the world, but maintained him at her own expense from that time unto this day." Pietersen said that he too wanted to promote the well-being of the boy and asked the authorities to officially recognize that Anthony was born the child of free parents, had been raised by free persons, and should therefore be declared free and capable of inheriting from Pietersen. Emmanuel Pietersen realized the tenuous status of Black people in the colony and sought to ensure that the child he and his wife had raised would always be recognized as a free person, despite also being Black. The council granted Pietersen's petition.

Pietersen used very deliberate language in his petition. He was careful to assert that Anthony had received a Christian baptism and that Dorothe Angola had cared for the child out of her "Christian affection." These were consequential claims in those early years for Black people desiring to be acknowledged as free. After all, the Dutch, English, and other Europeans operated at the time under the belief that Christians should not be enslaved, and part of their stated justification for enslaving Africans was that they considered them heathens. If Black people could then prove their Christianity through baptism or marriage in the Christian church, as occurred in New Amsterdam, they might logically be exempted from slavery.

It seems that the baptism loophole was effective for some time. Between 1639 and 1655, Black parents presented forty-nine children for baptism in the Dutch Reformed Church in New Netherland. But in a society become ever more dependent on the labor of enslaved people, laypeople as well as clergy grew concerned about the corre-

spondence between baptism and freedom, and Christianity and freedom.

What would later become New York closed this loophole for ma-
neuvering out of slavery. By 1656, the Dutch Reformed Church, caring more about saving slavery than saving souls, had stopped baptizing
Black people. "The Negroes occasionally request that we should baptize their children," wrote a clergyman who ministered to the forty
people Governor Peter Stuyvesant owned in Manhattan. "But we
have refused to do so, partly on account of their lack of knowledge
and of faith, and partly because of the worldly and perverse aims on
the part of the said Negroes. They wanted nothing else than to deliver
their children bodily from slavery, without striving for piety and
Christian virtues."

Ironically, the minister deemed Black parents' desires to free their
children "worldly and perverse" because of their emphasis on *physical*
freedom, presumably in contrast to the *spiritual* freedom of the Christian people who claimed ownership over them. Although the minister went on to say that when he deemed it appropriate, he did baptize
a few enslaved youth, he also noted, "Not to administer baptism
among them for the reasons given, is also the custom among our colleagues."

Over time, New Netherland and other colonies imposed more
and more restrictions against Black freedom. When Virginia codified
the fact that baptism would not free Black people from enslavement,
the language of the statute focused on "children that are slaves by
birth." In that colony, too, policy makers blocked parents from using
Christian baptism as a means of gaining freedom for their children.

In Virginia, Emmanuel and Frances Driggus took care of two
adopted children, one-year-old Jane and eight-year-old Elizabeth, in
addition to Ann, Thomas, and Frances, the three children who were
born to the couple. They all belonged to Captain Francis Pott, although Jane and Elizabeth were not enslaved but indentured for
terms of several years. To cover his debts, Pott mortgaged Emmanuel
and Frances and eventually was forced to turn them over to his creditor, who lived twenty miles away from Pott's farm, where all the children remained. Emmanuel, who had been given a cow and a calf by

Pott, was eventually able to save enough money to purchase Jane's freedom in 1652, thereby releasing her from her indenture at age eight, twenty-three years earlier than scheduled.

By the end of that same year, Pott prevailed in a lawsuit against his creditor, and Emmanuel and Frances Driggus returned to live on his property in Northampton. Seven years had elapsed since they had lived with their children. Upon their return to Northampton, Emmanuel Driggus faced a new threat to his ability to free himself and his family from slavery through the sale of his cattle—the county moved to prohibit enslaved people from engaging in trade. But Driggus was able to get Pott to put in writing the fact that Driggus legally owned the cattle and was allowed to sell them. Pott later restricted this prerogative, however, when he declared in court a few years later that no one should engage in trade with his slaves without his approval.

Just as Emmanuel Pietersen in New Amsterdam petitioned to protect the free status of his adopted child, Driggus sought to protect his ability to sustain some limited degree of economic autonomy in order to free his family.

More stunning for the Driggus family, though, was when Pott sold their eldest daughter, ten-year-old Ann, for five thousand pounds of tobacco. He also sold a younger son, Edward, four years old. These children were sold into lifetime enslavement.

Frances Driggus died a few years after her children were sold. Emmanuel remarried, and several years later, as a free man, he gave to his daughters Frances and Jane a bay mare "out of the Naturall love and affection." Jane was free and married; Frances's status is not clear.

Emmanuel Driggus was aware of the perilous lives of his daughters in the Virginia colony. His gift of a female horse who might produce other horses, he likely hoped, would provide his daughters, now in their twenties, with income that might render them a bit less vulnerable. After all, in the 1650s Virginia and other English colonies were racing toward full dependence on the forced labor of Black people.

UNFREE LABOR

NAKIA D. PARKER

—

IN HISTORY TEXTBOOKS AND IN POPULAR MEMORY, THE EN-slavement of people of African descent is often depicted as an unfortunate yet unavoidable occurrence in the otherwise glorious history of the American republic. Echoing this common sentiment, Republican senator Tom Cotton called slavery "the necessary evil upon which the union was built" in his objection to adding *The 1619 Project* to school curriculums. The United States was indeed built on chattel slavery, which deemed people of African descent inferior to white people and defined Black people as commodities to be bought, sold, insured, and willed. That was certainly evil. It was not, however, "necessary" or inevitable. The system of racialized slavery that is now seared into the American public consciousness took centuries to metastasize and mature.

The March 1655 court case of *Johnson v. Parker* in Northampton County, Virginia, exemplifies the insidious transformations in forced labor practices in the early American colonies. Anthony Johnson, the plaintiff in the case, was an African man who likely arrived in Virginia sometime around 1621 as a captive from Angola, transported across the Atlantic in the slave trade. In the course of thirty years, however, Johnson enjoyed a remarkable fate different from that of millions of African captives. Against insurmountable odds, Johnson survived the harrowing trek to the Americas known as the Middle Passage and eventually married, had children, secured his freedom, and acquired more than two hundred acres of land, livestock, and even indentured servants.

John Casor, another African man, was one of these servants. At the time of the lawsuit, he was working for Johnson under a contract. Unlike Johnson, Casor claimed he'd first come to Virginia not in captivity but as an indentured servant, and he therefore demanded his freedom after he believed he had fulfilled his indenture contract with Johnson. According to Casor, "Johnson had kept him his servant seaven yeares longer than hee ought [*sic*]." Casor likely knew that as an African man, he would face challenges in winning his freedom. In fact, fifteen years before Casor brought his case, in 1640, a Black indentured servant named John Punch ran away from his Virginia owners along with two white servants. After they were recaptured, the court sentenced the two white servants to thirty lashes and one extra year of servitude. Punch's punishment, however, was to "serve his said master or his assigns for the time of his natural Life here or elsewhere," thereby becoming the first person of African descent considered a "slave for life." Although the institution of chattel slavery had not yet been completely codified into law and racist ideologies connecting Blackness with enslavement were not yet fully formed, it was nonetheless clear at this time that servants of African descent were viewed as different from their white counterparts, subject to being held in servitude for an undefined period of time, unlike white servants, who had clear terms of indenture and were never considered slaves for life.

With the precedent that only people of African descent were held as slaves for life set before Casor, and with his claims of freedom apparently unheeded by Johnson, Casor eventually appealed to one of Johnson's white neighbors, Robert Parker, for help in his quest for freedom. Parker took Casor's side and, over Johnson's objections, took Casor out of Johnson's possession and to his own farm, "under pretense that the said Negro [Casor] is a free man." Johnson, after consulting with his wife, two sons, and son-in-law, reluctantly acceded to Casor's demands, even providing him "corne and leather," as "freedom dues." A few months later, however, Johnson reconsidered his choice and sued Parker in court for stealing Casor. Johnson asserted that Casor never had an indenture; on the contrary, "hee had him [Casor] for his life." The court ruled in Johnson's favor and ordered Casor to

"returne unto the service of his said master Anthony Johnson," de-
creeing that Robert Parker cover the costs of the court case.

   With the decision of the Northampton County Court, Casor became the first person of African descent in a civil case to be deemed
a "slave for life." Although Johnson initially agreed to free Casor from
his contract, the loss of his labor apparently proved too much to accept. Perhaps thinking about ensuring his financial standing and the
future of his family, Johnson decided that he needed to possess as
much property, both human and inanimate, as possible. And though
the court sided with him in this instance, Anthony Johnson and his
family faced increasing harassment and threats to his property from
his white neighbors. Around 1665, Johnson and his extended family
moved to Maryland. Other people of African descent who were able
to gain their freedom also bought land in the surrounding area and
formed a tight-knit community that provided much-needed support
in the face of rising discrimination and mistreatment of Black people.
Two years later, in 1667, Johnson's son, John, acquired forty-four acres
of land in Maryland and named the estate Angola, after the African
homeland his father had been torn away from over forty years before.

   Like Johnson, other masters of indentured servants in Virginia
also made calculated choices about which unfree laborers to manumit
or retain. In October 1657, Anne Barnehouse, the sister of Christopher Stafford, a white planter from England, followed the wishes
stated in his will to free his servant Mihill Gowen, a man of African
descent, and his son William, promising "never to trouble or molest
the said Mihill Gowen or his sone William or demand any service of
the said Mahill or his said sone William." Barnehouse, however, did
not free her servant Prosta, who was William's mother and perhaps
the partner of Gowen. Evidently, Barnehouse had no qualms about
obeying the manumission wishes of her brother but could not part
with her own servant, who was likely acutely aware of the differences
in status between herself, her son, and the father of her child. Five
years before the 1662 Virginia law of *partus sequitur ventrem* declared
that children followed the legal status of the mother, Barnehouse
likely realized that the productive and reproductive labor she could

extract from Prosta outweighed the morality of allowing her to enjoy freedom with her kin.

The English colonizers in the Chesapeake region were not the only Europeans to depend on Black people for labor. By the mid-seventeenth century, enslaved Africans comprised 20 percent of the population of New Netherland, the original homeland of the Lenape Indians—now occupied by Manhattan—making it the colony with the highest percentage of enslaved people at that time. Enslaved people of African descent performed all kinds of labor in the region for Dutch merchants of the West India Company. They cultivated small farms, built forts and churches, and protected the fledgling Dutch colony against Indian attacks.

Just like John Casor in Virginia, however, enslaved laborers of African descent in New Netherland used the labor they performed and the law as freedom strategies. Since enslaved Africans enjoyed the right to use the Dutch legal system, some individuals who participated on the side of the Dutch in conflicts with Indigenous nations petitioned—and often received—the status known as "half-freedom." The Dutch understood early on that fostering divisions between African-descended peoples and Native people could serve their interests by forcibly removing Indigenous people from their lands to free it for slave-based cultivation. Half-freedom was an appropriate term: those who had this status could not pass it on to their children, unlike the enslaved people in the English colonies, and had to pay the West India Company an annual tribute in exchange for working for themselves. Despite the limitations of this standing, Africans made the most of their circumstances and never stopped pursuing complete freedom.

Africans in early America lived in a society that blurred the lines between freedom and unfreedom, a world of constrained possibilities, a world that could provide only "half-freedom." And almost four hundred years later, Trayvon Martin, Michael Brown, Eric Garner, Sandra Bland, George Floyd, Breonna Taylor, and countless others serve as a stark and painful reminder that for people of African descent, the United States is still a place of "half-freedom."

UPON ARRIVAL

JERICHO BROWN

——

We'd like a list of what we lost
Think of those who landed in the Atlantic
The sharkiest of waters
Bonnetheads and thrashers
Spinners and blacktips
We are made of so much water
Bodies of water
Bodies walking upright on the mud at the bottom
The mud they must call nighttime
Oh there was some survival
Life
After life on the Atlantic—this present grief
So old we see through it
So thick we can touch it
And Jesus said of his wound Go on, touch it
I don't have the reach
I'm not qualified
I can't swim or walk or handle a hoe
I can't kill a man
Or write it down
A list of what we lost
The history of the wound
The history of the wound
That somebody bought them

That somebody brought them
To the shore of Virginia and then
Inland
Into the land of cliché
I'd rather know their faces
Their names
My love yes you
Whether you pray or not
If I knew your name
I'd ask you to help me
Imagine even a single tooth
I'd ask you to write that down
But there's not enough ink

I'd like to write a list of what we lost.

Think of those who landed in the Atlantic,

Think of life after life on the Atlantic—
    Sweet Jesus. A grief so thick I could touch it.

And Jesus said of his wound, Go on, touch it.
    But I don't have the reach. I'm not qualified.

And you? How's your reach? Are you qualified?
    Don't you know the history of the wound?

Here is the history of the wound:
    Somebody brought them. Somebody bought them.

Though I know who caught them, sold them,
        bought them,
    I'd rather focus on their faces, their names.

PART TWO

ELIZABETH KEYE

JENNIFER L. MORGAN

———

1662 Act XII [of the Virginia House of Burgesses]. Whereas some doubts have arisen whether children got by any Englishman upon a negro woman shall be slave or free, Be it therefore enacted and declared by this present grand assembly, that all children borne in this country shall be held bond or free only according to the condition of the mother—partus sequitur ventrem. And that if any Christian shall commit fornication with a negro man or woman, hee or shee soe offending shall pay double the fines imposed by the former act.

ELIZABETH KEYE WAS AN AFRICAN AMERICAN WOMAN WHO lived in colonial Virginia in the seventeenth century. She was the daughter of an enslaved African woman and the Englishman who owned her. As is so often the case, we can know nothing of the nature of their relationship except that it produced a daughter. Elizabeth Keye would instigate the single most important legislative act concerning the history of enslavement, race, and reproduction in the colonial Atlantic world.

As a child, Keye found herself misidentified on the estate where she was indentured. At some point in the late 1620s, Thomas Keye, a free white Englishman and member of the Virginia House of Burgesses, had impregnated her mother, an enslaved African-born woman (whose name we do not know). What this woman (who appears in the archives as "woman slave") hoped or believed about her daughter's future is utterly lost in the documentary record. What is clear is that her father's death threw that future into some confusion. Although Elizabeth had been placed in indenture as a child, after his death she (or her indenture) was sold to another Virginia landowner.

Selling the remaining term of an indenture was not uncommon, but because Elizabeth Keye was the daughter of an African woman, her race made her vulnerable to abuses that an Englishwoman would not have had to endure. Although the English embraced the system of African slavery elsewhere in the Atlantic, in Virginia they relied on indentured servants, the vast majority of whom were also themselves English. In the 1650s there were fewer than three hundred Africans in the colony, or about 1 percent of the population of English settlers. And yet Elizabeth understood that she was in danger, that her color could dictate her status.

Her status as Keye's daughter was never a secret; it was widely known that this young woman's father was a free Englishman. We learn from one witness that, out of ignorance or spite, Thomas Keye's other child, John, called Elizabeth "Black Besse." Mrs. Speke, the overseer's wife, "checked him and said[,] Sirra you must call her Sister for shee is your Sister." Whether or not Mrs. Speke's intervention was meant to take John Keye down a peg, it was recognition of Elizabeth's lineage. But her relative freedom, pinned as it was to a transgressive paternity that increasingly muddied the waters of property rights, was insufficient.

In 1655 Elizabeth Keye petitioned the courts for her freedom— and that of her new child—and thus became the first woman of African descent to do so in the English North American colonies. While we know very little about her, we can be confident that she had a precise understanding of the dangers that surrounded her as a result of the interrelated consequences of race and sex in colonial Virginia. She had been transferred, by then, to a third Englishman, whose executors listed her and her son among his "negroes" rather than his "servants." She had, by that time, been held for at least ten years longer than the terms of her 1636 indenture had specified. Her original freedom suit was granted, then overturned, and finally won when the father of her child and common-law husband, William Grinsted, an indentured Englishman who was knowledgeable in the law, brought her case to the General Assembly. On the day that her case was finally decided, July 31, 1656, she and Grinsted posted their banns (publicly announcing their intention to marry), and she and her descendants remained legally free well into the eighteenth century.

Less than six years later, the Virginia Assembly revisited this case. Perhaps the lawmakers understood that granting freedom to the children of women raped by free property-owning Englishmen would fundamentally undermine the labor system they relied upon. In 1662 they decreed that a child born to an African woman slave, no matter who the father was, would follow that woman into slavery. This piece of legislation encapsulated the early modern understanding of racial slavery—that it was a category of labor that African people and their descendants inherited.

How much did Elizabeth Keye know about the tide of racial slavery that was engulfing the Atlantic world? Enough to act decisively in an effort to protect herself and her children from the claims that she should be enslaved. She recognized, on some level, that she was embedded in racialized structures of meaning and labor. Her freedom was not assured, despite her father's prominence. When faced with the instability of her son's future, she came to understand that her ties to her child were exposed to destruction by the economic logic of racial slavery.

In this regard, she was prescient. The child of an African woman whose freedom and that of her children were dependent upon English men, Elizabeth may not have understood the role that her case would have in propelling the 1662 legislative act, but she did understand that the atmosphere in which she lived put her and her kin in jeopardy. The forces that moved Keye and the father of her children in and out of court were precisely those that anticipated both Keye's vulnerability and that of all Black women in a nascent slave society. The link between the Keye case and the 1662 act is evidence that legally sanctioned claims to lineage for Black Virginians were short-lived.

When racial slavery depended upon the transformation of children into property, Black women could not be legally allowed to produce kinship. The fact that they did, and that they would continue to do so despite the violations of slavery, is at the heart of the afterlife of reproductive slavery. Black women have struggled mightily to protect their children and, for that matter, their ability to give birth free of economic and racial violence. In the twenty-first century, African American women's ability to safely navigate the intrusion of the state into their reproductive autonomy continues to be at risk.

1664–1669

THE VIRGINIA LAW ON BAPTISM

JEMAR TISBY

═══

H OW EXACTLY DID CHRISTIANITY IN THE UNITED STATES become white? Of course we know that's not the reality. To this day, Black people remain the most Christian demographic in the country. But the statement, repeated in various ways throughout the centuries, that "Christianity is the white man's religion" has a basis in historical fact. After all, white Christians deliberately retrofitted religion to accommodate the rising racial caste system.

In 1667 the Virginia Assembly, a group of white Anglican men, passed a law that Christian baptism would not free an enslaved person in the colonies. "It is enacted and declared by this grand assembly," they wrote, "and the authority thereof, that the conferring of baptisme doth not alter the condition of their person as to his bondage or freedom."

In England it had been the custom that Christians could not enslave other Christians. Spiritual equality, if it meant anything, meant that Christians should promote and ensure the liberty of their religious sisters and brothers. In North America, however, the Anglican lawmakers had a dilemma. What would become of white supremacy and slavery if Christians insisted that they could not enslave other adherents to the faith?

The context for the new law was given in its preamble: "Whereas some doubts have risen whether children that are slaves by birth, and by the charity and piety of their owners made pertakers of the blessed sacrament of baptisme, should by virtue of their baptisme be made free."

Apparently, some slaveholders had concerns that their "charity and piety" in sharing the Christian message with enslaved children would result in the loss of unfree labor and income. Such a practice would also disrupt the ideology of white supremacy. It would be harder to maintain the social, economic, and religious superiority of white people if spiritual liberty translated into physical and material liberty for enslaved people as well.

The new law would, in the judgment of the legislators, assuage the fears of plantation owners so they could "more carefully endeavor the propagation of Christianity by permitting the children, though slaves, or those of greater growth if capable to be admitted to that sacrament." Under this law, white Christian missionaries could proselytize and the plantation owners could still have their profitable enslaved labor. The legislation helped harden the emerging racial hierarchy in the colonies.

These white Christian lawmakers chose to racialize religion and reinforce enslavement and white supremacy through religious laws and policies. While Christianity could have been a force for liberation and equality, under laws like the one passed by the Virginia Assembly in 1667, it became a cornerstone of white supremacy. According to many white Christians, their religion gave divine approbation to an emerging system of racial oppression and economic exploitation.

White Christian leaders made the double move of enshrining their bigotry in laws while simultaneously labeling the question of slavery as a "civil" or "political" issue outside the purview of the church. Not only did the religious, political, and economic establishment create policies to codify slavery and white supremacy, they also pushed those actions outside the realm of Christian ethics. To challenge slavery on moral grounds was to distract from the (selectively) spiritual mission of the church and impinge on the Christian liberty of white slaveholders.

White missionaries should not have been surprised, then, that they did not initially have much effectiveness in converting enslaved people to Christianity. Why would the enslaved adopt the religion of slave owners? What good to Black people was a foreign God preaching their perpetual bondage?

In spite of the hypocrisy of white Christian slave owners and missionaries, Black people still heard some of the dignifying and liberatory strains within the Christian message. The book of Exodus told of a God who delivered the Hebrews from slavery in Egypt. Enslaved Africans nurtured the hope of emancipation, too. They heard about the Promised Land awaiting the faithful followers of God and envisioned their freedom in a land of equity and justice. Enslaved people expressed their liberatory theology in "hush arbors" beyond the sight of slave owners. Their churchless church became the invisible institution. They composed and sang spirituals, finding within Christianity not only a source of daily endurance but also the motivation for protest and resistance.

But the faith of enslaved people often came in spite of and not because of the theology of white enslavers. The oppressed clearly saw the gap between Jesus Christ, who announced his ministry to "proclaim liberty to the captives," and the religion of racism and abuse preached by many white Christians.

Oppressed people must either reform or reject a religion that preaches spiritual salvation but has little to say about their physical and material conditions. The hypocrisy of white Christians who said their religion condemned darker-skinned people to perpetual slavery even as they worshiped a brown-skinned Jewish man who was put to death by an imperial power could hardly be starker, both then and now.

ANTIRACIST PROGRESS CAN ONLY be realized if people treat race, religion, and politics as distinct but inseparable and interrelated factors. America will not see peace between different racial and ethnic groups without working for change in faith communities, as well as in politics and law. Racial inequities are the result of racist policies, which have been justified by religion, especially Christianity.

Looking back on the past four hundred years, this nation's story of racism can seem almost inevitable. But it didn't have to be this way. At critical turning points throughout history, people made deliberate choices to construct and reinforce a racist America. Our generation has the opportunity to make different choices, ones that lead to greater human dignity and justice, but only if we pay heed to our history and respond with the truth and courage that confronting racism requires.

IN 1667 THOSE VIRGINIA lawmakers who insisted that baptism did not free an enslaved person also put themselves in bondage to a racialized corruption of Christianity. A recovery of the earthly and spiritual equality of all people, both in theory and in practice, is the only way to redeem religion from racism.

1669–1674

THE ROYAL AFRICAN COMPANY

DAVID A. LOVE

—

I

N NOVEMBER 1998, I FIRST VISITED LIVERPOOL WHILE WORK-
ing as a human rights campaigner and a spokesperson for Amnesty
International UK. During my journeys to this English port city, I
experienced the impact of the transatlantic slave trade in unexpected
ways.

I encountered Black Brits whose ancestors had arrived in England
hundreds of years earlier. They reminded me of the British role in the
triangular trade of Black people and goods across West Africa, Europe, and the Americas, and of the Middle Passage, which served as
an underwater resting place for millions of souls who succumbed to
the hellish journey warehoused in slave ship dungeons.

What struck me most about Liverpool was the extent to which
the city visibly and tangibly benefited from the slave trade. Evidence
of the wealth amassed from human trafficking is found in much of
the city's architecture. African heads and figures are carved into buildings and adorn such structures as the town hall and the Cunard
Building. The entrance to the Martins Bank (Barclays) Building—
designed by architect Herbert Rowse—features a relief by sculptor
George Herbert Tyson Smith of two African boys shackled at the
neck and ankles and carrying bags of money. It is "a reminder that
Liverpool was built by slavers' money and that its bankers grew fat off
the whipped backs of Africans when they were bankrolling cargoes of
strange fruit bound for the Americas."

The enslavement of human beings amounts to a grave violation of human rights. The institution of slavery is a sin, a form of genocide, and a system of racial oppression, exploitation, and intergenerational theft that robs people of their freedom of movement, expression, and self-determination. It endeavors to deny people their dignity and humanity, among other things. From the vantage point of the monarch, the oligarch, the slave trader, or the banker, however, human trafficking is first and foremost a for-profit endeavor, a business enterprise designed to enrich its partners and shareholders. Moreover, the profit motive justifies the abuses, and the attendant systems of racial oppression and white supremacy that certainly must follow.

Responsible for transporting more African people to the Americas than any other entity, the Royal African Company (RAC) of England was the most important institution involved in the transatlantic slave trade. Through this company, England developed its infrastructure of human trafficking and supplied Africans to meet the labor demands of the lucrative Caribbean sugar plantations. Between 1673 and 1683, England's share of the slave trade increased from 33 percent to three-quarters of the market—rendering the nation the global leader of the slave trade at the expense of the Dutch and the French. A precursor to British imperialism and colonialism, the trading company expanded England's role in the African continent, exploiting the gold and later the human resources on the West Coast in Gambia and Ghana.

The RAC was a business deal and a corporate monopoly designed to financially enrich the royal Stuart family—specifically King Charles II and his brother the Duke of York, who later became King James II—and to allow them independence from Parliament. Originally known as the Company of Royal Adventurers Trading to Africa, the company was granted a monopoly on the shipment of slaves to the Caribbean under the Navigation Act of 1660, which allowed only English-owned ships to enter colonial ports. Reorganized under a royal charter in 1672, the renamed Royal African Company was granted a legal monopoly on the British slave trade between the African continent and the West Indies and "had the whole, entire and only trade for buying and selling bartering and exchanging of for or with any Negroes, slaves, goods, wares, merchandise whatsoever." It was a joint stock company; its investors purchased shares and received returns on those shares. These stockholders elected a governor who was a member of the royal family, a subgovernor, deputy governor, and twenty-four assistants.

In addition to exporting slaves, the company also monopolized the trade in gold, ivory, *malagueta* pepper, and redwood dye. The company was authorized to declare martial law and amass troops, to establish plantations, forts, and factories, and to wage war or make peace with any non-Christian nation. RAC military forts existed across five thousand miles of coastline from Cape Salé in Morocco to the Cape of Good Hope in present-day South Africa. West Africans transported to the Caribbean and Virginia were branded on their chest with the company's initials.

A court on the West African coast was authorized to hear mercantile cases and matters involving the seizure of English interlopers who attempted to operate in violation of the company monopoly. In addition, the crown was entitled to claim two-thirds of the gold the company obtained, upon paying two-thirds of the mining expenses.

A royal proclamation addressed to John Leverett, governor of Massachusetts Bay Colony in 1674, granted the RAC exclusive rights to travel from America to Africa for the purposes of trade, and it forbade others from carrying "Negro Servants, Gold, Elephants teeth, or any other goods and merchandise."

Under the RAC, the slave trade brought considerable wealth to Britain and its cities, particularly the commercial center of London and the major trading ports of Liverpool and Bristol, where the slave ships originated. Ships from Liverpool carried 1.5 million enslaved Africans, or half of the human cargo kidnapped and transported by Britain.

While the RAC and the transatlantic slave trade are things of centuries past, the spirit they embody—of unbridled capitalism and monopolistic business schemes designed to monetize human suffering and reap corporate profits from a free and captive labor force—did not die with the slave trade. After all, section 1 of the Thirteenth Amendment to the Constitution—"Neither slavery nor involuntary servitude, except as a punishment for crime whereof the party shall have been duly convicted, shall exist within the United States, or any place subject to their jurisdiction"—provides a loophole allowing for enslavement to continue.

After the Emancipation Proclamation, slavery ended in name only, as the convict lease system allowed states to lease inmates to planters and industrialists to work on plantations, railroads, and coal mines in the late 1800s and early 1900s. Like slavery, convict leasing was highly profitable and cheap, requiring little capital investment and no expenditures for the healthcare of convicts, who died off and were buried in secret graveyards. Like the slave trade and the Royal African Company, the Jim Crow system of economic exploitation was perfectly legal. The convict lease system was made possible by the Black Codes, which were like vagrancy laws that criminalized minor offenses such as loitering, allowing Black people to be swept up and thrown into chain gangs.

And today, three and a half centuries after the Royal African Company received its charter, capitalism has continued to find a way to profit from—and exploit—Black bodies. Mass incarceration and prison labor are big business, and corporate America continues to extract every penny possible from the trauma and suffering of African Americans, creating new profit centers and intergenerational wealth streams. Unjust laws—enacted through lobbying and legalized bribery on the part of corporate America, corrections officers, the Fraternal Order of Police, and other groups—promote these predatory practices. The immigration industrial complex has criminalized undocumented immigration, and much as in the slave trade, private corporations profit from the detention of migrants and refugees as well as from the trafficking of babies and the separation of families. The Royal African Company may be long gone, but its spirit is very much alive.

BACON'S REBELLION

HEATHER C. MCGHEE

I FOUND THEIR NAMES ON A LIST THAT VIRGINIA GOVERNOR William Berkeley kept of the men executed for their part in a rebellion against his rule. My finger paused on "One Page," and I underlined what came next: "a carpenter, formerly my servant."

The description went on: "But for his violence used against the Royal Party, made a Colonel." Five names later I found what I was looking for again: "One Darby, from a servant made a Captain."

One Darby, one Page. Both were servants who became officers in Nathaniel Bacon's rebel army in 1676, an army that included hundreds of white "bondsmen" and enslaved Africans. They nearly succeeded in overthrowing the colonial government, burning the capital of Jamestown to the ground before Bacon's death. Governor Berkeley's list was the first time I'd seen names and descriptions of the men who followed Bacon and changed history.

I let my imagination wander. Was Page a white indentured servant and Darby an enslaved African? Had these two men experienced, in the brief months of rebellion in 1676, something that has eluded Americans ever since: working-class solidarity across race?

I first discovered Bacon's Rebellion while I was teaching myself American labor history. It's a history that otherwise is full of stories of white workers fighting workers of color to maintain their place in the hierarchy of capitalism: from Irish dockworkers chasing Black longshoremen out of their jobs in the nineteenth century to white factory workers leading "hate strikes" to oppose Black promotions in the twentieth. I heard the same story when I traveled to Canton, Mississippi, in the wake of a failed union drive in 2017 and talked to autoworkers. "The whites [were] against it because the Blacks [were] for it," one said. In the labor conflicts, the true victor was the boss, who used racial divisions as a wedge against organizing and kept employees competing for low wages.

In early colonial Virginia, work was brutal, often deadly, and for the large working class of Black, white, and Indigenous servants, it went unpaid and life was unfree. Even after servitude's end (still a possibility under the law for some Africans at this time), common people had few opportunities to acquire land or gainful work. The colonial elite disdained and feared the mass of "idle" freedmen and fretted over the possibility of insurrection among the enslaved. The tempestuous young newcomer Nathaniel Bacon tapped into the widespread discontent in the colony and rallied more than a thousand men, waging what some historians have called America's first revolution.

But as I read more about Bacon's Rebellion, a fuller picture came into focus. Searching through the writings of Bacon himself (a wealthy Englishman from the same social class as his enemy, Governor Berkeley), I found few if any references to class, land, or bondage. What Bacon sought was all-out war with neighboring Indigenous tribes. He rebelled because Berkeley had made alliances with some tribes and preferred negotiation to war. Bacon's anti-Native fervor was indiscriminate; his followers betrayed and massacred the group of Occaneechi people who helped them fight a group of Susquehannocks and relentlessly pursued a group of Pamunkey men, women, and children.

Knowing this, can we still think of Bacon's Rebellion as a classbased, multiracial uprising against slavery, landlessness, and servitude, as some have described it? Or was it just an early example of the powerful making the powerless fight one another, this time with white and Black united, initially against Indigenous Americans?

And again we confront the problem of history: it's usually the powerful who get to write it. Of the half-dozen or so remaining original documents about Bacon's Rebellion, all were written by landowning white men. With only Page's and Darby's names and absent their stories, we may never know what drove them to war.

What we do know, however, is that the rebellion turned these captives into officers and set them free. The last men to surrender after Bacon's death—not in battle but from dysentery—were a group of eighty Africans and twenty white men, who were tricked into surrendering with the promise of remaining free. Bacon had started his rebellion as an anti-Native crusade, but the multiracial alliance of landless freedmen, servants, and slaves who carried it on had their minds set on freedom.

But the governing white elite had their minds set on reinforcing slavery after putting down the rebellion. In 1680, four years after the rebellion, Virginia passed the Law for Preventing Negro Insurrections. It restricted the movement of enslaved people outside plantations; anyone found without a pass would be tortured with twenty lashes "well laid on" before being returned. At a time when white servants and African slaves often worked side by side, the hand of the law reached in to divide them. Prison time awaited "English, and other white men and women intermarrying with negros or mulattos." Already any indentured white servant caught running away with an enslaved African person was liable for their entire lost term of service, meaning that the servant risked becoming permanently unfree.

The law separated the members of the lowest class by color and lifted one higher than the other. The goal, as it has been ever since, was to offer just enough racial privileges for white workers to identify with their color instead of their class. The Virginia legislature ended the penalties imposed on rebels for the insurrection of 1676, but only the white ones, removing a source of lingering solidarity among them. Post-Bacon reforms forbade Black people to carry anything that could be considered a weapon, but they made sure that every manumitted indentured servant was given a musket. Even a free Indian or Black person was forbidden to "lift up his hand in opposition against any Christian," no matter the provocation.

A decade after Bacon, the governing class made a final decision to ensure the loyalty of white servants: simply have fewer of them. A critical mass of white working people threatened their racial slavery order, so Virginia plantation owners imported more Africans, whose rights they could drastically limit through legislation. By the end of the eighteenth century, the gentry were relying almost entirely on Africans for their labor. They stopped importing white servants from England, save to meet a Britain-imposed quota to ensure the presence of enough armed white people to defend against slave rebellions.

Why does Bacon—the myth and the reality—matter so much to those of us who care about justice today? I think we want to believe that there was once a time when people suffering from oppression together would stand up for one another, despite their color. We want to revel in the image of a Black person, perhaps like Darby, breaking his chains to become a captain in an army that brought a slaveholding colony to its knees. More desperately, now more than ever, we need to believe in the existence of a Page—a white man we'd call working-class today, refusing to settle for what W.E.B. Du Bois called the psychological wage of whiteness, and fighting instead for the freedom that can only be won in numbers.

Today, as in colonial Virginia, the wealthy and powerful maintain an unequal society with the complicity of white people who share color with them but class with almost everybody else. At the time of this writing, a man is in the White House who made promises to fight for white Americans by scapegoating immigrants and people of color, but his biggest policy accomplishment has been a massive tax handout for himself and other wealthy people.

Though my view of Bacon's Rebellion has changed over the years, I keep coming back to it. There's something vexingly American in the story, in the violence and in the hope—and in the lengths that the powerful will go to try to stop the most natural yearnings of all, for human connection and for freedom.

THE VIRGINIA LAW THAT FORBADE BEARING ARMS; OR THE VIRGINIA LAW THAT FORBADE ARMED SELF-DEFENSE

KELLIE CARTER JACKSON

———

B Y NOW, VIRGINIA WAS THE RINGLEADER OF SLAVERY. LAWS created there tended to have a "Simon says" effect, as other slaveholding colonies followed suit politically, economically, and socially. Enslavement "happened one law at a time, one person at a time," Frances Latimer explains.

Nearly 40 percent of North America's slave population lived in Virginia. And it was growing, along with the enslavers' fear of slave rebellions, especially after Bacon's Rebellion in 1676. Virginia's enslaved population grew from two thousand to three thousand in 1680 and to over sixteen thousand by 1700. The colony was becoming at risk of being an enslaved majority.

Virginia lawmakers responded by passing racist laws of control. They prohibited enslaved Africans from congregating in large numbers, even to bury their loved ones—and, notably, from bearing arms. They made it unlawful for an African American to own a gun, even for self-defense. The enslaved were not legally allowed to protect themselves from racist whites. If a white person struck an enslaved man or woman, striking back was a criminal offense.

If an enslaved person, in an effort to defend themselves, "lift[ed] up his hand in opposition against any Christian," the punishment was thirty lashes on their bare back—that is, if the Christian saw fit not to kill them. The law offered no space for the enslaved to defend themselves, protect loved ones, or even procure food by hunting game.

The irony is that most slaveholders violated these laws in their own interests. In 1723 Virginia allowed enslaved people to bear arms when hunting in the frontier regions. The enslaved held or transported guns while their owners hunted. Some enslaved people were given guns to keep birds off rice fields. In Lowcountry plantations, slave watchmen usually carried guns, and one county in the Chesapeake fined several masters for selling arms to their slaves. By the American Revolution, "eighty Guns, some Bayonets, swords, etc." were collected from the enslaved by their masters.

While it may seem reckless and self-endangering for masters to have violated gun laws like this, it speaks to planters' beliefs in their own military power. White nonslaveholding men from the militia could be signaled and employed at any moment. The punishment for rumors of uprisings, let alone rebellions themselves, was death.

But those were exceptions for the self-interest of individual planters: in general white Americans then and later considered it to be in their self-interest for Black Americans to remain unarmed. One U.S. Supreme Court justice argued, in the infamous *Dred Scott v. Sanford* decision in 1857, that one of the clear hazards of recognizing Black people as citizens was that it would allow them to "to keep and carry arms wherever they went."

Today the National Rifle Association (NRA) leads the charge in protecting the Second Amendment—a charge it has been leading since it began in 1871. But the NRA has never been a defender of African Americans who purchased weapons for self-defense against white terror. In the late 1960s, when Black Panthers carried weapons in public spaces, it was entirely legal in the state of California. When California passed some of the most restrictive gun laws in the country to disarm the Black Panthers, the NRA lent its support.

It is nearly impossible to disconnect gun ownership and race in America. Gun ownership has always been a tool to secure power— racist white power.

THE CODE NOIR

LAURENCE RALPH

━━

THE PERIOD OF THE 1680S WAS A TIME OF GROWTH AND EX-
pansion in the English colonies as Africans replaced European indentured servants, and slavery became commonplace. By 1685, when
Blacks were becoming more central to the plantation economy, the
conditions of slavery, especially the way whites treated Blacks, varied
based on location. In South Carolina, whites passed a law that "prohibited the exchange of goods between slaves or slaves and freemen
without their master's permission." In 1687 whites in Northern Neck,
Virginia, caught wind that enslaved people were organizing a revolt
under the guise of planning a funeral. They immediately crushed the
insurrection and then made it illegal for enslaved Blacks to bury their
dead.

Enslaved people began to flee harsh conditions in Virginia and
South Carolina to Spanish Florida. If an enslaved person made it
there and professed his belief that Roman Catholicism was "the True
Faith," the Spanish colonists would set him free. As a result, the first
Black town, St. Augustine, was founded by freedmen and -women in
1687. A year later Germantown Quakers wrote the first petition
against slavery ever drafted by a religious group in the English colonies. Just four years after the Quakers had brought enslaved people to
settle the frontier, they argued that it was immoral to treat human
beings as if they were cargo. This period also marks the tail end of the
Royal African Company's seventeen-year monopoly on transporting
enslaved people to the English colonies. But just as Black people who

lived in those colonies were deeply impacted by the decisions of the London-based trading company, the 1685 Code Noir, "one of the most extensive official documents on race, slavery, and freedom ever drawn up in Europe," transformed the lives of generations of Black people living in the geographical expanse that would eventually become the United States.

The Code Noir (or Black Code) was written by French politician Jean-Baptiste Colbert, who served as minister of finance for twenty-two years under Louis XIV. The goal of the Code Noir was to ensure the success of the sugar plantation economy. What France needed to do to maintain economic security, Colbert believed, was establish protocols for regulating enslaved people in the colonies. Colbert died an accomplished statesman at the age of sixty-four, but he was buried before the code was complete. In 1683 Colbert's eldest son, the Marquis de Seignelay, submitted the document to the king, and two years later Louis XIV ratified it.

In an edict that the king announced in March 1685, which concerned how order was to be enforced in "the French American islands," Louis XIV asserted that the purpose of the Code was to provide comfort to French officers living in colonies who were said to "need our authority and our justice . . . [in order] to regulate the status and condition of the slaves." As the majority of those living in the colonies were enslaved, the king meant for his white subjects to feel at ease.

In the security regime of the mercantilist period, the colonists' sense of safety was related to the way their mother country regulated and surveilled enslaved people, who were central to their nation's ambitions to conquer the globe. Louis XIV's attempts to "assist" his French officers living in the Americas, in other words, were inextricably bound to the process by which Spanish and European nations enlarged their power at the expense of rival nations through wars, purchases, treaties, and the enforcement of codes.

A remote part of the French Empire, Louisiana, was settled in 1699, though its most famous city—New Orleans—did not come under French control until 1718. The Code Noir was applied to Louisiana six years later, in 1724. Though Louisiana would eventually come under Spanish rule and then French rule again before being purchased by the United States, the territory was still controlled by the French in 1729 when John Mingo, a Black man who was enslaved in South Carolina, escaped to New Orleans. When Mingo arrived, a colonist granted his freedom, and he worked the land that the colonist hired him to break. Before long Mingo had saved enough money to purchase an enslaved woman, Therese, who also lived and worked on the plantation. John Mingo and Therese then moved in together and made a living by farming another colonist's land, for which they were granted a "salary and a portion of the yield."

As free Black people, John and Therese Mingo were rare but not completely alone. They joined the small population of free Black servants, drivers, hunters, artisans, and domestics who had accompanied French colonists when they arrived from Europe. The public record does not mention any Mingo children, but if Therese gave birth, her offspring were subject to the 1685 Code Noir. If John and Therese Mingo had a boy, they might have warned him that marrying an enslaved woman would turn his offspring into slaves. If they had a girl, they might have warned her about the perils of marrying an enslaved man. Having children with a white man was also dangerous under the Code, as both mother and child could become property of the New Orleans hospital. Since sexual relations with a white man could endanger her freedom and since marrying someone white was outlawed, it would have been reasonable for John and Therese to encourage their daughter to marry another free Black person.

Informed by the Code, their advice might have sounded something like this:

> Don't marry a slave; if you marry a slave, your life will be full of worry: if your slave husband were to carry a weapon, or even a large stick, you may find him flogged with his back bleeding at your doorstep; you would not be able to invite other slaves to your wedding; your husband could not sell sugar or fruits or vegetables or firewood or herbs at the market, and he could not

travel without a written note; if you or your husband were to be violated in any way he could never win a judgment; and if he were to strike his master, his mistress, or their children, his punishment would be death; know that if you were to save your money and purchase your husband's freedom, he would still have to maintain respect for his former master and his former master's family; rest assured, your children would be free despite the condition of their father; but for you, free girl, best not marry a slave at all.

In the system of chattel slavery from which Europe benefited, Black people were considered the property of colonists. However, they never stopped imagining ways to be free. Precisely because Black girls, in particular, were devalued, they were most likely to have their freedom purchased by family members. That is, "since girls and women had lower market values, they were more likely to be freed."

Despite the fact that free Blacks in New Orleans were a relatively large group compared to those living in other American cities, the legacy of the 1685 Code Noir should not be mistaken for a mythical story of progress in which the document traveled out of France and paved the way for freedom purchases, creating space for the emancipation of all Blacks. That mythology covers over the backlash to free Blacks in New Orleans under U.S. rule when the white planter class systematically excluded them from the halls of power. The legacy that I want to resurrect, rather, is the way that this piece of legislation helped colonial officers govern through enforcing and exploiting a society's racial divisions. What might be reduced to anti-Black sentiment or self-hate, in those imagined words of advice to a free Black girl, accurately reflect codified law that inscribed a racial caste system within New Orleans civil society.

In this way, our imagined advice given to the Mingo daughter also echoes the enduring dialogue about the law and the police that Black parents and their children have had for generations. (I am speaking of that coming-of-age conversation about racial awakening, commonly referred to as "the talk.") And thus, although one would never be able to prove it definitively, it would likewise be impossible to deny that the control, regulation, vigilance, and surveillance indicative of the 1685 Code Noir are still embedded in the place where the Mingos gained their freedom: New Orleans, the U.S. city that recently possessed the highest rate of incarceration.

THE GERMANTOWN PETITION AGAINST SLAVERY

Christopher J. Lebron

—

THE IDEA OF "ALLIES" OFTEN COMES UP IN OUR CURRENT resistance struggles. The #MeToo movement would do better if men were good allies in fighting the sexual predation of women; Black Lives Matter would benefit if whites were good allies in resisting racism and racist institutions; the queer movement would be stronger if cis-normative people were good allies in promoting understanding of gender fluidity and combating both ignorance and damaging public policies that limit access to traditionally gender-normed spaces.

But what makes a good ally? As it is used these days, it means someone who is not being directly harmed by the injustice in question yet who stands with those being harmed, even if it's against the self-interest of their identity privilege. In many ways, it asks more of the privileged than they are often willing to give but less than what those of us on the other side of that privilege need.

This was not the case in 1683, when thirteen families founded Germantown, a neighborhood in what would become the city of Philadelphia. Quakers were prominent among the founding families and, from this base, established a long-term presence in the city. History celebrates those of the Quaker faith as being reliably antislavery. But there were differences between early Quaker groups, as the 1688 Germantown petition shows.

In addition to being at the historical forefront of abolitionist tracts, the German Quaker petition represented a position that was importantly different from that of English Quakers. Although the English Quakers resisted the presence of slavery, their concern tended to focus on the inconsistency that slavery presented to the ostensible principles of this still-forming new country—a free land for free people. Thus for them, slavery was wrong because it impeded those of African descent from partaking of the bounty of the land as a reward for hard work and from participating in the processes that were collectively shaping the nascent nation.

These are fine abolitionist principles, but the German Quakers had a more fundamental disagreement with slavery: they found it an affront to the human condition. Consider the demands in the petition, written by its four authors, Gerret Hendericks, Derick up de Graeff, Francis Daniell Pastorius, and Abraham op den Graeff. They declared that Blacks

> are brought hither against their will and consent, and that many of them are stolen. Now, tho they are black, we can not conceive there is more liberty to have them slaves, as it is to have other white ones. . . . This makes an ill report in all those countries of Europe, where they hear off, that ye Quakers doe here handel men as they handel their ye cattle. . . .
>
> And in case you find it to be good to handel these blacks at that manner, we desire and require you hereby lovingly, that you may inform us herein, which at this time never was done, viz., that Christians have such a liberty to do so. To the end we shall be satisfied in this point, and satisfied likewise our good friends and acquaintances in our natif country, to whose it is a terror, or [fearful] thing, that men should be handeld so in Pennsylvania.

The most important part of the petition—the part that compelled historian Katharine Gerbner to describe it as "one of the first documents to make a humanitarian argument against slavery"—is the plain affirmation that Blacks are first and foremost human beings and not salable animals for toil and labor. A humanitarian argument is different from an argument based on inclusion and exclusion.

Inclusion—in this case, being included as beneficiaries of the bounty of America—is important, but it is not fundamental because if the people who want to be included are not considered worthy or even really people at all, then your commitment to inclusion will evaporate. But if you start from the idea that Blacks are indeed human, then every commitment to equality after that will be unshakable. And that is the thing to be learned from the 1688 petition. Blacks do not need allies who fight for our inclusion; rather, we need people who are possessed of the basic belief that we are human and that any arguments that depend on rejecting that proposition are tyrannical, unjust, and to be fought.

This may seem to be a semantic point. After all, can't allies do exactly that? Yes, but there's more to consider. By their very nature, alliances are agreements, explicitly or implicitly, and usually the most essential part of an alliance is that it is made for mutual benefit and advantage. But think about that. What does it mean to rely on a system of racial support founded on people entering into that kind of pragmatic agreement?

The 1688 Germantown petition is a model of, if nothing else, a quality that Black people need in white Americans—the uncompromising belief that what is wrong with racism is not that it inhibits full access to American goods and treasures but that it is an affront to the human standing of Black Americans. Black people don't need allies. We need decent people possessed of the moral conviction that our lives matter.

THE MIDDLE PASSAGE

MARY E. HICKS

===

FROM THE 1400S TO THE 1600S, PORTUGUESE MERCHANT interests on the vast coast of West Africa experienced the ebbs and flows of fortune characteristic of any form of early modern commerce. But the Portuguese were not exclusively involved in trading spices, textiles, specie, and other luxury goods; the fledgling empire increasingly specialized in the disreputable commerce "in human flesh and blood."

The tiny Iberian nation originated the Atlantic world's first transoceanic slave trade. It connected Europe with sub-Saharan Africa and the Americas through the brutal commerce of buying and selling human beings. The pioneering maritime technologies and trading strategies of the Portuguese made the once commercially insignificant territory into the preeminent importer of gold and enslaved men, women, and children on the continent in the fifteenth and sixteenth centuries.

The incursions of Dutch, English, and French traffickers slowly eroded the Portuguese monopoly. In the region surrounding Elmina—the most prolific gold-producing area in West Africa—the Portuguese were supplanted by the Dutch in 1637. The rush of European merchants to the Gold Coast following the Dutch victory prompted the once modest number of slaving ships trolling West African waters to metastasize. The number of enslaved people whom slavers violently embarked from the sandy strip of coast reached an average of 4,494 per year.

In the final decade of the seventeenth century, slave traders under Portugal's banner began to reassert their regional dominance by regaining the coveted *asiento* or commercial monopoly to supply enslaved laborers to Spanish America. In 1698 the ruler of Ardra, a powerful African polity to the east of Elmina, invited the Portuguese monarch to build a fortified trading post there in recognition of the nation's lucrative dealings in the port. Meanwhile in Brazil, Portugal's largest and most opulent colony, gold deposits were discovered in a remote, mountainous region west of Rio de Janeiro, which further stimulated Portuguese efforts to exploit a steady stream of laboring hands to mine for precious metals. But the Portuguese also exploited the expertise of another group of unlikely laborers.

West African mariners provided the critical labor necessary to make slaving voyages profitably efficient. And their seafaring skills became the hidden element in the slave trade's surging growth. A string of coastal communities, "Axim, Ackum, Boutroe, Tacorary, Commendo, Cormentim and Wineba," furnished Portuguese and other Europeans with highly skilled contracted canoemen to ferry goods and people from ship to shore, as well as carry provisions and trade goods along the coast.

Their expertise in fashioning lithe, maneuverable watercraft was unmatched. So too was their knowledge of the contours of coastal geographies and the rhythms of the powerful local surf, which often confounded European seamen. The canoes of the Fanti especially captivated European navigators for their size and complexity. These vessels, able to navigate on the open waters of the Atlantic, made a striking impression. Visitors noted "the bigger canoes . . . made from a single trunk, the largest in the Ethiopias of Guinea; some of them are large enough to hold eighty men, and they come from a hundred leagues or more up this river bringing yams in large quantities. . . . They also bring many slaves, cows, goats, and sheep." On larger craft, crewmen remained stationed for long periods, just as they would on European sailing ships, eating and sleeping aboard.

European slavers such as Jean Barbot called Gold Coast canoemen "the fittest and most experienced men to manage [to] paddle the canoes over the bars and breakings." Though at the behest of slaving ship captains and merchants, these laborers were not without leverage. They bargained for higher wages and used their proximity to transatlantic commerce to deal on their own behalf. As one European trader noted, "It was customary for Mina fishermen [canoemen] to go out in their canoes and contact ships from Portugal before they reached the [trading] castle. Out at sea they conducted private trade to the detriment of the [Portuguese] crown."

Maritime middlemen were vectors between avaricious European and American merchants and the West African brokers who sold them Black people. These middlemen occupied a paradoxical position within the transatlantic slave trade. They bore witness to and participated in heart-wrenching scenes of violence: enslaved peoples being shackled, branded, and forcibly moved aboard ships. Facing these disturbing scenes, as well as the inherent dangers of the Gold Coast's tumultuous waters, they carved out individual benefits for themselves on the margins of the infamous trade. Like many participants in the Middle Passage, the individual inducements for cooperation bound them to a ruthless process that enriched the few at the expense of many.

MAMA, WHERE YOU KEEP YOUR GUN?

PHILLIP B. WILLIAMS

———

If I had my way I'd have been a killer

—NINA SIMONE

In a box of baby pictures and green books,
old issues of *Jet* grave-stacked above.

Death at bay or death come close.

Next to the Bible full of obituaries haints ride
from here to Virginia, from now to 1676.

At the temple of my enemies wearing the face
of my enemies wearing the face of their fathers.

At the bay where the last indentured servant
kissed saltwater before taking notice, taking aim.

As a gris-gris between banknotes and abandoned bras.
Didn't know when but knew I would.

In the closet, beneath cobwebs wide as sails
above the first ships carrying the thirst of us.

Death at the bay. Death come close.

Where I mind my Black-ass business at.

A breeze the smell of salt seeps from the muzzle.

I keep it thus I is the crime.

Where rebellion evolves the tantrum.

In a lockbox under my bed
where the past writhes and births our semblant
     present-future
where to reach for the gun
is to reach for safety
in retrograde.

PART THREE

THE SELLING OF JOSEPH

BRANDON R. BYRD

━━

SAMUEL SEWALL, A WHITE BUSINESSMAN, RECORDED THE transaction in his typical fashion: "October 12. Shipped by Samuel Sewall, in the *James*, Job Prince, master, for Jamaica: 'Eight hogsheads of Bass Fish.'" The date of departure. The ship carrying his specified goods. The captain ensuring their safe arrival. Their final destination. His book of receipts repeated the mundane rhythms of his ships, of the seas.

The insatiable hunger for slaves lurked in its banality.

The whole business with the West Indies was simply unfortunate, Samuel thought. He had "been long and much dissatisfied with the Trade of fetching Negros from Guinea." He even "had a strong inclination to Write something about it." That the feeling "wore off" was no indictment of his godliness. Weren't "these Blackamores ... of the Posterity of Cham, and therefore ... under the curse of slavery"? Did their masters not bring them "out of a Pagan Country, into places where the Gospel is Preached"? Samuel felt some relief when his West Indian partners reminded him that there were reasons, both divine and natural, for the enslavement of Black people. A part of him wanted, all of him needed, to accept that "the Africans have Wars with one another: our Ships bring lawful Captives taken in those Wars," and to take comfort in the knowledge that "Abraham had servants bought with his Money, and born in his House." The idea of bondage as ancient and foretold, as divine and redemptive, quieted more troubling thoughts. It put his mind momentarily at ease.

The opening of the African trade, the breaking of the Royal African Company's monopoly, removed the comfort of abstraction. The growing number of enslaved people made Samuel recoil. "There is such a disparity in their Conditions, Color & Hair, that they can never embody with us, and grow up into orderly Families, to the Peopling of the Land," he wrote in his diary. These strangers will be the end of our experiment, he predicted.

But were they not men, "sons of Adam," too? Up close, Samuel could not help but notice enslaved people's "continual aspiring after their forbidden Liberty." His doubt resurfaced, the questions rose, until he began to buckle under the weight bearing down on his conscience. Had men misinterpreted the Scriptures, manipulated the stories of curses wrought and servants bought by the ancient prophets? Was the promise of conversion merely an apology for maintaining property in men? He suspected that the defenses of slavery might not hold up to scrutiny, that "the Numerousness of Slaves at this day in the Province, and the Uneasiness of them under their Slavery, hath put many upon thinking whether the Foundation of it be firmly and well laid." He had the feeling, the budding hope, that he was not alone in his suspicions.

He was thinking of ships laden with human souls, of the hundreds of lives bought and sold in Boston, when someone named Brother Belknap rushed in with a path to salvation. The petition being prepared for his General Court called "for the freeing of a Negro and his wife, who were unjustly held in Bondage." It was a portent. Providence. I am called of God, Samuel knew at once. He began writing his apology—the defense of the negroes that no colonist had dared to write before.

Samuel's plea for the slaves, his admonition to any freeman who would hold their fellow men as slaves, came as it had to, in the form of a sermon. Like any good preacher, he began with his argument: "FOR AS MUCH as Liberty is in real value next unto Life: None ought to part with it themselves, or deprive others of it, but upon most mature Consideration." His elaboration called on scripture to show that "all Men, as they are the Sons of Adam, are Coheirs; and have equal Right unto Liberty, and all other outward Comforts of Life." He reminded his fellow Christians that "GOD hath given the

Earth [with all Commodities] unto the sons of Adam ... And hath made of One Blood, all Nations of Men, for to dwell on all the face of the Earth." He summoned the story of Joseph, sold into slavery by his brothers although he "was rightfully no more a Slave to his Brethren, than they were to him." He lamented that "there should be more Caution used in buying a Horse, a little lifeless dust; than there is in purchasing Men and Women: Whenas they are the Offspring of GOD, and their Liberty is, Auro pretiosior Omni." More precious than gold.

Samuel understood the terrible doubts that plagued the minds of the men he hoped to sway. He remembered his own willingness to accept that God had made slaves of negroes, pagans, and the posterity of Ham. So he answered the objections of the skeptics to his attack on slavery. He showed the way to their own salvation, toward that elusive state of grace. Repent. Release your slaves. Stop the trade in men. "To persist in holding their Neighbours and Brethren under the Rigor of perpetual Bondage, seems to be no proper way of gaining Assurance that God ha's given them Spiritual Freedom." Manstealing was assuredly a path away from Heaven.

SAMUEL SEWALL WROTE the advertisement in his typical fashion.

SEVERAL IRISH MAID SERVANTS
TIME MOST OF THEM FOR FIVE YEARS ONE
IRISH MAN SERVANT WHO IS A GOOD
BARBER AND WIGGMAKER, ALSO FOUR
OR FIVE LIKELY NEGRO BOYS

He knew his business dismayed his uncle. Betrayed his namesake. He had read *The Selling of Joseph*, of course; the old man had seen to that. But he had also read the rebuttal from Judge John Saffin. He had been comforted by the argument that hierarchies were necessary, that bondage was natural, that the enslavement of negroes was part of an orderly, divine world. He had been convinced of his own godliness by the idea that "Cowardly and cruel are those Blacks innate."

He had made peace with what the province, with what his place in it, required. The doubts, the troubling idea that he was a man-stealer, a seller of his own brethren, had faded with each successful sale of a negro slave. Apprehension gave way to conviction. To self-assurance. To the unassailable belief that liberty required slavery. Capital was the real god of this new world, he thought. The future belonged to him; his uncle's protest was already forgotten.

THE VIRGINIA SLAVE CODES

KAI WRIGHT

—

It is hereby enacted, That all servants imported and brought into this country, by sea or land, who were not christians in their native country . . . shall be accounted and be slaves.

—ACT CONCERNING
SERVANTS AND SLAVES, SECTION 4

IT'S A TRUISM THAT WE SEE THE PAST AS FAR MORE DISTANT than it is in reality: my parents were adults before they could share bathrooms with white people; my grandmother was middle-aged before she could confidently enter a voting booth in Alabama. Yet these images fade easily into gentle sepia tones for me today. That's because it's safety, not wisdom, we're after when we look backward. We picture ugly things at a comfortable distance.

But Americans distort the past in other ways, too. We see horrible people as exceptional, and their many accomplices as mere captives of their times. We tell ourselves we would contain such wickedness if it arose today, because now we know better. We've learned. In our illusory past, progress has come in decisive and irrevocable strokes.

I wonder if that's how Mary and Anthony Johnson felt in 1652 when they petitioned the court for tax relief in Northampton County, Virginia. They had both been enslaved in their youth, but by midcentury they were free landowners, with four children and servants of their own.

They were part of a small Black population that had been in Virginia since colonists arrived in Jamestown, and they must have been optimistic, though they would've seen a lot of change in their lives.

They would have witnessed a developing debate among white Christians about whether Africans were fully human and thus entitled to the protection of God's love. They would have heard about each new law that came down from the legislature, as lawmakers tried to break up the colony's multiracial class of indentured servants. The Johnsons probably would have felt the shift as the colony reordered its mixed servant class into two distinct racial castes. They surely would have felt the cultural and economic space for free or indentured Black people steadily shrinking, as law after law codified who could have sex with whom; who had the legal standing to appeal to the courts when wronged and who had none; who could work or buy or pray their way out of servitude and who couldn't.

What would the Johnsons have thought about the future as this social reordering unfolded? Anthony and Mary did not live to see the Virginia General Assembly hand down the omnibus legislation that would define their heirs' lives and the next century and a half of American life:

> It is hereby enacted and declared, That baptism of slaves doth not exempt them from bondage; and that all children shall be bond or free, according to the condition of their mothers.
> —Act Concerning Servants and Slaves, section 36

Known colloquially as the "slave codes," the 1705 Act Concerning Servants and Slaves was an effort at finality. It put an end to decades of debating over how to make it clear that Virginia was a white man's colony, one in which a white man's colonial investment was secure, and one in which the law protected the white man's right to enslave Black people. It became the model for all the British colonies in North America. One colony after another codified its racial caste systems and assured white planters that they could enslave increasing numbers of Black people.

What's striking is the care that was taken to make it so. In the comfortingly distorted view of the past, American slavery came about in the passive tense. That's just the way things were back then. Slavery was an inherited reality, a long-standing if unsavory fact of trade and war. In reality, colonial legislatures consciously conceived American chattel slavery at the turn of the eighteenth century, and they spelled out its terms in painstaking regulatory detail. Virginia's slave codes contained forty-one sections and more than four thousand words.

> No master, mistress, or overseer of a family, shall knowingly permit any slave, not belonging to him or her, to be and remain upon his or her plantation, above four hours at any one time, without the leave of such slave's master, mistress, or overseer, on penalty of one hundred and fifty pounds of tobacco to the informer. —Act Concerning Servants and Slaves, section 32

The slave codes of 1705 are among American history's most striking evidence that our nation's greatest sins were achieved with clear forethought and determined maintenance. And in this case as in many others, white elites were incited to act by their fears.

Between 1680 and 1700, Virginia's enslaved Black population increased from 3,000 to 16,380, driven by a decreasing flow of white indentured servants from England and the fact that Africans had better survival rates on the colony's plantations. In the neighboring Carolinas, Black people were nearly a third of the population by 1672, a growth driven by the need for labor on the colony's booming rice plantations.

These demographics presented real threats to white planters, including a potential cross-racial labor movement. Plantation work was close and intimate, and it fostered a troubling solidarity between the growing Black population and white indentured servants. White planters could not afford for such a dangerous bond to form—which is why in 1705 Virginia's legislature did as much to codify white privilege as it did to establish Black subjugation.

> All masters and owners of servants, shall find and provide for their servants, wholesome and competent diet, clothing, and

lodging, by the discretion of the county court; and shall not, at
any time, give immoderate correction; neither shall, at any
time, whip a christian white servant naked, without an order
from a justice of the peace. —Act Concerning Servants and
Slaves, section 7

Still, there were just too many Black people, and they did not accept bondage. In the years leading up to and surrounding the slave
codes, Black defiance was widespread, with unrest stretching from the
plantations themselves all the way back to West Africa's Slave Coast.
New York passed its own code in 1705, motivated in part by the size
of its Black population.

White planters needed legal order to control the unruly and growing Black workforce upon which the colonies' wealth extraction depended. The slave codes provided it. They were among the first
American laws to carefully detail the terms and conditions for brutal-
izing Black people.

If any slave resist his master, or owner, or other person, by his
or her order, correcting such slave, and shall happen to be killed
in such correction, it shall not be accounted felony; but the
master, owner, and every such other person so giving correction, shall be free and acquit of all punishment and accusation
for the same, as if such incident had never happened. —Act
Concerning Servants and Slaves, section 34

The 1705 slave codes would not be the final word on anti-Black
violence. There would be many more laws: the Fugitive Slave Acts, the
post-Reconstruction "Black codes," the Jim Crow court rulings offering impunity for vigilante justice, the sentencing laws of the 1980s,
the police militarization of the 1994 Crime Bill, and today's ongoing
legal deference to cops who feel threatened by the unarmed Black
children they kill.

The myths Americans tell themselves about the past—that it is
distant, that people did bad things out of ignorance rather than mal-
ice, that the good guys won in the end—encourage a false faith in the

present. They allow us to believe our norms are fixed and that the forward march of progress may sometimes be delayed but never reversed. Bad times will get better, because they always have. We'll be safe.

But the past is close. The slave codes of 1705 are close. The past is filled with people who carried out evil acts with foresight and determination, supported by the complicity of their peers. It contains progress but just as many reactionary entrenchments of old power. White supremacy became the norm in America because white men who felt threatened wrote laws to foster it, then codified the violence necessary to maintain it. They can maintain it with the same intention today, if we allow it.

THE REVOLT IN NEW YORK

HERB BOYD

———

O N APRIL 6 OR 7, 1712, LESS THAN A YEAR AFTER NEW YORK City's municipal slave market opened for business, two dozen enslaved Africans "gathered in an orchard of Mr. Crook 'in the middle of town,'" according to Governor Robert Hunter.

They "had resolved to revenge themselves," the governor explained, "for some hard usage, they apprehended to have received from their masters." Harsher restrictions on the growing number of enslaved Africans in New York City had led to more resistance.

From the eleven captives brought to New York City in 1626, by 1700 the Black population had increased to more than six thousand, of whom approximately one thousand were enslaved to British owners. In the eighteenth century, depending on the time and place, there were more enslaved African Americans in New York than in some Southern states; more in New York City than in Charleston, South Carolina. In 1800 there were 20,613 enslaved Blacks in New York and 13,584 in Tennessee.

With the city's enslaved population increasing exponentially, harsher restrictions were imposed, and these measures, much like those in the South, only intensified the growing anger and discontent. Slave codes in New York forbade enslaved Africans to assemble in groups larger than three; any slave who broke the law was punished by forty lashes on the naked back; and slaveholders could punish enslaved people for any misdeed in any way they chose except killing them or cutting off their limbs. And any slave who plotted with others to murder his or her enslaver was tortured and killed.

But that did not stop the rebels in 1712.

Anglican chaplain Anthony Sharpe reported that the majority of the rebels were un-Christian "Koramantines and Pawpaws from the Akan-Asante society of the Gold Coast—probably imported within the previous year or two (so much for the assumption that newcomers from Africa were more docile)." Another account said the plotters tied "themselves to secrecy by sucking ye blood of each other's hand and reassuring themselves by accepting a charm from a free Negro."

Two Native Americans were among the rebels who set fire to a building and, armed with a few guns, clubs, and knives, waited for the whites to approach. "Several did, and were then attacked by the slaves who killed about nine men and seriously wounded five or six others."

Alarmed by the uprising and the deaths, Governor Hunter invoked martial law. The rebels hastily retreated into the woods. The next day the governor and his soldiers sealed off the island of Manhattan to prevent the rebels from escaping. "Hunted down," stated one report, "six of the conspirators cut their own throats (one man killing his wife and himself) rather than be captured."

While only about twenty-five enslaved people were involved in the rebellion, more than seventy others were arrested and brought to trial before a special court convened by the governor. Twenty-three were convicted of murder and two of attempted murder. Twenty were hanged outright, and others experienced excruciating forms of death, including being roasted, slow-turning, on a fire or broken on a wheel. Another had every bone of his body smashed by a man wielding a crowbar until he was dead. Six of them, however, including a pregnant woman, were pardoned. The means of punishment and modes of execution, lawmakers claimed, were consistent with the slave codes of 1708, since the rebels had conspired and wantonly killed members of the community.

After the trials and executions, even more stringent laws were enforced, and the Common Council ordered that no slave could travel about the city after dark without a lantern. The assembly enacted a new law that made manumission or emancipation prohibitively ex-

pensive for enslavers and stipulated that no freed slave could thence-
forth own a house or land in the colony.

The new laws were so restrictive that a free Black person became
rare in Manhattan. "The real legacy of the 1712 uprising was a new era
of routinized brutality and official cynicism toward slaves," said one
observer. "Crowds of townsfolk often gathered to watch slaves hanged
or burned to death for one offense or another."

Soon enslaved people were not allowed even to speak adversely to
a white person, lest they be publicly flogged at a whipping post, as was
the fate of one audaciously outspoken Black woman. She was tied to
a wagon, dragged through the streets, and subsequently transported
to another colony.

That woman, Robin, was just one of many Black New Yorkers who
lived in fear, waiting for the next knock on the door, or who watched
helplessly as a loved one was snatched from their loving grasp and
taken away. If these tragic acts were visited upon African Americans
in the North, it's no wonder that even more massive and deadly insurrections occurred in the South.

Things would get worse before they got better, and the hostility
vented on the Black population, slave or otherwise, was relentless and
vindictive. As such, it was only a matter of time before another band
of enslaved and outraged men and women would decide they could
no longer endure in silence the obdurate oppression, the lashes of
hatred and racism.

In 1741, nearly a generation after the militia put down the slave
revolt of 1712, white New Yorkers trembled again in the wake of a
rebellion, this one based on an even more elaborate conspiracy, and
this one including some white sympathizers. Time and again white
racism produced Black resistance. It is one of the longest-running
plotlines in African American history.

THE SLAVE MARKET

SASHA TURNER

——

IN 1714 THE "MEAL MARKET" STOOD IN THE CENTER OF NEW York City. Located where Wall Street meets the East River, between Pearl and Water Streets, the newly designated slave market became the government-authorized site for selling the city's enslaved people. Built by the municipal government, the Meal Market (so called because grains also were sold there) had been there for three years.

But New Yorkers had bought and sold humans for much longer than three years. As early as 1626, the Dutch had imported captive Africans into New York (then New Amsterdam), and starting in 1648 had traded for enslaved people directly with Angola. A New York census recorded settlers importing at least 209 enslaved people from Africa and 278 from the West Indies between 1700 and 1715.

Long before municipal authorities had slave markets, white New Yorkers traded enslaved people aboard ships and in merchant houses. They also traded humans on paper, through lease and mortgage agreements, wills, and private transfers. The slave market was more than a physical location. It was everywhere.

The growth of the slave market was dependent upon the belief that humans were a commodity whose only "socially relevant feature" was the price their bodies commanded. Chains and owner initials effaced tribal markings and clothing that had marked belonging, social distinction, and rank. Traders boiled the needs of these humans down to economic calculations of the cost of sustaining bare life. Investors dispensed food and medicine merely to keep laborers "wholesome," making them "grow likely for the market."

Just as speculators observed the changing height and size of children strictly with an eye on their labor readiness and market value, so, too, they assessed women of childbearing age based on the "possibilities of their wombs." From the 1662 Virginia law that decreed that all children born of Black women were slaves, to wills that included enslaved people as property, Euro-Americans used the power of language to enact a new reality that a human could be a commodity. The slave market was governed by the chattel principle.

In contrast to the plantation colonies, which purchased the enslaved by the shipload from the oceanic and domestic trades, New Yorkers bought and sold enslaved people individually or in small groups at commercial houses without public notice. The comparably fickle nature of slave ownership in New York made enslaved Africans vulnerable to multiple sales. One enslaved woman named Phyllis was sold six times between owners in Long Island, New York City, and New Jersey. Jack, a boy of twelve, was sold at least ten times to buyers on both sides of the Hudson. The exchangeability of enslaved children was especially pronounced in nonplantation settings like New York that marginally relied on slave labor. Enslaved children were frequently sold to neighbors, friends, and business associates by owners who had no need for more than one enslaved person or were unwilling to pay maintenance costs for an extra enslaved person.

The slave market was a space of exchange, not just an auction block. The mobility of the slave market as determined by slave exchangeability created a nuisance for well-to-do New Yorkers and government officials. A free-range slave market permitted tax-free slave sales, cheating municipal authorities of craved revenues. By the 1710s, enslaved people parading the streets scouting buyers or renters became bothersome to New Yorkers. New York merchants' and vessels' growing participation in the transatlantic slave trade further increased captive presence across the city.

After arriving only in small handfuls for decades, captives landed in New York at an accelerated pace as the eighteenth century went on. Between 1715 and 1741, some four thousand Africans arrived in New

York. The period between 1715 and 1718 accounted for the highest number of arrivals, approximately 40 percent of the total during that era.

Sellers relied on theatrics to create the illusion that humans were just another marketable commodity, valued at the price demanded, and that they were healthy and hardy laborers. Preparation of captives for the market began at least one week prior to opening sale. Agents refreshed them with water and food, filling out and strengthening their emaciated and exhausted bodies. To conceal the "undesired testimony [of] the violence and unsanitary conditions of the slave ships," agents bathed, shaved, and oiled the captives. From palm oil and lard to the more generic "Negro Oyle," traders used various forms of grease to polish captives' skin, giving them the illusion of health and vitality. Slaves marketed locally were similarly treated to extra rations and grooming. Eliminating evidence of aging, sickness, and ill and hard usage was integral to enhancing the value of enslaved people.

Market theatrics were especially crucial to New York's Wall Street. Enslaved people arriving in New York were mostly leftovers (called refuse slaves) from plantation colonies like Barbados and Virginia, where a handful of estates often cleared entire shipments. New Yorkers rarely bought shiploads of enslaved people, instead buying people individually or in small groups. Between 1715 and 1763, for example, only 16 out of 636 British slavers ported in New York, and then only after they had sold the majority of their cargo in the Caribbean and the American South. Captives arriving in the New York market had been twice rejected by Caribbean and Southern mainland buyers, because of perceived medical complaints, physical weakness, old age, and undesirable personal histories (infertility, rebelliousness, or criminal conviction). Traders fattened, polished, and preened refuse slaves as best they could to convince buyers their commodity held value.

Traders carefully staged the slave market to mask the humanity of people who had been turned into a commodity, making it into a theater of jollity and amusement. They plied buyers with wine and brandy while the auctioneer tickled them with jokes and antics, treating them to a lively show of the enslaved body, which was forced to be receptive to being touched and to feign happiness with their bondage. Dancing, jumping, singing, and parading the streets were commonplace "rituals of the marketplace" demonstrating slave value and, crucially, also denying emotions that would have betrayed the humanity of the enslaved.

Jollification and the threat of the lash, however, could not mask the sorrow of parting from loved ones and the revulsion at being fondled by lecherous buyers. The shame and humiliation that enslaved people suffered remained plainly visible in their tears and in the silent screams of their eyes.

MAROONS AND MARRONAGE

SYLVIANE A. DIOUF

—

O N JULY 16, 1720, THE *RUBY* LANDED IN LOUISIANA. AFTER fifty-four days at sea, 127 men, women, and children from Senegal and Gambia disembarked.

Naturalist Antoine Le Page du Pratz received "two good ones, which had fallen to me by lot. One was a young Negro about twenty, with his wife of the same age." After six months, the couple ran away. Native Americans captured them sixty miles away, and soon the husband "died of a defluxion on the breast, which he catched [*sic*] by running away into the woods."

To du Pratz, the couple had run away because they were lazy. The man's "youth and want of experience made him believe he might live without the toils of slavery," he said. In fact, the young Senegambians had chosen marronage over enslavement—emblematic of the fierce African resistance of the early 1700s.

Between 1700 and 1724, marronage, revolts, and more than fifty insurrections aboard slave ships caused much alarm throughout the British colonies. In the thirteen North American colonies, maroons— "runaways who hid[e] and lurk in obscure places," also called outliers— drew attention for the potential threat they posed.

In 1721 Virginia lieutenant governor Alexander Spotswood feared it would be difficult to apprehend "Negroes" who had settled in the Blue Ridge Mountains. Should their number increase, he thought they would endanger the frontier settlers and threaten the peace of the colony. Virginians and Marylanders knew maroon communities were well established in Jamaica, and to prevent a similar development, they instituted a policy of divide and conquer, offering Native Americans two guns and blankets or coats as a reward for each maroon they captured.

William Byrd II, the founder of Richmond, went so far as to recommend ending the slave trade, "lest [Africans] prove as troublesome and dangerous everywhere, as they have been lately in Jamaica.... We have mountains in Virginia too, to which they may retire as safely, and do as much mischief as they do in Jamaica." Lieutenant Governor William Bull of South Carolina warned that if the Cherokees were run out of the mountains, their land would become a "refuge to the runaway negroes ... who might be more troublesome and more difficult to reduce than the Negroes in the mountains of Jamaica."

The specter of Jamaica continued to be used whenever it was convenient, but unlike Jamaican maroons, most maroons in the colonies did not live in distant communities; they melted into their surroundings at the borderland of populated areas. They typically lived in underground, human-made caves, or dens as they called them, dug several feet underground and closed by well-camouflaged traps. Families, mothers with children, and friends could remain hidden there for years. They hunted, fished, and gathered fruit. They received food from friends and relatives and helped themselves to the pantries of plantation owners. They acquired clothes, salt, firearms, and ammunition through trade with free and enslaved Blacks and with poor whites. In the hinterland, maroon communities—comprising from twenty to eighty people—raised crops, poultry, and pigs. They, too, traded and appropriated what they could not produce.

Maroon communities remained a constant threat to slaveholding colonies. In the early 1700s, a North Carolina act deplored that "many Times Slaves run away and lie out hid and lurking in the Swamps, Woods and other Obscure Places, killing Cattle and Hogs, and committing other Injuries to the Inhabitants." Newspapers regularly reported on their numerous "depredations." Petitions to legislatures denounced the damage they caused to livestock, crops, and stores, as well as to the citizens' sense of safety, all the more because they traveled well armed. They encouraged desertion and often organized the liberation of loved ones.

In their "obscure places"—and more than any other population—maroons were attuned to the natural world. They found sustenance and protection in the environment; knowing it intimately was paramount to their survival. The popular image of the wilderness as dangerous and savage served them well. They built a parallel reputation as ferocious people who could measure up against wild beasts. But to them, danger and savagery lay in the slavers' world. "I felt safer among the alligators than among the white men," the maroon Tom Wilson once said.

Maroons' autonomy shattered the racist view of Black people as incapable of taking care of themselves. Besides, their very existence underlined the limits of the terror system used to control the enslaved population. Cornelia Carney—whose father and cousin and their friend were maroons—expressed a common sentiment when she said Black people were too smart for white people to catch them. Of course, that view was exaggerated. Maroons were captured and as a deterrent were tortured or gruesomely executed. Some gave up and returned to slavery. Some died in the woods.

But they had enough success stories to be an inspiration. The maroon Pattin, his wife, and their fifteen children lived underground for fifteen years and emerged only after the Civil War. In the Great Dismal Swamp, a Union soldier encountered children who had never seen a white man. Some maroons did not even know there had been a war.

In the end, the 1720s prediction that warring outliers would descend from the mountains did not materialize. Maroons did launch numerous assaults. Whenever they were outgunned and outnumbered, which was often, they employed the guerrilla tactic of disappearing. But American maroons were not antislavery insurrectionists. Individuals, families, and communities were the norm. They never had the numbers to lead a successful slave revolt. More than anything, they wanted to be left alone. When some plots were discovered, and during Nat Turner's revolt, they were suspected, but nothing could ever be substantiated.

Tenacious. Creative. Self-confident. Fearless. Resilient. They displayed all these qualities and more to their enslaved admirers. Maroons became folk heroes. In the 1930s, formerly enslaved men and women recalled their hard-won and defiant freedom. Maroons created an alternative to life in servitude, a free life in a slave society, a free life in a free state. Free Blacks and runaways were still subjected to white supremacy; only maroons were self-ruled. For three years, the maroon Essex endured hunger, frostbite, and the bites of hounds, but all these hardships were well worth it. When captured, he simply said, "I taste how it is to be free, en I didn' come back."

Soon, though, maroons disappeared from popular consciousness and scholarly research. But not the essence of marronage: self-determination and freedom outside of white hegemony. The heart of the maroon beat in the establishment of Black towns, the emigration to Black nations, movements for Black power, and Black institution building yesterday and today. Marronage outlived the maroons.

THE SPIRITUALS

Corey D. B. Walker

———

And so by fateful chance the Negro folk-song—rhythmic cry of the slave—stands today not simply as the sole American music, but as the most beautiful expression of human experience born this side the seas.

—W.E.B. DU BOIS, *The Souls of Black Folk*

WHAT IS THE SACRED SOUND OF FREEDOM? FOR CONTINENtal and diasporic Africans in North America in the early eighteenth century, the sound would inevitably have been polyphonic. Freedom would have been a sonic cacophony of beats, rhythms, and melodies, clapping and stomping in syncopated time that moved between and beyond purely notational patterns. It would have resembled, reflected, and refracted the stirrings of an Atlantic world in motion.

The sacred sounds of freedom in the Americas included "the syncretic Afro-Brazilian religions of *macumba* and Umbanda, the black Catholic *congado*, and the quasisacred remnants of the otherwise secular *batuque* circle dance." Eighteenth-century America served as a conjuring space for Black sacred sound. African religions—Abrahamic and indigenous—gave expression to the historical, cultural, and religious expressions of these communities. New world African communities deployed this sound in expressing the hopes, joys, dreams, histories, aspirations, and longings of a people with a history who were simultaneously an emerging people creating a new world. A dichotomous sacred and secular did not operate within this conjuring context. It was all one. Indeed, as the pioneering musicologist Eileen Southern notes, "The music is everywhere! Often, one needs only to stop and listen."

Enslaved communities in North America were ethnically diverse. These continental and diasporic Africans forged a new world community with a new sound. The music in these communities not only captured the diverse traditions and cultures of Africans, it also developed in dynamic ways to reflect the contingencies of life in North America. Sacred sound transmitted histories, traditions, stories, myths, religions, and culture. "Song texts generally reflected personal or community concerns. The texts might speak of everyday affairs or of historical events; texts might inform listeners of current happenings or praise or ridicule persons, including even those listening to the song. . . . But the most important texts belonged to the historical songs that recounted heroic deeds of the past and reminded the people of their traditions."

The sheer diversity, complexity, and variety of musical forms and styles point to the depth and character of this soundscape in motion. Scholars have attempted to understand this music in a number of ways. Musicologist Guthrie Ramsey reminds us, "A most striking quality of early black music historiography ideology is how writers— particularly African American ones—negotiated the generally accepted 'divide' between Euro-based and Afro-based aesthetic perspectives." Ramsey underscores the challenge of understanding eighteenth-century Black music: to develop an adequate knowledge of the music itself and translate it into an appropriate contemporary idiom. You run the risk of underdeveloping or overdetermining the immense African contributions shaping and forming the music when you make it conform to European-derived musicological registers. A further challenge is the need to hear the music absent the sound and play the music absent notes. You have to find another path to understanding.

Despite the diverse sources of Black sacred music in North America, spirituals were initially presented by Europeans in translation form, in the idioms of European notes and categories. But these translations were inadequate to the task of expressing the music's rhythmic texture and robust sound. Dena Epstein writes, "Afro-American music included many elements not present in European music and for which no provision had been made in the notational system. For example, Lucy McKim Garrison wrote in 1862: 'It is difficult to express the entire character of these negro ballads by mere musical notes and signs. The odd turns made in the throat; and the curious rhythmic effect produced by single voices chiming in at different irregular intervals, seem almost as impossible to place on score, as the singing of birds or the tones of an Æolian harp.'" The worlds of continental and diasporic Africans could not be fully represented by the notational representation of latter-day ethnographers and musicologists.

So what is the sound of Black freedom? Perhaps it is best to begin by thinking reflexively about the probing question posited by W.E.B. Du Bois: "Do the sorrow songs sing true?"

AFRICAN IDENTITIES

WALTER C. RUCKER

———

SAMBA BAMBARA, FORCED TO WATCH THE TORTURE AND hanging of an unnamed woman compatriot, stood at the precipice between this world and the next. On December 10, 1731, he awaited his execution.

The leader of a slave plot in French New Orleans, Samba had a complicated past. A decade earlier he had served as an interpreter for the French Company of the Indies near Galam, a gold-producing state along West Africa's Senegal River. Indirectly aiding and abetting the commerce in Black flesh, Samba reportedly led a 1722 revolt in Senegal that temporarily cost the French a trading post. When the fort was recaptured and Samba's role was revealed, French authorities exiled him into Louisiana slavery.

Upon arrival in the French colony, he reassumed his role as an interpreter and used his linguistic skills to help his fellow Bambaras, when they had to appear in court, receive reduced sentences by translating testimony used against them in a favorable manner. His role as translator and his intimate knowledge of the French elevated Samba to the role of leader of the New Orleans Bambara. He leveraged his leadership role to conspire with other Bambaras to massacre all whites from Pointe Coupée to Balize, to free all Bambaras, and to force all Atlantic Africans who were not Bambara into servitude.

At this early moment in the long arc of African American history, concepts of a single Black race and of pan-African unity did not exist. Notions of Black people being one people had yet to be embraced fully by Africans and their American-born kin. Samba Bambara's 1731 conspiracy was the product of a time when unifying labels like *Black* and *African* had yet to be internalized, had yet to reach their political potential.

In a period that saw the intensification of rivalries between the Spanish, French, and English crowns in North America, Atlantic Africans and American-born Creoles demonstrated their resilience in carving out freedom spaces in a hostile world. In November 1729, a number of enslaved women and men—many from the Bambara nation—joined a Natchez nation assault on a French outpost near present-day Natchez, Mississippi. They killed 237 French men, women, and children and burned Fort Rosalie to ash. Five years later, in June 1734, an enslaved woman named Marie-Joseph Angélique was accused of setting fire to the merchant quarter of Montreal to mask her attempted escape.

Surrounded by French and Spanish colonies on the North American mainland, the British colonies—numbering thirteen with the establishment of Georgia in 1733—faced the same realities and perils as their neighbors. Slavery and enslaved peoples were everywhere; thus, resistance was ubiquitous. By the 1730s, enslaved Africans and their descendants could be found in the Chesapeake colonies (Virginia and Maryland), the Lowcountry and Southern colonies (Georgia, South Carolina, and North Carolina), the middle colonies (New York, New Jersey, Delaware, and Pennsylvania), and the New England colonies (Massachusetts, Rhode Island, Connecticut, and New Hampshire). Even though Georgia banned slavery in 1735, enslaved Africans were present in the colony at its inception in 1733. In addition to hosting resident maroons, Georgia was part of an African corridor between British Carolina and Spanish Florida through which enslaved people seeking refuge in St. Augustine, and later Fort Mose, would travel. Indeed, Georgia was founded to serve as a military buffer to deter enslaved women and men from reaching freedom in Spanish Florida.

Within the thirteen British colonies, enslaved Africans and their descendants made the best of the hellish circumstances they faced. Key to their ability to survive were the ritual technologies carried with them across the Atlantic. These complex systems of belief and worship sustained them and, over time, became the cement that connected peoples from many African ethnic groups who had no prior history of contact. The sojourn into American enslavement, far from being a story about the Americanization of African peoples, was punctuated by cultural innovation and experimentation between enslaved Africans from varying backgrounds.

The epicenters of Black culture in colonial North America were wildly disparate. Though African-born captives and their American-born kin could be found in all thirteen colonies, they clustered principally in the Southern and Chesapeake colonies of the Carolinas, Virginia, and Maryland. By 1731, however, enslaved Africans accounted for 18 percent of the total population of New York City. In the 1730s, New York had the largest population of Black people of any colonial city north of Baltimore and was second only to Charleston as the urban region with the highest concentration of Africans in North America. Populating Chesapeake tobacco and Southern rice plantations as well as prosperous port cities in the urban North, enslaved peoples were critical to the commercial success of British colonial efforts.

Just as the colonies they came to were varied, enslaved Africans embarked on European slavers from a wide range of coastal regions. Of the 26,107 souls who were carried to British North America in the cargo holds of slavers between 1729 and 1734, known points of origin ranged from the Bight of Biafra (5,531 souls) and Greater Senegambia (4,730 souls) to West-Central Africa (4,636 souls) and the Gold Coast (513 souls). Moreover, within each coastal region were many polities and ethnolinguistic groups. The men and women who would be transformed by Europeans into enslaved "commodities" did not belong to "tribes" and did not live in "backwaters"; nor were they ignorant of the worlds around them. Some understood the intentions of Europeans and, as a result, developed rich folkloric traditions about them as witches, demons, or flesh-eating cannibals. Some imagined their fate across the ocean as a descent into a hellish world populated by evil spirits. Untold thousands met their fears with the hope that suicide would offer either relief or salvation. Others mobilized Africanized Christianity, Islam, or local religious faiths and ritual technologies to aid them in the travails ahead. Three generations into their sojourns in British North America, enslaved Africans and their descendants had not forgotten about Africa.

The creation of African nations or intentional communities was the principal means by which enslaved women and men maintained memories of their homelands. While European enslavers created many of the labels that identified the boundaries of these communities, these categories took on new meanings as enslaved Africans embraced them over time. Among the many ethnolinguistic labels that became part of a new African cultural geography in British North America were Bambara, Mandingo, and Gullah (Greater Senegambia); Eboe and Calabari (Bight of Biafra); Coromantee and Chamba (Gold Coast); Mina (Bight of Benin); and Congo and Angola (West-Central Africa). These identities were continuously reinforced by new streams of enslaved imports. Each of the thirteen British North American colonies witnessed fluctuations in the slave trade due to limited access to African coastal markets and the development of ethnic preferences. In this regard, Senegambians were heavily concentrated in South Carolina and Louisiana during the 1720s due, in part, to their proficiencies in cattle herding and rice cultivation. Enslaved peoples from the Bight of Biafra, widely regarded and rejected as "sickly" and "melancholy" "refuse" in prosperous colonies like Jamaica, were shipped to commercial backwaters like Virginia, where planters had less ability to influence the market. West-Central Africans from around modern-day Angola, representing 40 percent of the total traffic in enslaved Africans, were found everywhere in large numbers due to their ubiquity in the cargoes of slavers.

The slave trade into North America had flows and fluctuations across time and space, but it was patterned. As a result of the concentrations of specific Atlantic Africans in particular colonies and the formation of new African ethnic "nations," the developing slave cultures left indelible marks on what later became African American culture. Thus within the mother wit of many contemporary African Americans is the idea that dreaming about fish means that a close relative is pregnant (West-Central Africa). Some, especially in the

South Carolina and Georgia Lowcountry, have family memories of the ring shout (West-Central Africa), and many in and near Charleston still produce sweetgrass baskets (Greater Senegambia). Others, especially in Edenton, North Carolina, remember and continue to commemorate the Jonkonnu festival in December (Gold Coast).

Many African Americans still eat black-eyed peas at New Year's for good luck (Greater Senegambia). In the early twentieth century, some African Americans deployed prayer beads, prayed to the east multiple times each day while kneeling on mats, and were even interred—upon death—facing east (Greater Senegambia). Some recall that the folktale entitled "Brer Rabbit and the Tar Baby" has an ancient and dignified origin (Gold Coast and Greater Senegambia) that extends far beyond Disney's racist mangling of this epic tale in the 1946 movie *Song of the South*. All these expressions—aspects of mother wit, ritual technologies and knowledge systems, festivals, and folktales—emerged from the processes by which enslaved Africans from varied backgrounds shared cultural values, merged political interests, and became, over time, one people.

1734-1739

FROM FORT MOSE
TO SOUL CITY

Brentin Mock

——

BLACK REPUBLICANS OFTEN URGE BLACK DEMOCRATS TO "flee the plantation," meaning to join the Republican Party, or to cease using what they perceive as the victimizing language of civil rights and racial justice.

The "flee the plantation" cri de coeur is applied to conjure the memory of enslaved Africans escaping their forced labor camps in pursuit of freedom. For many Republicans, the Democratic Party, or liberals in general, represent the slaveholders, while the Republican Party represents emancipation. Alternately, Black Democrats often fancy themselves as emancipators from the Republicans and their plantations that are conserving the racist status quo. In reality, neither side can claim the title of emancipator.

The plantation is a powerful symbol, as the foundational unit for racial capitalism and chattel slavery in the United States. It represents the enduringly difficult living conditions of African Americans as well as the enduring reality that their labor goes primarily not to benefit themselves but to enhance the profits of white people. Neither Democrats nor Republicans, conservatives nor liberals, have been able to upend that racist order. Nor has either provided sanctuary for African Americans from "the plantation." In fact, the Black experience in America can be defined in large part as the never-ending search for refuge, sanctuary, and safe spaces to live, away from the plantation in all its forms, but to no avail.

One of the earliest hopes for Black sanctuary was Fort Mose, Florida, the first known free Black settlement in British North America. It was built in 1738 by Africans who had fled the plantations of the Carolinas for the Spanish settlement of St. Augustine in northeastern coastal Florida. While St. Augustine had a somewhat integrated population, comprising Indian tribes and formerly enslaved Africans who had been arriving there since as early as 1683, Fort Mose was established outside the city exclusively for the newer African refugees from the plantation. The Spanish policy, decreed by the crown in 1693, was that any enslaved person who made it to Spain's American territories would be at least eligible for freedom.

As South Carolina's enslaved African population swelled in the 1730s, particularly in Charleston, word began circulating about the opportunity for liberty in St. Augustine. All the enslaved would have to do was survive a journey of hundreds of miles of swamp, marsh, and sometimes-hostile Natives along the coast to reach Spanish Florida. But liberty would come in limited form. "Spanish bureaucrats attempted to count these people and to limit their physical mobility through increasingly restrictive racial legislation," explains historian Jane Landers. "Officials prohibited blacks from living unsupervised, or, worse, among the Indians. Curfews and pass systems developed, as did proposals to force unemployed blacks into fixed labor situations."

African migrants had to adopt the Spanish Catholic religion to gain entrance to St. Augustine. They were accepted as laborers and received wages, but only the lower rates paid to St. Augustine's Native residents.

While the migrants' living conditions were not as grueling here as in the Carolina plantations, where they had been treated as property, their situation in Spanish Florida might have been only slavery in a slightly more elegant font. They were still subject to European rule, and they were not in control of their destiny as long as they lived in the Spanish domain. This was but one of the earliest indicators that freedom for African Americans, no matter how promising, would never be complete, no matter where and when they moved throughout the North American landscape.

That tenuous freedom persisted after the Civil War. In 1887 the town of Eatonville was founded, just one hundred miles south of St. Augustine, outside Orlando. It was the first town to be "organized, governed and incorporated" by Black people. It existed in "relatively idyllic isolation" until the Supreme Court's 1954 *Brown v. Board of Education* decision imposed "forced integration." For African Americans, fleeing the plantation would rarely if ever mean finding safe harbor from white surveillance.

In the 1970s, civil rights activist Floyd McKissick gave the Black sanctuary experiment a shot when he founded Soul City. He planned to build a Black city—an urban oasis in the middle of rural North Carolina—from scratch. Soul City was to serve as a sanctuary from the racism that had taken the lives of Black leaders such as Martin Luther King, Jr., Malcolm X, and Medgar Evers—taking out the hopes and morale of many Black families in the process. Breaking ground in 1973, Soul City was the closest and most recent corollary to Fort Mose. But the trajectory to freedom was different: Soul City sought to draw African Americans to North Carolina, the general territory from which enslaved Africans had been escaping for Fort Mose some 240 years earlier.

Republicans of the 1970s were similar to the Florida Spaniards of the 1730s. President Richard Nixon's administration provided the initial funding and support for the building of Soul City. At the time, Nixon was looking to entice more African Americans into the Republican fold through the embrace of "Black capitalism," which he considered the only appropriate form for the popular new movement for Black Power. But slavery *was* capitalism. And it was capitalism that had lured rural and Southern Black workers to factories in cities, especially in the North and West in the mid-twentieth century, only to abandon many of those factories and cities by the century's end in search of cheaper, less-regulated, less-unionized shores. Nixon promised Black capitalism would be a solvent to the woes that racial capitalism created for Black people who were willing to break from the plantation of antiracist activism. But Nixon's motives were not genuine. It was a political ploy to siphon votes while hijacking the idea of Black Power for disempowering ends.

Similarly, in the 1730s the generosity that the Spanish Floridians

extended to Africans who had escaped enslavement was less than authentic. They positioned Fort Mose close to the northern Florida
border as a defensive buffer between St. Augustine and the potential
encroachment of British enslavers in the Carolinas and the newly
formed colony of Georgia in 1733.

Georgia's proximity allowed British militias to base-camp closer
to the Florida settlements. Spanish authorities needed Black laborers
to fortify Spain's economic investments throughout Florida, and they
armed and weaponized formerly enslaved Black militias to fend off
British invaders.

When Spain gave up Florida in 1763, it resettled some of its Black
subjects in Matanzas, Cuba, where, as Landers writes, "Spanish support was never sufficient," and the former Fort Mose inhabitants "suffered terrible privations." When Spain took Florida back in 1784, it
"made no effort to reestablish either Indian missions or the free black
town of Mose."

Similarly, for Soul City, when Nixon resigned under charges of
corruption in 1974, the federal government bailed on Soul City, allowing it to collapse before it had a chance to flourish. The "Soul Tech"
job training and business incubator center that was supposed to be
the anchor institution of Soul City became a county jail—a symbol of
the type of cities into which Black souls would be herded in the coming decades.

When Black conservatives urge their neighbors to flee the planta-
tion, it's not clear what or where they want Black people to flee to.
Neither Republicans nor Democrats have offered somewhere safe.
Certainly, African Americans have been creating sanctuaries in the
United States throughout history, since the genesis of Fort Mose, but
the United States has yet to honor any of them.

BEFORE REVOLUTION

Morgan Parker

—

Just crops. Just nooses. Wild
nerve. Soon as a hurricane gets
a name, it has breath, New lungs.

No use in looking back, only cost.
And so Man spat on the land, made her
take his name. Kingdom, Destiny, no other gods.

Before Jack Johnson. Before Malcolm. Before Nat Turner.
Before Bill Cosby. Before Cornel West.
Before Sly. Before Garvey. Before Stokely.

And Man say let freedom be a woman. Had to have her so
they took her. Just like a man
to name war lust

Before Colin Powell. Before Kanye West. Before Roc-a-
Fella. Before their heads were
cash, we were. Before Wall Street was a public

slave market on Wall Street. Feet and lemons
in the open. Before a flood, wickedness is
just another way to be almighty.

And there was
full moon, and there was half moon,

and there was new moon, solstice, harvest, waiting,
wading. Most of war
is waiting,
aftermath.
The Rapture was coming, all right.

Before freedom was something
else. Before this language. Before freedom of speech and
    freedom
of press and the anti-alien/inalienable right to shoot
    people,

before the Triangle Shirtwaist Factory fire, labor unions,
    Oakland Panthers
serving breakfast, the Philadelphia MOVE bombing,
    Fred Hampton's blood
on soaked mattress, there was war. There was always war.
    People always

got shot. Before African American but not before nigger,
    colored, Negro.
Before AAVE, before Black America. Before we voted
we won. Before New Orleans we invented jazz. Before
    this

revolution and that Revolution and this revelation.
Before California, before Rodney King, before Trayvon
    Martin, before justifiable
homicide, before manifest destiny, before they kept using
    this language.
Before Barack Obama, before Emmett Till, the crack
    epidemic,
the housing crash, opioids, ecstasy, before white flight.
Before Harriet Tubman before FloJo before Serena
    before Aretha.

Before Shirleys Chisholm and Bassey, before June Jordan
  and Juneteenth.
Before Roberta Flack sang "Go Up Moses." Before Phillis
  Wheatley, before
the Black Happy Birthday Song, before we could call
  spades
spades, before we wrote us down. Before Roberta Flack
  said
"Pharaoh doesn't want you, but he needs you.
My people." Before Sojourner, Ruby Bridges.
Before *Board of Education*, before railroads and Hawaiian
Airlines and Alaska Airlines and the NFL. Before the
  wars
on homelessness and poverty and terror and security
and Black trans women and Black women driving cars
  and Black girls
at pool parties and Black kids on playgrounds and corners
  and Black
veterans Black single mothers Black schizophrenics Black
professors Black athletes. Before we wasted all the water.
Before Flint, Michigan, Watergate, thoughts and prayers,
before semiautomatics. *"Without you there is no pharaoh."*
Before *The Arsenio Hall Show*. Before it was televised.
    Before Blaxploitation
and Lil' Kim and Dennis Rodman and before NYPD
  surveillance footage and
dash-cam footage the Lorraine Hotel and before Tamir
  Rice and Oscar Grant.
Before the West, west coast rap, west coast wineries,
  Mexican immigrants.
Before Ellis Island, before Japanese internment camps,
  before the gold rush,
cop shows, award shows, westerns, chain restaurants,
  Asian fusion,
the temperance movement and the suffragette movement

Hillary Clinton and Eleanor Roosevelt and Sandra
   Bullock in *The Blind Side*.
Before Jonestown. Before Selma. Before we almost lost
   Detroit.
Before Presidents of the United States of America.
   Before a noose
was a figure of speech. Before *unimaginable*
tragedy. No one put their hands over their hearts.

PART FOUR

THE STONO REBELLION

WESLEY LOWERY

———

I OFTEN THINK BACK TO A BALMY SPRING AFTERNOON WHEN I stood—my parents to my right and my two younger brothers to my left—beneath the rows of coffin-shaped pillars erected to chronicle a recent era of American terrorism.

We had traveled here, to Montgomery, Alabama, in early 2018, about one month after the grand opening of this exhibit: the National Memorial for Peace and Justice, which is a fancy name for what is a gut-punch of a memorial. It features 804 slabs of stone, suspended in midair as if hanging from tree branches, that represent every American county where a man, woman, or child was lynched.

We had come not only to see but to search. As we entered the walkway that snaked beneath the pillars, my father recited the names of four or five counties, primarily in rural North Carolina, and reminded us of various married names and divergent branches of his family tree. Our eyes searched the roster etched into each stone. We weren't looking for a specific name or incident—there aren't any known lynching victims in our lineage—but we knew it was possible, perhaps even likely, that at least one of those memorialized here would be recognizable as kin.

As my eyes interrogated each name of the slain, my ears drew me to a conversation just a few feet away, where another group stood, marveling, beneath a stone coffin. They appeared to be a family. They were all white. I can't recall precisely what I overheard. But I can't forget the realization, in that moment, that this family had no counties for which they'd been instructed to search.

This family was here to learn what my own had always known. While some nations vow never to forget, our American battle has always been over what we allow ourselves to remember.

Our historical record, we know, is subjective. Not every account is written down. The distinction between equity and injustice, riot and uprising, hinges on whose hand holds the pen. So often, it seems, our history is hiding from us, preventing the possibility that we dare look back and tell the truth—afraid of what doing so may require of us now.

Perhaps this is why we've been allowed to remember so little about the Stono Rebellion.

By the mid-eighteenth century, slavery had expanded so rapidly in the colony that would become the state of South Carolina that it was home to a Black majority. "Carolina looks more like a negro country than like a country settled by white people," Swiss traveler Samuel Dyssli wrote in 1737. "In Charleston and that neighborhood there are calculated to be always 20 blacks, who are called negroes, to one white man, but they are all slaves." The ratio wasn't quite that lopsided, but it was significant nonetheless. By 1740, Carolina's Black population was estimated at more than 39,100, while the white population stood at just 20,000.

But the booming population of enslaved people brought with it the same nightmare that has long tormented oppressive minorities: *what happens when they realize that they have us outnumbered?* Those fears were only exacerbated by a promise from the Spanish, eager to destabilize the British colonies, to free any enslaved person who made it to their territory in what is now Florida, specifically to St. Augustine. Soon the white slaveholders of Carolina would see their night terror come to life.

In the early hours of Sunday, September 9, 1739, about twenty Black rebels met on a bank of the Stono River, twenty miles southwest of Charleston, to carry out the plan that they had formed the night prior.

First, they marched to the Stono Bridge and broke into Hutchenson's store, which they robbed of guns and ammunition. The two white storekeepers were beheaded. Then they continued south, breaking into homes, executing the white families they found, and adding dozens of additional enslaved people to their ranks. At least twenty-three white Carolinians were left dead. The rebels are said to have acquired at least two drums, hoisted a flag, and indulged in defiant shouts of "Liberty!"

"Having found rum in some houses and drunk freely of it, they halted in an open field, and began to sing and dance, by way of triumph," wrote Alexander Hewatt, a white Charleston pastor, in his account of the uprising.

But the rebels would never make it to St. Augustine. In fact, most died in that very field—descended upon by an armed local militia.

The white residents vowed to never let this happen again. The colony's House of Assembly took steps to curtail the growing Black majority, implementing a ten-year moratorium on the importation of Black people and passing the Negro Act of 1740, which restricted the rights of enslaved people to assemble and educate themselves—undercutting the chances that future generations would discover the promise of freedom made by the Spanish to the South. For decades, white residents feared that some of the rebels, who had fled into the forest, would come back and again terrorize their towns.

The history we've been given recalls Stono—one of the bloodiest uprisings of enslaved people in the history of the land that would become America—as a cautionary tale, the story of the dangers of allowing Black men and women to dream of liberty. There's nothing to suggest that the rebels at Stono were political visionaries, that they aspired to overthrow the system of enslavement and plunder in which they lived each day as victims. They most likely just wanted to escape.

Generations of American storytellers have found that, when it comes to tales of uprising and rebellion, banishment digests easier than recollection. But what do we lose when we refuse to sit with the truth? What do we gain when we allow the rebels at Stono to tell their own story, when we see them not as rebels but as revolutionaries? What if the uprising, the riot, is not a story of disorder but one of a fearless fight for freedom?

History has left us just one known account of the rebellion from a nonwhite perspective, as part of the Federal Writers' Project in the 1930s. This is an interview with George Cato, purportedly a direct descendant—the great-great-grandson—of the rebellion's leader, whose family had orally preserved the details of the insurrection for nearly two hundred years.

"I sho' does come from dat old stock who had de misfortune to be slaves but who decided to be men, at one and de same," Cato told his interviewer. "De first Cato slave we knows 'bout was plum willin to lay down his life for de right, as he see it."

LUCY TERRY PRINCE

NAFISSA THOMPSON-SPIRES

———

A NINETY-SIX-YEAR-OLD BLACK WOMAN MASSAGES HER SPINE for a moment, kneads her Achilles, lifts her skirt slightly, secures her booted ankles into the stirrups, and starts on a long trek, "over the Green Mountains," to place flowers on the grave of her husband.

She has made the painful ride annually since 1794, and when she waves, a wry smile in her eyes, passersby remark, "Luce Bijah is still at it." Twenty years before, they shook their heads, incredulous, as Lucy Terry Prince rode home from making a successful stand before the Vermont supreme court. And since the eighteenth century, they sang her song with a knowing in their recitation.

Much of the extant research about Terry Prince focuses on the significance of her literary contributions. Born into slavery around 1730 and taken to Deerfield, Massachusetts, from Rhode Island, Terry Prince composed the first known poetry by an African American. She is customarily situated alongside Phillis Wheatley—the first African American with a published poetry book (1773)—and Jupiter Hammon, the first published African American poet, author of the 1761 broadside *An Evening Thought; Salvation by Christ With Penitential Cries.*

Terry Prince's "Bars Fight" remains the only known poetic work by its author and was preserved orally until its 1854 front-page regional print publication in the *Springfield Daily Republican* and later in Josiah Holland's 1855 *History of Western Massachusetts.* The ballad recounts the eponymous incident when "King George's War between England and France broke out in 1745, with the Abenaki Indians, who had been displaced from Massachusetts to northern New England and Canada, allying with the French."

What I'm most interested in here, however, is not the poem itself but the spirit and power structures that produced—and protected—Lucy Terry Prince. She stood before major government officials and is memorialized as an artist, but much of her life—including whether she actually "wrote" the poem—is shrouded in mystique and urban legends.

Baptized in 1735, Lucy was possibly born on the African continent and brought to Rhode Island, where she was purchased by Ebenezer Wells and subsequently moved to Deerfield. Church records confirm that in 1756 she married Abijah Prince, a free man who had secured his freedom after his master's death in 1749 and somehow purchased Lucy's freedom as well. They settled in Northfield, where Prince held "some real estate rights" to "three divisions of the undivided land." It is clear that the Terry Prince family, which soon included six children, was well known in their community. Neighbors called the brook bubbling through their property "Bijah's Brook," and their house "a place of resort for the young people of the 'Street,'" their front porch a pulpit, a site "where folks were entertained and enlightened by recitations, music, and poetry." Even if much of her mobility came through her husband, Terry Prince's rhetorical cunning made her a respected and noted figure in her own right.

Terry Prince's emancipation, freedom, and property already marked her as somewhat remarkable, and she made waves that could have ended in disaster in two different legal incidents. When in 1762 Bijah stood to inherit a hundred acres from a grantee in what is now Guilford, Vermont, Lucy and Bijah became entangled in an ongoing legal battle over this land with a white man who tried to claim it. As the case escalated through the 1790s, Lucy litigated before the Vermont supreme court, making her the first woman—and Black woman—to argue before the court and to win her case at that.

When liberal arts institution Williams College refused to admit her son Festus because of his race, Terry Prince advocated on his behalf during a three-hour argument. Her son was not admitted to the school, but we cannot understate the magnitude of Terry Prince's argumentation and willingness to take on white individuals and institutions in the eighteenth-century United States. Although race was not yet the fixed construct that it is today, Terry Prince's actions certainly could have compromised her and her family's safety.

When she died in 1821 at age ninety-seven, the Massachusetts paper *The Franklin Herald* published an obituary calling her "a woman of colour" and noting that "in this remarkable woman there was an assemblage of qualities rarely to be found among her sex. Her volubility was exceeded by none, and in general the fluency of her speech was not destitute of instruction and education. She was much respected among her acquaintance."

Even in death, Terry Prince was considered exceptional, and it is possible that she was exceptionally "strong" or stubborn.

A woman who held so many superlatives—the first to face off against the all-white and all-male supreme court, a vocal advocate for her child, and a town crier, a known eyewitness—likely occupied a fraught position, and we cannot underestimate how equally vulnerable and valuable her traits would have made her.

We need only to look to Anne Hutchinson—executed a century before Terry Prince's song—or to Nina Simone's "Backlash Blues" or to the case of Jacqueline Dixon for stories of "know-your-place aggression" and backlash against (Black) women who stood their ground. We cannot ignore the very real racial-sexual terror Terry Prince could have—and we don't know if she did—experienced for her actions.

Thus I do not want to risk emblematizing Terry Prince to the point of losing her humanity. As bell hooks and others have warned us, the danger in the myth of the strong, assertive Black woman is its elision of our pain and vulnerability. To fully see Lucy Terry Prince is to contextualize the conditions that made her choose to survive. Her song itself signals ongoing trauma from the incidents she witnessed. Phrases like "dreadful slaughter" and "killed outright" paint a painful scene still vivid in the psyche. And it is very likely that the named trauma of the Bars incident—and the unnamed traumas she experienced while enslaved and later as the mother of six children—affected her daily life. To maintain her safety and the safety of her family, Terry Prince would have had to tread skillfully, codeswitching between assertiveness and (performing) "knowing her place," as we have seen.

To that point, if we revisit the incident with Williams College, Terry Prince's insistence on her son's acceptance is actually in keeping with the cult of domesticity, which dictated that women took responsibility for the education of their children. It also helps that her magnum opus recounts the events of the Bars incident in a way that makes the white colonists look favorable and the Abenaki people the criminals. That her song was published posthumously and circulated orally during her lifetime rather than in print also makes it less a performance of gender or racial aberrance. When read another way, then, each of Terry Prince's seeming transgressions against the expectations of her gender and race and time—with perhaps the exception of her property battle—might equally resituate her within them.

I say all this not to withhold praise from Terry Prince for her very real accomplishments but to suggest that the way she achieved them is what is most exceptional. By working both within and against a system that seldom rewarded women for acting out—and living to tell—Terry Prince demonstrates the performative dexterity often required of African American women across history to survive, to avoid singing the backlash blues.

Her legacy extends beyond "Bars Fight" to a complex figure who must have suffered as much as she succeeded. A trickster, both a "respectable lady" and a bold troublemaker, Lucy Terry Prince should be the subject of more study—and new ballads, new songs.

1749–1754

RACE AND THE ENLIGHTENMENT

DOROTHY E. ROBERTS

———

IN THE 1700S, EUROPE EXPERIENCED AN INTELLECTUAL MOVE-
ment, known as the Age of Enlightenment, that set the course of
scientific theory and methods for the next three centuries. Leading
thinkers embraced reason over superstition and shifted the basis of
their conclusions about the universe from religious beliefs to secular
science, giving science the ultimate authority over truth and knowledge. In many respects, the Enlightenment advanced ways of understanding the natural world and human behavior, but it was also the
period when the modern scientific concept of race as a natural category was installed.

The expansion of the slave trade in the 1700s necessitated an expanding conceptual racial system of governance, spurring the change
among European intellectuals from theological to biological thinking. During the Enlightenment, race became an object of scientific
study, and scientists began to explain enslavement as a product of
nature. Racial science was deployed to explain unequal outcomes in
health, political status, and economic well-being as stemming from
natural racial differences rather than from racist policies.

By 1749, European naturalists had begun to use race as a category
for scientifically classifying human beings. The major groundwork for
modern biological typologies was laid by Carl Linnaeus, whose
twelve-edition catalog of living things, *Systema Naturae*, was published between 1735 and his death in 1778. Linnaeus divided *Homo*

sapiens into four natural varieties—*H. sapiens americanus, H. sapiens europaeus, H. sapiens asiaticus,* and *H. sapiens afer*—linked respectively to the Americas, Europe, Asia, and Africa, and he ascribed innate physical, social, and moral characteristics to each group. Although Linnaeus, like the biologists who succeeded him, claimed these racial categories were based on objective observations of nature, they were far from neutral. Eighteenth-century classifications positioned races in a hierarchy, placing Europeans at the top with the most positive traits ("Vigorous, muscular. Flowing blond hair. Very smart, inventive. Ruled by law"), and placing Africans at the bottom and with the most negative features ("Sluggish, lazy. Black kinky hair. Crafty, slow, careless. Ruled by caprice").

The Enlightenment is typically touted as a radical break from the Christian theology that preceded it. However, one aspect of its thinking transported from theology to science—the belief that some powerful force apart from human intervention divided all human beings into separate races. Many European theologians held that God created the races and made Europeans in His image. After the Enlightenment, with the Divine no longer an acceptable basis for scientific evidence, European scientists pointed to nature as producing innate distinctions between races. (A century later, after the publication of Darwin's *On the Origin of Species,* scientists began attributing race to evolution.) Thus, the racist theological concept of race survived the Enlightenment transition from "supernaturalist to scientific explanations of human origins and potential."

Benjamin Franklin, one of the most revered intellectuals of his day, was instrumental in importing Enlightenment thinking to the British colonies in North America. There, Enlightenment scientists' understanding of race served a critical political function: the view that nature had created racial distinctions resolved the contradiction between the Enlightenment ideals of liberty, equality, and tolerance and the enslavement of African people. The shift to secular thinking reinforced the view that Black people were innately and immutably inferior as a race and therefore were subject to permanent enslavement. After chattel slavery ended, the biological concept of race continued to shape the social and biological sciences, medical practice, and social policies, forming a scientific foundation for eugenics, Jim Crow, and post–civil rights color-blind ideology that ignores racism's persistent impact.

Excluding Black people from the emerging democracy was excused as an inevitable product of nature. Thomas Jefferson elucidated this racist scientific thinking in his 1781 treatise *Notes on the State of Virginia.* He justified the exclusion of Black people from the democracy he and Franklin had helped to create based on "the real distinctions which nature has made." He concluded: "This unfortunate difference in colour, and perhaps in faculty, is a powerful obstacle to the emancipation of these people."

Quaker preacher John Woolman had already disagreed with this racist line of thought in the 1750s. He wrote a religious treatise, *Some Considerations on the Keeping of Negroes,* in 1746 but didn't publish it until 1754, after abolitionist Anthony Benezet was elected to the Philadelphia yearly meeting press editorial board. Woolman urged his fellow Christians to see the evils of slavery by contesting enslavers' rationales for denying the equal humanity of Black people. He advocated not only for ending enslavement but also for refusing to benefit from enslaved labor until abolition was achieved. Benjamin Franklin's *Pennsylvania Gazette* advertised the publication of *Some Considerations on the Keeping of Negroes.* By the close of 1754, many Quakers had concluded that slavery was incompatible with Christianity and had begun to build an abolition movement. But the scientific understanding of race as a biological fact of nature was flourishing and would help to bolster slavery for decades to come.

Benjamin Franklin subscribed to the view not only that Black people were naturally distinct from white people but also that these distinctions necessitated differences in political status. In 1751 he authored *Observations Concerning the Increase of Mankind,* which argued that Anglo-Saxons should expand into the Americas because Europe was overpopulated. Franklin's claim depended in part on concerns about the "darkening" of certain parts of the Americas and its effect on the Anglo-Saxon inhabitants. "Who can now find the vacancy made in Sweden, France or other warlike nations, by the Plague of heroism forty Years ago; in France by the expulsion of the Protestants;

in England by the settlement of her Colonies; or in Guinea, by one hundred years' exportation of slaves, that has blacken'd half America?," he wrote.

Franklin explained in terms of natural distinctions between races why he did not want more Africans brought to the America that he and his enlightened colleagues were building:

> The number of purely white people in the world is proportionally very small. All Africa is black or tawny. Asia chiefly tawny. America (exclusive of the newcomers) wholly so. And in Europe, the Spaniards, Italians, French, Russians and Swedes are generally of what we call a swarthy complexion; as are the Germans also, the Saxons only excepted, who with the English make the principal body of white people on the face of the earth. I could wish their numbers were increased. And while we are, as I may call it, scouring our planet, by clearing America of woods, and so making this side of our globe reflect a brighter light to the eyes of inhabitants in Mars or Venus, why should we in the sight of superior beings, darken its people? Why increase the sons of Africa, by planting them in America, where we have so fair an opportunity, by excluding all blacks and tawneys, of increasing the lovely white and red? But perhaps I am partial to the complexion of my Country, for such kind of partiality is natural to Mankind.

Although Franklin supported abolishing the slave trade, he did not support Black people's freedom and equal citizenship in the American polity until later in his life. Rather, his central objective was to include white people only in the new nation he and his "enlightened" peers were creating.

BLACKNESS AND INDIGENEITY

KYLE T. MAYS

——

THE DISPOSSESSION OF MILLIONS OF NATIVE AMERICANS AND the simultaneous genocide and enslavement of Indigenous Africans remain two intertwining and parallel events that have fundamentally shaped the United States. These historical travesties continue today in the form of rampant anti-Black racism and anti-Indigenous erasure from the national consciousness.

The year 1754 was instrumental in prerevolutionary America. In that year the French and Indian War—a conflict between the British colonies, New France, and a host of Native American nations fighting on each side—emerged, an event that would change the dominant European population east of the Mississippi and lead into the modern world's first global conflict, the Seven Years' War (1756–63). The war ended with the Treaty of Paris, in which France ceded all land east of the Mississippi to Britain. After France was defeated, kinship was no longer a major part of Native-British relations as it had been with the French: the "British were the conquerors; the Indians were the subjects."

It was also a moment ripe with contradictions between freedom and unfreedom. For almost a century, Europeans had constructed Native North American peoples as savages in order to justify taking their land. Native people became central characters in how Europeans constructed their belonging to the "New World" as the original inhabitants of the land, thus erasing those Native people. In this way, they separated the European world from the Indigenous and African ones, creating a distinction between civilization and savagery, or human and nonhuman.

The population of this contested land comprised white men with property, indentured servants, enslaved Africans, and precariously placed Native peoples. As the British colonies and New France faced off, the combined power of anti-Black racism and African slavery became further entrenched in colonial society. For instance, between 1735 and 1750, Georgia was one of the few colonies that attempted to limit slavery, especially because of its close proximity to Spanish Florida. However, as Georgia's rice economy increased, its planters desired more enslaved people from West Africa. Between 1750 and 1755, Georgia's enslaved population increased nearly 3,500 percent.

Slavery became a further entrenched part of the colonies during the French and Indian War. In 1757 the Reverend Peter Fontaine of Virginia, the oldest of the original thirteen colonies, commented, "To live in Virginia without slaves is morally impossible."

This period also brought more interactions between people of African descent and Native North Americans. Paul Cuffe, born on January 17, 1759, was an early person of mixed ancestry, with both Indigenous African and North American Indigenous roots, born to Kofi (Akan), who was sold into slavery as a preteen, and to Ruth Moses (Wampanoag). After the Revolutionary War, Cuffe became one of the wealthiest Black shipping merchants of his time and played a central role in trying to establish a colony in Sierra Leone for people of African descent from the new United States. However, what is often missed in his history is that he represents some of the earliest Afro-Indigenous people in the United States—those with a relationship not only to the mark of Blackness but also to U.S. Indigenous roots. Cuffe had attempted to assert his North American Indigenous roots during his earlier years, but because of the rampant anti-Blackness, he would later more strongly identify as Black. What we can learn from Cuffe and others like him is that the first enslaved Africans did not lose their Indigenous roots—they maintained them as best as they could. They also often found possibilities in their encounters with Indigenous peoples in the United States.

Dispossession and enslavement were foundational to prerevolutionary America. However, they also created connections between Black and Indigenous peoples that might not have otherwise happened. These histories should serve as our opportunity to think about what it might mean for Black Americans not only to remember their foundational role in shaping American democracy but also to reflect on how they have always found kinship with Native American peoples. What would an alliance between Black and Native Americans look like today, and how would that continue to fundamentally change this country so that it not only met the founders' ideals of what democracy could look like but also radically reshaped them?

ONE BLACK BOY: THE GREAT LAKES AND THE MIDWEST

TIYA MILES

▬▬

THE RESOLUTION OF ARMED CONFLICT BETWEEN BRITISH troops and a multitribal Indigenous fighting force in May 1763 depended, in part, on the ownership of one Black boy. Did the child believe his chances for staying alive and perhaps gaining freedom were greater in his current condition, as the property of a British officer? Or did he think he might fare better under the authority of the Indigenous political and military leader who sought to obtain him? Did he even know that his life was on the trading floor, as officials in the besieged fort town of Detroit negotiated a potential cease-fire in the altercation known as Pontiac's War? Only a few words exist in the colonial archive to distinguish this child from any other in history: He was "a Negroe boy belonging to James [Kinchen]" desired as "a Valet de Chambre to Marshal Pontiac."

Pontiac, the Ottawa-Ojibwe military strategist for whom this conflict was named, had risen as a leader of his people in the wake of the French and Indian War. This prolonged battle between Britain and France had erupted in 1754 over control of land and trade on the North American mainland. After the French scored several victories, the British finally prevailed, forcing the French into a surrender following the decisive Battle of Quebec in 1759. France and Great Britain negotiated a peace treaty in Paris that officially ended the conflict in 1763, or so those representing these imperial powers thought.

French and British negotiators had failed to include members of the multiple Indigenous nations who occupied the Saint Lawrence River valley, Great Lakes, and Ohio River valley lands that they had contested. The new geopolitical order hampered Native American negotiating power, increased British settler presence, weakened Native traders' economic position, and contributed to the subsequent loss of Indigenous lands and lives. The British now controlled the region's military forts as well as the European side of the lucrative fur trade, and they treated Native trading partners with far less respect than had the French.

Some Native people refused to accept this dramatic change in circumstances. Pontiac counted himself as chief among them. Critically assessing the political landscape and embracing the bellicose message of the radical Delaware prophet Neolin, Pontiac organized a coalition of Ottawa, Ojibwe, Huron, Seneca, Delaware, Shawnee, and Miami defenders of the land. In addition to mounting surprise attacks on and seizures of British posts throughout the region, the coordinated plot included a siege of Detroit, a prosperous town and British stronghold on the western edge of European settlement, originally founded in 1701 by the French. Just as Pontiac held Detroit by the throat, blocking the residents' source of supplies at the Detroit River and taking two British officers captive, he stated the terms of his withdrawal. Pontiac would release Detroit if the British retreated to their original colonies east of the Allegheny Mountains and also left for Pontiac's exclusive use a certain "Negroe boy."

Pontiac's demand for a British evacuation and the exchange of one Black child said much about his clear understanding of how the balance of power was being reshaped in the Great Lakes. The British had expropriated, by military force and diplomatic fictions, massive swaths of lands and had acquired, by trade as well as by natural increase, thousands of enslaved people of African descent. Pontiac sought to reverse this order by calling for the British to depart, which would restore the most recent status quo, in which the less offensive French had occupied the inland forts. At the same time, he participated in the new order by attempting to muscle his way into Black slave ownership. By taking the boy for himself, the Ottawa leader would acquire not only a captive worker but also, and just as important, a visible status symbol in the form of a personal attendant of African descent.

Black boys and young men, though rare in Detroit and the upper Midwest, were highly sought after by members of the British merchant and military elite. By owning one, Pontiac could express without words his political and military equality to his European adversaries. After this moment, and especially during the Revolutionary War era that would soon follow, the enslavement of African-descended people as a specific group of racialized others would spread across a region where Indigenous slavery had formerly been the most common means of labor exploitation.

We do not know what became of this one Black boy. But we know that the British officers refused Pontiac's offer, and that his siege of Detroit and bold bid to oust the British failed by the autumn of 1763. The child, we can presume, remained the property of a British officer within the palisaded town of Detroit, where approximately sixty-five others of (usually) Indigenous American or (sometimes) African descent were held captive in the mid-1760s. As former British officers and military personnel joined the ranks of the merchants, the Black men and boys they preferred to own were put to work alongside Indigenous men and boys transporting supplies and beaver hides hundreds of miles across the Great Lakes and into upstate New York. James Sterling, a British merchant who moved to Detroit in 1761, kept records that revealed a growing transregional network of merchant elites who shared the labor of a few enslaved Black boys and men and helped one another track down and secure runaways. Early Detroit was fueled by the labor of people of color twice contained, by the walls of the town and by a series of agreements between French, British, and later American leaders permitting slavery's continuation.

The place that would eventually become the capital of the Michigan Territory grew practiced at confining and surveilling unfree people, ensuring the regular theft of their labor for economic, political, and symbolic ends. A century later the state of Michigan would perfect this practice of extractive entrapment. In 1838 the Michigan state legislature approved construction of the first state prison in Jackson. Coincidentally, or perhaps not, Michigan had formally abolished racial slavery just one year prior, with the ratification of its new state constitution in 1837. By 1843, prisoners were working for private contractors to produce farm equipment, textiles, tools, saddles, steam engines, barrels, and more at no pay. Michigan expanded the facility until in 1882 the castle-like fortress was said to be the largest walled prison in the world. The state assigned inmates to mine coal on public lands and soon had farming activities and factories operating on sixty-five enclosed acres.

Michigan is still home to one of the most extreme human containment systems in the United States. Its prison population has increased by 450 percent since 1973, and the state maintains a higher rate of imprisonment than most countries. African Americans are the largest incarcerated group by far in Michigan, with a total population of 14 percent and a penal population of 49 percent. Latinos and Native Americans are incarcerated in Michigan at rates equal to their population percentage. However, white Michiganders, who make up 77 percent of the general population, are underrepresented in the prison population at 46 percent. Racialized sentencing policies have much to do with these statistics. Historians Heather Ann Thompson and Matthew Lassiter, the founding codirectors of the Carceral State Project at the University of Michigan, point to "draconian" state legislation that by the 1990s included the infamous "lifer laws," which exacted life terms for narcotics possessions of over 650 grams and extinguished the opportunity for parole. As men and women were thrown behind bars for nonviolent offenses in the 1980s through the early 2000s, Detroit neighborhoods were gutted, children were orphaned, and voter rolls were depleted. And just as this Black prison population skyrocketed at the end of the twentieth century, the state loosened legislation to allow for an expansion of convict labor.

In the modern mass incarceration moment, the racialized "carceral landscape" of colonial Great Lakes slavery found an echo. The story of one Black boy foreshadowed the fate of too many Black prisoners.

1764–1769

PHILLIS WHEATLEY

ALEXIS PAULINE GUMBS

━━

WINTER SOLSTICE IN NEW ENGLAND, DECEMBER 21, 1767. The date Phillis Wheatley's first published poem saw the light of day was literally the day the sun shone least that year. So yes, let it be characterized by the potential of darkness. Let us consider the small flames of candles and whale oil lamps that the readers of the *Newport Mercury* would most likely have used to engage the first published poem by an African American, by an enslaved woman, by a daughter whose surviving memory was of her mother pouring water before the sun rose. Winter solstice and in the dark—what June Jordan would later call "the difficult miracle of Black poetry in America" was born.

We can imagine it was already cold when Phillis Wheatley sent the poem to post. Did she leave the house? Was some other person given the task to send her poem "On Messers Hussey and Coffin," from Boston to Newport?

In winter, the artist known as Phillis, who had nearly died on the slave-trading ship *Phillis,* was almost always sick. Was it the physical impact of surviving in the hold as a young girl before her front teeth even came in? A Middle Passage–borne chronic illness? Was the climate of New England incompatible with her constitution? Was she physically homesick, ripped from the warmth of the Wolof territories where scholars now imagine she was born?

She was well enough to append a note to the printer contextualizing her first published poem. Or is the note a poem as well? It uses

ALEXIS PAULINE GUMBS

the poetic device of alliteration to set the minds of the publishers at ease. The editors pass it along, so it reassures the (white) readers that the poet belongs. That she belongs, to somebody. Which is to say, she is owned by the prominent Wheatley family. And that this poem came, how curious, out of her interpretation of an astonishing tale she heard while she was doing what enslaved women are supposed to do, "tending table" for her owners.

In this note, before anything else, before even her name, she declares that "these lines" were "composed by a Negro Girl." Capital N capital G. And there it is. The absurd iteration of capitalism as capture: the object speaks. You know, from the perspective of the northern hemisphere of Earth, on the days surrounding the winter solstice, even the sun appears to stand still.

The Negro Girl, whom we now know as Phillis Wheatley, was very familiar with the New England audience who would be reading her first published poem. Like other enslaved people whose life and measure of safety depended on the absolute agency and control of their white captors, and who had no recourse to the law to protect themselves or each other, she had to know this audience better than they could bear to know themselves. And this, she tells the printer, who will print the telling, is the source of her poetry.

She was serving the characters in this poem dinner at the home of her captors. "Tending table" she says, abbreviating attendance and attuned to what she knows are the tendencies of the white readers she has access to in 1767, to underestimate the power, foresight, and layered use of voice available to a Negro Girl. How diminutive. *Do not be threatened*. How cute.

Though it was not yet published, earlier that year she had written a poem to her neighbors across the street, the loud young men of Cambridge. "Improve your privileges while they stay!" she admonishes. Is she referring to the bad behavior they demonstrated when there was a butter shortage on campus or the system of white privilege she wants to topple? Privileges don't last always, her phrasing seems to imply. Years later, when she does publish that poem in her collection, it will be much revised. This poet knows how privileged white people are about their bread and butter, slave commerce and trade. And so she must reassure them that she is just a benign eavesdropper in rhyme, tending, not overturning, their table.

However, her use of alliteration in her contextualizing note also reads to those of us coming along later as a claim for what the poet known as Solange recently called a Seat at the Table, an intervention into a language and literature that had heretofore failed to imagine her to "insert these lines composed by a Negro Girl."

Focusing on December 21, 1767, is already rereading the legacy of the Negro Girl known by multiple misspelled names. The poem that got her widespread acclaim and that was for years considered to be her first publication was an elegy for the famous Great Awakening evangelist George Whitefield. And indeed, much of her poetry is about death ("On death's domain intent I place my eyes," she says), mostly the deaths of white people. Prominent and powerful white people, or white people her prominent and powerful captors happened to entertain in their home.

But I find it significant that her first published poem is a poem of survival at sea—or almost dying at sea, a theme that she would write about for the rest of her life. Her later work returns to the gods of wind she references in this poem. Her most recently discovered poem, "Ocean," recounts her own return from England through a storm.

Of course, we must remember that the young poet had already almost died at sea in her first journey to the Americas, as she nearly wasted away in the hold of the *Phillis*. Is it too much to imagine that she returns to these scenes of violent ocean journeys to imagine another possibility for herself?

As James Levernier has noted, much of the poetry this Negro Girl published under the name Phillis Wheatley is of the "extraterrestrial and the supernatural." She writes about mythic characters, Greek gods, heaven and angels, the relevance of worlds beyond this world. She claims for herself the "tongue of a Seraphim," divine speech beyond the human scale. And therefore we could read this first published poem, about almost dying at sea, and the note that contextualizes it as the first act of Black speculative writing in English in the Americas.

This means that the note written ostensibly to the printer and the poem imagines me, Solange, Octavia Butler, and the rest of us as future readers, but also that her ocean poetry in general is a fantastic time-traveling navigation of what she calls "the tumult of life's tossing seas." In her poem "Ode to Neptune," she hails the sea god to keep "my Susannah" safe from a sea storm. An intimate prayer for her captor, Susannah Wheatley, syntactically reverses the logic of ownership. "[M]y Susannah" suggests her mistress belongs to her. In "To a Lady on her Coming to North America," she imagines, in the image of a white friend of the Wheatleys, privileges she would never have, depicting a woman with access to a climate more conducive to her own health and a return voyage that culminates in a healing reunion with her loving family, a longing especially poignant for someone kidnapped by slavers as a child.

In "To a Lady on Her Remarkable Preservation in a Hurricane in North Carolina," she describes a mother and daughter reunited after time separated by the sea. In "A Farewel to America," she says, "I mourn for health deny'd" from the perspective of someone living in bondage in a climate that makes her sick. In "Ocean," she voices her regret: "Oh had I staid!" This ostensibly refers to her fear that she will die during her return journey to Boston. It also could refer to the fact that Benjamin Franklin (to whom she planned to dedicate the book that this poem would have appeared in) suggested that she stay in England and live free from the Wheatley family. Does she regret the echoes of her second western transatlantic journey to care for the ailing Susannah Wheatley at the expense of her own autonomy?

Some scholars have noted that Phillis Wheatley's frequent writing about sea voyages demonstrated not only the reality of her life in a port town serving a merchant family but also the sense of her own divided life. Her own experience of what in Wolof cosmology is the space of death, a watery space that separates the living from the ancestors. In this case, the poet is separated by an ocean from her lineage and community.

Navigating that space through the supernatural and extraterrestrial technology of her own poetry may have given her access not only to those of us waiting for her in the future but also to those whom she lost, who indeed may have "made their beds down in the shades below" the boat, to use the imagery of this solstice poem. In her death-focused poetry of elegy and survival, is she making space to do the ancestral work she needs to do to honor the people who did not survive the Middle Passage with her? Who jumped or were thrown overboard during the journey of the ship *Phillis* that substantiated the future poet into a Negro Girl? Family? Community members? Her own parents? Who is actually sleeping in those beds?

In her invocation with seraphic ardor of the ocean beds in the shades, or (s)hades below, she links herself to contemporary musicians and speculative authors (including myself) who imagine the social lives of the captives submerged in the Atlantic as an ongoing space of engagement and accountability. She claims the power to heal with her words, to reach beyond her time, place, condition, and realm.

Maybe there should be limits on the extent to which I speculate on the ongoing spiritual work of an artist whose very body was stolen in an act of capitalist speculative value. Maybe there should be no limits at all. But what we do know is that on Winter Solstice 1767 a young poet made space for her own work and a layered journey in multiple directions across and through the ocean, backward and forward in time. Her own offering in the dark, black words, claimed by a Negro Girl. An intervention in print, facile in the shadows of the language of commerce. On solstice. And yes. Even the sun would wait.

1769–1774

DAVID GEORGE

WILLIAM J. BARBER II

━━

WHEN DAVID GEORGE WAS BORN IN ESSEX COUNTY, VIRginia, sometime around 1742, the man who claimed to own him and his parents was named Chapel. By his own testimony, George's parents "had not the fear of God before their eyes." But after his own religious conversion, George wrote as one who had both escaped bondage and learned the fear of the Lord that is, according to Proverbs 9:10, "the beginning of wisdom."

If the enslaver who had claimed to own George in colonial Virginia bore the name of a house of worship, Chapel's slaveholder religion did not define God for David George. A free man who was determined to free others through the good news he found in the Bible, George went on to establish the first Black Baptist church in the United States. In defiance of the first Chapel he had known, he established a chapel for freedom in the colonial South.

African Americans began to establish a shared religious life and culture in the late colonial period. While enslaved people from Africa had brought with them an array of cultures and religious practices, their Christian enslavers rationalized their use and abuse of enslaved people by investing in the salvation of their souls. The Society for the Propagation of the Gospel in Foreign Parts sent missionaries to catechize children like George who had been born into slavery, teaching that it was the spiritual duty of Christian enslavers to provide for the religious education of the people they held in bondage. This top-down effort to Christianize enslaved Africans met with limited success.

But the First Great Awakening, which swept through the colonies just before George was born, popularized an evangelical form of Christianity that emphasized the individual's decision to recognize their need for God's grace and accept Christ for themselves. The fear of God that George said his parents lacked became real to him through revivalist preaching that offered relief from that fear.

By the early 1760s, George had fled bondage in Virginia. He ventured south, negotiating a fugitive existence in and among Creek and Nautchee people as well as white settlers who were debating their loyalty to Britain. While Chapel's family for a short time reclaimed George as property, he escaped again, and unlike many who would travel northward on the Underground Railroad, he kept heading south.

Though he was Black according to the law of the plantation, George found another identity in the evangelical faith he embraced while living in South Carolina. After marrying and starting a family, he met a Black Baptist preacher, George Liele, who worked with a white minister, Brother Palmer.

White historians believe that the church they established together in Georgia was the first Black Baptist church in America, but it is more accurate to say that George joined and established a freedom church that interrupted the lies of racism. While the circumstances of the Revolutionary War took George and his family to Nova Scotia and Sierra Leone, the testimony he left us makes clear that he joined an interracial evangelical movement in the Georgia colony that offered him a way toward freedom for the rest of his earthly journey.

I was introduced to the freedom church that George joined and helped spread by my parents, William and Eleanor Barber. Though they were born two centuries after George, they told me stories of my father's family's fugitive existence among Black, white, and Native people in eastern North Carolina that also stretches back to the colonial period. The day I was born in the hospital in Indianapolis, Indiana, where my father was in graduate school at the time, he argued with the hospital administration to insist that I was not simply

"Negro." He was not ashamed of our African American heritage; he was, instead, determined to tell the truth about the fusion history he knew we had inherited in our place.

When we consider the origins of Black Christianity in America, I am equally determined to tell the truth about what we learn from stories like that of David George. Yes, he was a Black man determined to be free. But he did not negotiate his fugitive existence on his own. He worked with white, Black, and Native people to get away from the oppression he had been born into. And when he heard the good news of the gospel and became a preacher himself, he was not building up a "Black church." He was demonstrating the potential of a freedom church to interrupt the lies of slaveholder religion.

About 250 years have passed since David George received the call to preach good news to all people. But the tension between the Chapel he grew up knowing and the chapel he helped to build is still central in American life. Though slavery officially ended after the Civil War, the Christianity that blessed white supremacy did not go away. It doubled down on the Lost Cause, endorsed racial terrorism during the Redemption era, blessed the leaders of Jim Crow, and continues to endorse racist policies as traditional values under the guise of a "religious right." As a Christian minister myself, I understand why, for my entire ministry, the number of people who choose not to affiliate with any religious tradition has doubled each decade. An increasingly diverse America is tired of the old slaveholder religion.

But this is why the freedom church that David George joined in the late 1760s is so important. We who speak out in public life to insist that God cares about love, justice, and mercy and to call people of faith to stand with the poor, the uninsured, the undocumented, and the incarcerated are often accused of preaching something new. But those who claim "traditional values" to defend unjust policies do not represent the tradition of David George, George Liele, and Brother Palmer. They do not represent the Black, white, and Tuscaroran people of Free Union, North Carolina, who taught my people for generations that there is no way to worship Jesus without being concerned about justice in the world.

The United States has a moral tradition, deeply rooted in the faith of a freedom church, that has inspired movements for abolition, labor rights, women's rights, civil rights, and environmental justice. While that tradition has often been marginalized and overlooked, its values are no less traditional than those of the Chapel who claimed to own David George. To know George's story is to know that another kind of faith is possible. As James Baldwin said, "We made the world we are living in and we have to make it over again." But we don't have to make it from scratch. We can build on the faith of people like David George to become the nation we have never yet been.

THE AMERICAN REVOLUTION

MARTHA S. JONES

NOT EVERY REVOLUTIONARY MOMENT WAS MARKED BY THE firing of shots or the drafting of a declaration. In 1780 a woman known as Mumbet changed the course of the American Revolution when she sued for her freedom. She acted out of a turn of mind. She had been abused in the home of John Ashley, the man who claimed her as a slave.

It was time to preserve her life and get free. Mumbet believed that the law might help. Her home, in the newly independent state of Massachusetts, was governed by the aspirations of men like her owner who were free, white, and propertied. But those same men had produced a constitution that spoke directly to her: "All men are born free and equal, and have certain natural, essential, and unalienable rights; among which may be reckoned the right of enjoying and defending their lives and liberties; that of acquiring, possessing, and protecting property; in fine, that of seeking and obtaining their safety and happiness." These same rights, Mumbet argued in the court of common pleas in Great Barrington, Massachusetts, were also hers.

Even before Mumbet filed suit, her life had followed the course of the American Revolution in the way that so many enslaved people's lives did. As a household servant to the Ashley family in Sheffield, Massachusetts, she saw to the backbreaking and often dangerous work of keeping up a home in the late eighteenth century. She was also a silent figure in the parlor, in the dining room, and in the corridors, as politics, military strategy, and more were debated. There in 1773 John Ashley hosted a meeting that produced the Sheffield Declaration, a manifesto that challenged British tyranny and championed colonists' individual rights: "Mankind in a state of nature are equal, free, and independent of each other, and have a right to the undisturbed enjoyment of their lives, their liberty and property."

Ashley was among the local men who felt the strain when Parliament pressed back. In 1774 the Intolerable Acts punished Massachusetts colonists for their defiance by repealing their charter, imposing governance from England, and limiting town meetings. It was not a declaration of war, but it was a spark for the hostilities that would follow. This was Mumbet's political education, from which she gleaned new lessons about how to oppose her own bondage.

Both sides of the conflict understood that people like Mumbet could change the course of events. The British expressly tapped into enslaved people's ever-present pursuit of liberty through a series of military proclamations. First in the fall of 1775, John Murray, Fourth Earl of Dunmore and the British royal governor of Virginia, issued a proclamation that he hoped would advantage his troop strength while also destabilizing the colony's plantations. Dunmore declared "all indentured servants, Negroes, or others . . . free that are able and willing to bear arms."

In the summer of 1779, British Army general Sir Henry Clinton did much the same. From his headquarters in Westchester County, New York, Clinton deemed all enslaved persons belonging to American revolutionaries to be free. Neither proclamation won the British much military success. But the lessons went beyond how not to win a war. Enslaved people learned that they possessed genuine bargaining power against imperial-scale authority. Neither Dunmore nor Clinton had acted out of humanitarian or antislavery impulses. Instead, they had been forced to subordinate their commitments to slavery for a military advantage. It was a lesson that enslaved people carried into subsequent conflicts, including the Haitian Revolution and the American Civil War, where they would again trade military service for the promise of freedom.

Contradictions—the enslavement of some alongside calls for the liberty of others—were the foundation of the Ashley household in the 1770s. But perhaps Mumbet understood this juxtaposition differently: that the liberty of some in Massachusetts rested upon the bondage of others. Slavery and freedom were two parts of one society.

The words of Thomas Jefferson's 1776 Declaration of Independence emerged from a similar morass. When composing that galvanizing manifesto, Jefferson omitted language that would have condemned the slave trade. The Articles of Confederation, completed the following year in 1777, did not speak to the problem of slavery. It was a scheme that relegated human bondage to a matter to be regulated by the individual states.

Historians continue to debate the meaning of these silences. For Mumbet, these failures to speak directly to slavery and its future were not exactly an invitation. Her ongoing enslavement in the Ashley household showed how even in the midst of revolution, contradictions wrought of old inequalities could persist. Mumbet's claim to liberty appears all the more audacious in the face of the silence that characterized the founding texts.

Mumbet's freedom suit reflected her interpretation of what the Revolution might make possible. It was, however, no naïve impulse. She took her ideas to a local lawyer, another party to the Sheffield Declaration, Theodore Sedgwick. He was likely a known figure to Mumbet, someone who had joined deliberations over colonists' liberty in the Ashley home. Sedgwick was also a highly regarded lawyer who accepted Mumbet's case along with that of a man named Brom.

Some historians have suggested that Sedgwick aimed to test the full meaning of the new state constitution. It was, however, a jury that finally heard the claim. Mumbet was declared free by strangers who concluded that "Brom & Bett are not, nor were they at the time of the purchase of the original writ the legal Negro of the said John Ashley." Ashley initiated an appeal to the state high court but dropped it just a month later. Mumbet—newly self-baptized as Elizabeth Freeman—was a free woman who had put a nail into slavery's casket, at least in Massachusetts. Her case along with others ended enslavement in one New England state, a revolution that came about when an aggrieved woman seized upon revolutionary ideas.

Last summer I visited the place in Stockbridge, Massachusetts, where Elizabeth "Mumbet" Freeman was laid to rest in 1829. My trip was a pilgrimage in honor of a woman who changed the fates of Black Americans in Massachusetts. Her story is also a starting point for the long saga of how Black Americans have wrestled with constitutions. Freeman's story is but one in countless efforts by people of African descent to bend the aspirations set to paper by free, white, propertied men to their own ends.

I came to Stockbridge to honor this too-often-overlooked figure in U.S. constitutional history. There she is not forgotten. Still, buried in Theodore Sedgwick's family plot, Freeman is not honored as a figure of consequence in the epic battle for freedom over slavery in Massachusetts. Instead, her headstone is a tribute to her labor for Sedgwick's family in the years after winning her freedom. Her prominently sited marker tells of a loyal servant who had no equal "in her sphere," was trustworthy, dutiful, and efficient in the domestic realm, and was a tender friend and "good mother" to the white Sedgwicks.

It is another lesson in the politics of monuments. Freeman's burial site remains an incomplete and misleading monument to her life.

NOT WITHOUT SOME INSTANCES OF UNCOMMON CRUELTY

JUSTIN PHILLIP REED

—

Patrick Henry, addressing the Second
Virginia Convention, 1775, thrice mentioned
"chains," "slavery," "submission," the myth,
in transcription, refraining his Homeric
homoteleuton of royal blues—"We have
petitioned," "remonstrated," "supplicated,"
"prostrated," and "implored"—all before
demanding God deliver death or liberty.
That year in Virginia existed so many actual
slaves that Henry's echoes could have been
nine Negroes opportunely plotting in open
air, his shadow daring daydreams of out-
running streams of liquid sterling under
evening's seasickness of starlight and silence.

When Southern night shuffles the black
capacities of bull rustle, bark knots, clots
of nettle, I know insurrection is an act
of intellect. If not the slave's will to kill
to live free, what animates humanity's
heat for reason? Let me never fix my face
to say Wheatley's mistress mistreated her

with literacy. (I have also exalted Christ
until salvation and survival were two
tines of the same fork, and eaten.) It's just
this abolitionist's education takes me
at times for a fool, uses my gifts against me,
enters at ease assuming that because I enjoy
the music I haven't stashed the duller strings
and meanwhile practiced strangulation.

Not all rebels yell. Not all run. Not all
of Carolina is a complacent swamp.
This is a gator road. This, the Isle of Wait.
My people stay places eponymous for
plantations, patriots—Marion, Sumter,
many Greene streets. They stay like
depressions in plaster walls or knives
in their never-owned tapestries war routes
gallantly streak. Militia-secreted creeks
taper to tap hiss in pots where rice still
whitens and rises. Remembering's expensive
if you can't afford to know what is owed.
My people's self-retention inside this theft
is investment—enviable, thick-leggedness
of shall-not-be-movement. They don't move
easily from home (again) or (back) to tears.

No one has liberated my mouth except
to give me more elaborate things to do
with these teeth. Assume I mean nothing
by it, that the overwrought rhyme lucy-
terries mastery as a matter of fact, a draught
to steal them off to sleep, a loose leaf,
a draft on the way to someday seal them
up in it. They still have their guns, still

go to separate church. No, sir, this poem
torched none of the houses on the road,
merely wrote: *Here was a row of angels,*
molting, folded—stars, aligned—and the reddest
gullet of God hollered their ankles to powder.

PART FIVE

1779–1784

SAVANNAH, GEORGIA

DAINA RAMEY BERRY

———

NESTLED ALONG THE ATLANTIC COASTLINE, PARALLELED by the Savannah River, the city of Savannah is the oldest urban center in the Peach State. Established in 1733 by King George II's 1732 charter, the colony was an experiment to provide British debtors and war criminals a second chance at life in the New World. Thus 114 colonists set sail across the Atlantic on the *Anne,* arriving in February 1733. They "were expected to become farmers and citizen-soldiers on a hostile and desolate frontier," and they worked hard to create amicable relations with the Yamacraw Indians.

Between 1779 and 1784, Savannah residents experienced changes in the economy, in the population, and in social and religious institutions. They witnessed the importation of enslaved people from various regions of West Africa, the growth of religious public worship through the Second Great Awakening, and severe losses during the American Revolution's Siege of Savannah.

Savannah had been planned by William Bull of South Carolina and James Oglethorpe, the British leader sent to establish the colony, and it included a series of squares, wards, and trust lots. Planners intended to create a city that would resemble London. Each ward was "built around central squares with trust lots on the east and west sides of the squares for public buildings and churches, and tything lots for the settlers' homes on the north and south sides of the squares."

With so many enslaved people residing in those wards, in many ways Savannah was nothing like London. There is not a singular way to think about the lives of people of African descent in Savannah, especially between 1779 and 1784. Many and varied factors and circumstances were in play, including the tremendous restrictions of slavery, the freedom some experienced as a result of war, and the spiritual expression realized through religious conversions.

Even though Georgia was the only colonial region that issued a ban on slavery from its inception in 1733, colonists from South Carolina and other regions brought enslaved people to the city before the ban was lifted by a royal decree in 1751. At that time there were about four hundred enslaved people in Savannah. This means that for them, life in the budding urban center may have been difficult because many worked in the homes of their enslavers and had little contact with other people of African descent.

Some of the early descriptions of experiences in the city from an African perspective come from Olaudah Equiano, an Igbo captive, in the 1760s. Equiano shared his nearly fatal public beating by a well-known physician, his time in jail after the beating, as well as his recovery aided by another prominent physician, in his memoir, *The Interesting Narrative of Olaudah Equiano* (1789). The shipping and slave-trading industry brought Equiano and thousands of other African captives to the city.

African people forced into the belly of slave ships crossed the Atlantic and came to Savannah through several different routes, but beginning in the late 1760s, Africans came directly from West Africa. While the trade continued and the colony grew, enslaved Africans and their descendants contributed to a growing religious community. During Equiano's time in Savannah, he witnessed a moving sermon by George Whitefield. The spirit-filled preaching, such as was common within the African and African American community, impressed him greatly.

Savannah was home to the First African Baptist Church (established in 1777), hailed as the oldest Black church in North America. Reverend Andrew Bryan, an enslaved preacher who became the second leader of this congregation in 1782, used a rice barn on his enslaver's property for services. Bryan later bought property in Oglethorpe Ward to build a church.

In January 1788, a white minister named Abraham Marshall visited Savannah with one of his Black colleagues, Jesse Peters, and the two baptized more than forty members. Marshall also ordained Bryan. Church membership continued to grow, from 575 members in 1788 to 2,795 in 1831.

In the fall of 1779, while people of African descent worked and worshiped, some had the opportunity to fight for their liberty during the American Revolution. Savannah was home to the second-deadliest battle of the Revolutionary War: the Siege of Savannah. American allies along with the French failed to ward off the British navy when it increased its occupation of the Savannah River by adding "two row galleys." British Captain Hyde Parker ordered "twelve negroes" to serve as part of the crew.

This military strategy to enlist troops of African descent represented a significant moment in African American history. Guides of African descent "were instrumental in the defense of Savannah" because these men knew the waterways better than anyone in uniform. Fighting against the Franco-American forces, the British enlisted some "two hundred negroes" to help with "skirmishes on the outskirts of the city." At the same time, Savannah residents feared armed Blacks and petitioned to disarm them because they walked around with "great insolence."

By October 1779, the American colonists had suffered 752 casualties. When the French tried to lend some naval support, the prepared British sank six French ships in the Savannah River—a humiliating and costly loss for French general Count d'Estaing. D'Estaing's army of 3,600 contained 545 people of African descent, many from Saint Domingue (later Haiti). An estimated 1,094 of these soldiers, including 650 French troops, lost their lives.

One of the reasons for the British success is that they also used African American guides and laborers. Quimano Dolly was one African American who helped the British capture Savannah by bringing troops through a swamp area behind the city. At the end of the war, nearly four thousand people of African descent left Savannah and headed to Florida, the Caribbean, and Canada.

But many Black people remained. Today African Americans represent 54 percent of the population, the First African Baptist Church still stands, and the battle sites of the American Revolution are recognized in city parks, on historical landmarks, and through the oral traditions of Africans and their descendants. The freedom dreams of the Revolutionary War remain the freedom dreams of today.

THE U.S. CONSTITUTION

DONNA BRAZILE

——

MY NAME IS RICHARD ALLEN. I WAS BORN ENSLAVED AND died a Methodist bishop.

I am an African, and an American. In my lifetime, 1760–1831, I had two enslavers. Both were relatively good men by my own standards and those of my fellow citizens. Still, slavery was a bitter pill to swallow.

My emotions never accepted that my mind, my learning, my labor, my character, my hands, were someone's personal property. Beginning with the first awareness of my condition, I thought without rest of freedom. I often felt that one day I would be free.

Benjamin Chew of Philadelphia was my first owner. When I was eight, he sold my parents, my siblings, and me to a Delaware planter of modest means. Stokley Sturgis and his wife were aging, kind people. They didn't work me very hard. In fact, I didn't know hard work until I left them to earn back my body.

When I was ten, the Boston Massacre took place. All people, both enslaved and free, were living and moving and breathing in an ether of expectation. It hit me hard that Crispus Attucks, a man like me, was the first to give his life. In 1776 we learned the news that the Declaration of Independence was signed and issued. Its message had a deep impact.

The following year, at age seventeen, I became severely aware of my personal deficiencies, my moral shortcomings. They weighed heavily. I struggled daily with these feelings. Then Freeborn Garretson, a white preacher, came. I listened and converted to Methodism.

I was hungry for spiritual discipline and guidance. I took Scripture to heart, especially the teachings of Christ. They were words to live by, and I lived by them.

My life changed.

Then Sturgis's life changed. He had been attending our meetings when, at one of them, Reverend Garretson said that slave owners had been "weighed in the balance and found wanting." That struck Sturgis squarely in the heart. He saw he could no longer own slaves.

Sturgis told me I should leave, find work, and pay him what he had paid for me. By age twenty-six in 1786, I had bought my body, literally earned my freedom.

It was in some ways harder to be a free man. Now—no mistake—the ideals of the American Revolution, the words of the Declaration, had triggered the fall of slavery in the northern states.

Although unable to endure the hypocrisy of slavery, most northern white citizens could not bring themselves to be social equals. Accordingly, they did all they could to squelch opportunity for free American Africans.

I felt for those newly freed. Few whites would make loans to buy homes. Those who did, mostly abolitionist Quakers, were tight in reviewing and granting them. It was hard to get jobs. It was hard just to live. We even found it hard to be dead—we were not allowed to own cemeteries in which to bury our deceased.

This conflict, dealing with the hypocrisy of slavery while building a foundation of "All men are created equal," was an ongoing contest throughout the country. It became the primary discord at the Constitutional Convention.

"A nation, without a national government, is, in my view, an awful spectacle," wrote Alexander Hamilton. If the United States were to survive as a nation, it would need a central government. That reality, that overriding necessity, drove the convention's compromises with slavery.

Because of my faith, I was less judgmental and more forgiving than were many about this hypocrisy. We were instructed to "do good" to those who hated and despitefully misused us. Those weren't just words; they were a command. I obeyed.

With other American Africans, I had been attending services at St. George's in Philadelphia. One Sunday an elder was standing at the door and told us to go to the gallery. We took seats in the same location as where we used to sit downstairs. No sooner had we touched our seats than a prayer was announced, so we got on our knees.

I was focused on the prayer when I heard a commotion of tussling and angry low voices. I looked up to see a trustee pulling my friend and colleague, Absalom Jones, off his knees, saying, "You must not kneel here!"

Jones said he would get up when prayer was finished. The trustee would not have that. Jones was told to rise immediately or he would be forced to rise. The prayer ended just then.

We rose as one and left as one, never to return to St. George's. The abuse and affront were the harder to bear since we had contributed largely of our monies and given our labor generously to laying the church floor and building the gallery.

We were shut out of St. George's by 1787. The Constitutional Convention was in town. There, too, we were shut out. The most vigorous debates were over allowing slavery without building it into our new institutions.

I read the U.S. Constitution. Nowhere are the words *slave* or *slavery* to be found. Abraham Lincoln later told a Cooper Union audience that "this mode of alluding to slaves and slavery, instead of speaking of them, was employed on purpose to exclude from the Constitution the idea that there could be property in man."

It is an honest and realistic argument that slavery became incorporated into the Constitution without naming it because slavery was considered on its way to extinction. To many, the Constitutional Convention compromises were but a temporary accommodation.

Some see only the hypocrisy. They admit of no decent impulses at all in the convention's compromises—and refuse to tolerate slavery's existence for a while longer as a necessity, with the intent that it should in time be no more.

But named or not, slavery was there in writing, a presence allowed by the Constitution. As for myself, I had been owned by good men who wouldn't be able to see their own sin for years. But I knew of my own sins. And I have a Lord who commands me to forgive. So I forgave and did not sit in judgment.

While I did not judge souls, I did judge behavior. It was my decision, and that of my fellow worshipers, never to return to St. George's Methodist Church. Jones and I, therefore, sought to establish a Free African Society (FAS) based on faith but not affiliated with any church. Today it would be called nondenominational. Following the example of the Constitution, we drew up a preamble, then outlined its purpose and functions.

The FAS would be a self-help group for those recently freed African Americans who were adrift in a hostile society that actively sought to deny them opportunities to advance. The society cultivated and mentored new leaders. It formed a warm community, provided a social life, constructed a network of people who cared.

It was needed. In 1780 there were but 240 freed Americans of African descent in Philadelphia. But by the next census ten years later, the city had 1,849 freed men and women.

I am greatly satisfied that FAS served as a model for many leaders and prophets who would come after me, including W.E.B. Du Bois and Dr. Martin Luther King, Jr.

When we withdrew from St. George's, we rented a storeroom to continue worshiping. This was much opposed by a church leader who visited us twice on the subject, using persuasion ranging from belittling to beseeching.

There are several twists to this story, but the ending is that we settled on a lot on Fifth Street, where I later turned the first shovel for construction. This led, eventually, to the first Independent African church in April 1816, an institution that continues to this day, the African Methodist Episcopal Church, consisting of 2.5 million members.

It saddens me that with all the blood spilled—drawn first by the lash, then by the sword, later drained by dogs, clubs, bombs, and guns during the civil rights era—today the federal courts are reversing the human rights gains so long in coming, so dearly won. And doing it with the facade that racism is no longer with us.

I was a poor vessel whom God used to give gifts to his oppressed— the tools to free them. American Africans have served a vital function in this democracy. We have been the flint against which the Almighty has sparked this country's struggle to live out the proposition that "all men are created equal."

Whether we are entering a period of regression, or are on the verge of reaching the mountaintop, the tools He gave me are still available: self-help groups, faith and self-discipline, community, and moral leadership as constants from the home to the nation.

SALLY HEMINGS

ANNETTE GORDON-REED

—

IN AUGUST 1789, SALLY HEMINGS WAS LIVING AT THE HÔTEL de Langeac on the rue de Berri, just off the Champs-Élysées in Paris. She had arrived about two years earlier after living in London for two weeks at the home of John and Abigail Adams.

Hemings had accompanied Mary (Polly) Jefferson, the nine-year-old daughter of Thomas Jefferson, on an Atlantic voyage from Virginia that lasted five weeks. Jefferson was in Paris serving as the American minister to France. John Adams was the American minister in London. He and his wife had agreed to receive Jefferson's daughter and her traveling companion, and to keep Polly until her father could arrive and bring her to Paris.

Jefferson had asked for a "careful Negro woman" to accompany Polly. Then the woman was to return to Virginia. He had suggested Isabel Hern, who was about twenty-eight years old. Hern was unable to make the trip, having recently given birth. So Jefferson's in-laws, Francis and Elizabeth Eppes, with whom Polly and Sally were staying, sent fourteen-year-old Sally Hemings instead.

In the convoluted world of Virginia slavery and family, Sally Hemings's father was John Wayles, the father of Jefferson's deceased wife, Martha, and also of Elizabeth Eppes. So the little girl whom Hemings helped bring across the ocean was her half-niece. When she arrived in Paris, Hemings joined her brother James, who had been in the city since 1784, having come over with Jefferson and Jefferson's eldest daughter, Martha (Patsy).

A great deal had taken place during Hemings's stay in Paris, both within the Hôtel de Langeac and outside it. France had witnessed the fall of the Bastille in July 1789, which is often seen as the beginning of the French Revolution. In truth, much had been happening on that front since Hemings's arrival. The signs of discord in the society were everywhere. Demonstrators amassed in the neighborhood where Hemings lived, outside her residence, actually, shouting about the new world that was to come. Paris was on fire with talk of politics among men and women of all classes.

Hemings's neighborhood was a relatively new one, and though the overall number of Black people in Paris was small, the section of Paris where the Hôtel de Langeac was located had the city's largest concentration of people of color. It was an active community whose members kept tabs on one another's fortunes, alerting each other to developments that were taking place in their community.

Perhaps people kept tabs on the fate of Sally Hemings. As her son Madison Hemings explained, during her time in Paris she had become "Mr. Jefferson's concubine." It is not known when this occurred, but the evidence indicates that it was near the end of her time in the city. In fact, it is very likely that by August 1789, sixteen-year-old Hemings was either newly pregnant or about to become pregnant.

Jefferson had been planning a leave of absence to return his daughters and, most likely, Hemings to Virginia. He was set to come back to Paris and finish his time as minister. When Hemings learned of Jefferson's plans, she balked. She was not alone; none of the young people who were living at the hotel—Jefferson's daughters and his protégé William Short, who had come from Virginia to be Jefferson's secretary—wanted to leave. James Hemings could expect to return with Jefferson.

The Hemings siblings knew that the law in France gave them an easy shot at freedom. Jefferson knew this, too, and was defensive about it, which is probably why he paid both Hemings siblings wages, and paid them well. James was the *chef de cuisine* at the Hôtel de Langeac, and Sally was lady's maid to Jefferson's daughters and likely Jefferson's chambermaid.

It was a heady time for both brother and sister. They were nomi-

nally free, receiving wages near the top of the scale for French servants, and living in the midst of a revolution that promised a new
world for people on the bottom of the social scale. Hemings had her
own money, but Jefferson had started buying her clothing, and there
is reason to think she was attending balls with Patsy Jefferson as an
attendant.

Both Hemings siblings would have had every reason to think they
had a chance to make it in the new society being born. James hired a
tutor to teach him proper French. It is not known whether Sally was
included, though her son mentioned her facility with the language.
Most important, Sally Hemings did not want to be enslaved again.
Jefferson wanted to bring her back to Virginia, and when he met with
her resistance, he promised her that if she came home with him, she
would live a life of privilege, and that any children they had would be
free upon reaching the age of twenty-one. Madison Hemings said
that his mother "implicitly relied" on Jefferson's promises and decided
to return to Virginia.

Hemings, her brother James, and the Jeffersons set sail for the
United States in October 1789. They landed in Norfolk, Virginia, in
November. After visiting relatives, the group arrived at Monticello
just before Christmas. The next reference to Sally Hemings in Jefferson's records is a letter written around September 1790, saying that
at some point in the spring, she had been too ill to make a trip. Other
letters from that time make clear that Hemings's status had changed:
she ceased to be a lady's maid for Jefferson's daughters once they returned to the United States. It is not known when Hemings gave
birth, but the child she had upon her return to Virginia apparently
did not survive infancy.

As things turned out, Jefferson did not return to Paris. He accepted President Washington's invitation to serve as U.S. secretary of
state and left for New York, then the nation's capital, in March 1790.
James Hemings, who continued to be paid regular wages, accompanied him. They were soon joined by Robert Hemings, the eldest of
the Hemings-Wayles children. Sally Hemings remained at Monticello and disappears from Jefferson family records. When the capital
moved to Philadelphia temporarily, starting in 1791, the Hemings

brothers continued to work for Jefferson. Jefferson referred to Sally Hemings in a letter instructing that she was to be sent the bedding she used while in France.

Jefferson's position as secretary of state kept him away from Monticello a great deal from 1790 until his retirement in 1794. In fact, during that four-year period, he was at Monticello a total of only about five nonconsecutive months. Hemings conceived no children during this time. She likely spent this period with her mother and the rest of her family. She did not become pregnant again until Jefferson retired from Washington's cabinet and returned home at the end of 1794. Hemings conceived her second child in January 1795. She would, in the word of a visitor to Monticello, "cohabit" with Jefferson for thirty-seven years, bearing seven children, four of whom lived to adulthood, all of whom were freed when they became adults.

1794-1799

THE FUGITIVE SLAVE ACT

DEIRDRE COOPER OWENS

——

IN 1788 A NEW WESTERN NATION ESTABLISHED ITSELF AS A
fledgling republic that privileged the democratic process for its most
respected citizens: white male property owners over twenty-one years
old. At the cornerstone of its democratic process was the vote. Overwhelmingly, white male voters created clauses in the U.S. Constitution that attended to slavery, one of the new nation's most pressing
political issues. Article IV, Section 2, Clause 3 of the Constitution not
only protected slavery as an American institution but also protected
slave owners whose human property liberated themselves into either
free states or territories.

In 1789 voters elected their first president, the former general and
Revolutionary War hero George Washington. He was one of the
wealthiest and most politically connected slave owners in the United
States, whose presence eventually established the presidency as a position that was amenable to men who made up what would later be
known as the slaveocracy—the slave-owning ruling class that ran the
country. It comes as no surprise that from 1789, when Washington
was elected, until 1877, when General Ulysses Grant ended his presidency under Reconstruction, more American presidents (twelve)
owned slaves than those who did not (six). As a result of the seem-
ingly enduring and lucrative industry based on human bondage, the
United States gave birth to a small but politically mighty abolitionist
movement.

During the early 1790s, powerful slave owners put more teeth into

Article IV of the Constitution to protect their assets, enslaved people. In 1793 Congress passed the Fugitive Slave Act, which deemed it a federal crime to aid any fugitive from slavery:

> *And be it further enacted,* That any person who shall knowingly and willingly obstruct or hinder such claimant, his agent, or attorney, in so seizing or arresting such fugitive from labor, or shall rescue such fugitive from such claimant, his agent or attorney, when so arrested pursuant to the authority herein given and declared; or shall harbor or conceal such person after notice that he or she was a fugitive from labor, as aforesaid, shall, for either of the said offences, forfeit and pay the sum of five hundred dollars. Which penalty may be recovered by and for the benefit of such claimant, by action of debt, in any Court proper to try the same, saving moreover to the person claiming such labor or service his right of action for or on account of the said injuries, or either of them.

Anyone who provided assistance to a fugitive risked a hefty fine and whatever other punishment local officials decided to mete out. Fugitives would then be re-enslaved. The nation's leaders were responding to the proliferation of abolitionist societies in northern states. They were also responding to the Black men, women, and children who decided to live in freedom rather than in slavery.

For George Washington, the very act he signed into being haunted him until death. Ona Judge, a twenty-two-year-old enslaved woman, owned by Washington, ran away from his household in the summer of 1793, when Washington signed the nation's most powerful Fugitive Slave Act. Washington immediately placed an ad for her recapture, and insinuated in the ad that he did not know what provocation caused Judge to run away. He seemed to not imagine that a human being held in lifelong bondage might desire freedom, especially from his plantation. Ona Judge remained in the free state of New Hampshire as a fugitive from slavery until her death in 1848.

Washington would have been in the middle of a political maelstrom, had he re-enslaved a poor bondwoman who simply wanted freedom in a nation that had prioritized that value in its own fight for freedom from Britain. Although the existence of slavery and powerful laws to protect those invested in maintaining the system were in place, the Fugitive Slave Act amplified the role of the fugitive slave catcher.

In the aftermath of the 1793 Fugitive Slave Act, slave catchers proliferated. The men who patrolled slave states, free states, and territories created even more fear in the hearts of enslaved people thinking of running away. If a fugitive slave was caught and re-enslaved, the emotional and physical costs would be dire. Slave catchers were motivated by money and also performed a civic duty to a slaveholding nation that protected slavery at any cost. This constitutional protection of slavery helped to create a cottage industry where white duplicity, anti-Black violence, and the privileging of property rights over human rights reigned.

African Americans, especially those who were free, immediately responded to the Fugitive Slave Act. They created political abolitionist organizations that addressed the need for discretion in their liberation work, raised funds for runaways, and advocated the use of armed tactical violence in the name of self-defense. Black abolitionists recognized violence as an inherently American language that white supporters of slavery understood quite well. Although white abolitionists advanced moral suasion as the central tenet in dismantling slavery, Black abolitionists understood that white America would need more than fiery speeches to dissuade them from supporting slavery.

These leaders were also emboldened by leaders of the Haitian Revolution that began in August 1791. Black people in Haiti, who were engaged in a bloody fight for freedom from their French slave masters, used tactical violence as a means for liberation. Enslaved people in the United States were inspired by the Haitian example. In 1795 in Louisiana, still a Spanish colony, African-born slaves, mainly men, developed a plan to revolt. In Pointe Coupée, Louisiana, fifty-seven slaves and three white men dedicated themselves to destroying slave owners' property, seizing arms, and killing white slave masters. As happened with most slave rebellions, they were betrayed by informants, in this case by Indian people of the Tunica tribe, and almost half of the enslaved conspirators were beheaded. Although the revolt did not happen, the Pointe Coupée Conspiracy served as a potent reminder for white people that enslaved people would fight back. Despite reigning ideologies that espoused so-called truths about Black people's docility and intellectual inferiority, slave conspiracies not only confirmed white people's fear of an impending "race war" between angry Blacks and defensive whites but also showed the nation that people of African descent would fight for their right to live and die as free people.

The 1793 Fugitive Slave Act was one of the first federal laws to provide universal protection for slave owners against loss of property in enslaved people. It codified anti-Blackness and white supremacy because it signaled that a white person's claim to stolen property was inherently more important than a Black person's right to freedom and liberty. It reified that the United States was a nation divided, one that established freedom with whiteness and servitude with Blackness. Most critically for Black people, whether enslaved or free, the United States proved to be hostile to their freedom and hypocritical in its claims for justice and liberty.

In 1850 Congress passed an even more restrictive Fugitive Slave Act, and in the 1860s a violent and bloody civil war exposed the nation's deep history of anti-Blackness and its commitment to honoring the propertied rather than all its people, especially those of African descent. For African Americans, the Fugitive Slave Acts meant that their fight for freedom and civil rights would be a long and dangerous one. Yet they forged a political consciousness in Black America that extended beyond the borders of the United States and had ties in a developing Black diaspora.

HIGHER EDUCATION

CRAIG STEVEN WILDER

———

At the end of the American Revolution, Francisco de Miranda—a mercenary and future dictator of Venezuela—visited the College of New Jersey (now Princeton University) during a journey through the United States. He found it to be a "well regulated" college despite the absence of President John Witherspoon, who was off fundraising. He approvingly examined the model solar system, which was not working, and then toured the town. However, when he reached nearby New Brunswick, de Miranda wrote nothing about Queen's College (now Rutgers University).

One might dismiss that as an oversight if it had not happened repeatedly. In 1794 Moreau de Saint-Méry—a Martiniquais lawyer who had practiced in Cap François (Cap-Haïtien) before the Haitian Revolution—visited Princeton. He was disappointed with Nassau Hall, the main campus building that was once the architectural jewel of the British American colonies. He offered modest compliments to the library and still-broken orrery, recorded the tuition and fees, and even took an informal census of students from the South and the West Indies. In New Brunswick, Saint-Méry noticed that a bridge had collapsed across the Raritan River, but he too made no mention of Queen's College.

A couple of years later, Isaac Weld, a topographer from Ireland, surveyed the region. He ridiculed the College of New Jersey: the main building was a plain stone structure, the museum but a couple of display cases, the vaunted orrery useless, and the library just a collection of old theology texts in no graceful order. All colleges in the United States were really grammar schools, he judged. His stage ride into New Brunswick seemed to confirm that verdict. "There is nothing deserving attention in it," Weld concluded of the village, "excepting it be the very neat and commodious wooden bridge that has been thrown across the Raritan River."

There was a reason Rutgers wasn't even on the radar for visitors. The Revolutionary War had left the campus "wasted & destroyed" and scattered the students, as a Rutgers president appealed to the New Jersey legislature, and the whole college was but "a naked charter and little else."

The Revolution had strained and fractured the new country's educational infrastructure. British and American forces had used college campuses for headquarters, barracks, and hospitals. The governors of Harvard in Cambridge, Yale in New Haven, King's College (now Columbia University) in New York City, the College of Philadelphia (now the University of Pennsylvania), and the College of Rhode Island (now Brown University) in Providence had had to close their schools or relocate to interior towns as British forces attacked vulnerable port cities. The officers of Rutgers and Princeton dispersed their students and faculties as the fighting approached their gates. British troops targeted the College of William and Mary in Virginia and burned a portion of the campus while French soldiers camped there. Because of its remote location, Dartmouth College in New Hampshire was spared physical damage but emerged from the Revolution in fiscal crisis.

But a renaissance was near. The revival of the slave trade in New England and the mid-Atlantic and the expansion of plantation slavery in the South allowed white Americans to rescue the old colonial colleges from the wreckage of war and raise eighteen new colleges before the turn of the century. In less than two decades, the slave economy underwrote an academic revolution that tripled the number of colleges and transformed the nation's intellectual geography.

The expansion of higher education tracked the southward and westward movements of plantation slavery. The Presbyterians founded seven new schools, five of them in the South. The Episcopalians built three Southern colleges. North Carolina, Georgia, and Tennessee established public universities. Governor Thomas Jefferson and the Virginia legislature chartered Transylvania College in Kentucky, the first college west of the Alleghenies.

Early American colleges preyed upon the bodies, labor, and lives of enslaved Black people. In 1789 Bishop John Carroll and the Roman Catholic clergy founded Georgetown College (now Georgetown University) in what would soon become the new federal district. Carroll's small community of Catholic priests began planning a church with national reach, administered from Georgetown and funded by slavery.

Catholic clerics and families, emboldened by the promise of religious freedom, had ventured into Kentucky after the Revolution, where they established a base for the church's southern and western expansion. A few years later Father Patrick Smyth, a visitor from Ireland, published a scathing account of his tenure in the United States that revealed the brutal realities of "institutional slavery." The Maryland slave plantations were sources and sites of clerical immorality and improvidence, he warned. The Irish priest detailed multiple abuses. A contemporary offered some additional insight into Father Smyth's urgent protests. During his tour of Maryland, the French republican Brissot de Warville exposed the public secret of systemic rape on the church's plantations. The priests were "keeping harems of Negro women, from whom was born a mixed race," Warville charged, while pleading for the abolition of slavery and the cultivation of some "more moral and profitable crop" than tobacco.

In the decades after the Revolution, human slavery allowed the United States to establish a system of public and private colleges and universities, and the inhumanities of that relationship would echo through the history of American higher education.

COTTON

Kiese Laymon

———

BLAME COTTON.

Grandmama is massaging the tummies of teacakes in her kitchen. The smell, and only the smell, will make it to tomorrow. I'm watching Walter Payton run to and from yesterday on CBS.

Everyone on Grandmama's TV, in Grandmama's kitchen, is wearing cotton.

I hear a Black man stomp his butter brown boots onto her porch.

I am eight years old, wearing a cotton V-neck, and I feel good.

There are four bangs outside Grandmama's screen door. No one who knocks on Grandmama's screen in the summer knocks more than three times. Most folks don't knock at all. They simply press their faces as close to the screen as possible and say, "Hey, Ms. Cat. Y'all good?"

On this summer day, Grandmama is asking who in the world is up in there banging on her door like the police.

No one in the world is banging on Grandmama's door like the police.

Outside the screen door stands an old Black man with frown lines even deeper than Grandmama's. The depth of those frown lines, the heavy hang of both lips, the creases beneath his graying eyes, give this old Black man's familiar face a symmetry I find sexy. In addition to his butter brown boots, his lean ashen body is held up in these sky-blue overalls. Tucked under his right armpit is a huge wrinkled paper sack.

And as with most of the old Black men of Forest, Mississippi, I can see the imprint of what I assume is a small .22 in his front bib pocket.

Over a supper of collard greens, black-eyed peas, and squirrel dumplings that I just refuse to eat because the squirrel in the dumpling looks just like the squirrels on her pecan trees, Grandmama tells me not to dare call this man my great-granddaddy. "Call him Albert Payton," Grandmama says right in front of his face. "That's who he always been to me. Albert. Payton."

I usually sleep in Grandmama's bed, but that night she asks me to sleep in one of the two beds in what she calls her back bedroom.

"Why I gotta sleep in the same room with that man?" I whisper to her. "I don't even know that joker. And he smell funny."

"Because I said so." Grandmama laughs. "He liable to steal everything that ain't nailed down if he don't . . ." She trails off.

"If he don't what?"

"If he don't have as many good folks watching him as he can find, if you know what I mean." Whenever Grandmama says "if you know what I mean," I always feel grown. And like most grown folks, I never ask her to clarify what she actually means. I just smirk and nod up and down super slowly.

That night, while Grandmama sleeps in the bedroom next to ours, I watch Albert Payton, lying on his back, go in the bib pocket of his overalls, and take out his gun and a bulb of cotton. I watch him place this gun and bulb of cotton on the ironing board next to his bed.

I'd never felt on cotton. I'd felt cotton on my body. I'd seen cotton a few times driving from Jackson to the Delta. But I'd never felt on cotton.

So while my grandmama's father sleeps, I get up and I grab the bulb of cotton. I gently feel the seeds. The nearly crumbling brown flower holding the actual cloud is twisted in more ways than one. I smell it. I can't smell anything. I smell it again. I smell Grandmama. But it's her house.

Over the next few days, I learn that my great-grandfather, who was a shitty father to every child he fathered, was a wizard at picking cotton. He doesn't talk, so when I ask questions, Grandmama answers them.

Why are your hands so rough?

"All that cotton."

Why do the joints in your fingers look swole?

"All that cotton."

Why don't he talk to us?

"All that cotton."

When Grandmama and her father go to bed, I look through these old encyclopedias Grandmama bought for my mama and them when they were children. I'm confused about how or when my great-grandfather could have picked cotton. I don't find much in the encyclopedias, but my mama has a book called *Slavery in the United States* by Charles Ball. She's using the book published in the 1800s to finish her dissertation on *Poverty, Politics, and Public Policy in the South.*

This is usually the kind of book Mama won't let me read because she thinks it will give me nightmares.

Ball writes,

> Surely if anything can justify a man in taking his life into his own hands, and terminating his existence, no one can attach blame to the slaves on many of the cotton plantations of the south, when they cut short their breath, and the agonies of the present being, by a single stroke. What is life worth, amidst hunger, nakedness and excessive toil, under the continually uplifted lash?

I'm not sure what he means by "cut short their breath." But I understand the question "What is life worth?"

My grandmama hates her father because of his inability to be there with her. That night I blame cotton. Even though Grandmama hates her father, she lets him in, offers him food, gives him a bed.

I blame cotton.

There is a gun and a bulb of cotton in my great-grandfather's overall bib. I don't really even notice the gun.

I blame cotton.

I ask Grandmama the next day if her father really picked cotton.

"That's the only reason he here," she says.

I don't know what she means. But I know we are in a seven-hundred-square-foot pink shotgun house surrounded by a garden we eat out of every day. I know there are a father and child in my house who were never paid fairly for work they did in houses, in chicken plants, and in cotton fields.

I blame cotton.

Thirty years later, when I drive to the University of Mississippi to accept a fellowship, I will see acres and acres of cotton on Highway 6, right down the road from where I'm supposed to stay that year.

I will accept the fellowship because of cotton.

When the land is freed, so will be all the cotton and all the money made off the suffering that white folks made cotton bring to Black folks in Mississippi and the entire South.

I go to sleep every night with a bulb of cotton on the dresser next to my bed, not because I want to remember. I will always remember. But the cotton helps me imagine. It helps me wake up. It helps me fight. It helps me realize that there are millions of ways to win. But in this country, they're all rooted in Black bodies, Black deaths, Black imaginations, Black families.

And cotton.

THE LOUISIANA REBELLION

CLINT SMITH

——

IN WALLACE, LOUISIANA, AT THE FAR EDGE OF THE WHITney Plantation, between the wooden white fence demarcating ownership of the land and the red brick path leading you through it, is a plot of earth where the dark heads of fifty-five Black men sit on metal stakes, robust silver beams that push their necks toward the sky.

The heads are not real. They are ceramic renderings of a violent past, but from a distance the human likeness is so unsettling that you need to get closer just to be sure. In the warmer months, gnats and flies swarm around them, while wasps begin nesting on the underside of their open necks. The bugs hum together around the decapitated figurines like an army of small drones. The area beneath the rows of heads is an interspersing of brown and red mulch, creating the illusion that the land beneath these skulls is, similar to the faces, covered in dry blood. Each of the faces is nameless, with the exception of the ten that rest at the front. Mathurin. Cook. Gilbert. Amar. Lindor. Joseph. Dagobert. Komina. Hippolite. Charles. These were the leaders of the largest slave rebellion in American history. These were the people who decided that enough was enough.

On a rainy southern Louisiana evening in January 1811, Charles Deslondes, a mixed-race slave driver, led the rebellion.

Composed of hundreds of people, Deslondes's army advanced along the serpentine path of southern Louisiana's River Road to New Orleans with a military discipline that surprised many of its adversaries. It is remarkable to consider that hundreds of enslaved people—

people who came from different countries, with different native languages, who had different tribal affiliations—were able to organize themselves as effectively as they did. The layered cacophony of their languages merged together into a single organized voice.

On the German Coast of Louisiana—named for the German immigrants who settled there—where the rebellion was taking place, roughly 60 percent of the total population was enslaved. The fear of armed insurrection had long been in the air.

That fear escalated over the course of the Haitian Revolution (1791–1804), in which Haitian slaves rose up against the French to create the first Black-led republic in the world. The successful uprising had both political and social import. The French army was defeated so badly—80 percent of the soldiers sent to the island died—that Napoleon, looking to cut his losses and refocus his attention on his military battles in Europe, sold the entire Louisiana territory to Thomas Jefferson's negotiators for a paltry $15 million, about four cents an acre. Without the success of the Haitian Revolution, Napoleon would not likely have sold a landmass that doubled the size of the then–United States. Jefferson was simply looking to purchase New Orleans in order to gain access to the heart of the Mississippi River. For enslaved people throughout the rest of the New World, the victory in Haiti served as inspiration for what was possible.

Even William C. C. Claiborne, the governor of the territory that would become the state of Louisiana in 1812, wanted the territory to stop importing enslaved people from Haiti, fearing that some of them might have taken part in the Haitian Revolution. He didn't want to run the risk of bringing that revolutionary ideology to his state. In 1804 he wrote to then–Secretary of State James Madison to share his concern. "At present I am well assured, there is nothing to fear either from the Mulatto or Negro population," he began, attempting to assuage any immediate fears the president may have had, "but at some future period, this quarter of Union must (I fear) experience in some degree the Misfortunes of St. Domingue [Haiti], and that period will be hastened if the people should be indulged by Congress with a continuance of the African trade." Claiborne said that he would attempt "to prevent the bringing in, of slaves that have been concerned in the insurrections of St. Domingo."

As the men marched along the bends of the river—drums rumbling, flags held high above their heads—they attacked several plantations with an assortment of knives, machetes, muskets, and other scavenged weapons, killing white men and destroying property in their wake. The groundwork for the uprising had been laid for several months through careful and secretive planning, the planners even using code language so as not to tip off anyone unsympathetic to their cause. At first, the surprise held. The farther along the river they marched, the more men joined and the more weapons they were able to accrue. They wielded clubs and farm tools and the knives that they used to slice sugarcane in the fields. Still, not all the enslaved fighters had guns, and because of that, it would take only a small number of armed troops to put them down. And ultimately that was what happened.

Within forty-eight hours, local militia and federal troops suppressed the rebellion. Many of the rebels were slaughtered on site, decapitated and their heads posted on stakes that lined the levee as a warning to other enslaved people that this was the price of rebellion. Naval officer Samuel Hambleton wrote: "They were brung here for the sake of their Heads, which decorate our Levee, all the way up the coast. I am told they look like crows sitting on long poles."

Deslondes briefly escaped the initial wave of slaughter by hiding in the swamp, but he was quickly captured and executed—his hands were chopped off, the femur bone in his leg was shattered by bullets, and he was burned atop a bale of straw.

Compared to other rebellions, like those of Nat Turner and John Brown, the 1811 slave revolt has received little historical attention. There are no notes of what was said between the co-conspirators, little that gives us insight into what Charles may have been thinking. But what is undoubtedly true is that each of the people assembled that evening knew the risk of their involvement.

In the immediate aftermath of the uprising, now that slave owners' worst fears had come to fruition, the backlash was brutal. Alarmed slaveholders in Louisiana invested resources in training local militia, and slave patrols began surveying slave quarters with increasing frequency and violence. Commodore John Shaw captured the planters' sense of fear that pushed them to respond with such violence against those who participated in the insurrection, and make them an example to the larger enslaved population: "Had not the most prompt and energetic measures been thus taken, the whole coast would have exhibited a general sense of devastation; every description of property would have been consumed; and the country laid waste by Rioters."

Meanwhile, the federal government committed to defending the institution of slavery by officially granting Louisiana statehood, as a slave state, in 1812. Louisiana remained a state until 1861, when it seceded from the Union. In a speech at the time, Louisiana's commissioner made the state's priorities clear: "Louisiana looks to the formation of a Southern confederacy to preserve the blessings of African slavery."

My mind wanders back to the exhibit in front of me. I look at Charles's floating head and imagine the smell of his charred flesh lacing the air, the cackle of dissolving skin melting into the earth. The wind blows, and I can almost taste the mingling of burned flesh and scorched soil, the mix of sweat and swamp water that lathered his body before he was captured by the bloodhounds who chased him down. I look at the rest of the bodiless figurines, observing the ridges in their tortured faces and adjusting my feet along the uneven brick path to find comfort where none would be found.

QUEER SEXUALITY

RAQUEL WILLIS

—

T O BE BLACK AND TO BE A GENDER OR SEXUAL MINORITY IS to carry a mixture of identities that have been chronicled historically in a piecemeal manner. This makes it difficult to acquire records that clearly reveal the existence of queer identities and experiences in the United States during the nineteenth century. After all, terms like *gay, lesbian, bisexual, transgender,* and *queer* did not exist then or weren't being used in the manner they are used today.

But by examining the history of queerness in West and Central Africa, uncovering the dominant cisgender and heterosexual mores of the time (and why that social order needed to be maintained), and exploring the concepts of fugitivity and surveillance, we can surmise a great deal about queer Blackness during this era.

First, in attempting to uncover the lives of Black queer folks in the 1810s, we must look to the origin cultures of their groups. Between 1720 and 1770, while the North American colonies received shipments of enslaved Africans from at least eight coastal regions of the continent, at least 60 percent came from West and Central Africa. Another snapshot figure of shipments of enslaved Africans from the first decade of the nineteenth century reveals that at least 35 percent were still coming from West and Central Africa. In examining the existence of queer behaviors and identities in these African regions, we may find that early examples of Black queerness were also imported into the United States.

As Stephen O. Murray and Will Roscoe assert, "African homosexuality is neither random nor incidental—it is a consistent and logical feature of African societies and belief systems." Going further, they share documentation, from as early as the 1600s to the early twentieth century, of what by today's standards Western cultures would refer to as queerness. In West Africa, there was the tradition-ally feminine dress and sexual behavior of young men of Sudan's Mossi tribe's royal court, and homosexual behavior among enslaved millet farmers in present-day Mali. The Dagara society of southern Burkina Faso had a role for gender-nonconforming mediation. Ho-mosexual behaviors are documented within both Hausa and Yoruba communities, and interviews and local lore describe multigendered societal roles and sexually fluid behaviors in Central Africa, especially in present-day Congo and Sudan.

Even with limited documentation of their potential origin cul-tures and the cultural aspects that later evolved in the same regions, enslaved Africans could have brought hidden alternative gender and sexual behaviors and identities with them to the United States. In the absence of first-person accounts from the antebellum period, it may be useful to employ the approach of historians like Daina Ramey Berry and Leslie M. Harris: examining runaway advertisements for evidence of how enslaved people's intimate relationships thrived and survived. They also offer a definition of sexuality to ground their un-derstanding of it: "the range of emotional and physical practices that have grown up around human reproduction and non-reproductive intimate expression, practices rooted in cultural beliefs and reflective and expressive of love but also of oppressive power."

Berry and Harris's volume emphasizes the importance of the doc-umentation of enslaved people running away from their enslaved cir-cumstances, as a viable means to preserve relationships and "evade capture and to subvert capitalistic control over their bodies." Those who ran away employed other methods, such as masquerading as a different class or even as another person, to evade capture. In the *Ra-leigh Register*'s September 9, 1814, issue, an enslaver, Laurence Battle, shared that an enslaved man he owned named Spencer had the "in-tention to pass for a free man, and may perhaps change his clothes and alter his name; and may have procured from some villain a free pass." Historian Sharon Block deduces that this method could be used by runaways to "transcend their laboring status" and more freely navigate society undetected.

Runaway advertisements are not the only sources that offer a glimpse into the lives of enslaved fugitives, and by proxy, gender and sexual minorities whose status would have been criminalized in American society. However, most documentation of these individuals deemed society's undesirables would have been connected to attempts to reprimand them punitively. "One of the unfortunate things is that a lot of the ways queer and trans bodies appear in the archives is through surveillance and moments of institutional crisis due to their identities," said Jessica Marie Johnson, a Johns Hopkins University historian. Run-ins with the law offer some of the few markers of their lives.

There are other instances of gender-nonconforming figures during the nineteenth century. On June 11, 1836, Mary Jones (also known as Peter Sewally) testified in court after being arrested for stealing one of her sex work clients' wallet and money. She testified:

> I have been in the practice of waiting upon Girls of ill fame and made up their Beds and received the Company at the door and received the money for rooms and they induced me to dress in Women's Clothes, saying I looked so much better in them and I have always attended parties among the people of my own Colour dressed in this way—and in New Orleans I always dressed in this way.

"Folks like Mary Waters, Mary Jones, and Thomasina Hall come up in court records in explosions of conversations that fixate on their gender and race," Johnson says. "It's probably one of the biggest similarities we have in how women of color are treated now, especially being policed, scrutinized, surveilled, and possibly not given justice in court. That's a legacy of an earlier preoccupation."

The existence of queer behaviors and modes of expression, and the larger white society's need to police these expressions by Black gender and sexual minorities, have long existed on this soil. As Johnson explains, "Policing gender, race, and the boundaries of these things has always been the work of creating laborers, separating communities and people from their humanity. A lot of categories we're dealing with in present-day are legacies of that period."

REMEMBERING THE ALBANY 3

ISHMAEL REED

—

For Edwidge

Like Caonabo
Anacaona
Padre Jean
And Macandal before
Boukman got his
Guabancex and Ogun on
Saint-Domingue flowed with the blood of France
Dread spread to Guadalupe, Jamaica and
The slaveholding North
Not only in the South but Albany, New York
Virginia masters slept with their lights turned
On
They feared that it might happen up here
Slaves roaming from plantation to plantation
Their minds set on decapitation

Said Jefferson's man
Jupiter: There wasn't no
Sword of Damocles over the enslavers' beds
It was a machete that Iman Boukman held
I overheard Tom talking to his friends
About how they could wrench the
Settler French from danger
Wasn't gone be no cinch. Ha!

He was all for the French having their liberty
But condemned his "property" to a life of slavery
They was afraid that Boukman would cross the sea
And interrupt their lives of comfort and ease
While we lived on pork, cornmeal and day old fish
They recruited French chefs to
Prepare their dish
Had all the pretty women at their
Beck and call
Said Monsieur La Rochefoucauld
After visiting Monticello
Tom's Greco Roman involuntary
Bordello
"I have even seen, and particularly at Mr. Jefferson's, slaves
Who have neither in their color nor features a single
Trace of their origins."
Tom couldn't keep his children out of sight
He was a founding father all right
Sally Hemings wasn't the only one
There were at least two others by whom
He had daughters and sons
They weren't treated like the other
Slaves whose wounds were
Smeared with brine
After his overseers got
Drunk on Tom's imported wine
He and his friends thought that
Haitian rebels would rob them
Of their gains
The ones they stole from Indians whom
They murdered and maimed

Tom called the rebels "Cannibals"
When it seems to me that
He was the one who was a

Consumer of men
Worked them 24/7 without a fee
While he studied Plato's philosophy

The Albany Dutch shared the planters' fears
The Schuylers, the Ten Eycks and
The Rensselaers
When arson broke out
They blamed the Haitians
Saw Haitians under their beds
Behind the door and
In the basement

But finding none arrested their
Slaves
Pompey was the first who was taken in
He was grilled until he finally bent
If you name the conspirators we'll
Set you free, they lied
Just like they lied to the Central Park 5
He named two teenage girls Bet and
Dinah
Said that they helped him burn a
Barn that belonged to Gansevoort
Another Dutchman who prospered
From stolen loot
They were found and jailed
For the Albany conflagration
All three were sent to the gallows
By the kind of Albany jury
That acquitted the
Murderers of Amadou Diallo

The Gov. said the facts of the
Case didn't make sense
And tried to postpone their sentence

But the Albany mob was lusting for a kill
The girls were hanged on Pinkster hill
And Pompey was hanged a little later
Pompey was called a rogue
The girls were called "wenches"
But for others they were liberators

Their arson sparked
Fires in other places
Boston, New York, Georgia and Ohio
Their owners learned
That it's not only Gabriel's
Army from whom you have to scurry
But teenagers like the Albany 3
About whom you have to
Worry
Black Lives Matter!

PART SIX

DENMARK VESEY

ROBERT JONES, JR.

—

RAPPER KANYE WEST, WHO EMERGED AN ADMIRER OF DONALD Trump, once suggested that slavery was a choice. From his limited understanding of history, he attempted to convey the idea that Black people never resisted their enslavers. As such, the subjugation of enslaved people was the fault of the subjugated who failed to resist.

Clearly, West was unfamiliar with the story of Denmark Vesey, who planned a powerful insurrection in Charleston, South Carolina, in 1822.

Enslaved until he purchased his freedom from lottery winnings (which did not, however, permit him to purchase the freedom of his wife and children), Vesey initially lived quietly as a carpenter around whom white people felt safe. So safe, in fact, that he rented or owned a house in the heart of Charleston only a few blocks away from the mayor and the governor. He gathered with other Blacks at his residence to plot the overthrow of slavery.

In 1800 Vesey, at about thirty-three, must have noticed that Black people made up over 77 percent of the population of Charleston. It was the Blackest city in the country—and one of the most heavily policed. It seems that wherever the Black body is present, whether in solitary or in a multitude, whites feel threatened, perhaps by the ghosts of their own sins for which they have never atoned.

Given the size of their majority, it is not difficult to determine why Vesey imagined that he, along with the rest of the Black population, could overthrow the city. He planned to raid the banks and artillery storages and leave almost every one of its white citizens, young and old, massacred in the streets, then escape to Haiti. The Haitian Revolution must have inspired Vesey's plans since he had once been enslaved on the island to work the sugarcane fields. Smartly, he had faked an epileptic seizure to get out of doing such drudgery and had been brought to Charleston.

For Vesey, Blackness was a unifier that superseded geography. Seeking a community of radical Black spirit, he joined the new African Methodist Episcopal (AME) Church, founded in 1817 in Charleston. But in 1818, the city shut it down because the whites feared Black people congregating and discovering that their lot was in fact neither ordained nor written in the sky. However, by then it was too late. Vesey had already found among its clergy and believers kindred spirits. For this was a moment when the Black church could be relied upon as a site of revolutionary, liberatory action rather than for what it has more recently been known: respectability, docility, anti-queerness, and greed—a shadow version of whiteness.

A brutally anti-Black city, despite its Black majority, Charleston was home to the Work House, a former sugar factory that had been converted into a torture chamber for Black people. Charleston must have shown Vesey the same untold cruelties that all Black America would witness in 2015 when one Dylann Storm Roof, after being welcomed into the open arms of the congregation of Charleston's Emanuel African Methodist Episcopal Church, opened fire and murdered nine of them in the middle of prayer.

Vesey made it clear to all his lieutenants that they were to recruit to his army only Black people who loved Black people, not those striving to be white. He was distrustful of Charleston's biracial population, particularly the bourgeois class, whom he saw as having, at best, split loyalties. (However, he did recruit at least three biracial men into his army.) What he achieved in terms of organization is remarkable: he recruited as many as nine thousand Black people under the single banner of their own liberation, willing to risk life and limb to attain the dignity afforded to horseflies but denied to them.

What must have stung no less acutely than a lash from the whip, however, was that Vesey's meticulous strategies were undone by other

Black people. As much as by the superior military strength and numbers of the white opposing force, the possibility of Black liberation is often undermined by Black people who have been so successfully indoctrinated by white supremacist principles that the idea of mass Black freedom is threatening or, worse, unimaginable. What motivated these men (alarmingly, there is no record of any women being recruited either to aid in the rebellion or to undermine it, though they must have certainly played a significant role) to act on behalf of white masters to determine the specifics of the uprising can only be guessed at, but chief among the likely causes are cowardice and pragmatism. That they were scared was obvious; of what, however, deserves more consideration.

From these men, long dead, we will never have definitive answers. But perhaps answers can be found in questioning contemporary figures like Kanye West, U.S. Supreme Court justice Clarence Thomas, former secretary of state Condoleezza Rice, attorney Larry Elder, political commentator Candace Owens, or any other Black person whose actions are direct descendants of the same fealty to racist systems that undid Vesey and company's chances at achieving humanity.

Vesey's strategy was gruesome by necessity, yet it paled in comparison to the infinite horrors enacted by all who participated in the capture, transport, enslavement, abuse, rape, disfigurement, and murder of Black people during the enterprise known as antebellum slavery. Upon being betrayed, in the summer of 1822 Vesey and thirty-nine of his followers were executed by hanging. All transcripts of the trials were ordered destroyed by the judges (though at least one copy, discovered accidentally, survived the purge) for fear that it might inspire Black people to engage heartily in their human right to self-defense.

The Black people who attended the public executions to witness and give their respects were threatened with arrest and flogging if they dared to show any public sign of mourning. Their docility and acquiescence, however phony, were made mandatory so as to assure the white populace of Charleston, and the entire United States, that all the power still rested in white hands, and that despite the cruelties enacted upon them, Black people had nothing but boundless love in their hearts for white people. This myth of Black docility, alongside a gut-level fear of a Black uprising, is the American empire's motivation for enforcing supplication through unjust laws, sealing a social contract that punishes the wretched for daring to recognize their own dignity, and rewarding them for conceding to the pretense of the empire's innocence. The only peace to be had is through thorough capitulation and assimilation. These are the principles upon which bigotry is built.

However, as Vesey surely understood, the enslaver's morality should not be the morality of the enslaved. If it is wrong to enslave, then it is right to free oneself from enslavement. The means by which that freedom is achieved is above moral speculation, with one exception: once attained, one must remember: Wash the blood from the hands. Never turn the (t)error inward. Discontinue the abject failures of humanity that lead one to regard other people as property, lest the cycle begin again, this time with the blade pointed at one's own throat.

1824–1829

FREEDOM'S JOURNAL

PAMELA NEWKIRK

FOR A QUARTER OF A CENTURY, I HAVE TAUGHT A COURSE
that surveys media portrayals of marginalized groups, including racial, ethnic, and religious minorities and the LGBTQI population, in
film, on television, and in the popular press. Each year the course
begins with an examination of *Freedom's Journal* (1827–1829). It was
America's first African American–owned and –operated newspaper
and, from its New York City office, it unflinchingly challenged de-
meaning depictions of Black people in the press. "We wish to plead
our own cause," the editors proclaimed in their first editorial on
March 16, 1827. "Too long have others spoken for us. Too long has the
publick been deceived by misrepresentations, in things which concern
us dearly. Our vices and our degradation are ever arrayed against us,
but our Virtues are passed by unnoticed. From the press and the pulpit we have suffered much by being incorrectly represented."

This editorial was penned by founding editors John B. Russwurm,
who a year earlier had become the first African American graduate of
Bowdoin College, and Samuel E. Cornish, an abolitionist and freed-
man who organized New York City's first Black Presbyterian congregation. Their critique came just fifteen weeks before New York State,
on July 4, effectively emancipated enslaved Blacks, and nearly four
decades before the Emancipation Proclamation, followed by the
Thirteenth Amendment, commenced the journey to an uncertain
freedom for others.

In cataloging the derisive and destructive portrayals of Africans and their descendants, the editors extended their critique to progressive whites. "Men whom we equally love and admire have not hesitated to represent us disadvantageously, without becoming personally acquainted with the true state of things, nor discerning between virtue and vice among us.

"And what is still more lamentable," they added, "our friends, to whom we concede all the principles of humanity and religion, from these very causes seem to have fallen into the current of popular feeling and are imperceptibly floating on the stream—actually living in the practice of prejudice, while they abjure it in theory and feel it not in their hearts." From their Lower Manhattan office at 236 Church Street, the editors hoped to "arrest the progress of prejudice" while shielding Africans and their descendants from its wrath.

For two years the newspaper reached African Americans in eleven northern states and the District of Columbia, and it circulated as far away as Haiti, Europe, and Canada. It inspired the publication of two dozen other Black newspapers before the Civil War. Every year I hope my twenty-first-century New York University students will see the nearly two-hundred-year-old paper as little more than a significant relic of a dystopian past. However, the critique leveled in that first editorial still resonates for them. In their case studies of contemporary media portrayals, they continue to find glaring patterns of bias in the pervasive depictions of African Americans, which reserve extra scorn for Black men.

Whether analyzing news coverage in some of the nation's most respected newspapers and magazines, or depictions of Blacks in film and on television, my students find that African Americans are too often relegated to narratives related to crime, sports, and pathology. For far too many Americans, these depictions are more authentic renderings of African American life than are the daily strivings of the actual people who evade detection: the ordinary and extraordinary fathers, brothers, mothers, and sisters who languish on the margins. It's unlikely that the average African American is cognizant of the extent to which these portrayals shape and misshape the contours of their own lives: how the preponderance of stereotypes in film, crime shows, news stories, and music videos reduces them to specters whose walking, driving, or standing can result in a store clerk's surveillance or a fatal encounter with police. And these images have gone far to sustain a rigid racial caste system resulting in the overpolicing and the mass incarceration of Black and Brown men, as well as a culture of exclusion in many of the most influential fields.

Despite the major strides African Americans have made since Russwurm and Cornish's day, they remain disproportionately underrepresented in practically every influential field, including journalism: between 2002 and 2015, the number of Black journalists in mainstream newspapers actually declined from 2,951 to 1,560.

In radio, people of color, while comprising roughly 39 percent of the population, held just 14.5 percent of newsroom jobs and were only 7.2 percent of general managers and 8.2 percent of news directors, according to the 2019 annual survey conducted by the Radio Television Digital News Association. In television, people of color held about 22.8 percent of newsroom jobs at network affiliates, and were just 7.4 percent of general managers and 13.4 percent of news directors. African Americans, at 12 percent of the news staff, had achieved near proportional representation but were only 5.4 percent of news directors, down from 6.7 percent in 2018.

Meanwhile the Black press, once a staple of African American life, has become as marginalized as those it had sought to represent. As mainstream media prominently covered the civil rights movement, the reliance on Black newspapers waned. The circulation of leading newspapers including *The Chicago Defender, The Pittsburgh Courier,* and *The Baltimore Afro-American* peaked in 1945 at 257,000, 202,000, and 137,000, respectively, but by 1970 it stood at just 33,000, 20,000, and 33,000. While unfiltered Black voices can still be found offline and online in *Essence, The Root,* and the sprinkling of African American newspapers around the country, the centuries-long struggle to sustain a free Black press continues.

In 2019 the iconic *Ebony* magazine was compelled to sell its historically significant archives in a bankruptcy auction. Black Entertainment Television, founded by Robert L. Johnson, once featured news and politically oriented programming along with music videos and entertainment. However, in 2002 it shifted its focus to entertainment, and in 2005, the year it was sold to Viacom, it canceled its nightly news show. Like a number of other Black-interest outlets, it is no longer Black-owned and has drawn criticism for its programming.

Despite the fanfare over the occasional triumphs, Black voices—like those of other people of color—remain muted in film. *Hollywood Diversity Report: Five Years of Progress and Missed Opportunities,* a 2018 study conducted by UCLA, found that in the top two hundred theatrical releases in 2016, people of color comprised just 8 percent of screenwriters and 12.6 percent of directors.

Moreover, the kind of stereotypes condemned in *Freedom's Journal* persist. A study by the University of Southern California's Viterbi School of Engineering used artificial intelligence to analyze one thousand recent films and found that many continued to reinforce stereotypes of racial minorities, with African American characters more likely to curse.

Given the critical issues facing African Americans—including a starkly unjust criminal justice system and persistent racial disparities detected on practically every social indicator—it is clear that Black people still need to plead our own cause. While in recent decades the luster of the Black press has faded, the legacy of *Freedom's Journal* can be glimpsed in the unbridled voices found on social media; in some Black-owned or -operated outlets; and in the cracks and crevices of mass media. The continuing quest by Black journalists to depict the breadth of the African American experience and to combat injustice recalls the audaciousness and valor of the trailblazing founders of *Freedom's Journal.*

MARIA STEWART

KATHRYN SOPHIA BELLE

———

I WAS FIRST INTRODUCED TO MARIA W. STEWART (1803–79) as a student at Spelman College in a feminist theory course brilliantly taught by Beverly Guy-Sheftall. The primary text for the course—Sheftall's classic edited collection, *Words of Fire: An Anthology of African American Feminist Thought* (1995)—begins with Stewart. Perhaps for this reason, she has always stood out to me as a foundational Black feminist and philosophical figure. Stewart offers what I have termed proto-intersectionality—an early Black feminist articulation of intersecting identities and oppressions along the lines of race, gender, and class.

Stewart was born free in Connecticut, orphaned at five years old, and worked as a servant for a minister in her youth. She later worked as a teacher in New York, Baltimore, and Washington, D.C., where she also served as a matron of the Freeman's Hospital. She became a prominent speaker and writer—though that was short-lived due to racism and sexism. Nevertheless, several of her essays and speeches were published in *The Liberator,* and she self-published two edited collections of her written works. She created her own legacy through her speeches, writings, and activism against race and gender oppression. But in the historical record, she is often presented through the lens of her relationships with prominent men: as the widow of James W. Stewart, a friend of David Walker, a correspondent of Alexander Crummell, and a friend and professional affiliate of William Lloyd Garrison.

Stewart has been identified as the first woman in the United States to speak publicly to an audience composed of men and women, and also as America's first Black woman political writer. Her speech in September 1832 was organized by the Afric-American Female Intelligence Society of Boston. It was a time when "women did not speak in public," as Paula Giddings explains, "especially on serious issues like civil rights, and most especially, feminism." And they especially did not speak publicly before a "promiscuous" audience of both men and women.

Beyond the significance of this historic first, Marilyn Richardson argues, "Her original synthesis of religious, abolitionist, and feminist concerns places her squarely in the forefront of black female activist and literary tradition only now beginning to be acknowledged as of integral significance to the understanding of the history of black thought and culture in America." Richardson also describes Stewart as offering a "triple consciousness, as she demonstrates the creative struggle of a woman attempting to establish both a literary voice and an historical mirror for her experience as 'an American, a Negro,' and a woman."

Stewart made her public appearances, speeches, and writings during the time of the Second Great Awakening, the Nat Turner Revolt, and intense debates about slavery—from more militant abolitionism (as expressed in William Lloyd Garrison's *The Liberator*, for example) to concerted efforts for the colonization or repatriation of free Black people to Africa by the American Colonization Society. *The Liberator* published several of Stewart's writings, including "Religion and the Pure Principles of Morality, The Sure Foundation on Which We Must Build" (October 8, 1831); "An Address Delivered Before the Afric-American Female Intelligence Society of America" (April 28, 1832); "Cause for Encouragement: Composed upon Hearing the Editors' Account of the Late Convention in Philadelphia" (letter to the editor, July 14, 1832); "Lecture Delivered at the Franklin Hall" (speech delivered September 21, 1832); "An Address Delivered at the African Masonic Hall" (March 2, 1833; speech delivered February 27); and "Mrs. Stewart's Farewell Address to Her Friends in the City of Boston" (September 21, 1833).

These writings shed light on her proto-intersectional ideas. In her 1831 pamphlet "Religion and the Pure Principles of Morality, The Sure Foundation on Which We Must Build," Stewart critiqued both the prevailing racist assumption that Blacks were an inferior race and the sexist paternalism of men, all while calling on Black women to have more agency. She named race, gender, and class oppression in the form of economic exploitation of the labor of the "fair daughters of Africa." She admonished Black women to wake up, rise up, and support one another through cooperative economies to gain economic independence. She considered a range of possibilities for Black women, from mothers and educators to intellectually and economically empowered contributors to the community. She called on Black women to "possess the spirit of men, bold and enterprising, fearless and undaunted. Sue for your rights and privileges. Know the reason you cannot attain them."

In 1832 Stewart delivered a lecture at Franklin Hall in Boston. She called out racial prejudice and its specific impact on Black women and girls, limiting them to servile labor and ignoring their qualities beyond that service. In her 1833 "Farewell Address to Her Friends in the City of Boston," she outlined diverse roles and expectations for women, especially Black women. Offering examples of women in the Bible as well as women from various cultures (Greek, Roman, Jewish, Ethiopian, and even "barbarous nations"), Stewart again made the case for Black women in particular to publicly demand their rights. And in her 1833 "Address Delivered at the African Masonic Hall," Stewart critiqued Black men for their "talk, without effort." The "gross neglect, on your part, causes my blood to boil within me."

Beginning with Maria W. Stewart, Black women have been offering intersectional analyses of identity and oppression since at least the early nineteenth century. In addition to her foundational insights about intersecting identities and oppressions, Stewart has also been analyzed from the perspective of her religious and theological insights and interventions, her rhetorical strategies, and her appeals to sympathetic violence.

THE NATIONAL NEGRO CONVENTIONS

Eugene Scott

——

MORE THAN 150 YEARS AFTER BLACK AMERICANS EXPERI-
enced the first tastes of freedom, a question still dominates the minds
of those deeply invested in the fate of the descendants of the enslaved:
what does it mean to be Black and free in the United States? Throughout the history of Black America, the media have played a significant
role in finding answers to the most pressing race questions. And in
many ways they continue to do so. However, in an era when many
media outlets show little interest in grappling with these questions
while others are simply struggling to remain viable, the ability—or
willingness—of the press to replicate what it was once so effective at
doing is concerning.

Since Black people first arrived in what would become the United
States, freedom was without question their greatest desire. And that
continued to be the case in those decades leading up to the abolition
of slavery, even as attempts at emancipation became more frequent.
But exactly what emancipation would look like for Black Americans
was still unclear and debatable. While some Black thinkers and abolitionists entertained ideas of citizenship, others believed that formerly enslaved people could never be treated equally and with respect,
so they advocated for racial separatism or emigration to the Caribbean or western Africa. Activists grappled with these ideas publicly
and privately, but there was a need for a robust gathering where the
leaders of the time could discuss the future of Black people. In 1834

those of great influence who were concerned with the state—and fate—of Black people in America congregated to find answers at National Negro Conventions, gatherings aimed at moving America toward abolition at the very least, in the hope that the formerly enslaved would command a more respected standing in the country and across the globe.

In the decades leading up to the Civil War, the question of what it meant to be Black in the United States was largely obvious but still diverse in its answer. In 1830, of the nearly 13 million people in the United States, 2 million were enslaved. This large ratio, combined with an increase in slave rebellions, like those led by Nat Turner and Denmark Vesey, had white enslavers on edge, as they realized that aggressive fights for freedom by the enslaved would become more frequent—and more violent—until freedom was granted. Although these rebellions often ended tragically, they gave many Black people hope. The desire for freedom spread across slave states, as some former slaves successfully reached the temporary promised land: free states. During this time the population of free Black Americans, particularly in the northern and western United States, was growing. However, most Black Americans remained enslaved, leading those who were experiencing freedom—and the white people who supported them—to increase their attention to arriving to the place where all were free. Freedom from slavery was certainly the initial goal for Black people. But as the movement to eradicate slavery grew, a new question arose: what would it mean to be Black in a postslavery America?

During the late 1830s, Black thought leaders, businesspeople, clergy, and many of their white counterparts gathered to answer this burgeoning question at the National Negro Conventions, events whose popularity was made known mainly through the efforts of the press. Two specific publications—*Freedom's Journal,* the country's first Black newspaper, and *The Liberator,* an abolitionist newspaper founded by William Lloyd Garrison—played major roles in gathering Black leaders from across the nation to answer this fundamental question while also seeking solutions for more complex ones. These publications, by elevating the National Negro Conventions, allowed

Black people and abolitionists to form networks to move America toward freeing—and advancing the lives of—enslaved people, with a level of urgency and efficiency that was previously unseen. Without them, influential minds could hardly have gathered to develop the strategies required for Black people to receive the justice they had long been denied. This model would be replicated decades later, when the Black press played an influential role in pointing leaders in the Black community (and those who supported them) toward the NAACP's national conventions; the National Urban League's State of Black America; and other events aimed at zeroing in on the most pressing issues facing Black Americans.

One of the most significant contributions of the National Negro Conventions was their vision to encourage the continued gathering of those who cared about the future of Black people in the United States and beyond. Those in attendance gave much attention to the freeing of Black people, but they also recognized that there were issues plaguing the Black community beyond the need for emancipation. They gave significant attention to topics related to the global fate of Black people and internal conflicts within the Black community related to gender and even diversity of political thought. For them, freedom for Black people went beyond freedom from slavery. It also meant having their humanity acknowledged and having the ability to live their lives to the fullest.

The meaning of freedom pertaining to Black people is a question much older than the United States. Quests to determine and experience a free life for Black Americans reach back to the earliest colonial settlements. Yet centuries later, de facto segregation continues, mass incarceration remains prevalent, and significant gaps between the lived experiences of Black and white people in health, education, and wealth persist. The question remains prevalent today and in many ways has taken on deeper significance. Although slavery has been legally abolished, freedom for many Black Americans seems like a far cry from the vision of freedom described by the founders in the Constitution.

1839–1844

RACIAL PASSING

ALLYSON HOBBS

════

OCTOBER 4, 1842

GEORGE LATIMER AND HIS PREGNANT WIFE, REBECCA, MADE a desperate leap for liberty. They escaped from Norfolk, Virginia, hiding in the hold of a ship for nine hours. They stole away to Baltimore, then to Philadelphia, before arriving in Boston.

Four days after Latimer's escape, Latimer's owner, James Gray, described Latimer's complexion as "a bright yellow" in an advertisement. Latimer was able to pass as white, so he "travelled as a gentleman" while his wife traveled as his servant. While boarding the ship in Norfolk, Latimer walked by a man he knew. He quickly pulled his Quaker hat over his eyes, entered the first-class cabin, and was not recognized.

In antebellum America, runaway slaves wore white skin like a cloak. Racial ambiguity, appropriate dress—Latimer's Quaker hat, for instance—and proper comportment could mask one's enslaved status and provide a strategy for escape. Once Latimer was seated in the first-class cabin, it would have been impolite for a passenger or a conductor to question his racial identity.

Tactical or strategic passing—passing temporarily with a particular purpose in mind—was born out of a dogged desire for freedom. In later historical periods, this type of passing would allow racially ambiguous men and women to access employment opportunities, to travel without humiliation, and to attend elite colleges. In the antebellum period, passing was connected to a larger struggle and to strivings for freedom.

The countless men and women who passed successfully demonstrate that even in the most totalizing systems, there is always some slack. Passing was an expedient means of securing one's freedom, and in its broadest formulation, it became a crucial channel through which African Americans called for the recognition of their humanity. The desperate acts of enslaved men and women were not freighted with the internal conflicts, tensions, or moral angst of other historical periods. Surrounded by loss, enslaved people were motivated by a desire to be reunited with their families, not to leave them behind. Many runaway slaves neither imagined nor desired to begin new lives as white. They simply wanted to be free.

Latimer had been beaten severely while he was enslaved, sometimes in front of his wife. When he was returning from the market with Rebecca, his owner struck him with a stick across his jaw, bruising his skin. His owner followed Latimer to a store, where he hit him with a stick nearly twenty times. Latimer said that if he were captured, he expected to be "beaten and whipped 39 lashes, and perhaps to be washed in pickle afterwards."

"We all know on a certain, almost intuitive level that violence is inseparable from slavery," historian Nell Painter has written. "We readily acknowledge the existence of certain conventions associated with slavery: the use of physical violence to make slaves obedient and submissive, the unquestioned right of owners to use people they owned in whatever ways they wished."

Shortly after Latimer and his wife reached Boston, James Gray arrived in the city and had Latimer arrested on a charge of larceny. Nearly three hundred Black men gathered around the courthouse to prevent Latimer from being returned to Gray, who planned to send Latimer back to Virginia. A chaotic meeting in Faneuil Hall roused public sympathy for Latimer and sharpened abolitionists' demands for legislation to protect fugitive slaves.

Latimer's escape took place in 1842, the same year as *Prigg v. Pennsylvania*. This decision allowed states to forbid officials from cooperating with federal legislation like the Fugitive Slave Act of 1793, which guaranteed slave owners the right to recover runaway slaves. The *Prigg* decision was later overturned by the Fugitive Slave Act of 1850, which required free states to support the capture and delivery of fugitive slaves, even if it meant deputizing local law enforcement.

In November 1842, Latimer's supporters in Boston founded a newspaper, the *Latimer Journal and North Star*. With a circulation of twenty thousand, the *Journal* sought to raise public support for fugitive slaves among antislavery Bostonians. In an interview, an editor asked Latimer if he had ever led Gray or anyone else to believe that he wanted to return to Norfolk. "No, never," Latimer declared. "I would rather die than go back." James Gray tried to get Latimer to return willingly, to avoid all the trouble and the chaos created by the meeting in Faneuil Hall. Gray promised to "serve [Latimer] well." Latimer turned his back on Gray and stated bluntly: "Mr. Gray, when you get me back to Norfolk you may kill me."

What about Rebecca? We know very little about her besides what was published in an advertisement after she escaped:

RANAWAY from the subscriber last evening, negro Woman REBECCA, in company (as is supposed) with her husband, George Latimer, belonging to Mr. James B. Gray, of this place. She is about 20 years of age, dark mulatto or copper colored, good countenance, bland voice and self-possessed and easy in her manners when addressed.—She was married in February last [1842] and at this time obviously enceinte [pregnant]. She will in all probability endeavor to reach some one of the free States. All persons are hereby cautioned against harboring said slave, and masters of vessels from carrying her from this port. The above reward [$50] will be paid upon delivery to Mary D. Sayer.

Rebecca must have ached for freedom just as desperately as her husband did, not only for herself but also for the unborn child that she carried on their perilous journey.

Who was Mary D. Sayer? Did she own Rebecca? Perhaps her husband did. Her status as a white woman may have depended on

Rebecca's labor. Perhaps Sayer stood high on the social ladder (but never at the top, a space occupied exclusively by white men). She lived with the discomfort of knowing that, as Painter explains, white men had unfettered sexual access to all women and saw "women—whether slave or free, wealthy or impoverished, cultured or untutored, black or white—as interchangeable." There was nothing that Mary Sayer could do to prevent her husband from sleeping with enslaved women, who in turn were forced to be readily available sexual partners.

On November 18, 1842, Latimer was finally manumitted for $400 and could not be returned to Virginia. In 1843 approximately sixty-five thousand residents signed a petition, which led to passage of the "Latimer Law," a liberty law that (1) prevented state officials from assisting in the arrest of fugitive slaves, (2) forbade the use of jails to detain fugitive slaves, and (3) formally separated Massachusetts residents from any connection with slavery. Judges, justices of the peace, and other state officers could not legally assist in the arrest of any fugitive slave.

In an autobiographical sketch published in the same year as the Latimer Law, Latimer wrote that he had always imagined running away, even as a child. He would roll up his sleeve and wonder, "Can this flesh belong to any man as horses do?"

We can only imagine the conversation that George and Rebecca Latimer shared as they lay in the hold of the ship for nine hours during their flight from Norfolk. Maybe they pictured their lives as free people. Maybe they talked about their dreams for their child and touched Rebecca's growing stomach. Maybe they worried that George's disguise as a white man might fail. Maybe they did not speak a word to each other. What we do know is that these two souls believed deeply in their humanity, and that they risked everything for it to be recognized.

1844–1849

JAMES MCCUNE SMITH, M.D.

HARRIET A. WASHINGTON

═══

The Negro "with us" is not an actual physical being of flesh
and bones and blood, but a hideous monster of the mind,
ugly beyond all physical portraying . . . that haunts with
grim presence the precincts of this republic, shaking his
gory locks over legislative halls and family prayers.

—JAMES MCCUNE SMITH, M.D.

THE UNIVERSITY OF GLASGOW BEGAN ITS 2020–21 ACADEMIC
year with the unveiling of the £90.6 million James McCune Smith
Learning Hub. This steel-and-glass shrine to modernity also celebrates the past, because it is named for one of the institution's most
revered alumni—James McCune Smith, M.D. (1813–65), who graduated as valedictorian of the medical school in 1837.

Today thirty annual university scholarships and the annual James
McCune Smith Memorial Lecture bear his name, as do signs in
Glasgow's historic "slave walk." The McCune Smith Café offers Scot-
tish delicacies, an "anticolonialist menu," and African coffees on the
site of his former Duke Street home.

But in New York City, this Renaissance man—erudite classicist,
writer, abolitionist, apothecary, and statistician who was also the first
African American to be awarded a formal medical degree—is all but
forgotten.

He was born to a white father and an enslaved mother who later earned her freedom, as did James. He grew up in Lower Manhattan's Fourth Ward, where at the African Free School number two on Mulberry Street he earned excellent grades, achieved fluency in Greek and Latin, and displayed a rare facility for writing. He wished to attend university and study medicine, but every U.S. university to which he applied rejected him—evidence of the race-based exclusion that was widely practiced in both Northern and Southern schools, sometimes into the 1960s.

McCune Smith was, however, accepted by the elite University of Glasgow, and local abolitionist groups raised funds that enabled him to sail in 1832 to Scotland. There he earned academic laurels, assumed leadership in the Glasgow Emancipation Society, and inspired the university to eschew its significant profits from enslavement.

Yet McCune Smith was determined to return home after graduation and wield his education against American enslavement. He sailed back to New York City in May 1837.

Once ensconced in New York, McCune Smith proved far more than an incisive abolitionist who wrote for Frederick Douglass's *The North Star*. He opened a medical practice in Manhattan, established the nation's first African American apothecary, and served as the physician of the New York Colored Orphans Asylum. He married Malvina Barnet, and they started a family.

A few years into the 1840s, McCune Smith undertook a key refutation of racial pseudoscience—the U.S. Census of 1840. The "monster of the mind" to which this essay's epigraph refers was promulgated by our nation's most influential nineteenth-century scientists, including Louis Agassiz, Samuel Cartwright, Josiah Nott, and Samuel Morton. They pronounced African Americans to be acutely inferior, unintelligent, and animalistic but strong and designed for subtropical servitude. Their screeds lent the weight of medical science to proslavery arguments.

The results of the 1840 census, which by the time of McCune Smith's review in 1844 were under the ultimate control of Secretary of State John C. Calhoun, showed data on the health of both white and Black Americans, the latter of which were divided into categories of "free" and "enslaved." According to these data, enslaved Black Americans enjoyed much better health than free ones, particularly mental health. Free African Americans were eleven times more likely than enslaved ones to be mentally ill, he found. Enslavement was therefore beneficial, according to the census data, and freedom could prove fatal.

Except for protests by one physician, antislavery activists offered only pallid rebuttals, while McCune Smith analyzed the data and found it rife with fraud and error. He demonstrated that many of the figures were specious or invented and that by every meaningful measure, from life expectancy to disease rates to mental health, free Blacks enjoyed far superior health than the enslaved.

McCune Smith presented his detailed report to the U.S. Senate in 1844. Former president John Quincy Adams, then serving in the House of Representatives, ordered an investigation, but Calhoun, a slavery advocate and former medical student, appointed a proslavery crony who pronounced the census flawless. Thus the 1840 census was never formally corrected, and enslavement was held to be necessary for African American health.

McCune Smith continued his abolition work despite snubs. The New York Academy of Medicine refused to consider his fellowship application, a slight that was mitigated by his posthumous acceptance at my request in 2018. After the orphans' asylum was burned to the ground by rioting whites in the 1863 draft riots, he relocated his family to Williamsburg, Brooklyn, for safety. He had planned to leave New York for an academic position at Wilberforce University in Ohio but was unable to do so because of an illness.

James McCune Smith, who fought enslavement valiantly on two continents, lived to see it banned by the Thirteenth Amendment before his 1865 death.

The distortion of medicine to support nineteenth-century enslavement is more than a shameful bit of history. Contemporary research reveals a widespread belief among physicians that, for example, Blacks are impervious to pain. Bias also persists in the dramatic underrepresentation of African American men among the nation's eighteen thousand medical students: they make up 6 percent of the country's population but less than 2 percent of medical students. And that number is falling: their peak year for medical school graduation was 1978.

OREGON

MITCHELL S. JACKSON

———

BACK WHEN I WAS A YOUNGIN LIVING IN PORTLAND, OREGON, almost my whole block was Black. There was the old woman across the street, whose blinds were forever cracked, the easier to spy on us juveniles and snitch to our parents or guardians. There was the lil patna Poobear, who lived a couple houses down and whose front porch could've doubled as a junkyard. There was Ms. Mary in the middle of the block, whose cherry tree was the most fertile in the land but who would chase you off her lawn with a switch should you dare to pick a single sweet orb. There were the Mayfields at the end of the block, a family with huge Doberman pinschers stalking behind a fence too short to keep them from bounding it and turning canine-petrified me into doggie grub.

In a shabby duplex across from the Mayfields lived a Native American family (foolish me, I called them Indians in those days), whose yard always featured a dismantled car on cinder blocks. Back then, us neighborhood kids would build go-carts and race them down a hill, or we would stage concerts using upturned coffee cans, or on special summer days, we would chase down the ice cream truck and cop frozen treats—ice cream sandwiches were my fave—and lounge in someone's front yard and hold tacit speed-licking contests. As far as I can recall, there was but one white person on the block, an old woman who didn't much engage with the rest of us. This was the 1980s, and my block was situated in Northeast Portland, what us denizens came to call the NEP.

The NEP was one of the few mostly Black neighborhoods in the city. Because of that fact, because I didn't venture much outside my neighborhood as a kid, and because I was ignorant of my state and city's racial history, I knew not that I was living in a white man's land, that it had been intended as one from its founding, and that Black folks had long been an unwanted presence.

The lone person, on record, to be expelled from Oregon was a fair-skinned Black man named Jacob Vanderpool, purportedly a sailor from the West Indies. Vanderpool had arrived by ship in what was then the Oregon Territory (Oregon didn't achieve statehood until 1859) and settled in Oregon City, where he opened a boardinghouse/saloon. Vanderpool must've been one helluva businessman because the following year, August 1851, a man named Theophilus Magruder, himself the owner of a hostelry, complained that Vanderpool's presence in Oregon City was a violation of the territory's exclusion law, passed in 1844.

The case went to trial later that month. Vanderpool's lawyer claimed the law violated several provisions of the U.S. Constitution, that the Oregon legislature hadn't owned the jurisdiction to create it in the first place, and also that the charge itself had not been executed properly. But strong defense be damned, the very next day, August 26, 1851, the judge ruled Vanderpool guilty of violating the exclusion law and ordered him "removed from said territory within thirty days."

Another expulsion order on Oregon's historical ledgers occurred in September 1851 and involved brothers O. B. Francis and Abner Hunt Francis, free Blacks who owned a mercantile store in downtown Portland. Abner was also an abolitionist and friend of Frederick Douglass. Historians theorize that the brothers' business and anti-slavery ties aroused the concerns of racist whites, and therefore while Abner was away, O.B. (and his wife) were ordered to leave the territory within six months. On appeal to the Oregon supreme court in September 1851, that judgment was shortened to four months. Abner, implicating himself in the expulsion, published a letter about his and his brother's plight in Douglass's newspaper, *The North Star:* "even in the so-called free territory of Oregon, the colored American citizen, though he may possess all the qualities and qualifications which make

a man a good citizen, is driven out like a beast in the forest." Fortu-
nately for the Francis brothers, 225 local citizens signed a petition that
allowed them to remain in Oregon on an exception. Though lawmakers spent beaucoup time debating said petition, in the end, they tabled
it and never revisited it.

A third expulsion order targeted a man named Morris Thomas,
who was married to a woman named Jane Snowdon. Like those targeted for ousting before him, he was an entrepreneur, his business a
barbershop. As in the case of the Francis brothers, local citizens, 128
of them, filed a petition asking that Thomas and his family be spared
expulsion.

About the time I reached the era of double-digit birthdays, folks
who never had to worry one bit about being kicked out of the state
or the city (most often white men in shabby suits) were roaming our
neighborhood. They weren't door-to-door salesmen hawking encyclopedias or water purifiers, but door-to-door home buyers. And
they were offering residents, some of them our grand- and great-
grandparents, cash for abodes some had owned for decades. Those
deals must've seemed sweet or else the best of an inevitable swindle,
because people started selling.

By the mid-1990s, many of the neighborhood's residents were
white. By the early 2000s, forget about it, almost all the families from
the old neighborhood were gone, which is also to say, Northeast Portland had become what most of Portland is, what most of Oregon is, a
place that nurtures whiteness. While the tactics for its whitening, for
the most part, didn't involve foreclosures or blatant evictions, its
transformation featured racialized expulsion nonetheless.

Though it was amended in 1849, the legal means to expel Vanderpool, the Francis brothers, and Thomas, as well as the ethos of Oregon
as a white monolith, had been established in 1844 via the Oregon Territory's exclusion law. Of the numerous people responsible for the
racist writ, the lion's share of onus belongs to a certain few: a Native
surnamed Cockstock, a free Black man named James Saules, and
white men named Elijah White and Peter Burnett.

So it goes, Saules had been beefing with Cockstock in a land dispute. In the resulting confrontation, two white men, along with

Cockstock, were killed. A few weeks later Saules was involved in an-other dispute, and this time he threatened a white settler that he'd incite the Natives to violence against him. For making that threat, Saules was arrested and, in time, handed over to Elijah White, an Indian subagent. White wrote a letter to the secretary of war in D.C., calling Blacks "dangerous subjects" and arguing that Saules and every other negro "ought to be transported" and their "immigration prohib-ited."

As one might guess, the secretary of war was the wrong contact for White to complain to. However, White's cause was soon taken up by an Oregon politician named Peter Burnett. It was Burnett who had written the 1844 exclusion law and its revision, who had proposed it to Oregon's territorial government, who had convinced the white men who composed that government to pass his racist legislation—the lone law of its kind passed by states admitted into the union.

And now, what do we have all these decades hence? The U.S. Cen-sus Bureau's American Community Survey (ACS) 2016 statistics (for the year 2015) note that the population of whites in the state of Ore-gon is 84.89 percent and the percentage of Blacks is 1.90 percent. In Portland, the figures are 77.37 percent for whites and 5.7 percent for Blacks. Compare those numbers to the 2016 national statistics, where whites comprise between 61.3 and 76.9 percent of the population de-pending on whether Hispanics and Latinos identifying as white are included (which is an essay in itself), and Blacks are 12.7 percent. You needn't be an analyst to glean that in my fair state, in my beloved city, my people are scant, scant by design.

As it turns out, white folks, the ones who made us scarce in the NEP and who compose a majority everywhere in Oregon, love them some ice cream just as much as my old neighborhood crew did. In the new NEP, there's a famous ice cream parlor named Salt & Straw, so famous that people sometimes line up for a block for the chance to taste its artisanal flavors. (Anyone for Mummy's Pumpkin Spice Po-tion, or Black Cat Licorice and Lavender, or Cinnamon Snickerdoo-dle?)

Back in 2015, during a street fair just a few blocks from where I grew up that now attracts thousands, a sixteen-year-old Black boy fired a gun into a crowd, wounding two teenage boys and a twenty-five-year-old woman. Per protocol, the police taped off the crime scene. They also ordered Salt & Straw closed. One would think the would-be customers would've respected the gravity of the incident and set aside their ice cream hopes for the day. But on the contrary, before it was closed, two dozen or so more people approached the crime scene tape not to inquire about victims but to beseech the police to let them past to cop their frozen treats. Others snapped selfies using the crime scene as a backdrop, some cracking jokes about dessert-fueled motives. Others dined at restaurants just a few feet from where police searched for shell casings. It's oh so obvious to me that the people who transmuted that crime scene into a collective case of blatant, damn near parodic insouciance were reflecting the ethos of that long-ago territorial government, one set on nixing eternal the presence of my people for the supposed safety, privilege, and prosperity of a great white monolith.

DRED SCOTT

JOHN A. POWELL

———

THE MOST ELEMENTAL QUESTIONS OF AMERICAN CITIZENSHIP, democracy, and identity were ill defined and surprisingly undetermined by colonial, revolutionary, common law, and antebellum traditions. The Constitution itself, prior to 1868, failed to specify the precise nature of national citizenship, and how it was to be defined or acquired, despite the fact that in two major provisions (Article IV, Section 2, and Article III, Section 2), it extended to citizens critical protections and privileges that it denied to noncitizens. It was also not entirely clear about on what basis new territories might be admitted to the Union as states, or how the territories should be governed.

The period 1854 to 1859 crystallized disastrous answers to these questions with calamitous consequences, including Bleeding Kansas, the dissolution of the Whig Party and the formation of the Republican Party, the acrimonious debates over slavery in the territories, and the doctrine of popular sovereignty. The idea of popular sovereignty was epitomized by the Lincoln-Douglas debates and, above all, by the infamous *Dred Scott* decision, a combustible mixture that exacerbated a sectional crisis and precipitated the Civil War.

The entire tapestry of American history may contain no more singularly revealing or defining event than the infamous *Dred Scott* decision. In his Pulitzer Prize–winning book on the case, Don Fehrenbacher asserts that *Dred Scott* is "a point of illumination, casting light upon more than a century of American" law and politics that preceded it. This tells only half the story. The light of *Dred Scott* also extends forward in time, straight through the nineteenth and twentieth centuries and well into the twenty-first.

Dred Scott was, among other things, a complex, multifaceted case addressing aspects of territorial sovereignty, the constitutionality of the Missouri Compromise's prohibition of slavery above the 36° 30′ latitude line, and the meaning of American citizenship. However, the case is best known for the indelible scar etched by an overreaching chief justice, Roger B. Taney. Writing on behalf of the Court, Taney held that persons of African descent—whether free or slave—were not, and could never become, citizens of the United States. Some today still embrace this claim.

To resolve the issue of whether Dred Scott and his wife and children could file suit against John Sanford for their freedom—on the basis of their sojourn in either a free state or a free territory—the Court did not have to overturn part of the Missouri Compromise or draw a race line into American citizenship. Instead, it could easily have dismissed the case on the grounds of standing. Or it could have said that Dred Scott's return to a slave state meant that the condition of slavery reattached. Or that a formerly enslaved person, who had won their freedom and became a state citizen, was also a federal citizen, as some Southern theories—under which federal citizenship was derivative of state citizenship—would suggest. Or it could have held that a freeborn African American, born a citizen of a state, was also a federal citizen.

But the Supreme Court did none of these things. Instead, it held that no person of African descent, whether born free or slave, whether manumitted or held in chains, or whether a citizen of a state or not, was a federal citizen nor could they ever become one. In so doing, Taney not only inverted the states' rights paradigm and nationalized the denial of citizenship to African descendants, stripping northern Black citizens of their federal citizenship rights, but he also denied states the ability to do anything about it.

In Taney's view, the framers of the Constitution did not intend to include members of the "enslaved African race" because they did not consider them to be members of their political community that framed that instrument. Chief Justice Taney explained his reasoning in the harshest terms: "They had for more than a century before been regarded as beings of an inferior order, and altogether unfit to associate with the white race, either in social or political relations; and so far inferior, that they had no rights which the white man was bound to respect; and that the negro might justly and lawfully be reduced to slavery for his benefit." Thus, persons of African descent were not members of the political community; nor could they benefit from the instruments that were formed for the benefit and protection of the (white) people of the United States; nor were they "members of the political communities in the several states."

The *Dred Scott* decision not only extended the protections of slavery nationally, but it stripped free Black citizens of free states of their federal citizenship status and rights. And it made whiteness, and white identity, the sine qua non of American national citizenship. This legacy lives with us still. Whenever restrictive immigration laws and travel bans are erected primarily against nonwhite peoples, *Dred Scott* casts its long shadow in the continuing predicate of whiteness as a condition of fitness for American citizenship.

Since citizenship is the primary distributive decision we make, and the political community defines the polity, *Dred Scott* posed a simple question: who belongs? And Chief Justice Taney's answer to that question was unequivocal. In that sense, *Dred Scott* is the fulcrum of American identity. It defines, through who is included and who is excluded, the very nature of our national and civic identity.

Since *Dred Scott* has never been formally overturned by the Supreme Court, it was left up to the political branches to do so. Virtually every instrument expanding equality has taken aim at *Dred Scott*. The Thirteenth Amendment was the first volley, limiting slavery. The next step was the Civil Rights Act of 1866, and, more directly, the Fourteenth Amendment, which defined that federal and state citizenship are acquired by birthright citizenship, by being born or naturalized in the United States. It extended critical protections to those citizens (and all persons) with the equal protection clause, the due process clause, and the privileges and immunities clause, among others.

But in truth, the overturning of *Dred Scott* is an ongoing and incomplete project. The Immigration and Naturalization Act of 1965, which ended national quotas on immigration, and the Twenty-fourth Amendment, which banned poll taxes as a condition of voting, are also part of that project. Every effort to extend equality into the heart of American citizenship, to erase the race line drawn by Chief Justice Taney, and to enlarge the "we" who belong to the American project continues the work of overturning *Dred Scott*.

Also implicated is the extent to which these questions can be left to democratic majorities or even empowered pluralities. Indeed, the doctrine of popular sovereignty would have left these questions to a vote. But true equality cannot be left to the whims of an electorate—it is the predicate for democracy and the vote, not their product. This, too, is a lesson from the period of the late 1850s: that a constitution or declaration constitutes the "we," and that this act of constituting structures all other distributive decisions and identity itself. Thus, who we are, and who belongs, is the most fundamental question that we have ever asked or can ever ask. We are still struggling to get the answer to this question right. We are still coming up short.

COMPROMISE

DONIKA KELLY

I.

They tied it to the land like a dog,
the idea: compromise—which

the land alone is incapable of exacting
absent, on the one white hand, the North,

on the other white hand, the South;
incapable, absent the parchment

declarations and debate, all of which,
alongside the hoe the shovel the plow

the whip, broke the land open like skin.
A latitude welled with blood.

II.

To tell right it, refuse the theory
offered: the promise of property futures
masquerading as balance, the premise
of nearly, but not quite, a person. Refuse.

Hear instead Maria Stewart: *And such is the powerful
force of prejudice. Let our girls possess
what amiable qualities of soul they may . . .*

it is impossible for scarce an individual of them
to rise above the condition of servants.

Hear Bethany Veney: *I have imagined myself*
with a young girl's ambition, working hard . . .
getting a little home with a garden . . . bringing
my sisters and brothers to share with me
these blessings of freedom.

Hear Mattie J. Jackson: *The days of sadness*
for mistress were days of joy for us.
We shouted and laughed
to the top of our voices.

Hear Lucy Anne Delaney: "*You have no business*
to whip me. I don't belong to you" . . .
I rebelled against such government.

III.

Say the compromise is between a woman
who feels pain and another woman who feels
pain. Say both women are torn after giving birth
and from both arise a smell like rot, a pain
from being rotted inside. Say *fistula*.
Say only one woman is whole. Say the other
is ⅗ths. Which one do you sew with silver,
with pig gut, with lead? Whoever says, sews.
Whoever's sewn gets no laudanum. Say *cure*.
Call it *technique*. Call it *science*. Whoever
calls it, keeps it, no matter Anarcha,
who took, after thirty procedures, the needle
and silk. A new compromise: take down
the statue, hooded and noosed, put into storage.
Concede: still only one woman is whole.

IV.

Concede in favor of balance.
Let the state petition for statehood.
Let the state say who is free.
Let the state enslave.
Let the state set the terms
            for enslavement: three years.
            The Lash Law.
Let the state set the clock for exile
    once the term is complete.
Let the state call it grace:
            three years for women,
            two years for men.
Let the state refuse to ratify
    the amendments: 14th and 15th.
Let the state Jim Crow before Jim Crow:
    whites-only on every border.
Let the state keep its balance
    in 1959 and '73,
    on campus in 1988,
    or on the light rail in 2017:
            a bat in its hand, a knife
            in its hand, blood on its hand.

V.

They set the terms, rigged
the clock, the ship, colonized
the land. They would see us

free but gone.
Compromise.

But we convened,
decided the land that held
our blood, our kin—

decided we would stay,
show that one way
could be another.

VI.

Track the fissure of the first compromise,
then the second, then another running
fugitive through the foundation.

Follow it one century
to my great-grandmother's birth.
A century more: just past her death.

It wasn't that long ago
I was sitting on her porch swing,
hoping for a breeze.

It wasn't that long ago
we were in the twenty-fourth state,
our bodies undoing the roads.

It wasn't that long ago,
the latitude migrated, anchored
to the southern border: history looped.

This isn't America.

It's nothing else.

PART SEVEN

FREDERICK DOUGLASS

ADAM SERWER

━━

BY 1859, FREDERICK DOUGLASS WAS A FUGITIVE AGAIN.
The formerly enslaved Douglass had famously escaped bondage in 1838, fled north, and become one of the most eloquent abolitionist orators in the country. But in October 1859 his friend John Brown had led a failed raid on the federal arsenal in Harper's Ferry, Virginia, hoping to start a slave insurrection and end the peculiar institution for good. Douglass knew of Brown's scheme but had declined to participate. Yet his association with Brown had made him a wanted man, and he fled to Britain rather than face trial in Virginia.

Douglass would later write in his autobiography *Life and Times of Frederick Douglass* that he felt Brown "was about to rivet the fetters more firmly than ever on the limbs of the enslaved." Despite Brown's entreaties, Douglass recalled, "my discretion or my cowardice made me proof against the dear old man's eloquence—perhaps it was something of both which determined my course."

As for his escape, "I knew if my enemies could not prove me guilty of the offence of being with John Brown, they could prove that I was Frederick Douglass," the orator wrote, "and I knew that all Virginia, were I once in her clutches, would say 'Let him be hanged.'" He took pleasure in the irony, however, that it was the men who wanted him clapped in chains who would themselves soon rise up in armed insurrection. Perhaps, Douglass wrote, the Democrats on the Senate committee investigating Brown's failed rebellion "saw that by using their senatorial power in search of rebels they might be whetting a knife for their own throats."

If Brown was a lone radical in 1859, several events would enlist the North in a quest for the violent abolition of slavery by 1861. In the interim, Douglass had quietly returned to the United States to mourn the death of his ten-year-old daughter, Annie. As the Southern Confederacy rose, each state proclaiming the principle of human bondage at the center of the rebellion, Douglass was convinced the North would ultimately see the necessity of abolishing slavery. After all, the catalyst for the South's secession was the election of Abraham Lincoln, who by that point had merely vowed to limit slavery's expansion, not to abolish it. But if the South could not maintain its control over American democracy through the expansion of slave states, then it would destroy it through insurrection.

During this period, Douglass became more than just an orator or a journalist: he became a prophet of a United States who embodied the courage of its convictions, a country that, as Douglass put it, "shall not brand the Declaration of Independence as a lie." At the time, it was horror to the white South and a foolish dream to much of the white North. Today Douglass's vision of America is so pervasive that even its strongest opponents pretend to believe in it: an America that actually recognizes that all are created equal, where the rights of citizenship are not abridged on the basis of accidents of birth.

"The republic was undergoing a second founding, and Douglass felt more than ready to be one of its fathers," historian David Blight writes in his biography of Douglass. "The old nation might now be bludgeoned into ruin, and a new one imagined."

Yet Douglass also understood intimately that much of the white North, and not just the South, would have to drastically revise its vision of America. Although Northern states had abolished slavery, most had also severely restricted Black rights and suffrage. Right up until the beginning of the war, many Northern whites, even those hostile to slavery, saw abolitionists as just as culpable for the sectional conflict as slave owners. Abolitionists faced murder, censorship, and mob violence, even in Northern states like Pennsylvania and New Hampshire.

In his speeches and writings, Douglass laid out his vision of this new America. "We stand in our place today and wage war, not merely for our selves, but for the whole world; not for this generation, but for unborn generations, and for all time," Douglass declared in his "Mission of the War" speech in 1864. The North, Douglass insisted, was "like the south, fighting for National unity; a unity of which the great principles of liberty and equality, and not slavery and class superiority, are the corner stone."

One of the most crucial developments in what Douglass hoped, and many in the white North feared, would become an "abolition war" was the recruitment of Black soldiers. By 1862, President Abraham Lincoln had authorized the recruitment of Black troops, and two of Douglass's sons, Charles and Lewis, had enlisted. But the Northern reaction to that decision illustrated another one of Douglass's observations, that an America that truly lived up to its own beliefs would have to confront prejudice in the North as much as rebellion in the South.

"The recruitment of black soldiers did not produce an instantaneous change in northern racial attitudes. Indeed, to some degree it intensified the Democratic backlash against emancipation and exacerbated racial tensions in the army," the historian James McPherson writes in *Battle Cry of Freedom*. "The black regiments reflected the Jim Crow mores of the society that reluctantly accepted them: they were segregated, given less pay than white soldiers, commanded by white officers some of whom regarded their men as 'niggers,' and intended for use mainly as garrison and labor battalions."

Douglass was no stranger to such attitudes. "It came to be a no[t] uncommon thing to hear men denouncing South Carolina and Massachusetts in the same breath," Douglass wrote, "and in the same measure of disapproval." He had faced jeering racist mobs at his Northern speeches; he had bitterly denounced the Lincoln administration's flirtations with "colonizing" the Black population of the United States to Africa; and he had warned the proslavery "peace camp" that "as to giving the slave States new guarantees for the safety of slavery . . . the South does not want them, and the North could not give them if the South could accept them."

When Lincoln issued the Emancipation Proclamation in 1863, Douglass would get his abolition war. Yet Douglass understood that many in the North believed that "abolition, though now a vast power, is still odious." Such people, he said, "despise the only measure that can save the country"—that is, the end of slavery.

Douglass predicted in 1863 that "a mightier work than the abolition of slavery" lay ahead. This was an understatement. The lingering hatred of abolition and racial equality, North and South, would eventually cement into a fierce opposition to Black political rights. Early in Reconstruction, Douglass would be provided with a glimpse of the North's lingering ambivalence toward Black freedom. Elected a delegate to the National Loyalists' Convention in 1866, he would be urged by his Republican colleagues not to attend.

"They dreaded the clamor of social equality and amalgamation which would be raised against the party, in consequence of this startling innovation," Douglass wrote of it years later. "They, dear fellows, found it much more agreeable to talk of the principles of liberty as glittering generalities, than to reduce those principles to practice."

Southern rebellion had forced the Union to adopt Brown's methods for the abolition of slavery, but it was nevertheless a long way from Douglass's vision of inclusive nationhood. Only Southern intransigence and violent resistance would persuade Republicans in Congress to adopt the Fourteenth and Fifteenth amendments, establishing birthright citizenship and barring discrimination in voting on the basis of race. Although a believer in woman suffrage, Douglass would endure a bitter split with his white feminist allies, who saw the Fifteenth Amendment's enfranchisement of Black men but not women as a grave insult, disgusted that "Patrick, Sambo, Hans, and Yung Tung" would be enfranchised before them.

But the freedoms of the Reconstruction amendments would be short-lived, at least for Black people. Whether because of the terrorism of the white supremacist so-called Redeemers in the South who overthrew the Reconstruction governments by force and intimidation, or because of the Republican-appointed Supreme Court justices who rendered the Reconstruction amendments to the Constitution useless to the emancipated, Douglass's dream of a new nation proved more elusive than it must have seemed at the war's end.

"The Reconstruction amendments do not occupy the prominent place in public consciousness of other pivotal documents of our history, such as the Bill of Rights and Declaration of Independence," the historian Eric Foner has written. "But even if we are unaware of it, Reconstruction remains part of our lives, or to put it another way, key issues confronting American society today are in some ways Reconstruction questions."

Even today, American political conflicts are defined by the limits of American citizenship and who is allowed to claim it. In this sense, Douglass understood that until Black Americans could claim full citizenship, the nation he envisioned could not exist.

"Men talk of the Negro problem. There is no Negro problem," Douglass declared in 1894, as the shadow of Jim Crow fell across the nation. "The problem is whether the American people have honesty enough, loyalty enough, honor enough, patriotism enough to live up to their Constitution." More than a century later, that problem is still with us.

THE CIVIL WAR

JAMELLE BOUIE

——

BY AUGUST 1864, AS GENERAL WILLIAM T. SHERMAN PREPARED his forces for an assault on Atlanta, nearly 400,000 enslaved people had escaped to Union lines. They had won themselves freedom in the process.

As fighting intensified, tens of thousands would join the Union Army as soldiers alongside their freeborn counterparts. By the war's end, approximately 180,000 African Americans fought in thirty-nine major engagements as soldiers in the U.S. Colored Troops.

But the significance of Black soldiers went beyond their military prowess. Every revolution produces a class of people committed to its fulfillment. The Civil War was no exception. The free and freed men who took up arms for the Union would, in the war's aftermath, become an important force for equal rights and democracy, part of a vanguard of Americans who fought to give meaning to the great sacrifice of the war.

At the start of the Civil War, the Lincoln administration didn't want Black soldiers. When "300 reliable colored free citizens" of Washington, D.C., offered to defend the city from Confederate attack, the War Department rejected them. Likewise, at various points in 1861 and 1862, President Lincoln pushed back against efforts to arm former slaves. When battlefield commanders tried to organize Black regiments in Kansas, occupied Louisiana, and the Sea Islands of South Carolina, the Lincoln administration refused to authorize them.

Lincoln's resistance was met with the pressure and advocacy of abolitionists, Black leaders, and radical Republicans. These advocates made the case that the Union could win the war and end slavery if it embraced African Americans as soldiers.

Lincoln eventually relented. On January 1, 1863, he issued the Emancipation Proclamation, freeing slaves in all the seceded states except specified areas of Louisiana and Virginia. The proclamation also stated that former slaves would be "received into armed service of the United States to garrison forts" and "to man vessels of all sorts." Black enlistment had arrived. By March, Secretary of War Edwin Stanton had sent Adjutant General Lorenzo Thomas to organize regiments of African American soldiers in the Mississippi Valley. Other army camps sprang up near Baltimore, Philadelphia, and Washington, D.C., where thousands of Black Americans enlisted.

Black soldiers fought and died under the Union flag. In doing so, they didn't just help win the war and abolish slavery, they also set the terms for the aftermath. Frederick Douglass recognized this: "Once let the black man get upon his person the brass letters, U.S.; let him get an eagle on his button, and a musket on his shoulder and bullets in his pocket," declared Douglass in 1863, "and there is no power on earth which can deny that he has earned the right to citizenship."

Service to the nation gave Black Americans a claim on freedom and citizenship. Lincoln recognized this, too, in an 1863 letter. "If they stake their lives for us they must be prompted by the strongest motive—even the promise of freedom. And the promise being made, must be kept."

And then there were the soldiers. In fighting for the freedom of themselves and their families, many of the men of the U.S. Colored Troops came to understand themselves as political actors, committed to the Union cause, to republican government, and to the values of American democracy.

You could see this on the ground when African American soldiers interacted with freed people. As part of the federal occupying force in the South, notes the historian Eric Foner, Black soldiers emerged as "apostles of black equality," spreading "ideas of land ownership and political equality" among the former slaves.

Indeed, the first years of Reconstruction saw intense struggle and rapid social change across the South. But the most dramatic transformations were in those towns and cities and villages where Black troops and Black veterans inspired local confidence and sparked political mobilization. Historian Steven Hahn notes how, in one district of Charleston, South Carolina, in 1867, hundreds of Black laborers had assembled as a military company, wearing "old army uniforms," marching and drilling, for the sake of protecting themselves and negotiating better prices with landowning planters.

It's too much to say that Black soldiers and veterans were the driving force behind the political organization of freed people. Black men, women, and children of all ages played important and critical roles in shaping and sustaining communities as they embarked on new paths forged by freedom. But Black soldiers and veterans had an important role in particular forms of mobilization. By 1868, most Union-occupied areas of the former Confederate South had vibrant Union Leagues, formed to "protect, strengthen, and defend all loyal men without regard to sect, condition, or race" as well as to sponsor political events and provide forums for discussion among freed people.

Black veterans of the Civil War were among the key organizers for Union Leagues, traveling throughout the South to help mobilize rural Blacks into organizations that quickly became tools for collective empowerment and defense. Working through Union Leagues, freed people established schools, opened cooperative stores, and mobilized to challenge white political power at a local level.

Black soldiers and veterans were also at the forefront of the monumental effort in 1867 and 1868 to craft new constitutions for the former Confederate states. A substantial number of delegates to these constitutional conventions had been enslaved themselves. And many had come to prominence and leadership through their activities in the Union Army, their participation in the Union Leagues, and their efforts to organize their communities for mutual benefit. The importance of these new constitutions cannot be overstated. They were the foundation for a new kind of democracy, one rooted in equal citizenship and full civil standing, one with new opportunities, and new possibilities, for freed people throughout the South.

The 1868 election was the first one where African Americans had a say in the nation's next president. Not surprisingly, prospective Black voters in the South faced vigilante violence from whites who wanted to reestablish the hierarchies and relations of the antebellum past. It was against this violence that Black soldiers and veterans, again, stepped into the fray. In New Orleans, for example, "several republican clubs of colored men, in uniform, with torches and a drum corps, paraded through the streets" to the county courthouse to cast their ballot.

The second half of the 1860s, from the late years of the Civil War to the impeachment of President Andrew Johnson and the start of Radical Reconstruction, was one of the most tumultuous periods in American history, a time of rapid, unprecedented change across the entire society. African Americans, free and freed, played a critical, world-historical part in driving that change.

It's in that fulcrum of transformation that Black soldiers were a revolutionary force. By joining the conflict, they turned a war for union into a war for emancipation. In the wake of the fighting, as millions worked to build a new society in the South, they helped guide, organize, and defend. In doing so, they established a tradition: not just of military service, but of using the fruits of that service to help secure rights for the community at large. It's why, when Black Americans mobilized themselves to challenge racism and race hierarchy in the twentieth century, Black soldiers would again be at the forefront of the struggle, urging "double victory," against tyranny both abroad and at home.

RECONSTRUCTION

MICHAEL HARRIOT

━━

WHAT YOU ARE ABOUT TO READ IS THE STORY OF THE FIRST war on terror.

No . . . wait.

This is actually the origin story of second-wave white supremacy known as "Jim Crow laws."

This is a war narrative. This is a horror story, but it's also a suspense thriller that ends in triumph. It also ends in tragedy. It's a true story about a fantastic myth. This is a narrative, nonfiction account of the all-American fairy tale of liberty and justice for all.

Behold, the untold story of the Great American Race War.

Before we begin, we shall introduce our hero.

The hero of this drama is Black people. *All Black people.* The free Blacks; the uncloaked maroons; the Black elite; the preachers and reverends; the doormen and doctors; the sharecroppers and soldiers— they are all protagonists in our epic adventure.

Spoiler alert: the hero of this story does not die.

Ever.

This hero is long-suffering but unkillable. Bloody *and* unbowed. In this story—and in all the subsequent sequels, now and forever—this hero almost never wins. But we still get to be the heroes of all true American stories simply because we are indestructible. Try as they might, we will never be extinguished.

Ever.

Our story begins at the end of the War for White Supremacy.

Also known as the "War for Slaveholders' Rights"; the "War of White Tears"; or more recently, "Conflict for Future Racist Monuments." Demographic historian David J. Hacker contends that this war's death toll could possibly outweigh the combined total of all the casualties of the nation's other wars. (Whatever one chooses to call it, just remember: no war is civil.)

By 1869, the worst fears of the Confederate white supremacists had all come true.

The Thirteenth and Fourteenth amendments to the U.S. Constitution had been ratified, abolishing slavery, guaranteeing citizenship, and promising equal protection under the law. The treasonous states that previously decided they didn't want to be a part of the United States if they couldn't own Black people were now occupied by Union troops, some led by Black freedmen. Then came the last straw:

On February 26, 1869, the U.S. Congress passed the proposal that would become the Fifteenth Amendment to the Constitution of the United States, proclaiming that the right to vote "shall not be denied or abridged by the United States or by any State on account of race, color, or previous condition of servitude." According to the U.S. Commission on Civil Rights, the legislation resulted in more than 700,000 Black people registered as voters, slightly outnumbering the number of white voters in the South. In some states, the Black population equaled or surpassed the white population. But for the first time in decades, white Democrats—the original racists—were a minority in the South.

Something had to be done, so they started a war.

While many historians describe Reconstruction as a period of "racial unrest" marked by lynchings and "race riots," it was undoubtedly a war. The network of terror cells that sprang up during Reconstruction was no different from the organized militias of the American Revolution or the ragtag Confederate squads. Although they went by many names, including the White League, the White Knights, the Knights of the White Camellia, and—the most famous of all—the "Circle of Brothers" known as the Ku Klux Klan, the loose confederation of historically white fraternities had one common goal: to overthrow the government and create their own white supremacist state.

Ku Klux Klan members in North Carolina lynched so many Black voters in 1870 that Governor William Woods Holden declared an insurrection and suspended habeas corpus (the right against unlawful detention), imposing martial law in two counties. After Klansmen assassinated Republican state senator John W. Stephens—along with Wyatt Outlaw, a Black town commissioner—Holden had no choice but to hire Union colonel George Washington Kirk to quell the violence. Kirk and three hundred soldiers traveled to North Carolina, arresting some of the most prominent men in the state for conspiring with the Klan—including ex-congressman John Kerr—for fueling what would become known as the Kirk-Holden War.

But the Klan's rampage worked.

Battered by rampant murder and intimidation, the Tarheel State's Black voters were successfully suppressed in the 1870 statewide elections. When Democrats won control of the state legislature, their first order of business was to impeach Holden for treating Klansmen too harshly. None of the more than one hundred terror leaders arrested in the Kirk-Holden War were ever charged with a crime. But on December 4, 1870, William Woods Holden became the first governor in American history to be removed from office.

North Carolina's Klansmen had successfully overthrown their state's government.

It was not the first time, and it would not be the last.

In June 1869, thirty-three Georgia legislators were officially removed from office when the state's supreme court ruled 2–1 that "there is no existing law of this State which confers the right upon the colored citizens thereof to hold office." The decision, however, was largely ceremonial. By the time the court handed down the decision, the Klan had already driven the "Original 33" from office, slaughtered at least a dozen antiexpulsion protesters in the Camilla Massacre, and forced Republican governor Rufus Bullock to ask for military intervention. One-quarter of the Original 33 would be killed by white supremacist violence, and Governor Bullock would be "obliged" by the Klan to resign the governorship and flee the state in 1871.

In Eutaw, Alabama, Black voters so outnumbered their white counterparts that in the 1868 presidential election, Republican Ulysses S. Grant easily won Greene County by more than two thousand votes.

But on October 25, 1870, two weeks before the gubernatorial election, white radicals opened fire on thousands of Black citizens at a political rally. Because of the Eutaw Massacre, Black voters were bullied into staying home on election day, allowing Robert Lindsay, the Democratic candidate for governor, to win the county by forty-three votes.

In Laurens, South Carolina, "ten or twelve persons" were slaughtered the day after the 1870 state elections. A congressional committee investigating Klan violence heard accounts of white and Black ballot-casters being "waited upon" after voting, which sounds biblically scary. Being attacked by dingy-robed horseback riders is one thing, but being "waited upon" sounds like Stephen King–novelesque, next-level racism.

In an attempt to vanquish the Klan's reign of fear, Congress passed a series of three increasingly restrictive laws aimed at curbing the terror groups' power. The Enforcement Act of 1870 prohibited groups from banding together, using force, or even wearing disguises to violate the constitutional rights of other citizens—namely the right to vote.

It did not work.

The Second Enforcement Act was similar but imposed harsher fines and allowed federal oversight of local and federal elections. It was cute but, of course, it didn't work, either. It wasn't necessarily the *elections* that concerned Black voters, it was the fireworks at the Klan afterparties that caused so much consternation. It's almost like Congress didn't hear that whole "waited upon" part. Still, they gave it one more try.

The Third Enforcement Act gave the president the right to suspend habeas corpus, an extraordinarily controversial power to hand to the commander in chief. Outside wartime, the United Sates has never invoked the authority to suspend this constitutionally guaranteed right, but Congress thought it was the only way to win this rapidly escalating race war. They didn't even try to pretend why they passed the legislation by calling it something like the "Patriot Act" or the "Please Be Nice to Black People Law of 1870."

They called it the Ku Klux Klan Act.

It did not work.

In 1871 the Klan continued its Klannish ways by slaughtering

thirty people in Meridian, Mississippi. No one knows how many people a white militia mob murdered on Easter Sunday in Colfax, Louisiana, in 1873. A military report lists eighty-one Black men; another
fifteen to twenty bodies were fished out of the Red River, and another
eighteen were secretly buried, according to historian Charles Lane. In
August 1874, the White League killed at least a dozen freedmen in
Couschatta, Louisiana. One month after the Couschatta Massacre,
five thousand members of the Crescent City White League successfully overthrew the state government and installed the Democrat
John McEnery as governor. Although their victory was quickly erased
by federal troops, the White League later erected a monument to
their cause, containing the following inscription:

> McEnery and Penn having been elected governor and
> lieutenant-governor by the white people, were duly installed by
> this overthrow of carpetbag government, ousting the usurpers,
> Governor Kellogg (white) and Lieutenant-Governor Antoine
> (colored).
>
> United States troops took over the state government and re
> instated the usurpers but the national election of November 1876
> recognized white supremacy in the South and gave us our state.

By now, you may be wondering, where is our hero?

Well, perhaps the most inconceivable thing about this story is neither the details of the horrific massacres nor the fact that—for the
most part—Black people haven't even succumbed to the primal seduction of vengeance. (Remember, the ones who were "waited upon"
outnumbered the waiters.) *There were more of us* than them, yet we did
not reciprocate the terror. Still, that is not the magnificent part.

The most marvelous, unbelievable thing about Black people in
America is that they exist. Every imaginable monstrosity that evil can
conjure has been inflicted on this population, yet they have not been
extinguished.

The hero remains.

Still.

And that is the most wondrous part of all.

ATLANTA

TERA W. HUNTER

———

I N LATE 1879, ERNEST INGERSOLL, A MICHIGAN-BORN NAT-
uralist and explorer, visited Atlanta. He was writing an article for
Harper's Magazine trumpeting the rise of the New South city since
the Civil War.

Ingersoll was most impressed by the railroad industry, the ancil-
lary businesses it stimulated, and the cushy lifestyles of the emergent
industrial elites who profited from the city's explosion. But he did not
ignore the sights and sounds of the downtrodden elements, which
struck contrasting poses alongside the prosperity.

"A feature of the city to which no well-ordered resident will be
likely to direct a stranger's attention is Shermantown," he wrote. The
place was so named because during the Civil War it had been occupied by U.S. general William T. Sherman, when he carried out his
famous raid against the Confederates heading to the coast. Shermantown is a "random collection of huts forming a dense negro settlement in the heart of an otherwise attractive portion of the place,"
Ingersoll noted. "The women 'take in washing' and the males as far as
our observation taught us, devote their time to the lordly occupation
of sunning themselves."

An ink drawing of Shermantown accompanied the article, which
complements Ingersoll's commentary overly determined by his ad-
mittedly tutored "observations," but it also offers readers additional
information that insiders of Black urban life in the late 1870s might
have seen differently. Ingersoll inferred disorder where one could have

seen a consciously arranged village, poverty aside. Houses were drawn as dilapidated dwellings and looked fragile as though they were temporary shelter, built out of found wood and scraps of material.

Housing in the city was scarce as the population exploded after the Civil War and recovery from the war's destruction was slow, which meant makeshift units were the norm for the influx of poor residents. The shacks, arranged in a semicircle, appear to have been built close enough together that little space passed between them. Some have rickety stairs leading up to doorways pitched off the ground, which allowed individuals to perch themselves and look out into the communal space in the center. Chickens and pigs wander about the yards, signs that rural people brought their survival skills with them to the city. The houses surround a well and a canopy that covers the implements of the washing trade, such as buckets and scrub boards. Women are shown walking with a basket of dirty laundry and doing the wash.

Men are shown, by contrast, hanging out but not engaged in work. Though Ingersoll noted Black men's presence in other parts of the city, however insidious he found their occupations, as "brush fiends," chair vendors, street musicians, and blackface minstrels, he leaned on the stereotypes of lazy Black men "sunning themselves" in Shermantown. Progress in the form of physical construction of the city in Ingersoll's mind popped up like magic, without the human ingenuity of (Black and white) manual labor behind it. He did not connect the dots between Atlanta's fast growth and economic development and the contributions of Black men as draymen, painters, brick masons, carpenters, brakemen, and factory workers.

Jim Crow had not yet settled in rigidly in 1879, which meant Blacks and whites lived in proximity in the still relatively new postwar city. But the signs of racial and economic inequalities were already being written into the physical landscape. Shermantown, just east of downtown, was the site of one of the largest Black settlements, though it otherwise mirrored the rest of the city's demographics. Black residents were located in all the city's wards. They dominated none of them but made up sizable clusters in several areas. They lived in low-lying areas where water and sewer systems were exclusively enjoyed by downtown businesses and wealthy white residents. Light sketches of houses perched on a hill at the top of the drawing depict the typical arrangement of good housing lording over poor stock in the bottoms.

Black clusters were subject not only to floods but also to sewage literally draining down from the hills. City laws allowed garbage to be dumped in Black and poor neighborhoods, in addition to the natural flow of malodorous human waste of the better-offs. Potable water for drinking and bathing could only be siphoned from wells. Ingersoll seemed not to notice these health hazards of uneven development, claiming that "drainage is therefore excellent" and "epidemics are unheard of and the locality is an island of health in the treacherous yellow-fever climate of its region."

There is much beneath the surface that Ingersoll, in pigeonholing Blackness, could not see. Shermantown was a vibrant settlement. It was the home of Big Bethel A.M.E. Church, the first Black church in the city, dating back to the antebellum era. The church in turn housed the first school for freed people in 1865, organized by James Tate, a grocer and former slave, then taken over by the American Missionary Association a year later and named the Storrs School. Wheat Street Baptist Church and the First Congregational Church were also located there. Wheat Street itself was a major street that housed an inchoate Black business district that would later become famous as Auburn Avenue, still thriving today. And it was home to the growing popularity of commercial leisure, especially outlets for music and dance.

Shermantown, like the other Black neighborhoods, was a haven for newly freed people in search of life in the city that would enhance their autonomy and allow them to escape the strictures of bondage. At the center of this effort to create community were women, the majority of the city's Black population. And essential to their existence was work. They were half of the Black workforce.

These women did impress Ingersoll, if nothing else, because of their ubiquity: "There are certain features that strike the stranger's eye. On Mondays you may see tall, straight negro girls marching through the streets carrying enormous bundles of soiled clothes upon their heads," he wrote. Domestic work was the primary occupation of Black women, and within that, laundry work dominated. By the time

Ingersoll was visiting the city, laundry work was growing by leaps and bounds. There were more washerwomen than there were casual laborers among men (the largest single category of men's work). Over the course of the 1870s, the number of Black washerwomen increased by 150 percent.

A number of factors fed this expansion. Black women were forced into domestic service, but they gravitated to the jobs that gave them the most autonomy. Whereas under slavery, domestics lived and worked under the close supervision of slaveholders, under freedom, Black women were determined to live on their own. They refused to live in the homes of employers even when they chose to be general housekeepers and cooks. But taking in wash gave them the most flexibility. It changed the dynamic of the conventional employer-employee relationship by giving the washerwomen more control over their labor. Women picked up loads of dirty clothes and brought them back to their homes, just as the lithograph depicted. Married women and those with children especially found the flexibility of the work attractive, as it allowed them to take care of their children and perform other chores intermittently.

The popularity of washerwomen was also driven by demand. As more whites moved into the city, they desired a variety of housekeeping services. Laundry work was among the most arduous household chores for women, and any who could afford to do so preferred to send out their wash for others to literally do their dirty work. Even some poor whites, only slightly better off, took advantage of Black women's labor.

The community life that was invisible to Ingersoll's sightseeing enabled more than women's work. Just two years before, the washerwomen had started to mobilize, deciding to adopt a uniform rate of pay for their labor. And in 1879 they gathered to form the first organization, a protective association, modeled on the prolific mutual aid societies founded by African Americans in the postwar South. Two years later this would all build up to the launch of the largest strike in the city's history.

The broader context of these working-class mobilizations was a thriving grassroots political culture that persisted beyond the formal end of Reconstruction. Neighborhoods like Shermantown were bases for community organizing. Mass meetings were held in churches and halls where men, women, and children gathered to deliberate on the important issues of the day: to demand the hiring of Black teachers and police officers, jobs on the state railroads, more public schools, and the provision of potable water and sewer lines.

These political mobilizations were intensifying when Ingersoll visited. African American men came close to winning city council elections, defeated only by the last-minute scramble by white voters who shrank the field of candidates and closed ranks. Only men could legally vote, but women eagerly engaged in local Republican politics, much to the chagrin of employers who complained about their absenteeism as a result of their partisan work.

Shermantown of 1879 was by no means unique. The limitations of racial and economic oppression and the collective efforts to push against them were common in Black communities throughout the South and the nation. Truth be told, similar disparities persist today. Despite progress since the civil rights era, African Americans are disproportionately confined to inferior, overpriced housing, live near hazardous waste sites, and even lack clean drinking water in places like Flint, Michigan, Ingersoll's home state. And yet, out of the shabbiest of conditions, miracles have been made.

Dreams have been deferred but not always defeated.

JOHN WAYNE NILES

WILLIAM A. DARITY, JR.

——

IN THE EARLY 1880S, JOHN WAYNE NILES PROPOSED A TER-
ritorial reparations program under the aegis of his all-Black Indemnity Party. It arrived during the period between the unmet promise of
the Black demand for slavery restitution in the form of forty-acre
land grants and Callie House's 1890s movement claiming pensions
for the formerly enslaved. While Callie House's National Ex-Slave
Mutual Relief, Bounty, and Pension Association reached a membership numbering in the hundreds of thousands, Niles's Indemnity
Party probably never exceeded two thousand members. But the notoriety of his efforts extended much further than the scale of his political party. His personal notoriety as a swindler stretched nationwide.
His numerous exploits were covered in newspapers from New York to
San Francisco.

In 1883 he brought a petition to the U.S. Congress seeking an al-
location of separate public lands for settlement of the "colored folk"
living in the South. In 1884 he mysteriously vanished from the national eye and historical record. It is unclear what happened to him
after 1883, and precisely when or how he died.

John Wayne Niles was born in 1842, the son of a white man and a
Black woman in Mississippi. In adulthood, white reporters described
him variously as "a burly and muscular negro, weighing over two hundred pounds, light in color, with features rather Caucasian than Sen-
egambian, and with a winning and self-confident rather than an

intelligent expression," as "[a] heavily built colored man," and as "the most remarkable negro in the Southwest."

Niles may have been semiliterate, but evidently he was a remarkable orator with uncanny powers of persuasion. Not only did he have a convincing impact on "the more illiterate of his own race," but he included well-heeled white bankers among the victims of his artistry as a con man.

In 1869, in Tennessee, he had been incarcerated for killing a man, but somehow obtained a pardon from the governor long before his sentence was complete. Upon release from prison, Niles moved to Kentucky and became engaged with the Exodusters movement, the effort to form settlements in Kansas on the part of Black immigrants to the state. He joined the Nicodemus, Kansas, colony project in a leadership capacity and arrived at the settlement site in 1877. Apparently he left a wife and children behind in Kentucky, and there is no evidence that he was with them again after his migration to Kansas.

His presence in Nicodemus leaves a contradictory trail. While most of the Black settlers applauded Niles for the community's survival in mid-1878 in the midst of food shortages and viewed him with admiration, he also developed a reputation as a nineteenth-century hustler, a scoundrel always on the make.

In 1881, during his time in Nicodemus, he managed to obtain a substantial loan from banker Jay J. Smith, by offering as collateral fifteen hundred bushels of corn he said he had bought from local Blacks at twenty cents a bushel. Niles convinced Smith not only that he had this large amount of corn in his possession but also that he anticipated he could resell it at thirty cents a bushel—and required a loan to tide him over until the price of corn reached a suitable level.

When Smith learned that local Black farmers had not raised an amount of corn that even approached the quantity that Niles claimed to have, he brought Niles to trial on charges of fraud. Drawing upon his oratorical prowess, Niles successfully defended himself against a team of professional lawyers hired by the banker without calling a single witness. In a stem-winding, three-hour statement, described by one observer as both "eloquent and soulful," Niles drew the attention of the all-white jury not only to the plight of the Black man in the near aftermath of slavery but to their own experience of oppressive encounters with local banks. Niles won his case. "The judge who criticized the 'jurymen for ignoring the evidence and their instructions,' the county attorney, the assisting lawyers, and the bankers were all astonished at the verdict," according to a report.

Even W. H. Smith, president of the Nicodemus colony, saw Niles's efforts to obtain support and resources for the settlement as unauthorized, dishonest, and self-serving. Always seeming to try to outrun any deterioration in his reputation, Niles left Nicodemus shortly after his exoneration in the "corn trial" and moved to Phillips County, Arkansas.

Niles's idea of a land reparations program for all Blacks seems to have taken seed in Nicodemus. However, it came to fruition in Arkansas, where Niles formed the Indemnity Party, an all-Black political party seeking reparations and providing an alternative to the Republican Party for Black voters in the state. The charge immediately was made that any diversion of the Black vote from the Republican Party would give the more explicitly white supremacist Democratic Party a greater opportunity for electoral success. This parallels the contemporary claim—given the post-Dixiecrat reversal of the postures of the two major parties—that any withdrawal of Black votes from the Democratic Party in search of a specific "Black agenda" only will give the now overtly racist Republican Party an additional critical leg up in national politics.

Not only were local whites discontented about Niles's political activity, they also were disturbed by his alleged involvement in additional scams. But it was the formation and promotion of the Indemnity Party that seemed to draw the greatest ire.

Many people schemed to bring Niles down because of his political activities. In 1882 Niles owned a store in Lee County, Arkansas, where he sold whiskey without a license. Initially he was arrested and convicted on multiple charges of violating state law and ordered to pay $1,200 in fines. But the Black community rose in his support, and after he spent a few days in jail, it raised the full amount and paid off his fine. However, he was rearrested immediately for violating federal laws by selling liquor without a license. This time, despite a renewed outcry from the Black community, he was convicted again and ordered to pay $400 and spend four months in state prison.

At the end of his sentence, Niles left Arkansas for Washington, D.C., and proceeded to actively promote the Indemnity Party's project. Niles sought to obtain public land where Blacks could live separately and independently of whites. It would constitute a space for Black settlement of six thousand square miles or almost 4 million acres.

Niles advanced this proposal in the latter half of 1883, and by early October he was making the case in writing to the president and the Department of Justice. He also indicated that an all-Black political party could come together and possibly nominate Frederick Douglass as its presidential candidate. Niles argued that it was necessary to "declare war against the Republican Party" for its failure to fulfill its promises for two decades.

The climate for the Indemnity Party's plan was not propitious. Respectable voices in the Black community were hostile. On October 15, 1883, the Supreme Court struck down the Civil Rights Act of 1875, an act that had prohibited discrimination in access to hotels, trains, and other public sites. On November 3, 1883, the Danville (Virginia) Massacre resulted in massive loss of Black lives and destruction of Black property. The massacre was followed by the November 6, 1883, election, when Virginia senator William Mahone and the Readjuster Party lost control of the state to the Democratic Party.

Ultimately, it was America's officialdom who shut down Niles's project. Attorney General Benjamin Harris Brewster deflected the Indemnity Party's petition in two steps. First, he invoked a states' rights argument that the territory sought was under the jurisdiction of the state of Arkansas and beyond the approval of the federal government for Black settlement. Second, Brewster said if satisfaction was not forthcoming from the state of Arkansas, Niles ultimately could appeal to the U.S. Supreme Court—the same Court that just had struck down the Civil Rights Act of 1875.

With Kansas senator John James Ingalls's successful motion to table the Indemnity Party's petition for homesteads for Black Americans on the floor of Congress, this chapter of the Black reparations movement came to an end. Subsequent claims for reparations consistently have been met by resistance from elite Blacks and by concerted efforts to discredit advocates. Unfortunately, Niles's personal history had given his opponents plenty of ammunition, but implementation of his core idea—provision of land grants for the formerly enslaved—would have forever altered the trajectory of America's racial and economic history.

PHILADELPHIA

KALI NICOLE GROSS

===

WHEN CHRISTOPHER J. PERRY LAUNCHED THE *PHILADEL-phia Tribune* on November 28, 1884, he had no way of knowing that it would become the longest-running independent Black newspaper in the nation. Yet he was confident in the future success of the *Tribune* because it was unabashedly written by Black people for Black people. Or as Perry described it, the *Tribune's* purpose was to "lead the masses to appreciate their best interests and to suggest the best means for attaining deserved ends." The clear imperative and sense of urgency are evident in his words. With good reason, too.

Between 1870 and 1890, Philadelphia's African American community nearly doubled in size. This steady stream of Black migrants sparked white fears of rising urban crime. Police officers profiled African Americans using surveillance methods that a decade later would be codified into official policing practices. Patrolmen were directed to report on and detain all those who appeared to be poor or loiterers from outside the state. Such tactics found Black people especially vulnerable in a city that already had a long history of disproportionately incarcerating them. Philadelphia was home to the country's first penitentiary, the Walnut Street Jail, founded in 1790, in anticipation of Black freedom after Pennsylvania passed one of the earliest acts of gradual abolition in 1780.

Building on a legacy of biased justice, police officers in Perry's time employed a muscular surveillance of suspected members of the "crime class." Between 1884 and 1887, the force had a clarified admin-

istrative hierarchy and a detective squad overseen by a former Secret
Service operative. Coercion in custody was routine, as police beating
prisoners was, for the most part, tolerated as a part of the job. Most
African Americans arrested by Philadelphia police and sentenced
by its justice system were charged with crimes against property. But
in 1885, one recent Black migrant to the city would be arrested for
murder.

The majority of the migrants hailed from Virginia and Maryland,
but smaller numbers of African Americans came from New England.
Such was the case with Annie E. Cutler, a twenty-one-year-old Black
woman who lived and worked in the heart of the City of Brotherly
Love. Laboring as a cook, Annie had a solid job at a saloon at 835
Race Street. Perhaps because of her schooling and pedigree (she had
had eight years of private education in her hometown of Newport,
Rhode Island), Annie enjoyed an amicable relationship with her
white employers, the Mettlers. She also maintained a close, intimate
relationship with the man she expected to wed, William H. Knight.
The two had been dating for years. She had followed him from Newport to Philadelphia, after falling in love with him in the summer of
1882.

Despite the perils of anti-Blackness, the city held exciting activities for young couples. There were "jook joints" and pubs, theaters,
concerts, dances, and parks for leisurely strolls. It also offered a measure of anonymity that permitted brazen, even reckless kinds of social
and sexual attachments. Lovers' quarrels were fairly common, and
shouting matches could easily devolve into more violent melees, particularly in underground haunts where liquor and carousing mixed in
combustible ways.

Yet the violence that erupted between Annie and William did not
occur while they were in the throes of a heated argument in a hot,
packed dance hall; nor did it burst forth in a private space where the
two might have cuddled up from time to time. It happened a few
steps away from 1025 Arch Street, where William worked as a waiter,
on a crisp spring evening in late April, in front of several witnesses.

William had been heading home when he passed and ignored
Annie on the sidewalk. He had recently broken her heart by ending

their engagement with the news he had married another woman. His new wife was expecting their first child. William's failure to acknowledge Annie served as the final straw. In a statement read before the court, Annie said: "He did not look at me, and passed without appearing to see me.... This enraged me more than ever. Without knowing what I was doing I took a pistol and shot him." Not just once, either. William was struck twice and died from his injuries. Shocked witnesses disarmed Annie and detained her for the authorities. According to their accounts, she wanted to know if William was dead and begged them to let her "give him the balance of it." An officer came and arrested her. She was charged with murder.

Attorney Elijah J. Fox initially handled her case. Though it seemed open and shut, details about her motives emerged. Annie had shared her wages with William for years in anticipation of their marriage. She had also shared her body. She charged that William had "ruined" her and then married another. Prior to the night of the shooting, Annie had written two letters—both were entered into evidence. One was to the Mettlers, apologizing and thanking them for their kindness. The second was to her mother, apologizing for what she was about to do. Reading like a suicide note, the letter contained her request to be buried in a plain white box.

Under the circumstances, Fox advised Annie to plead guilty, likely to elicit mercy from the court. Whatever Fox's logic, it was the wrong move. The judge found Annie guilty of murder in the first degree. She burst into tears upon hearing the verdict. Fox asked that the sentence be postponed. It was. In the weeks that followed, Annie's family, employers, and a growing number of concerned citizens worked to secure a pardon.

On October 16, 1885, Thomas E. White, Esq., presented Annie's statement to the court. She said that shortly before their fatal encounter, William had beaten her during an argument, and that she had been driven to alcohol and despair. She said she purchased the gun as protection because she feared that he might strike her again when she confronted him. Judge Mitchell was unconvinced, particularly because the two letters indicated premeditation and because Annie had tested the gun ahead of the meeting to make certain it worked. "The sentence of the law is that you, Annie E. Cutler," the judge said, "be taken hence to whence you came, and there hanged by the neck until you are dead. And may God have mercy upon your soul."

Undoubtedly, they were terrifying words for any prisoner to hear, but considering many Philadelphians' long-standing aversion to capital punishment, Annie had a strong chance of having her sentence commuted. After the hearing, her attorney, her family, her supporters—a bevy of elite Blacks and whites among them—and the Pennsylvania Prison Society swung into action to press the board of pardons.

The specter of a double standard in the case was troubling. White women received the benefit of the doubt from the justice system and in similar cases were afforded mercy as fallen women. Wealthy Black men like Robert Purvis, who had famously financed abolitionist causes and William Garrison Lloyd's paper *The Liberator*, and elite Black and white men such as William Still, John Wanamaker, and J. C. Strawbridge, all advocated for mercy and signed petitions asking that Annie's sentence be commuted. Even the Citizens' Suffrage Association took up Annie's cause. Not everyone agreed. Edward M. Davis tendered his resignation from the group, citing its engagement in matters that were not "directly connected with the cause of attaining woman's equality at the ballot." His resignation was accepted.

Annie's support grew, and her counsel submitted a request for commutation, asking not for life imprisonment but for a fair sentence given the aggravating circumstances, including that Annie had been poorly advised by her first attorney. Their efforts were rewarded. Annie's sentence was commuted to eight years at Eastern State Penitentiary. Incarcerated Blacks had disproportionately higher rates of death at Eastern, but compared to a hangman's scaffold, the new sentence seemed like a win.

Annie's crime, sentence, and commutation played out in detail in local presses, with the *Tribune* likely among them. Unfortunately, the earliest archived issues of the *Tribune* begin in 1912. The case stirred people and mobilized collective, interracial action against the state-sanctioned killing of a Black woman. Even against the era's rising racist tides, women and men in Philadelphia organized against the judicial double standards because they knew not just that tolerating them would amount to an unfair outcome for Annie Cutler but that such an imbalance ultimately held dangers for all.

LYNCHING

CRYSTAL N. FEIMSTER

———

> I found that in order to justify these horrible atrocities [lynchings] to the world, the Negro was being branded as a race of rapists, who were especially mad after white women. I found that white men who had created a race of mulattos by raping and consorting with Negro women were still doing so wherever they could, these same white men lynched, burned, and tortured Negro men for doing the same thing with white women, even when the white women were willing victims.

IDA B. WELLS-BARNETT

IN HIS WIDELY ACCEPTED 1889 STUDY, *THE PLANTATION Negro as Freeman,* Southern historian Philip Alexander Bruce alleged a dangerous moral regression among post-emancipation African Americans. Black people, Bruce maintained, had undergone a salutary civilizing process through enslavement that was tragically ended by emancipation.

For Bruce, the most striking example was the alleged "increase" of "that most frightful crime," the rape of white women by Black men. Adding insult to injury, Bruce blamed the supposedly hypersexual Black women. Black men are "so accustomed to the wantonness of the women of his own race" that they are "unable to gauge the terrible character of this offense against the integrity of virtuous womanhood."

Bruce's construction of the Black male rapist functioned to reinforce a variety of racist ideas in the South: that only white women were chaste and respectable; that Black womanhood was immoral and unredeemable; and that white men were honorable and civilized. The spread of such ideas in the early 1890s justified an unprecedented period of lynching.

Ida B. Wells-Barnett, the mother of the nineteenth-century antilynching movement, was among the first to publicly challenge the racist ideas about Black men and women that Southern whites deployed to excuse their mob violence. Wells-Barnett, born into slavery during the Civil War, lost her parents to yellow fever at sixteen. She was a teacher-turned-journalist who co-owned the *Memphis Free Speech*. She launched her antilynching crusade in 1892, after a white mob of economic competitors murdered three prospering Black Memphis store owners, one of whom was a close friend.

She urged African Americans to fight back, with guns if necessary and through economic pressure. Spurred by her scathing editorials, thousands migrated to Oklahoma, while those who stayed in Memphis boycotted the newly opened streetcar line. Wells-Barnett began investigating other lynchings and soon discovered that many were designed to suppress the economic and political rights of Black people. When she published an editorial arguing that "nobody in this section of the country believes the old threadbare lie that Negro men rape white women," a white mob destroyed her press. Wells-Barnett, in New York at the time, received warnings not to return to Memphis at the cost of her life.

Far from being silenced by this attack, Wells-Barnett transformed herself into the architect of an international crusade. In exile from Memphis, she wrote for the *New York Age* and in 1892 published her first antilynching pamphlet, *Southern Horrors: Lynch Law in All Its Phases*, which offered an incisive analysis of the economic roots of lynching and linked violence against Black men with the sexual exploitation of Black women by white men. Wells-Barnett revealed that less than 30 percent of all lynchings involved the charge of rape, let alone the conviction. She also documented consensual sexual contact between Black men and white women and insisted that lynching functioned to keep Black folks terrorized, politically disenfranchised, and economically dependent.

From the inception of her crusade, Wells-Barnett claimed that white hysteria about the rape of white women by Black men effectively masked violence against women—both Black and white. "To justify their own barbarism," she argued, Southern white men "assume a chivalry which they do not possess." Lynching, she explained, was not about protecting Southern womanhood but had everything to do with shoring up white men's social, economic, and political power—in other words, white male supremacy. Desperate to control white women's sexual behavior and maintain sexual control over Black women, Southern white men had created a scapegoat in the animalized figure of the Black rapist. Wells-Barnett argued that the focus and attention on the image of the Black rapist concealed lynching's motives and masked violence against Black women who were victims of sexual assault and lynching.

While Wells-Barnett advocated Black self-defense and self-help, she also hoped to turn white public opinion against the South, where most lynchings took place. In 1893 and again in 1894, she traveled to England, where she inspired the formation of the British Anti-Lynching Society and published *The Red Record* in 1895. By the end of her second British tour, Wells-Barnett had made lynching a cause célèbre among British reformers. White American men found that in the eyes of the "civilized" world, their tolerance of racial violence had cast them in the unsightly position of unmanly savages. Her skillful manipulation of dominant cultural themes did not stop lynching, but it did put mob violence on the American reform agenda and made visible sexual assault against Black women.

Highlighting Black women's victimization and white men's disregard for law and order, Wells-Barnett challenged the racial double standard embedded in the rape-lynch discourse. In *The Red Record*, under the heading "Suspected, Innocent and Lynched," Wells-Barnett reported the 1893 lynching of Benjamin Jackson; his wife, Mahala Jackson; his mother-in-law, Lou Carter; and Rufus Bigley in Quincy, Mississippi. She explained that the two women, accused of well poisoning, were hung by a white mob even after they were found innocent of the charges against them. Wells-Barnett argued that neither their innocence nor their sex served to "protect the women from the demands of the Christian white people of that section of the country. In any other land and with any other people, the fact that [these two accused persons] were women would have pleaded in their favor for protection and fair play." Wells-Barnett argued that mob violence against Black women was not only barbaric but ran counter to the rape-lynch discourse. The accusation of rape, she argued, could not explain why Black women were "put to death with unspeakable savagery."

Wells-Barnett constructed an antilynching argument that addressed the inconsistencies produced not only by female victims of lynching but also by Black female victims of white men's sexual assault. In *The Red Record*, under the heading "Color Line Justice," Wells-Barnett provided numerous examples of Black women and girls raped by white men. She opened the section with this report: "In Baltimore, Maryland, a gang of white ruffians assaulted a respectable colored girl who was out walking with a young man of her own race. They held her escort and outraged the girl. It was a deed dastardly enough to arouse Southern blood, which gives its horror of rape as excuse for lawlessness, but she was a colored woman. The case went to the courts, and they were acquitted." Black women, she argued, were protected neither by mob violence nor by the courts.

PLESSY V. FERGUSON

BLAIR L. M. KELLEY

———

AT THE BEGINNING OF OUR CONVERSATION, KEITH PLESSY lets me know that if I google Homer Plessy, historic images of mixed-race men pop up, but none of the images are actually of him. He tells me that the man with the full beard is P.B.S. Pinchback, a Union Army officer and the former lieutenant governor of Louisiana. The clean-shaven gentleman, who is also not Plessy, is Daniel Desdunes, the son of organizer Rodolphe Desdunes and the first man selected by the Citizens' Committee to test the legality of interstate segregation. This isn't the first time Keith Plessy, whose fourth-great-grandfather was also Homer Plessy's grandfather, has told me a search of the Internet will not turn up a real picture of Homer Plessy.

He mentioned this when we first met eight years ago, not realizing he kept repeating the same complaint. His repetition underscores his abiding frustration with the error of misidentification and the other omissions that shape our landscapes. Keith Plessy wants to correct those mistakes and reshape how we understand the legacy of *Plessy v. Ferguson* (1896).

Those familiar with the outlines of the legal battle for civil rights know that the U.S. Supreme Court case *Plessy v. Ferguson* served as the legal foundation for de jure racial segregation. This failed test case was put forward by the small group of Creole of Color New Orleans activists called the Citizens' Committee. The case set the precedent of "separate but equal" that stood for more than half a century. Indeed, when viewed strictly as a story about legal history, *Plessy* is the top of a slippery slope down to an American South where Jim Crow segregation marked every landscape. However, my conversations with Keith Plessy remind me that this historic case must be considered in the context of the particularities of place and time—then and now. *Plessy v. Ferguson* was the manifestation of the African American opposition to segregationist attempts to shame and degrade Black train passengers. While elite Creole of Color leaders organized the Citizens' Committee, African Americans from all walks of life supported the effort—more than 110 organizations and thirty individuals donated to the cause. Likewise, in this moment, when our collective memories about the past are hotly contested, it will be the work of like-minded people who will harness accurate histories of the past to better address our present.

I suspect that there is no extant picture of Homer Plessy because he was working-class and probably did not have his picture taken often if at all. In the 1890s, a portrait was a luxury. Black scholars and race leaders, not shoemakers, had portraits. Even if there was once a picture, in a city that suffers from floods, winds, and weather, so much family history has been lost. In addition to the visual silence, there is an archival one; none of the extant correspondence between the members of the Citizens' Committee and their attorney, Albion Tourgée, includes any personal, political, or professional reference to Plessy. In the elder Desdunes's 1911 book *Nos Hommes et Notre Histoire* (Our People and Our History), a history of the Creole of Color community in New Orleans, the only mention of Plessy reports that "the Committee engaged Mr. Homere [*sic*] Plessy as its representative."

Like his well-known forebear, Keith Plessy is a working-class activist and a New Orleans native. He has worked as a bellman at the New Orleans Marriot on Canal Street for nearly as long as the centrally located modern hotel has existed. Along with filmmaker Phoebe Ferguson, a descendant of Judge John Howard Ferguson, the local judge whose decision against Homer Plessy connected his name to the case forever, Keith established the Plessy and Ferguson Foundation in 2004. They are working to increase public understanding of this historic case. To date, their organization has erected five historical markers in the city and state, worked to have June 7 declared

Homer A. Plessy Day, and led the charge for New Orleans to have the street where Homer Plessy boarded the East Louisiana railcar designated Homer Plessy Way.

Well before the Louisiana Purchase in 1803, New Orleans was home to one of the largest communities of *gens de couleur libre*, or free people of color, in the South, where people of mixed European, Native American, and African descent battled to establish themselves as free in a slave society. Some were manumitted, educated, and propertied by their European fathers, while others had migrated to the port city from Haiti and Cuba. Plessy's paternal grandfather, Germain Plessy, was a white Frenchman who fled to New Orleans in the wake of the Haitian Revolution and had a family with a free woman of color. But when Keith Plessy told me his family history, he began with his great-grandmother, Agnes Mathieu, who successfully sued for her freedom in the courts after a slaveholder refused to honor his promise to allow her to purchase her freedom. He connected her determined advocacy with Homer Plessy's and, implicitly, with his own.

Working-class Creoles of Color like Plessy were set apart from both the elite Creoles of Color—the New Orleans equivalents of the "talented tenth"—and the masses of Black workers whose ancestors had been in bondage. Plessy was a shoemaker. Keith Plessy said he was "raised to the trade" that his stepfather, Victor Dupart, passed down. But Dupart passed down a legacy of activism as well; he had been active in the 1873 Unification movement, a short-lived but valiant effort to halt political, social, and economic discrimination. Dupart was one of the published signatories of the movement's *Appeal for the Unification of the People of Louisiana*.

At the time of the arrest in 1892, Plessy lived with his wife in a rented house on North Claiborne Avenue, a beautiful tree-lined thoroughfare in the Faubourg Tremé, an integrated working-class neighborhood on the French side of Canal Street. He served as the vice president of a local education reform organization, the Justice, Protective, Educational and Social Club, that resisted racism in New Orleans schools. Perhaps Plessy saw the work of the Citizens' Committee as an extension of his own interest in fighting segregation. The committee held mass meetings in Congregation Hall, just steps from

Plessy's home. We can't know exactly what connected him to the effort. Maybe he was drawn by a flyer to attend a meeting of the Citizens' Committee. Perhaps because of his racial ambiguity, relative youth, and interest in activism, he was asked to volunteer on the Citizens' Committee. These ambiguities remind us why Keith Plessy is digging. So much of this past is long gone.

When I googled Homer Plessy's 1892 home address, 1108 North Claiborne Avenue, I saw nothing but concrete. The shotgun house where Plessy lived with his young wife is long gone, razed in 1968 to construct Highway 10. There is no remnant of his life on a tree-lined street so wide that children played ball on the grassy neutral ground in the middle. You'll see no hint as to why that avenue was the site of Black Mardi Gras, where the Zulus and Mardi Gras Indians would parade annually. As in so much of the country, the historic landscape of the lives of Tremé's everyday Black working men and women is gone, wiped away by politicians seeking urban renewal and labeling Black property as blighted. Homer Plessy put his life on the line to fight to preserve his citizenship, yet policy makers and planners saw the landscape of his New Orleans as disposable. The work of preservation that Keith Plessy is doing is urgent. The landscapes of African American history are as vulnerable to gentrification today as they were decades ago to eminent domain and urban renewal. But this work has a hold on him, perhaps because Homer Plessy is still with us. As Keith Plessy said, when "you start looking for your ancestors, you find out they have been looking for you all along."

JOHN WAYNE NILES
... .--. . .- -.- ... / - ---
ERMIAS JOSEPH ASGHEDOM

MAHOGANY L. BROWNE

——

Gunshot wound
is a violent way to say gone missing
Your body will be laid to rest
by your family's devoted palms

Black people will always find each other
in the passage between death and America
A country designed in an image of rot
But we've always been able to ferment the good
knuckle deep in prayer despite the steel

- .... .-.- / .-- .. .-. .-./ -.-. --- .. / ... .--- .-./ -.-- --- .. .-.-/ -. .-.- / -. .-.-.- .- / -.../ .- .-.-.- .- .. .-.- .-.-

Eat well
Sleep sound
Faith in the hands that raise children and wheat

This is what happens when you blind divine and brilliant
A smoke signal is sent to snuff you clean off this good land
Your land
The way your blood is righteous in the toiled soil
Until a home

a community
a church
is centered
start boom then born

Migration for freedom is a drinking gourd anthem
Is a liberation of black & black & brown dot link & link our dna

-.-..- .-..…..- --- .-.-..-/ - --- / --- -.- .-..- ….. --- -- .- .-.-/ .-- ./ .-- ..-.-..-../ -...-./ ..-..-..-..-.-

Listen
The time is ours
Blow the doubt to bits

Missing gone say
Hush
The secret to Nicodemus
beats beneath the sternum in Compton
beneath the solid stretch of acre in Mississippi and Detroit
and the crown of our labor chant
a river returning to the source

A reddening dusk   that will never settle on the
        backs   of our people

PART EIGHT

BOOKER T. WASHINGTON

DERRICK ALRIDGE

——

THROUGHOUT MY YEARS OF TEACHING COURSES IN AFRICAN American educational history and studies, I have always been excited to discuss Booker T. Washington. My excitement stems from engaging the complexity of the man and scrutinizing the ways he is presented in scholarly works and contemporary textbooks. Washington is often referred to as the "Wizard of Tuskegee." His politics, which are described as "accommodationist," are typically referred to as the "Tuskegee Machine."

Typically, in my classes, some students support Washington's pragmatic approach and his advocacy for Black people. They admire his focus on education as a means of making a living, while forgoing civil rights for the time being. Other students view Washington's approach as representing acquiescence to white supremacy. I often agree with aspects of both viewpoints, and I try to help my students understand this complex man in the context of his time.

At the turn of the twentieth century, the United States perceived that it had a problem, in the form of 9 million Black Americans who sought the rights of full citizenship. The so-called "Negro problem," sometimes referred to as the "Negro question," was of such great concern that politicians and scholars alike examined the "problem" and proposed measures to address it. Some believed that with proper training and the passage of time, Black people could evolve intellectually to become productive members of American society. Others viewed Black people as inherently inferior and incapable of full integration into society. Among African Americans, Booker Taliaferro Washington emerged as a representative of his race who offered a pragmatic approach to addressing the "Negro problem." He was so revered as a great "Negro" leader of his time that historian August Meier has called the period between 1880 and 1915 the "age of Booker T. Washington."

Washington emerged on the national scene on September 18, 1895, at the Cotton States International Exposition in Atlanta. His speech, commonly known as the "Atlanta Compromise," offered pragmatic suggestions for resolving the "Negro problem." Washington observed that after Emancipation, Black Americans had started "at the top instead of at the bottom," emphasizing political participation and holding seats in Congress during Reconstruction. Washington argued that instead of engaging in politics and pursuing civil rights, Black people should have pursued training in the trades and agriculture to obtain the skills to make a living.

In making his point, Washington offered the analogy of a ship lost at sea for many days hailing another ship for help, indicating that its crew was dying of thirst. Washington related how each time the crew of the lost ship called for water, the crew of the other ship replied, "Cast down your bucket where you are." The crew of the lost ship finally cast down their buckets and retrieved fresh water from the Amazon River, enabling the crew to survive.

For Washington's audience, the lost ship represented Black America. Washington encouraged African Americans to heed the advice given to the crew of the ship: "'Cast down your bucket where you are.' Cast it down, making friends in every manly way of the people of all races, by whom you are surrounded." He encouraged them to cast down their bucket in "agriculture, mechanics, in commerce, in domestic service, and in the professions." Addressing whites' fears about the commingling of Black and white people, he noted, "In all things that are purely social we can be as separate as the fingers, yet one as the hand in all things essential to mutual progress."

When I teach Washington, I always begin with his Atlanta Compromise speech. I have read and taught the speech and heard it recited countless times over the past few decades. I consistently struggle with certain passages, particularly Washington's statement, "The wisest among my race understand that the agitation of questions of social equality is the extremist folly." While much of his message sounds like appeasement of the white South, a closer reading reveals that these are the words of an extremely pragmatic and politically astute man dedicated to the future of his race. I therefore challenge my students and myself to "step into Washington's time." This means remembering that in 1896 *Plessy v. Ferguson* had established the "separate but equal" doctrine, upholding Jim Crow laws throughout the South. Moreover, 541 African Americans were lynched between 1899 and 1904. These realities offer crucial context for understanding Washington's views.

Though Washington published several books, I always assign his autobiography *Up from Slavery* as the central text in studying his life and thought. *Up from Slavery* reads like an inspiring Horatio Alger story, yet as Ishmael Reed notes, the story is even more impressive because Washington was born into slavery and founded a university. Published in 1901, the book recounts how Washington received no education as a slave but had vivid memories of seeing children sitting at desks in a schoolhouse. Going to school, he believed, "would be about the same as getting into paradise."

Washington's book recounts the valuable lessons he learned from his mother and stepfather, as well as from his own work in coal mines. He describes the lessons of tidiness and cleanliness he gleaned from Mrs. Ruffner, a woman for whom he once worked. He also tells of his odyssey traveling by foot, wagon, and car five hundred miles to the Hampton Institute; the mentorship he received from Union general Samuel Chapman Armstrong; and his founding of the Tuskegee Institute.

Each time I teach *Up from Slavery*, my students and I ponder how much of the book reflects Washington's true thoughts and feelings. We consider to what extent the work might reflect a mythology of himself and of Blacks as a people that he wanted to convey to the country at that particular moment in time. In the end, we typically conclude that, like most other biographies, the book reflects both the real Washington and a mythological Washington.

In addition to *Up from Slavery*, I have my students read Washington's collection of published papers, his correspondence, and passages from books about Washington. We discuss how he sometimes made jokes about Black Americans that appealed to white audiences; these jokes often chastised Black people for having an obsession with learning the classics before learning to make a living.

At the same time, it is clear that behind the scenes Washington advocated for Black civil rights. For example, he stated the following in the *Birmingham Age-Herald* in 1904:

> Within the last fortnight three members of my race have been burned at the stake; of these one was a woman. Not one of the three was charged with any crime even remotely connected with the abuse of a white woman. In every case murder was the sole accusation. All of these burnings took place in broad daylight, and two of them occurred on Sunday afternoon in sight of a Christian church.

The years 1899 to 1904 were pivotal in African American history broadly and in the life of Booker T. Washington in particular. During this period, *Up from Slavery* was published and became the best-selling autobiography of an African American, a distinction it retained until the 1965 publication of *The Autobiography of Malcolm X*. Students of history who engage the life and thought of Booker T. Washington by reading *Up from Slavery* and other primary sources that provide insight into his life, thought, and vision for Black people will gain deeper insight into the complexity and multidimensional leadership of African Americans in the twentieth century.

1904–1909

JACK JOHNSON

HOWARD BRYANT

▬

STARTING IN 1898, TWO YEARS AFTER *PLESSY,* PUBLIC accommodations in the South—streetcars, bathrooms, buses, restaurants, down to something as simple as a drinking fountain—were segregated in a coordinated legislative assault. These laws were passed in every Southern state, from Louisiana and Mississippi to Georgia and Tennessee. By 1902, no segment of Southern society contained social ambiguity. In the North, Midwest, and West, there was equal unambiguity in regard to hierarchy. The American empire was a white one—and this was also evident in the realm of sports.

During this period, baseball and several of its nascent organized leagues had been integrated. White players, aware of the empire and their place in it, systematically removed the Black players from the field. They did this first not by edict but by violence. A late-nineteenth-century second baseman named Frank Grant had his calves and shins pierced so often by white players sliding deliberately into his legs—instead of the base—that he began wearing thin slabs of wood to protect them.

By the turn of the century, no organized white league fielded Black players. By the time of the first World Series in 1903, Black players were excluded from professional baseball.

But that very same year, a mirror was placed in the face of white supremacy. The mirror existed in reality, in the flesh and blood, fist and muscle, of a Black boxer, Jack Johnson. Born in 1878 in Galveston,

Texas, Jack Johnson, whose full name was John Arthur Johnson, became the World Colored Heavyweight champion in 1903.

Away from the speeches and the laws and the treaties that could
be broken when backed by a gun, the true arena of white supremacy
was inside the ring, one-on-one.

The white champions were protected by racism, by their refusal to
fight Black champions. While John L. Sullivan and Jim Jeffries, the
iconic names of early white boxing, built their legend without fear of
losing to a Black man, those who encountered Jack Johnson were not
as fortunate. It would take more than two thousand fights before a
white champion accepted Johnson's challenge to fight—and finally
put white supremacy to the test.

In 1908 in Australia, Johnson destroyed Tommy Burns to become
the first Black man to win the heavyweight title. The writer Jack London, ringside for the fight, looked at Johnson in the ring, holding the
mirror up to white America—the entire white race, actually—and saw
the mediocre reflection of Burns, who could not beat Johnson or save
them. It was London who birthed the term the "great white hope."

That ignited the search for a fighter, as *The New York Times* would
write often, who could restore the dignity of the white race. The search
reintroduced Jeffries, spawned the "fight of the century," and articulated the white desire—through the defeat of this singular symbolic
Black man—to prove that its quest for white empire was not constructed on a faulty blueprint. London, in his account of the Johnson-
Burns fight, had offered these final words: "But one thing remains.
Jeffries must emerge from his alfalfa farm and remove that smile from
Johnson's face. Jeff, it's up to you."

But in 1910 Johnson pummeled and humiliated the unretired,
now-mediocre Jeffries. White rioting resulted in the deaths of twenty-
six Black people in incidents across the country.

The spectacle Johnson created in the ring showed America what it
truly was: a nation that espoused the aspiration to freedom and equality but demanded white supremacy. His challenge shifted from inside
the ring to outside it. Johnson, once he became a national figure, took
on the characteristics of myth quickly and completely. Symbolically,
he represented the Black male in the white nightmare: strong and

indomitable—and oversexed in his preference and appetite for white women. He became so symbolic that his existence appears almost to be a caricature or a deliberate construction of the prototypical embodiment of all white fears of Black masculinity.

By extension, Johnson also became symbolic of Black freedom—the freedom to wear gold teeth, to kiss white women in public, to marry them in private (and thus to be desired and not repulsed), to drive expensive cars, to take America's material ostentatiousness—the fruits of empire intended only for whiteness—and keep it all for himself. Johnson did all this and more at a time when most Black Americans were laboring to survive in homes and fields.

In 1910 Congress passed the White Slave Traffic Act, prohibiting the transporting of white women across state lines. That brought Johnson down, eventually sending him to prison due to his marriage to a white woman. He then became the rallying point for a quest for reputational rehabilitation for the ensuing century.

What happens to the person when they become a symbol? Can they be recovered? Can they exist beyond what they embody? In this wrestling over symbols, the individual is sacrificed. They become the unknown. Johnson's eternal value to the American story has never received the balance of most historical figures who are viewed as part person, part of the times in which they lived. Johnson is almost completely defined by his time period—what his presence meant to the white order, his threat to empire. While rogue to some Blacks, offensive to others, inspiration to others still, he was just a man—except to whites who viewed him as a threat. America is unwilling, except in the strictest academic terms, to label Johnson's years the most calculatedly racist period of the twentieth century, and because of that unwillingness, it talks about itself through Johnson.

So this fascinating man of morbid defiance—neither heroic nor villainous—lives on as an almost mythological barometer. There is, in all this, a certain exploitation at work, for the price Johnson paid was not the 117 years he and his reputation lived unpardoned for the crime of marrying a white woman. Rather, America's inability to reconcile even the clearest truths about its foundations meant his personal humanity has never received the proper priority. It was never about him.

THE BLACK PUBLIC INTELLECTUAL

BEVERLY GUY-SHEFTALL

═══

THE ACCEPTANCE OF AFRICAN AMERICAN WOMEN AS intellectuals—thinking women—has been elusive, but we have a long history as producers of knowledge, even when that production has not been fully recognized.

An example is the American Negro Academy (ANA), the first learned society of persons of African descent in the United States, which was founded in Washington, D.C., in March 1897 by seventy-eight-year-old Reverend Alexander Crummell. Born in New York City and educated at Queens' College, Cambridge, Reverend Crummell was an Episcopalian minister, educator, and missionary, as well as one of the most prominent and visionary nineteenth-century Black intellectuals. The ANA did not bar women from membership (limiting them to fifty), but during its thirty-one-year existence it remained an all-male organization from 1897 to 1924. Its constitution announces itself as "an organization of authors, scholars, artists, and those distinguished in other walks of life, men of African descent, for the promotion of Letters, Science, and Art." Its overall goal was to "lead and protect their people" and be a mighty "weapon to secure equality and destroy racism."

The ANA's specific objectives were to defend Black people against racist attacks; publish scholarship about the Black experience by Black authors; foster higher education and intellectual projects; promote literature, science, and art in the Black community; and create a

Black intellectual elite, whom W.E.B. Du Bois would later conceptu-
alize as the "talented tenth." During this era, many Black women intellectuals made outstanding contributions, among them Anna Julia
Cooper, Mary Church Terrell, Frances Ellen Watkins Harper, Fannie
Barrier Williams, Josephine St. Pierre Ruffin, and Ida Wells-Barnett.
Yet not one of them was ever invited to join the ANA. Though they
believed a natural alliance existed between them and Black men, they
were rejected on the basis of their sex.

More recently, a small group of predominantly Black feminist
scholars has been responsible for reconstructing the androcentric African American intellectual and activist tradition by making visible
Black women's significant contributions to political discourse on a
range of issues going back to the nineteenth century. An example of
these reclamation projects is my own 1995 collection, *Words of Fire: An
Anthology of African American Feminist Thought*, which makes the case
for a robust Black women's intellectual tradition dating back to 1831,
with the publication of Maria Stewart's speeches.

The period 1909–14 was pivotal in the annals of African American
political history. Perhaps the best-known civil rights occurrence was
the founding of the National Association for the Advancement of
Colored People (NAACP) in 1909. Ida Wells-Barnett, the legendary
antilynching crusader, journalist, newspaper editor, clubwoman, and
suffragist, was one of only two Black women signers of the 1908 call
for the establishment of the organization.

Less well known than the NAACP was the founding, by white
reformer Frances Kellor, of the New York–based National League for
the Protection of Colored Women in 1905. Four years later Nannie
Helen Burroughs founded the National Training School for Women
and Girls in Washington, D.C. In 1910 the league merged with the
Committee for the Improvement of Industrial Conditions Among
Negroes in New York. Renamed the National League on Urban Conditions Among Negroes, it was a precursor of the National Urban
League, founded in 1920.

Other significant developments in Black political history during
this period include Margaret Murray Washington's 1912 founding of
National Notes, the newsletter of the influential National Association

of Colored Women (established in 1896); and the founding of the
Universal Negro Improvement Association (UNIA) by Marcus Garvey and Amy Jacques Garvey in Jamaica in 1914.

Ida B. Wells-Barnett's "Lynch Law in America," written in 1900,
is a powerful critique of the institutionalized racism and sexism that
render Black men and women vulnerable to previously unspeakable
acts of violence. Less visible in the annals of history is her militant
struggle for woman suffrage. In the summer of 1913, Illinois had
passed the landmark Equal Suffrage Act, which granted women in
the state limited suffrage. That year, in one of this period's most significant yet historically occluded political occurrences, Wells-Barnett
founded the Alpha Suffrage Club in Chicago. It was the first Black
woman suffrage organization, committed to enhancing Black wom-
en's civic profile by encouraging them to vote for and help elect Black
candidates, especially men; in 1915 it would be critical to the election
of Oscar De Priest as the first Black alderman in Chicago.

Wells-Barnett founded the club because Black women were prohibited from joining white suffrage organizations, such as the National American Women Suffrage Association (NAWSA). In 1913
NAWSA organized the Woman Suffrage Parade in Washington,
D.C., to garner broad support for the passage of the Nineteenth
Amendment. But because Southern white women were opposed to
integration and to granting suffrage to Black women, the parade's
organizers informed club president Wells-Barnett that she and her
sixty-five members could march only in the segregated Black section
at the back of the parade.

As instructed by the NAWSA organizers, most Black women, including club members, participated in the march at the rear, but
Wells-Barnett refused. When the all-white Chicago delegation drew
near, she left the crowd and joined that procession. The *Chicago Daily
Tribune* captured an iconic image of Wells-Barnett marching with
the Illinois delegation.

By 1916, the Alpha Suffrage Club had nearly two hundred members and published a newsletter entitled *The Alpha Suffrage Record*.

Ignoring or minimizing the political work and writing of African
American women such as Ida Wells-Barnett renders invisible the im-

portant ways these women have contributed to a broad range of social justice initiatives, such as the passage of antilynching legislation, the attainment of voting rights for women regardless of race and national origin, and the election of Black officials. Black freedom struggles and women's liberation movements since then would not have been possible without the courageous and visionary leadership of Ida Wells-Barnett and the brilliant strategizing of women's organizations such as the Alpha Suffrage Club in the early twentieth century.

THE GREAT MIGRATION

ISABEL WILKERSON

——

THEY FLED AS IF UNDER A SPELL OR A HIGH FEVER. "THEY left as though they were fleeing some curse," wrote the scholar Emmett J. Scott. "They were willing to make almost any sacrifice to obtain a railroad ticket, and they left with the intention of staying."

It was the middle of the second decade of the twentieth century, and the vast majority of African Americans were still bound to the South, to the blood-and-tear-stained soil of their enslaved foreparents. It had been twenty years since *Plessy v. Ferguson* formalized an authoritarian Jim Crow regime that controlled every aspect of life for African Americans, from where they could sit in a railroad car to which door they could walk into at a theater to the menial labors to which they were consigned. They were now bearing the full weight of a racial caste system intended to resurrect the hierarchy of slavery and were living under the daily terror of its brutal enforcement.

By this time, an African American was being lynched every four days somewhere in the American South, and for the majority of African Americans, as the Southern writer David Cohn would later put it, "their fate was in the laps of the gods."

The incendiary film *Birth of a Nation* premiered in 1915, romanticizing the Lost Cause of the Confederacy, glorifying the very violence to which African Americans were being subjected, and helping to revive the Ku Klux Klan. Across the Atlantic Ocean, the nations of Europe were at war in what was being called the War to End All Wars, which had begun in 1914 and had disrupted European immigration to the United States just as the industrial North needed more workers for its factories and steel mills. Northern labor agents traveled to the South to recruit cheap Black labor, and word spread among Black Southerners that the North was opening up.

It was then that a silent pilgrimage took its first tentative steps, within the borders of this country. It began without warning or notice or very much in the way of understanding by those outside its reach. The nation's servant class was now breaking free of the South, in quiet rivulets at first and then in a sea of ultimately 6 million people whose actions would reshape racial distribution of the United States. It would come to be called the Great Migration.

Its beginning is traced to the winter of 1916, when *The Chicago Defender* made note in a single paragraph that that February, several hundred Black families had quietly departed Selma, Alabama, declaring, according to the newspaper's brief citation, that the "treatment doesn't warrant staying."

This was the start of what would become a leaderless revolution, one of the largest mass relocations in American history. It would come to dwarf in size and scope the California gold rush of the 1850s, with its 100,000 participants, and the 1930s Dust Bowl migration of some 300,000 people from Oklahoma and Arkansas to California. But more remarkably, it reshaped the racial makeup of the country as we know it, and it was the first mass act of independence for a people who were in bondage in this country far longer than they have been free.

The families from Selma, and the millions who followed, carried the same hopes as anyone who ever crossed the Atlantic or the Rio Grande. Over the decades of the Great Migration, a good portion of all Black Americans alive picked up and left the tobacco farms of Virginia, the rice plantations of South Carolina, the cotton fields in East Texas and Mississippi, and the villages and backwoods of the remaining Southern states. They set out for cities they had whispered of or had seen in a mail-order catalog.

They followed three major streams, paralleling the railroad lines that carried them to what they hoped would be freedom. Those in Florida, Georgia, South Carolina, North Carolina, and Virginia went up the East Coast to Washington, D.C., Baltimore, Philadelphia, New York, and Boston. Those in Alabama, Mississippi, Tennessee, and Arkansas went to Chicago, Cleveland, Detroit, Milwaukee, Minneapolis, and elsewhere in the Midwest. Those in Louisiana, Texas, and Oklahoma went to Los Angeles, Oakland, Seattle, and elsewhere on the West Coast.

They were seeking political asylum within their own country, not unlike refugees in other parts of the world fleeing famine, war, and pestilence, only they were fleeing Southern terror. In May 1916, just months into the migration, fifteen thousand men, women, and children gathered to watch eighteen-year-old Jesse Washington be burned alive in Waco, Texas. The crowd, one of the largest ever gathered to witness a lynching, chanted, "Burn, burn, burn," as Washington was lowered into the flames. It was a reminder to those contemplating the migration that, however heartbroken they were to leave the loved ones who chose to stay, the region of their birth was not changing anytime soon.

"Oftentimes, just to go away," wrote John Dollard, a Yale anthropologist who would later study the rural South, "is one of the most aggressive things that another person can do, and if the means of expressing discontent are limited, as in this case, it is one of the few ways in which pressure can be put."

As it was, in the early years of the Great Migration, the South did everything it could to keep the people from leaving. Southern authorities resorted to coercion to keep their cheap labor in place. In Albany, Georgia, the police came and tore up the tickets of colored passengers waiting to board. A minister in South Carolina, having seen his parishioners off, was arrested at the station on the charge of helping colored people get out. In Savannah, the police arrested every colored person at the station regardless of where he or she was going. In Summit, Mississippi, authorities closed the ticket office and did not let northbound trains stop when there were large groups of colored people waiting to get on.

Instead of stemming the tide, the blockades and arrests "served to intensify the desire to leave," wrote the sociologist Charles S. Johnson, "and to provide further reasons for going."

The refugees could not know what was in store for them and for their descendants at their destinations or what effect their exodus would have on the country. In the receiving stations of the North and West, they faced a headwind of resistance and hostility. Redlining and restrictive covenants would keep them trapped in segregated colonies in the cities to which they fled. Many unions would deny them membership, keeping their wages lower than those of their white immigrant counterparts. And after the war, during the Red Summer of 1919, racial tensions and resentments boiled over as race riots erupted in cities across the country.

The riot in Chicago began on July 27, 1919, when a seventeen-year-old Black boy named Eugene Williams, swimming along the shore of Lake Michigan, drifted past an invisible line in the water into the white side of the Twenty-ninth Street beach. He drowned after someone hurled a rock at him. Within hours, a riot was in full cry, coursing through the South and Southwest Sides of the city for thirteen days, killing 38 people (23 Blacks and 15 whites) and injuring 537 others (342 Blacks, 178 whites, the rest unrecorded), and not ending until a state militia subdued it.

And yet despite outbreaks such as these, 6 million Black Southerners chose to seek the relative freedoms of the North and West, where they built churches and civic clubs, made enough money to send some back home to their loved ones in the South, could send their children to schools open for full semesters rather than tied to the schedule of the cotton field, and sent a message to the South that African Americans had options and were willing to take them.

"I went to the station to see a friend who was leaving," a person quoted by Emmett J. Scott observed shortly after the migration began. "I could not get in the station. There were so many people turning like bees in a hive."

The Great Migration grew out of the unmet promises made after the Civil War, and the sheer weight of it helped push the country toward the civil rights revolutions of the 1960s. It would proceed in waves in the following decades, not ending until the 1970s, and it would set in motion changes in the North and South that no one, not even the people doing the leaving, could have imagined at the start of it or dreamed would take nearly a lifetime to play out. When the migration began, 90 percent of all African Americans were living in the South. By the time it was over, 47 percent of all African Americans were living in the North and West. A rural people had become urban, and a Southern people had spread themselves all over the nation. They fled north and west as they did during slavery.

It was a "folk movement of inestimable moment," the Mississippi historian Neil McMillen said.

And more than that, it was the second big step the nation's servant class ever took without asking.

1919–1924

RED SUMMER

MICHELLE DUSTER

——

I CAME OF AGE ON THE SOUTH SIDE OF CHICAGO IN THE WAKE of the 1968 urban rebellions. Too young to remember the mass destruction, violence, and tensions of the actual rebellions, I knew only that the South and West Sides of the city did not have the same prosperous look and opportunities as downtown Chicago and the North Side. The sharp racial division between white, Black, Asian, and Hispanic neighborhoods within the city was normal to me.

The magnet high school I attended was located on the other side of the city, so every day I commuted for an hour and a half each way through various Black neighborhoods on the South Side, crossed through the racially diverse downtown area, then over to another Black section on the Near West Side. Public transportation ran with varying efficiency depending on the part of the city in which I traveled. Boarded-up buildings, vacant lots, concentrated high-rise public housing units, fast-food places, barbershops, nail salons, bars, liquor stores, factories, and steel mills were prevalent in Black neighborhoods. The racial concentration also produced many Black-owned companies such as Soft Sheen, Johnson Publishing Company, Parker House Sausage, Army & Lou's Soul Food Restaurant, *The Chicago Defender*, and Seaway Bank. The racial concentration was similar to what my great-grandmother, Ida B. Wells, saw as a Chicago resident all those years ago.

As I navigated the city, I knew there were certain neighborhoods to avoid, such as Bridgeport, Marquette Park, Humboldt Park, and

Canaryville, because of the racist hostility demonstrated by the white people who lived there. Stories of Black people being beaten with bats, bricks, or other weapons, if they were unfortunate enough to end up in that part of town, were well known. I also remember hearing stories of Black people having bricks thrown through their windows or experiencing bombings or other forms of harassment when they tried to cross the deeply entrenched racial line and move into certain predominantly white neighborhoods.

Little did I know that the divide, hostility, and violence were a continuum of the issues that caused the 1919 Race Riot, in which thirty-eight people—twenty-three Black and fifteen white—were killed and over five hundred were injured. The tension had been fueled by a combination of several factors that included job opportunities, housing availability, and the dynamics of World War I. Chicago was among many cities that experienced riots, which gave the summer of 1919 the nickname "Red Summer."

During the Great Migration, the population of Black people in Chicago increased by 148 percent, while the area of the city that welcomed them remained the same. White people did everything they could to keep Black people separate. Restrictive covenants were enforced and redlining was in full force to confine Black people to a small thirty-block section of the city known as the Black Belt.

Near the Black Belt was a neighborhood dominated by white Irish and Lithuanian immigrants who mostly worked in the stockyards. Their attempts to unionize, plus a shortage of workers due to World War I, induced the stockyard owners to bring in Black migrants to work, undercutting the employment of white men. Resentment and tension rose between the two groups.

In addition, Black soldiers returned from World War I, where they had fought for democracy overseas only to be met with resentment and violence once they got home. The sight of their uniforms created ire among racist white people. Trained to fight, the Black veterans were not willing to accept second-class citizenship.

Racial tension gradually increased, and on July 27, 1919, it boiled over into a full-blown white invasion of Black neighborhoods. The violence mostly took place on the South Side, near the stockyards, which was inhabited by working-class white immigrants, and in the Black Belt area. In the aftermath, at the beginning of 1920, a deep level of suspicion between Black Americans and white immigrants remained.

City and state leaders and officials decided to "study" the problem. The Chicago Commission on Race Relations was formed and was led by Black sociologist Charles S. Johnson. After two and a half years, a 651-page report titled *The Negro in Chicago: A Study of Race Relations and a Race Riot* was produced, which included findings of systemic racism along with almost five dozen recommendations on how to solve some of the problems. To this day, the city has yet to implement most of them.

Over one hundred years after the riot, Chicago boasts a diverse population that is almost equally—30 percent each—white, Black, and Hispanic, and about 5 percent Asian. Over 30 percent of residents speak a language other than English. However, there remains extreme housing segregation as a remnant of official redlining and restrictive covenants that were enacted in the early 1920s, the "white flight" that took place in the 1950s and '60s, and public policies that concentrated racialized poverty and underinvestment in predominantly Black neighborhoods.

During Mayor Richard J. Daley's reign over the city from 1955 to 1976, high-rise public housing units were built in Black neighborhoods, creating a high concentration of racialized poverty. During Mayor Michael Bilandic's term, there was benign neglect of the Black sections of town, which was demonstrated during the 1979 blizzard: the streets in the downtown area were cleaned, while the Black neighborhoods remained buried in snow. The next mayor, Jane Byrne, campaigned on the promise of equal snow removal for all neighborhoods. When Harold Washington was elected in 1983 as the first Black mayor, he was met with a virulent group of aldermen nicknamed the "Vrdolyak 29" who did everything in their power to block his initiatives.

Twenty years later, when Mayor Richard M. Daley, the son of the earlier Mayor Daley, dismantled high-rise public housing units, residents faced many barriers to moving into predominantly white areas of the city. The reality of the resulting "mixed-income housing" was that poor Black people moved into lower- or middle-class Black neighborhoods. The idea of Black Chicagoans sharing in educational, economic, and housing opportunity was hard fought against, as was evident in the early 2010s, when Mayor Rahm Emanuel closed more than fifty schools and several mental health clinics in predominantly Black neighborhoods on the South and West Sides. That decision, combined with the uneven distribution of tax incremental financing (TIF) money, led to significant investment in downtown and the North Side and contributed to the underdevelopment of the South and West Sides. These developments represented a continuum of policies that negatively affect Black people, who still live in highly segregated neighborhoods.

After the 1919 Chicago Race Riot, the city responded by implementing and maintaining policies that kept racial segregation in place. One hundred years later the city is considered "global," boasts gleaming tall buildings, and is home to many multinational corporations. Its residents also have a thirty-year discrepancy in life expectancy, depending on the neighborhood in which they reside. Racial disparities are evident in education, employment, income, home ownership, property values, crime, relationship with the police, access to healthcare and healthy food—all related to racially segregated neighborhoods.

For decades Chicago has worked to overcome deeply entrenched racial separation and divisions that have been part of the fabric and makeup of the city. The 2019 election of Mayor Lori Lightfoot—the first African American and openly lesbian woman to hold the position—could be a step toward the progress the city needs. The fact that Lightfoot is a North Sider married to a white woman challenges some of the racial and geographic divides. And the fact that she won all fifty wards during the election suggests that residents in every part of the city were ready for a change. In the twenty-first century, Chicago might finally live up to the promises and expectations outlined by the Chicago Commission on Race Relations in the aftermath of the 1919 Race Riot.

THE HARLEM RENAISSANCE

FARAH JASMINE GRIFFIN

———

BY THE SUMMER OF 1924, WHEN INFLUENTIAL OBSERVERS began to take note of the artistic flowering known as the Harlem Renaissance, Harlem was already an exciting and vibrant Black enclave.

Blacks had started moving to the area in the early decades of the century and it could boast at least four major publications. Socialists Chandler Owen and A. Philip Randolph founded *The Messenger* and published editorials exploring "The New Negro" as early as 1920. They asserted an ascendant political and economic militancy among the new generation of Black people who populated Harlem. In addition to *The Messenger*, *The Crisis* (1910), published by the NAACP and edited by the formidable W.E.B. Du Bois, Marcus Garvey's *Negro World* (1918), and the Urban League's magazine *Opportunity* (1923) were all important shapers of an emerging Black public sphere.

The *Crisis* literary editor Jessie Fauset published many of the young writers who would become literary lights of the Renaissance. However, in 1924 *Opportunity* upstaged both *The Crisis* and Fauset by announcing itself as the vehicle that would usher Harlem's writers to mainstream publishers, critics, and reviewers.

In March 1924, sociologist Charles Johnson, director of the Urban League and editor of *Opportunity*, hosted a now-legendary dinner at the Civic Club, widely hailed as "the first act of the Harlem Renaissance." The dinner was not so much the start of the Renaissance as its public coming-out. The evening was planned as a tribute to Fauset for her tireless efforts on behalf of Black writers and for the publication of her novel *There Is Confusion*. Instead, the event served to highlight the younger writers and offered them valuable introductions to members of the white literary establishment who were in attendance.

Two writers who would become the brightest stars of the Harlem Renaissance, Langston Hughes and Zora Neale Hurston, were absent that evening. Having already published works in *The Crisis* and *Opportunity*, both were on the brink of very promising literary careers, but neither had relocated to New York. By August 1924, the literary flowering that had started with the publication of Jean Toomer's *Cane* in 1923 was fully under way, attracting a bevy of young artists drawn by the energy, community, and opportunity of the Black Mecca.

Significantly, a future literary great made his arrival in Harlem that summer as well. James A. Baldwin was born at Harlem Hospital in August 1924. He would come of age in a Harlem shaped by, but quite different from, the heady days of the 1920s.

In spite of the cultural ascendancy of Harlem, the summer of 1924 offered continued challenges to Black people. That summer the Ku Klux Klan was present and influential at both the Democratic and Republican national conventions, and lynching was still prevalent throughout the South. Harlem was fully aware of these horrific conditions, as many of its inhabitants had fled virulent racism. Once they arrived in Harlem, they devoted themselves to the fight against it. If the artists sought creative freedom, they also saw themselves as participants in a larger movement that asserted the humanity of Black people. Johnson, Du Bois, and others saw the arts as central to the struggle for full citizenship.

In 1925 Howard University philosopher Alain Locke guest-edited a special issue of the journal *Survey Graphic*, titled "Harlem: Mecca of the New Negro." Devoted to life in Harlem, featuring essays by Booker T. Washington, Marcus Garvey, W.E.B. Du Bois, and a number of promising younger writers, the special issue quickly sold out. Its popularity led to the anthology *The New Negro*, also edited by Locke and published in 1925, which according to Arnold Rampersad not only served to "certify the existence of a great awakening in Black America but also to endow it with a Bible."

Meanwhile in 1925 Hughes, who first published in *The Crisis*, and Hurston, whose writings would appear in *Opportunity*, came from Washington, D.C., to Harlem. The painter Aaron Douglas relocated as well. In May the *New York Herald Tribune* became the first publication to use the phrase "Negro Renaissance" to describe the flowering of art. *The Crisis* launched its literary prizes and a research project on the social conditions of American Blacks. The first prizes were issued in August 1925.

Although best known for an abundance of literary work, the Renaissance produced music and visual art as well. Louis Armstrong parted with his mentor King Oliver to join the Fletcher Henderson Orchestra and came to the city that was as big as his sound—New York. Bessie Smith and other blues queens were among the most popular musical artists of the day. Both Hurston and Hughes attended rent parties and after-hours joints where they might hear Duke Ellington, Fats Waller, and Willie "the Lion" Smith, musical giants who would join the partying crowd after they'd finished performing in some of Harlem's whites-only clubs. Also in attendance were Black workers and Black debutantes, whites in search of a little excitement, and members of Harlem's thrilling, vibrant, and brilliant queer community.

Like their contemporaries, Hurston and Hughes found sponsors among wealthy whites, philanthropist friends of the Negro. Amy Spingarn, an artist and philanthropist, gave Hughes the funds he needed to attend Lincoln University. Hurston met Annie Nathan Meyer, author and founder of Barnard College, at the second *Opportunity* dinner in March 1925. Meyer offered her a spot at Barnard that evening and later helped her find the resources she needed to attend.

In 1926 some of the movement's inherent tensions surfaced. Nowhere is this more notable than in two of the year's most significant publications, the singular issue of the journal *FIRE!!* and "The Negro Artist and the Racial Mountain" by Langston Hughes. "The Negro Artist and the Racial Mountain" is the aesthetic manifesto of a generation. It is boldly assertive, unabashedly in love with Black people, and insistent on the value of Black vernacular culture. Hughes's metaphor of the racial mountain takes on several meanings. Here it is an "urge within the race toward whiteness." It is that which the Black artist must climb "in order to discover himself and his people." It is the rocky road, but one that ends with the younger Black artists "building temples for tomorrow . . . on top of the mountain, free within ourselves." If "Racial Mountain" provides the theory, *FIRE!!* is the practice.

FIRE!! appeared only once, in November 1926, but remains a lasting document of the period. Having been nurtured and chided by their elders, Hughes, Hurston, and Douglas, along with Wallace Thurman, Richard Bruce Nugent, and others, joined forces to produce a groundbreaking publication. The issue contained fiction, drama, essays, and visual imagery focusing on both urban and rural Blacks. The group met at Hurston's or Douglas's apartment, where they edited manuscripts, made design decisions, and produced a work by Black people free of the oversight of their Black elders and white funders. The issue contained Nugent's beautiful and impressionistic story of queer desire, "Smoke, Lilies and Jade"; Hurston's "Color Struck and Sweat"; poetry by Hughes, Countee Cullen, and Helene Johnson; and drawings by Douglas and others. It was a beautiful hand grenade, a modernist gem.

At the beginning of 1927, Hurston received a fellowship under the direction of Columbia's Franz Boas. Armed with a pistol and driving herself, she ventured south to collect folklore in a land where the threat of racial violence, lynching, and rape was real. She would spend the next two years there collecting material that she eventually published in the groundbreaking *Mules and Men*.

If Hurston turned her attention to folklore, 1928 saw the ascendancy of the novel as preferred form: Claude McKay's *Home to Harlem*. Du Bois's *Dark Princess*. Jessie Fauset's *Plum Bun*. Newcomer Nella Larsen's *Quicksand*. Larsen, who would later be dubbed the "mystery woman of the Harlem Renaissance," was for a brief moment a favorite writer of Du Bois for her depiction of the Black elite and the talented tenth, and what he saw as her critical dissection of the absurdity of racial classification. What he missed was her exploration of female sexual desire and her critique of the elite's adherence to respectability and its own racial hypocrisy. *Quicksand* would be followed by *Passing* in 1929. Both novels were critical successes and ensured Larsen a prominent place among Harlem's literary lights.

In the shadows of the literary lights, economic desperation was growing among Harlem's Black residents. Whites owned more than 80 percent of Harlem businesses. But following the Wall Street crash in October 1929, fewer and fewer white people came to Harlem in search of a good time. When Hurston returned to Harlem that year, she confronted enormous poverty and Harlem friends "all tired and worn out—looking like death eating crackers." But when she visited her white benefactor, Charlotte Osgood Mason, there was no evidence of the Great Depression in her penthouse. She ate caviar and capon.

THE GREAT DEPRESSION

ROBIN D. G. KELLEY

———

The Fascist racketeers were no fools. They understood the psychology of their starving victims. Their appeal to them was irresistible. It went something like this: "Run the niggers back to the country where they came from—Africa! They steal the jobs away from us white men because they lower wages. Our motto is therefore: *America for Americans!*"

ANYONE LIVING IN DONALD TRUMP'S AMERICA WILL FIND these words eerily familiar; the author's name, not so much. When Angelo Herndon penned this passage over eight decades ago, the twenty-four-year-old with a sixth-grade education was one of the most famous Black men in America. He had spent almost three years in a Georgia jail cell, about five years in Southern coal mines, and at least two years as a Communist organizer in the Deep South.

Herndon's conviction under Georgia's insurrection statute and his subsequent defense made the handsome young radical a cause célèbre. His story upends typical Great Depression images of despondent men and women in breadlines and soup kitchens, waiting for Franklin D. Roosevelt's New Deal to save the day.

Instead, the story of thousands of Angelo Herndons is a story of Black antifascism.

As American finance capital eagerly floated loans to the Italian dictator Benito Mussolini, and *Fortune, The Saturday Evening Post,* and *The New Republic* ran admiring spreads on Italian Fascism, Black radicals called out and resisted homegrown fascism in the form of lynch law, the suppression of workers' organizations and virtually all forms of dissent, and the denial of civil and democratic rights to Black citizens. As this was the state of affairs in much of the United States long before Mussolini's rise, Black radicals not only anticipated fascism, they resisted before it was considered a crisis. As Herndon aptly put it, his case was "a symbol of the clash between Democracy and Fascism."

Born Eugene Angelo Braxton on May 6, 1913 or 1914, he and his seven siblings grew up poor mainly in Alabama, though by his own account he was born in Wyoming, Ohio. His parents, Paul Braxton and Harriet Herndon, both hailed from the Black Belt town of Union Church, just southeast of Montgomery, in Bullock County, Alabama. Angelo was barely five years old when their father succumbed to "miners' pneumonia" and his death sent Harriet and her children back to Union Church, where she sharecropped to make ends meet. In 1926 Angelo (thirteen) and Leo (fifteen) worked in the coalfields of Lexington, Kentucky, before moving in with their aunt Sallie Herndon in Birmingham, Alabama.

In 1930 Angelo was working for the Tennessee Coal and Iron company in Birmingham when the fledgling Communist Party began organizing there. He was primed for its message of militant class struggle and racial justice, having once dreamed of organizing "some kind of a secret society that was to arm itself with guns and ammunition and retaliate against the Ku Klux Klan and the American Legion." On May 22, he attended his first Communist-led mass meeting and listened to party leaders denounce racism, segregation, and lynching, and demand that Black people have the right to equality and national self-determination—that is, the right of the subjugated Black majority in the South to secede from the United States and form a truly democratic government if they so desired. This position, adopted by the Communist International in 1928, promoted not separatism but rather the rights of a subjugated nation to choose. Consequently, the policy led the party to greater support for civil rights and racial justice. Impressed with the Communists for fighting for all workers and for advocating openly for "Negro rights," teenaged Angelo joined the party that night.

Using his birth name, Eugene Braxton, he immediately threw himself into the work, organizing coal miners, the unemployed, and sharecroppers, and spending many a night in an Alabama jail cell. The political situation heated up in March 1931, when nine young Black men were pulled from a freight train near Paint Rock, Alabama, and falsely accused of raping two white women. Following a hasty trial, all the defendants except the youngest were sentenced to death. The Communist-led International Labor Defense (ILD) built an international campaign to defend the "Scottsboro Boys," eventually leading to their release.

Meanwhile, in the fall of 1931, the party dispatched Herndon to Atlanta. The reputedly liberal city had become a hotbed of fascism. Between March and May 1930, Atlanta police arrested six Communist leaders—Morris H. Powers, Joseph Carr, Mary Dalton, and Ann Burlak, all white—and African Americans Herbert Newton and Henry Storey. The state charged the Atlanta Six, as they came to be known, under a nineteenth-century statute that made it potentially a capital crime for anyone to incite insurrection or distribute insurrectionary literature.

Liberals across the country objected to this arcane law largely on the grounds that it violated free speech. Most white Atlantans, however, were less concerned with the party's incendiary literature than with its interracialism. That white women and Black men had attended an antilynching meeting together was an egregious violation of Southern conduct and the primary reason for their arrests.

Unemployment fueled the party's growth in Atlanta, which in turn fueled the fascist movement. During the summer of 1930, about 150 Atlanta business leaders, American Legionnaires, and key figures in law enforcement founded the American Fascisti Association and Order of Black Shirts. Their goals were to "foster the principles of white supremacy" and make the city (and its jobs) white. The Black Shirts held a march on August 22, 1930, carrying placards that read "Niggers, back to the cotton fields—city jobs are for white folks."

Since the Black Shirts were of the better class, the anti-insurrection statute did not apply to them, though they earned the ire of merchants and housewives who feared losing access to cheap Black labor, and of unemployed white men who got black shirts but no jobs. By 1932, the city began denying Black Shirts parade permits and charters, though racial terror and discrimination continued unabated.

As the Atlanta Six appealed their case, Angelo Herndon became the next victim caught in the web of Georgia's insurrection statute. On June 30, 1932, he led a march of over one thousand Black and white workers to city hall that forced the city to add $6,000 to local relief aid. Twelve days later Herndon was arrested while picking up his mail, and police searched his room without a warrant. They discovered a small cache of leaflets, pamphlets, Communist newspapers, and books by George Padmore and Bishop William Montgomery Brown.

Initially charged simply for being a Communist, on July 22 Herndon was indicted for violating the insurrection statute. The ILD retained two local Black lawyers, John H. Geer and Benjamin Davis, Jr., the latter a scion of a prominent Black Republican family who would go on to become a national leader in the Communist Party.

The rabidly anti-Communist prosecutor, John Hudson, sought the death penalty for Herndon for possessing the material. But Davis and Geer showed that the material in Herndon's possession was readily available in the public library. And Davis turned the tables by insisting that "lynching is insurrection" and that the systematic exclusion of Black people from the jury pool was a violation of Herndon's rights, rendering any indictment against him invalid.

On January 18, 1933, an all-white jury found Herndon guilty but spared him execution by sentencing him to eighteen to twenty years on the chain gang. After securing his release on bail in October 1934, the ILD sent Herndon on a national tour to talk about his case in the larger struggle against class oppression, racial injustice, and fascism. "Today, when the world is in danger of being pushed into another blood-bath," he warned in one of his stump speeches, "when Negroes are being shot down and lynched wholesale, when every sort of outrage is taking place against the masses of people—today is the time to act."

The tour ended after the U.S. Supreme Court rejected his appeal, sending him back to prison in October 1935. His legal team then turned to the insurrection statute itself and succeeded in convincing a Fulton County Superior Court judge that the law was unconstitutional. Herndon was released again on bond three months after he returned to prison. Predictably, the Georgia supreme court rejected the lower court's ruling, setting the stage for a second appeal to the U.S. Supreme Court, which in 1937 in a 5–4 decision finally struck down Georgia's insurrection statute, vacating Herndon's conviction for good.

But in 1935, as Herndon crisscrossed the country fighting for his life, the Nazis consolidated power in Germany, Japan occupied Manchuria, Britain and France tightened their grip on the colonies, and Mussolini invaded Ethiopia. Black radicals heeded Herndon's plea "to act," mobilizing in defense of Ethiopia, resisting lynch law in the South, organizing a global anticolonial movement, and defending Republican Spain from the fascists.

Angelo's brother, Milton Herndon, died fighting Franco's troops in the Spanish Civil War. He told his men why he was there: "Yesterday, Ethiopia. Today, Spain. Tomorrow, maybe America. Fascism won't stop anywhere—until we stop it." His words still ring true.

ZORA NEALE HURSTON

BERNICE L. MCFADDEN

—

WHEN I WAS A CHILD, USING THE WORDS *AIN'T, HUH,* AND *hey* would reap an icy gaze from an elder or, worse, a pinch or slap, followed by the correction:

Bernice, the word is:

Isn't. Yes. Hello.

Historically, so-called Bad English or improper grammar was attributed to poor and uneducated people. It was considered lazy English, created by "lazy" Blacks, those Africans who were enslaved in America and worked from can't see to can't see, bonded people who were quite literally worked to death.

My siblings and I were educated in private schools and spent summers in Barbados. We children were neither poor nor uneducated, so that sort of language was unacceptable in my household. We were expected to speak proper English if we aspired to be accepted and respected in the white world.

I grew up in a family that was Southern on my maternal side and Caribbean on my paternal side. These relatives had migrated and immigrated to New York, stubbornly clinging to the customs of their birth homes. So I was raised in a family full of interesting and complex dialects, all of which I adopted.

Truth is, Standard American English has never felt comfortable on my tongue. It is as unnatural to me as swimming fully clothed in the ocean. Today, even in middle age, I still speak in a dialect that I lovingly refer to as Yankee Bajan.

I discovered Zora Neale Hurston in the summer of 1987. I was twenty-one years old and an aspiring writer unsure of what or whom I wanted to write about.

When I opened *Their Eyes Were Watching God*, I was immediately struck by Hurston's use of dialect, and a door in my mind creaked loudly ajar.

In 1934 Hurston published her first novel, *Jonah's Gourd Vine*. It was well received by readers and critics alike. Hurston was celebrated for her use of Negro dialect. "*Jonah's Gourd Vine* can be called without fear of exaggeration the most vital and original novel about the American Negro that has yet been written by a member of the Negro race," wrote Margaret Wallace in *The New York Times*. "Miss Hurston, who is a graduate of Barnard College and student of anthropology, has made the study of Negro folklore her special province. This may very well account for the brilliantly authentic flavor of her novel and for her excellent rendition of Negro dialect."

Perhaps Hurston's well-worded and sophisticated prose, set in contrast to the dialogue, led Wallace to assume that Hurston's education was what allowed her to expertly mimic the Southern Negro dialect. It probably never occurred to Wallace that this achievement was the result not of an education at a prominent academic institution but of Hurston's bilinguality. After all, Zora had been born in Alabama and raised in Florida, in towns populated by Black people. The people and their ways of communicating weren't foreign to her—she was writing about home.

Black language, now known as African American Vernacular English (AAVE), was born in the American South during slavery when bonded people, separated from their familial tribes, mixed with Africans who spoke different languages. In an effort to communicate with their fellow men and women—and their captors—they stitched together scraps of several languages, including that of their enslavers, and created the melodic and nuanced dialect that Hurston used in her work, a dialect that still survives today.

In 1936 Hurston was awarded a Guggenheim Fellowship to study the folk religions of Jamaica and Haiti. While in Haiti, she wrote, in just seven weeks' time, *Their Eyes Were Watching God*, a story that she said "had been dammed up in me."

Published in the fall of 1937, during the Great Depression, *Their Eyes Were Watching God* centers on Janie Crawford, who finds herself married to the controlling Jody, a man who does not allow her to speak or communicate with friends. In contrast, when she meets Tea Cake, he is happy to hear what she has to say, encouraging her to share her thoughts and engage with others. This new relationship forges a feeling of empowerment and joy within Janie.

In *Their Eyes Were Watching God*, Jody can be construed as a metaphor for white people eager to silence the thoughts and expressions of Black people.

But Zora Neale Hurston would not be muted.

The publication of *Their Eyes Were Watching God* was met with criticism. The harshest came from Richard Wright, who accused Hurston of writing into and not above the stereotypes and tropes that had plagued Black people from slavery into Jim Crow. It was his stance that if a Black person took up a pen to write, that pen should be used as a sword to wage war against the oppressive white racist regime. Anything less was a frivolous waste of ink and paper. "Miss Hurston can write, but her prose is cloaked in that facile sensuality that has dogged Negro expression since the days of Phillis Wheatley," Wright wrote.

> Her dialogue manages to catch the psychological movements of the Negro folk-mind in their pure simplicity, but that's as far as it goes.
>
> Miss Hurston *voluntarily* continues in her novel the tradition which was *forced* upon the Negro in the theatre, that is, the minstrel technique that makes the "white folks" laugh. Her characters eat and laugh and cry and work and kill; they swing like a pendulum eternally in that safe and narrow orbit in which America likes to see the Negro live: between laughter and tears.

Their Eyes Were Watching God was taken out of print in 1938 and remained in obscurity for forty years, until writer Alice Walker brought it back into the national spotlight. It was reissued in 1973, and the classic remains in print to this day.

Had Hurston bent to the will of her critics, she might have received her flowers while she was still alive. Ever the nonconformist, the willful Hurston, in her next book, yet again put the politics of race aside in favor of presenting Black people in all their glorious authenticity.

By the time Hurston published *Tell My Horse* in 1938, she was struggling financially. *Tell My Horse* is a travelogue of sorts, outlining the customs, superstitions, folk traditions, and religions found in Haiti and Jamaica. Hurston defied genre assignment by mixing and melding anthropology, folklore, and personal experience. This infuriated her critics. "It is a pity, therefore, that her real talents produced a work so badly—even carelessly—performed! She pays practically no attention to grammar or sentence structure," complained Reece Stuart, Jr.

One of Hurston's biographers, Robert Hemenway, describes *Tell My Horse* as "Hurston's poorest book, chiefly because of its form." Later that year Hurston reviewed Richard Wright's novel *Uncle Tom's Children* and had no qualms about repaying his unkindness, saying that Wright's writing was "so grim that the Dismal Swamp of race hatred must be where they live." Too much, too little, too late, Hurston's star had fallen and was slowly burning away in the cold, looming shadow of Richard Wright.

In 1939 Hurston returned to Florida and went to work for the Federal Writers' Project. Working alongside folklorist Stetson Kennedy, she and others collected songs and folktales from the culturally rich communities that dotted the Sunshine State. Hurston respected and revered the many iterations of Black language found in America and abroad and charged herself to do her part in collecting and preserving it for future generations.

For this, I am grateful God sent Zora Neale Hurston into the world. She has been a steady guide on this literary journey of mine. It is because of her refusal to participate in the contempt and erasure of Black dialect that I am able to proudly embrace and celebrate my bilinguality on and off the page.

GOD DON COME, he send. —Barbadian saying

COILED AND UNLEASHED

PATRICIA SMITH

———

A whole people's tumble into raw, untested century began
with one man, penning his serpentine sojourn up from slavery—
I am not quite sure of the exact place or exact date of my birth,
but . . . I must have been born somewhere and at some time.
He began as another baby shoved directly into the wrong air.
Eavesdropping on the whispered blue archives of a scarring
passage—the passage that taught so well the gracelessness
of chains—Booker T. slowly untangled the acrid truths of his
own mother's bondage. He knew how gingerly his people
had to sidle toward that blaring northern star. And words,
like feral soldiers, lined up for him, crafting that careful story—
his stern and measured gospel, the only breath in his body.

Screeching a story that feels like the only breath in his body,
Du Bois upended Booker, angled for agitation, commanded
there be nothing hushed and unhurried about our freedom.
He preferred the uncompromising clench, the coil, the strident
voice and stalwart stride. *Make yourself do unpleasant things*
so as to gain the upper hand of your soul. He meant the soul
of Black folk, and that soul's upper hand was a fist—pierce
and pummel at the sleek white wall, prelude to the unfeigned,
unslaved voice. Restraint had no role or reason in revolution.
Between the tenets of those two men, a race strived to untangle
its convoluted root, urged its whole self forward, and hurtled
toward the door America had fought so hard to keep closed.

A thousand clamorous truths lurked behind that thick door.
To coax them loose, pens scarred its surface, keyboards clicked
and spat. In Chicago, which was destined to be ours, Black word
became Black bellow, warning of the menace seething behind
Jim Crow's burgeoning growl. Word was soundtrack, it was
solace, salvage, defender of the defenseless. The Black word
would learn to hide in the deep pockets of Pullman porters,
cooing the brethren north, it would slip on the silken shouts
of Hughes, Brooks, and Ida B., sing to soldiers of boundaries
that wailed their color. The *Defender* and *Crisis* harbored
the merciless Black word, the *us to us,* the tongue of tenement,
of chittlins and factory, spinning the fractured tale of that

furious north star and where it had always meant to lead us.
It led us to Madame CJ Walker, who slathered Black crowns
with grease that clung and stank like flowers, oil that crackled
under a toothed and rabid heat. She schooled us in that sweet
torture until we shamed our own mirrors, until our whole nappy
heads spat glow. And she raised fists of her own damned money,
from *us to us.* Blue-black and hallelujah-crowned, Madame CJ
Walker American-dreamed. The star led us to the sharecroppers'
boy, who knew no star was the end of free, who drove his body up
through ice and into a startling sky. Matthew Henson stepped into
that sky and planted the flag of a country that was not yet his.
Mahri-Pahluk, the Inuit called him. *Matthew. The Kind One.*

That furious star kept leading us north, and north—five decades
after Lincoln dragged ink across the only edict that mattered,
a wary Jubilee spanned the year. Soon after—as if a lock had
clicked open—frenzied migrants, wide-eyed and beguiled,
surged into depots in New York, Chicago, Detroit, Cleveland
Philly and Pittsburgh, clutching our strapped cloth cases, with
tabasco leaking from the waxed paper seams of what was left
of our lunches. Dizzied by a conjured glare, we streamed into
tenements, placed mementos of our other selves on shadowbox

shelves, declared ourselves blessed, and sent hallelujahs back
down south, in carefully scripted letters that sloshed our new
city's cracked concrete with gold. *You got to come see, Pearl,*

it's better up here. Amos, there a job for every man who want one.
And Amos worked to beat the willful red dust off his hat and he
came, Pearl wrapped fried bread and peppered pork scraps
for the journey and she came, Annie cried loud in front
of her granddaddy's slantways old house and she came, Otis beat
down the little-boy fear in his belly and he came, Earl put one last
flower on Mary's grave and he came, Esther slow-folded all her
country clothes and she came, Willie started bragging all around
Mississippi 'bout some paycheck he didn't have yet and he came,
Eunice, Nona's baby girl, got her tangled hair pressed and plaited
for the first time and she came, we came, hauling even the things
we dreamed of owning, we came, loosing the noose, stepping

gingerly into the gaping mouths of cities, we came, just stunned
enough. We wrangled with wary merchants, waged war with
vermin, dragged our feet through bloodied butcher shop sawdust.
Some found jobs revolving around bland ritual—the putting in
or taking out or hammering on or the pulling apart of things.
We calmed the fussy clockwork of white babies, held them to
the wrong breast. We scarred skillets for another family's beans
and meat. We dug with *ain't-a-thang-different-but-the-dirt,* 'cause
all that black gold is buried somewhere. We were told that
all those vexing daily battles were ours, but real wars belonged to
everyone. Once again, we lunged lockstep into questions that white
American men had vowed to answer with their breath and bodies.

It was called the first war in the world, but it wasn't, it couldn't have
been, because we had forever been tending to wounds. When
that war shuddered to its close, the very same America held out
its skeletal arms and begged the brown soldiers back inside—
inside where their names were still a street-spat venom. Inside,
while their bodies still dripped from the thickest branches of trees,

inside, where they were whispered to be not men, but fractions
of men. They returned to their homes in South Carolina and Texas,
in DC and Chicago, in Omaha and Arkansas, and the air had not
changed there. So the summer turned red and exploded, blood
splattering storefronts, a war inside a quavering peace. Snarling
white men killed to feed their hatred of hue, killed 1000 of us

to make America great again, to siphon all that dark trouble from
between its shores. We fought back, coiling and unleashing a fury
threaded in our stolen names. Incensed by our ease upon our own
streets, our stolen names gracing storefronts, our control over
our own lives, they torched the landscape flat in Tulsa, ignored
the screams of its rightful citizens and curious children, they set us
to flame. Wherever we were, whenever we dared upright, wherever
we breathed out loud, they were—damning the boys in Scottsboro,
disregarding the vile savage rampaging through men in Tuskegee.
But, dammit, we phoenix, we. We renaissance and odes inked
in tumult. We Billie warbling a fruit gone strange. And we still be
Marian sanctifying that stage, singing her America while America
said *There ain't a damned thing here that sounds like that.*

PART NINE

1939–1944

THE BLACK SOLDIER

CHAD WILLIAMS

——

ISAAC WOODARD WANTED TO BE A SOLDIER. ONE OF NINE children in a family of sharecroppers, he grew up in rural South Carolina, hoping, like so many other African Americans in the Jim Crow South, for a better life.

His opportunity came. At the age of twenty-three, on October 14, 1942, he traveled to Fort Jackson and enlisted in the U.S. Army. He would become one of approximately 1.2 million Black men and women who served in World War II.

On the eve of American entry into the war, the place of Black soldiers in the nation's military was dire. In the summer of 1940, when Congress began debating a peacetime draft, fewer than five thousand Black soldiers were in the entire U.S. Army. Black World War I veterans Rayford Logan and Charles Hamilton Houston, still scarred by their experiences, testified that Jim Crow in the military had to end. The September 1940 Selective Service Act, the first peacetime draft in American history, prohibited racial discrimination in the administration of the draft, but it did not outlaw segregation.

The NAACP and civil rights activists pressured President Franklin D. Roosevelt and the War Department to reform the military and address racism affecting Black workers. The government responded by appointing Judge William Hastie as a special adviser to Secretary of War Henry Stimson and by promoting Colonel Benjamin O. Davis, Sr., to brigadier general, making him the first Black flag officer in the history of the U.S. military. Despite these concessions, the

armed forces remained segregated and the defense industries systematically excluded African Americans. In January 1941, longtime labor
organizer A. Philip Randolph proposed a mass march on Washington, threatening to have some one hundred thousand African Americans descend on the nation's capital. On June 25, just days before the
march, President Roosevelt issued Executive Order 8802, banning
discrimination in the defense industries and creating the Fair Employment Practices Commission.

The United States entered World War II following the December 7, 1941, attack on Pearl Harbor. During the surprise bombard-
ment, a Black naval messman, Dorie Miller, manned an antiaircraft
gun and shot down at least two Japanese planes. Miller became a
powerful symbol of African American patriotic loyalty and commitment to the war effort. But Black people, as represented by the "double V" slogan, were committed not just to victory against fascism
abroad but to victory against racism at home as well.

They faced an arduous battle. Approximately 2.5 million African
Americans registered for the draft, a process rife with discrimination.
Of the more than 1 million men inducted into the military through
the draft, 75 percent served in the army. When they arrived at training
camps, especially those located in the South, Black draftees endured
humiliation and abuse. The army rigidly enforced racial segregation,
often treating German POWs with more respect than Black servicemen. When Black soldiers went off base, they posed both a real and
symbolic threat to Jim Crow and frequently clashed with local whites.

As in World War I, the military consigned the majority of Black
troops to labor and service units. Racist ideas that Black men lacked
the cognitive ability to be effective combatants and officers continued
to pervade the thinking of War Department officials. This belief,
however, did not stop the military from putting Black servicemen in
harm's way, both abroad and on the home front. In the summer of
1944, Black dockworkers stationed at Port Chicago, California, refused to work following two munition explosions that resulted in 320
deaths, 202 of whom were African American. The navy court-
martialed fifty men on charges of mutiny and sentenced them to
eight to fifteen years of hard labor.

During the war, the military deployed approximately half a million African American soldiers overseas. Although service units, like the 320th Barrage Balloon Battalion and the 490th Port Battalion, were present from D-Day on, the army initially had no intention of using Black soldiers as combatants on the European front. Pressure from civil rights organizations and the Black press eventually forced the army to send the reactivated 92nd "Buffaloes" Division to Italy in the summer of 1944. As in World War I, the division's racist officers lacked faith in the men under their command and derided their allegedly poor performance in combat. The all-Black 93rd Division arrived in the Pacific Theater in early 1944. It finally saw action during the New Guinea campaign. Most Black troops in the Pacific, however, toiled in support capacities. Isaac Woodard, who served as a longshoreman in the 429th Port Battalion, arrived on New Guinea in October 1944, loading and unloading ships.

In spite of discrimination, Black servicemen did make significant contributions and took advantage of limited opportunities. During the Battle of the Bulge in December 1944, the army found itself in desperate need of replacement troops. In January 1945, over the objections of his senior officers, Supreme Commander Dwight Eisenhower called for a limited number of Black volunteers to fight alongside white soldiers. The 761st Tank Battalion distinguished itself on the European front and was in combat until the final days of the war. The navy grudgingly opened its ranks to Black volunteers. Although the majority of the sixty-five thousand Black seamen continued to serve as messmen, the navy did commission the first Black officers in its history, and one ship, the *Mason,* had an all-Black crew. The Marine Corps proved most willing to accept Black servicemen in its forces. While the approximately twenty thousand Black Marines trained at a segregated facility in Montford Point, North Carolina, and never saw combat, they paved the way for future enlistees.

The most significant examples of racial progress in the military occurred in the Air Corps. Bending to pressure, on January 9, 1941, the War Department agreed to the creation of the 99th Pursuit Squadron with headquarters located in Tuskegee, Alabama. Benjamin O. Davis, Jr., was part of the first graduating class of cadets and subsequently took command of the squadron. The War Department's refusal to send them into battle was the last straw for Judge William Hastie, who resigned in protest in January 1943. Manpower needs and pressure from First Lady Eleanor Roosevelt ultimately put them in action, first in North Africa and then in Italy. In February 1944, the 99th was joined by the 100th, 301st, and 302nd squadrons, becoming the 332nd Fighter Group. By the end of the war, 992 men became pilots, with 450 serving overseas. Used primarily as bomber escorts, the fighters of the 332nd flew 1,578 missions with over fifteen thousand individual sorties and won numerous commendations.

Black women, too, took advantage of opportunities created by the war. Along with entering the industrial workforce by the thousands, they served in the military, enduring both racism and sexism throughout their experiences. They made up approximately 4 percent of the fifteen thousand enlistees in the Women's Army Corps (WACs); Charity Adams Earley became the first African American female WAC officer. The navy's Women Accepted for Volunteer Emergency Services (WAVES), established by Congress in 1942, was originally all white. But at President Roosevelt's insistence, the WAVES began accepting African American volunteers in 1944, and seventy-two Black women ultimately underwent training.

After the war came to an end on September 2, 1945, African Americans immediately began to wonder if their service and sacrifice had been in vain. The military did not award Medals of Honor to any Black soldiers and largely ignored their contributions to the war effort. As they returned to their homes across the country and especially in the South, their expectations for freedom and increased rights were met with fierce resistance. In the spring and summer of 1946, white supremacists killed several Black veterans and attacked countless others.

On February 12, 1946, Isaac Woodard was almost home. He had distinguished himself during the war, rising to become a sergeant and earning several medals. He returned to the United States on January 15 and received his official discharge on February 12 at Camp Gordon, Georgia. There he got on a Greyhound bus along with other newly minted veterans and headed for Winnsboro, South Carolina, to be reunited with his wife, Rosa.

During the ride, when Woodard asked the white bus driver to use the restroom, they got into a heated argument. When the bus stopped in Batesburg, South Carolina, the driver called for local police to remove Woodard. Two white officers arrived, forcibly took Woodard off the bus, and viciously beat him with their batons before dragging his unconscious body to jail. When Woodard awoke the next morning, his face battered and covered in dried blood, he could not see. Both his eyes had been destroyed, leaving the twenty-seven-year-old veteran permanently blind.

News of Woodard's blinding shocked Black America. It offered a brutal reminder that while the foreign war might have ended, the domestic war for civil rights raged on. The NAACP, led by Executive Secretary Walter White, used the incident to pressure President Harry Truman to act. In December 1946, Truman established the President's Committee on Civil Rights. And on July 26, 1948, in response to its recommendations and to continued agitation from A. Philip Randolph, Truman issued Executive Order 9981. The order abolished segregation in the armed forces. Black veterans such as Medgar Evers, Amzie Moore, and Robert Williams, inspired by their war service, became key leaders in the civil rights movement of the 1950s and '60s. World War II transformed African Americans and ultimately changed the course of American history.

THE BLACK LEFT

RUSSELL RICKFORD

———

THOUGH AFRICAN AMERICANS JOINED IN THE JUBILANT CEL-ebrations of peace when the Second World War came to an end in 1945, many among them remained skeptical about the U.S. war effort, seeing it as nothing more than a white man's fight.

The more radical thrust of African American demands—which included meaningful global peace, decolonization, and thorough-going human rights in their own country—sought not merely greater inclusion of "minorities" in the capitalist apparatus but a basic reorganization of political and economic arrangements. It was the Black left that embodied this expansive agenda. From activist-intellectual W.E.B. Du Bois's 1946 *An Appeal to the World* (a report on U.S. racial oppression submitted to the fledgling United Nations), to socialist crusader Claudia Jones's 1949 essay, "An End to the Neglect of the Problems of the Negro Woman!," the Black American manifestos of the day imagined liberation as the wholesale redistribution of power and wealth.

But society was moving in a different direction. The early postwar years produced great waves of political and social reaction, delivering a stunning rebuke to just conceptions of peacetime reconversion. The intensification of national hostilities with the Soviet Union reinforced efforts to crush bold prescriptions for reform within the United States. Black activists of all political inclinations were among the targets of the retrograde forces that combined to stymie progressive change. The organs of hyperpatriotism—from the congressional body known as the House Un-American Activities Committee to local segregationist, antilabor, and anti-Communist groups—harbored special enmity for leftists, whom they attempted to discredit by labeling them "subversives."

It was in Peekskill, New York, however, that the savagery of racist reaction surfaced most dramatically in 1949. The occasion was a Paul Robeson concert. A star of stage and screen, the fifty-one-year-old Robeson was one of the world's foremost entertainers. He was also a stalwart activist who fought tirelessly for the causes of decolonization, labor, and human rights. Robeson was an antifascist and an internationalist who lent his prodigious talents to trade union struggles across the globe. He had battled lynching and segregation while promoting Black militancy and cultural pride. He was an ally of the Communist Party; an outspoken admirer of the Soviet Union (which he cherished for its anticolonial and antiracist policies); and an opponent of the Cold War who called for peaceful coexistence of the superpowers.

In short, Robeson was everything the far right despised. When he was named headliner of a civil rights benefit concert set to take place in Peekskill in late August 1949, some of his most committed foes resolved to block the performance.

Earlier that spring, news outlets had quoted Robeson (somewhat inaccurately) as proclaiming, at the Paris Peace Conference, that African Americans would refuse to participate in a war against the Soviet Union. The gist of the statement Robeson had actually made was that Black America's true fight lay at home, in the land of Jim Crow.

This overwhelmingly defined the African American worldview after the smoke cleared from World War II. Black people had nurtured their own visions of the war, recasting a struggle against fascism as a crusade against white supremacy. Now they were determined to translate that ideal into a quest for full democracy at home.

On the one hand, that meant preserving the gains—including increased access to industrial jobs and unions—that mass Black mobilization and the exigencies of wartime production had enabled. On the other hand, African Americans believed that the cataclysm of global war heralded a new racial order that they could help construct.

Having helped defeat Adolf Hitler and his ideology of racial hierarchy, Black people increasingly resented Jim Crow and other domestic regimes of second-class citizenship. Indignation became migration as thousands (and eventually millions) of Black Southerners journeyed to northern, western, and eastern cities, expanding an African American exodus that had accelerated during the war, laying the groundwork for the burgeoning and restive Black communities of the postwar years.

War had weakened the colonial empires of Europe; everywhere, it seemed, subject peoples were pressing for self-rule. Black Americans watched this upsurge with a sense of expectation, seeing India's 1947 independence and the nascent freedom campaigns of other "colored" populations as closely aligned with their own efforts to restructure U.S. society.

There were signs that some African American aspirations might be realized. In 1944 and 1948, respectively, the Supreme Court struck down the whites-only primary election system and ruled that racially restrictive housing covenants could not be enforced. By 1948, President Truman had been pressured into desegregating the military and the federal bureaucracy. He had already impaneled a Committee on Civil Rights whose 1947 report, *To Secure These Rights*, offered a stark assessment of structural racism nationwide. In 1947 as well, Jackie Robinson broke the color line in major league baseball, and the Congress of Racial Equality, a civil rights outfit, organized the Journey of Reconciliation, a campaign to test compliance with a new law banning segregation on interstate buses.

But any departure from the tenets of militarism and Negro acquiescence enraged ultranationalists and bigots. In 1946 a South Carolina policeman beat veteran Isaac Woodard so badly it ruptured his eyes and left him blind. In 1947 Georgia sharecropper Rosa Lee Ingram was sentenced to death, along with her two sons, after all three family members repelled the vicious assault of a white man. And in the same year, the Trenton Six were wrongfully convicted of murder by an all-white jury in New Jersey.

And then there was Robeson. Amid the outcry about his alleged Paris declaration, several of his concerts were canceled. In the Westchester County town of Peekskill, as the date of his performance approached, some residents felt justified in engineering a campaign of aggression against the singer. The American Legion and the Chamber of Commerce denounced the upcoming recital as "un-American" and called for it to be vigorously contested. "The time for tolerant silence that signifies approval is running out," an area newspaper asserted.

These provocations had the desired effect. When the day of the concert arrived, such a menacing swarm of anti-Robeson demonstrators appeared at the outdoor performance site that the event was called off. That evening roving bands of self-styled patriots attacked concertgoers trapped on the show ground. A cross was burned. Anti-Black and anti-Semitic epithets were hurled. "Lynch Robeson!" the mob chanted. As Robeson supporters attempted to exit the grounds, they were brutally stoned or beaten, and many of their vehicles were overturned. Police stood by amid the mayhem, sneering at victims or hoisting their billy clubs and joining in the ambush.

Robeson was defiant. Buoyed by a massive rally in Manhattan's Harlem neighborhood, where well-wishers marched in his defense, the singer vowed to return to the Peekskill area. The concert was rescheduled for the following weekend. This time Robeson was able to perform, his rich baritone echoing in the hills. To ensure his safety and that of the concertgoers, a large contingent of Black and white trade unionists formed a perimeter around the grounds. There they stood, shoulder to shoulder, throughout the concert. But when it ended and attendees began to leave, throngs of right-wing protesters, including supporters of veterans groups, again unleashed a torrent of violence. Assailants bludgeoned audience members or fanned out along a roadside to shower departing cars with rocks, shattering windshields and bloodying the asphalt.

Observers around the world viewed the Peekskill riots as a portent. As the Cold War deepened, the United States was lurching to the right, and the most regressive social elements felt emboldened. Seeing Peekskill as a call to arms, jingoists nationwide soon adopted a chilling new slogan: "Wake up, America! Peekskill did!"

A future generation, in retrospect, might have recognized the symptoms of creeping fascism that marked the Peekskill affair: hatred wrapped in the banner of patriotism; collusion of business interests, nativists, and racists; incitement by high officials and the media; and exaltation of violence as a redemptive force. African Americans remembered Peekskill as the acceleration of the powerful currents of tyranny that they would have to confront even more assiduously in years to come.

1949–1954

THE ROAD TO BROWN V. BOARD OF EDUCATION

S H E R R I L Y N I F I L L

═══

IN 1948 U.S. OFFICIALS VIGOROUSLY PROSECUTED GERMAN war criminals in Nuremberg for enforcing anti-Semitic policies, practices, and laws that advanced a theory of ethnic and religious inferiority of Jews. At the same time, state officials across the American South were enforcing segregationist policies, practices, and laws that advanced a theory of white supremacy and the racial inferiority of African Americans, undisturbed by the federal government.

In the small town of Hearne, Texas, starting in the fall of 1947, the contrast between the U.S. fight against Nazism abroad and its embrace of a rigid racial caste system at home was dramatized in a battle over segregated schools. The standoff between African American parents in Hearne and the local white school superintendent drew the attention of Thurgood Marshall. Just eight years earlier the brilliant and determined young African American lawyer from Baltimore had founded the NAACP Legal Defense and Educational Fund (LDF). Marshall became the LDF's first president and its director-counsel in 1940. Seventy-three years later, I became the LDF's seventh president and director-counsel.

The story of LDF's brilliant strategy to successfully challenge the constitutionality of racial segregation has been documented and chronicled in multiple books and articles. The strategy culminated in *Brown v. Board of Education,* a monumental 1954 landmark legal decision that literally changed the course of twentieth-century America. The Supreme Court, led by Chief Justice Earl Warren, decided that "separate educational facilities are inherently unequal" and deprive Black children of the constitutional right to equal protection of the laws. The decision cracked the load-bearing wall of legal segregation. Within ten years, the principles vindicated in *Brown* were successfully deployed to challenge segregation laws in the United States.

The rather unknown story that unfolded in Hearne, Texas, captures the historical significance of *Brown*. Black parents were powerfully affected by the contrast between the U.S. stance against Nazis on the global stage and the embrace of Jim Crow at home. Their postwar ambitions for their children ran headlong into the determination of Southern whites to reinforce segregation. In communities around the South, Black parents sought and received the assistance of local NAACP lawyers to challenge the absence of school facilities for their children, or substandard educational facilities and investment in Black schools.

In Hearne the challenge was initiated by C. G. Jennings, the stepfather of thirteen-year-old twins, Doris Raye and Doris Faye Jennings. In August 1947, he tried to register his daughters at the white high school. His request was refused, and he engaged local counsel.

A few weeks later, in September 1947, African American parents initiated a mass boycott. Maceo Smith, who led the NAACP in Dallas, contacted Marshall about the situation in Hearne.

A year earlier, the Blackshear School, the high school designated for Black students, had burned down. No one expected the Black students to now attend the nearby white school due to a Texas law segregating students. The school superintendent announced that $300,000 would be devoted to the construction of a new school for Black students, and a $70,000 bond issue was placed on the ballot. Although Black children outnumbered white students in Hearne, the physical plant of the existing high school for white students was estimated to have a value of $3.5 million. The building that would be haphazardly renovated into the "new" Black high school was, in fact, the dilapidated barracks that had just recently housed German soldiers during the war.

When Black parents learned about the city's plans, they felt compelled to take matters into their own hands. According to reports in the local African American newspaper, "these buildings were sawed in half, dragged to the school location, and joined together with no apparent regard for physical beauty or concealing their prison camp appearance." The complaint later filed by parents in *Jennings v. Hearne Independent School District* further described the school as "a fire hazard," "overcrowded and . . . unfurnished with modern equipment," and with "inadequate lighting." All in all, the Black parents deemed the building "unsafe for occupancy," and the indignity of educating their children in a prisoner of war barracks was an insult too ugly to be borne.

White officials and local newspapers disparaged the parents' school boycott and the Jennings suit as an attempt by the NAACP to "stir up trouble." On September 28, Thurgood Marshall—who recognized the importance of challenging media distortions to his litigation efforts—fired back at the editorial board of *The Dallas Morning News* with a lengthy letter.

As African American parents in Hearne kept their children home from school, one hundred miles away in Houston, Black schoolteacher Henry Eman Doyle was the sole law student registered at Texas State University for Negroes, a hastily organized three-room "school" created by the State of Texas after Marshall won a case brought on behalf of Heman Sweatt, a Black student who had been barred from registering at the University of Texas Law School. The three-room school, located in the basement of the state capitol, was the state's attempt to comply with the *Plessy v. Ferguson* "separate but equal" doctrine that required states to provide a public law school for Black students if they excluded Black students from flagship public law schools.

Marshall took his challenge to federal court, and in 1950 the Supreme Court would find that Texas's crude attempts were in vain, and that at least in the area of law education, separate could not be equal. *Sweatt* is widely regarded as the final case that set the successful stage for the frontal attack on segregation that became *Brown v. Board of Education*.

Meanwhile, some federal judges found the courage to defy South-

ern mores and uphold the constitutional guarantee of equal protection. In South Carolina, federal court judge Julius Waties Waring, the
scion of a respected Charleston family with deep Confederate roots,
issued a series of decisions in cases tried by Marshall that suggested
that federal judges might play a role in protecting civil rights. Waring's searing, powerful dissent in *Briggs v. Elliot,* the South Carolina
Brown case, became the template for the Supreme Court's decision in
Brown. Here Judge Waring first articulated the concept that "segregation is per se inequality"—a full-on rebuke of *Plessy v. Ferguson* that
Chief Justice Warren later paraphrased in *Brown.*

But civil rights lawyers, and the African American parents they
represented, were also emboldened after World War II. And it was
their energy and uncompromising demands that shifted the landscape. By 1951, African American students were making their own
demands. In Prince Edward County, Virginia, sixteen-year-old Barbara Johns led her classmates at Moton High School in a walkout
and boycott of their segregated school. Her action prodded Marshall
and the LDF lawyers to file *Davis v. Prince Edward County, Virginia,*
one of the four *Brown* cases.

Back in Hearne, by the time African American parents began
organizing to challenge the dilapidated "new" high school for their
children, Marshall already had his hands full with cases, all of which
would become landmarks in their own right. This may be in part
why the Hearne case is not widely known. It was one of a cadre
of small, unsuccessful cases extending back to Marshall's late 1930s
schoolteacher-pay-equality cases in Maryland and Virginia. But
these cases played a powerful role in shaping the thinking of LDF
lawyers about what was possible in their litigation challenging Jim
Crow. And it powerfully demonstrated the civil rights challenge confronting the United States in those early postwar years. As Thurgood
Marshall wrote in his 1948 letter to the editors of *The Dallas Morning
News,* "I think that before this country takes up the position that I
must demand complete equality of right of citizens of all other countries throughout the world, we must first demonstrate our good faith
by showing that in this country our Negro Americans are recognized
as full citizens with complete equality."

1954–1959

BLACK ARTS

Imani Perry

—

O N MAY 17, 1954, THE AXIS OF AMERICAN HISTORY SHIFTED
when the unanimous Supreme Court opinion in *Brown v. Board of
Education* declared that separate was in fact not equal, and that legally
mandated segregation was unconstitutional. It was front-page news
around the world, and the opinion was printed in full in American
papers.

Desegregation would prove an arduous process, marked by violence and unapologetic resistance in many corners of white America.
Nevertheless, the *Brown* decision had immediate significance because
it indicated that finally, after decades of aversion and refusal, the Supreme Court would be on the side of the Fourteenth Amendment.
The decision concluded a hard-fought multidecade legal strategy by
the NAACP. The victory fueled the coming two decades of African
American protest and organizing and America's second Reconstruction.

Brown fueled not only Black activists but also Black artists who
explored social conditions and the human imagination necessary to
transform them. In prior years, many Black artists had been chas-
tened and chastised by McCarthyism. Black artists were among those
blacklisted for holding leftist politics or simply for being outspoken
against American racism. Organizations were fractured and shut-
tered, and careers were destroyed. Black art communities were subject
to surveillance, closed doors, and punitive measures.

And so in 1954, Black artists and writers found themselves at something of a crossroads. McCarthyism was waning. *Brown* was a beginning, and the FBI surveillance of Black activists under the COINTELPRO program had not yet begun. Possibility, however fraught, was refreshed. And these artists claimed new space.

In November 1955, James Baldwin followed two novels, *Go Tell It on the Mountain* and *Giovanni's Room,* with a collection of essays, *Notes of a Native Son.* The book fairly crackled with his refusal to apologize for who he was and where he came from. The essays were both autobiographical and critical. His pen was unflinching.

In the first section, Baldwin took his predecessors to task. He subjected Harriet Beecher Stowe, Richard Wright, and the filmmakers who made *Carmen Jones* to withering critiques for their too-narrow depictions of Black life, thought, and feeling. Baldwin sought to claim the expansiveness he saw in Black history and culture. In the second section of the book, he depicted the conditions of Black life, North and South, including Jim Crow in Princeton, New Jersey. Baldwin placed himself as a global figure, in France and Switzerland. Unfamiliar ground gave him a sense of solidarity with other oppressed peoples and nuanced his and his readers' understanding of race and racism as a global problem.

This drive to expand the terrain of Black humanity in the public sphere was evident in the work of other artists. Elizabeth Catlett, already recognized as an exceptional visual artist who worked largely in prints, began to sculpt in the 1950s. A graduate of Howard University and the child of a Tuskegee professor, Catlett had settled in Mexico to escape the tentacles of McCarthyism. She had been scrutinized and harassed more than most in retaliation against her leftist politics. And she did not break. She sculpted smooth, sensual, and solemn pieces, and her fully rounded Black subjects—both of historic significance and of the folk—grew under her hands. Her landmark 1957 print *Sharecropper* is the image of a Black woman—serious and dignified—beneath a hat shielding her from the sun. *Niña* depicts a Mexican girl in profile, with the brown skin of an Indigenous child and her hair in plaits. In both prints, along with many other works, Catlett wove together key elements of her artistic imagination—

a fight against economic exploitation, sexism, and racism—with unseen yet quintessentially American faces.

Black American artists of the 1950s found common ground and purpose with Black artists abroad. In 1958 the Nigerian novelist Chinua Achebe published *Things Fall Apart*, considered one of the most important and widely read novels in the English language. Published two years before Nigerian independence, the novel tells a story of the infiltration and domination of the West at the dawn of colonialism. Achebe's protagonist, Okonkwo, a man with a clear history and place in his Ibo community, confronts the world-destroying forces of the colonial order and the missionaries who served as the moral justification for British incursion. The anticolonial novel had a global impact. It also brought Achebe into contact with Baldwin and the playwright Lorraine Hansberry.

Baldwin's younger but similarly genius friend, a protector and a thinking partner, Lorraine Hansberry transformed American theater in March 1959. Her play *A Raisin in the Sun* was the first written by a Black woman to be produced on Broadway. It was a runaway success, and that year Hansberry won the Drama Critics Circle Award. The play tells the story of a Chicago South Side family living in a squalid kitchenette apartment whose patriarch has died, leaving them with a $10,000 insurance check. The question of what to do with the check is the primary plot device.

Around it, Hansberry crafts a masterful ensemble of characters who dream in the face of a deeply racist society. The title of the play comes from Langston Hughes's poem "Harlem," also colloquially known by its introductory question, "What happens to a dream deferred?" Each character lives with that prospect. Walter Lee Younger longs for wealth and status of the sort he sees in the lives of the white men he drives around. His wife, Ruth, is a domestic worker who is contemplating an abortion and is desperate for a home of her own. Beneatha, Walter's younger sister, aspires to be a doctor and is also exploring her identity and the idea of freedom in part by means of a West African suitor, a student in the independence movement. And the elder Lena, Walter and Beneatha's mother, betrays every Mammy stereotype with the force of her moral guidance and her reminder that freedom is the purpose of life.

At the conclusion to the play, the Younger family moves into a home in a white neighborhood. They aren't wanted there and are almost certain to encounter violent retaliation for claiming a place in the American landscape. The family is heroic in their insistence on facing the mobs, reminding the audience of the question at the heart of the American project: is equality a deliberate fiction or an end for which people will fight?

These works by Baldwin, Catlett, Achebe, Hansberry, and others provide a glimpse of the moment after the *Brown* decision. All these artists were accustomed to loss: the grief of lives cruelly limited by racism, sexism, homophobia, and imperialism. But they insisted that Black life was not mere endurance but a victory of spirit in the form of human complexity, imagination, resistance, breadth, and depth, precisely the resources that were essential for the coming revolutions.

1959–1964

THE CIVIL RIGHTS MOVEMENT

CHARLES E. COBB, JR.

⸻

A CRITICALLY IMPORTANT ASPECT OF THE FREEDOM STRUG-
gle that intensified in the 1960s was the convergence of young people
with people the ages of their parents and grandparents who were willing to share their networks and experiences. In some respects, this has
always been true but in my view never more so than during the 1960s.

How did this happen, and why was it important?

On February 1, 1960, four eighteen-year-old students attending
North Carolina Agricultural and Technical College (now University),
in Greensboro, walked into an F. W. Woolworth department store.
After purchasing a few school items, they sat down at the lunch counter and tried to order soft drinks and doughnuts. They were denied
service, but they refused to leave. They remained seated at the counter
until the store closed. The next day more students returned to sit in,
and within two months sit-ins involving thousands were unfolding in
some thirty Southern cities, largely emanating from historically Black
colleges and universities.

There had been similar protests in previous decades, most recently
in 1957 at the Royal Ice Cream Parlor in Durham, North Carolina. In
1935 Howard University student Kenneth Clark, the psychologist
who would become famous because of his instrumental work in the
Brown v. Board of Education case, was arrested while protesting with
fellow students against segregated restaurants in Washington, D.C.
In 1943 Howard University law student Pauli Murray led university
women in protest against segregated restaurants near her campus. In

1950 Mary Church Terrell led protests against segregation that included a sit-in at Thompson's Restaurant in downtown Washington, D.C. The Montgomery Bus Boycott took place from 1955 to 1956. But the Greensboro sit-ins and those that followed would have far greater impact in battering the walls of segregation.

The sit-ins did two things. They gave rise to the Student Nonviolent Coordinating Committee (SNCC), and they revitalized—with Black student energy—the Congress of Racial Equality (CORE), which in 1960 was largely northern and largely white. More than most, as they evolved, these two organizations pushed forward the old tradition of grassroots community organizing. After all, enslaved Africans had not sat in at plantation manor dining rooms or marched in nonviolent protest on auction blocks. Rather, they had organized escapes, secret schools, rebellions, sabotages, and work slowdowns, and sometimes even assassinations, which was one of the biggest fears of white owners living on plantations and being served their meals by enslaved Black people.

Ella Baker, someone who should be much better known, was critical in the organizing that emerged from the sit-ins. Her activism brought together generations of Black struggle. The 1960 surge in youth activism drew her immediate attention. Recognizing that the activist leaders did not know one another, she decided they needed to meet and exchange ideas. On Easter weekend in 1960, she brought them together for a student leadership conference, held at Shaw University in Raleigh, North Carolina. She had received $800 for this purpose from Reverend Martin Luther King, Jr., who was also very conscious of this new wave of young activism. King wanted to see the formation of a student wing to the Southern Christian Leadership Conference (SCLC), an organization he had formed after the Montgomery Bus Boycott. Baker was the SCLC's temporary executive director and one of the South's most respected political organizers. As the NAACP director of branches in the 1940s, she had organized chapters throughout the region.

Almost from the opening of the conference, she suggested to the student leaders that they might want to consider forming their own organization. She had long been uncomfortable with the male supremacist attitude found among many in the SCLC leadership and was on the way out of the organization.

More important than her discontent over how the SCLC responded to her suggestions and ideas because she was a woman, she was also disappointed at the SCLC's lack of commitment to community organizing, notwithstanding Septima Clark's Citizenship School program. Leadership was top-down. As Reverend King said following his selection as pastor of Dexter Avenue Church in Montgomery, Alabama, "Authority flows from the pulpit to the pew, not from the pew to the pulpit."

"You have begun something that is bigger than a hamburger," Ella Baker told the conference in her opening address. To make real change, she stressed, you must organize from the bottom up, empowering those at the bottom. Years later, elaborating on leadership, she would say,

> In government service and political life I have always felt it was a handicap for oppressed people to depend so largely on a leader, because unfortunately in our culture, the charismatic leader usually becomes a leader because he has found a spot in the public limelight. . . . There is also the danger in our culture that, because a person is called upon to give public statements and is acclaimed by the establishment, such a person gets to the point of believing he is the movement . . . and they don't do the work of actually organizing people.

The emphasis on community organizing does not diminish the importance of legal strategies such as those that led to the 1954 *Brown v. Board of Education* decision or the lobbying of Congress. Other currents, such as the effects of World War II, certainly shaped the civil rights struggle in this era as well.

Ella Baker was the most important influence on SNCC's movement into the organizing that powered Black struggle in the South. In less than a year, a small core of students left their college campuses

to work as full-time organizers in the Black Belt South. In many instances, they traveled in the network Baker had built as NAACP director of branches. A similar process was under way with CORE,
especially in Louisiana and North Carolina. And in the rural counties
of the Black Belt, these young "field secretaries" quickly learned that
to most who lived there, restaurant desegregation was unimportant.
In the Black Belt, gaining power to control their lives meant gaining
the vote, which seemed to offer the best path toward change and empowerment.

The rampant violence that organizers from SNCC and CORE
encountered as they attempted to mobilize and organize for voting
rights is still largely untold. It was not the kind of violence wielded
against the marches in Selma or Birmingham but rather assassinations and bombings in out-of-the-way places that never commanded
press attention. It included beatings on the steps of county courthouses.

And this violence was protected by local and state authority. The
reluctance of the federal government to provide any protection is also
an important and too often ignored part of this story. The civil rights
movement is in many ways best described as a slow process during
which organizers learned to dig in and win enough trust with people
to challenge a system—and *system* must be emphasized here—that
had been in place virtually since the Civil War.

The Black Belt communities, however, were not entirely or even
mostly submissive to white terror. There was strength beneath the
surface. As the civil rights movement reached these rural communities where Black people were concentrated, residents on plantations
and in small towns chose carefully, reading the political climate surrounding their lives with the same care they used to anticipate weather
or crops. Not until the passage of the 1965 Voting Rights Act did
Black people in significant numbers begin to show up at county
courthouses to register to vote. Still, even at less visible levels, they
gave support, sometimes only verbal. They fed organizers in their
homes and protected them, sometimes with weapons. They opened
church doors. World War II and Korean War veterans were especially
supportive of the movement. Having been told that they were fight-

ing for freedom and democracy overseas, they were unwilling to accept anything less at home.

We are now in another era of intense activism, shaped by young movements such as Black Lives Matter. The political work and grassroots organizing of civil rights activists of the 1950s and '60s paved the way.

1964–1969

BLACK POWER

PENIEL JOSEPH

———

I FIRST ENCOUNTERED BLACK POWER THROUGH MALCOLM X. As a junior high school student in New York City during the 1980s, I saw his image while watching the extraordinary *Eyes on the Prize* television documentary.

Malcolm's bold critique of white supremacy, Western colonialism, and anti-Black racial violence embodied the Black Power movement. All this seemed to contrast with the passionate call for Black citizenship through nonviolent suffering extolled by Dr. Martin Luther King, Jr., another figure covered extensively in the documentary.

Contemporary social justice movements, ranging from Black Lives Matter (BLM) to efforts to end mass incarceration, stand on the shoulders of Black Power activists who led a sprawling, intersectional, multigenerational human rights movement whose universal call for justice has been obscured by its basis in the particular struggle of Black people.

Malcolm X represents Black Power's most crucial avatar. On August 20, 1964, Malcolm appeared at the Organization of African Unity's Cairo conference, where he lobbied African heads of state to publicly denounce America's mistreatment of Blacks as a human rights violation. The most vocal opponent of white supremacy of his generation, Malcolm defined Black Power as a radical movement for political, economic, and cultural self-determination, one rooted in anticolonial, antiracist, and anti-imperial politics. Malcolm challenged the Black community—most pointedly King and other civil rights activists—to reimagine the struggle for Black citizenship as part of a global pan-African and human rights struggle.

Although Black Power would burst onto the national stage with Stokely Carmichael's call for "Black Power!" in the evening humidity of Greenwood, Mississippi, two years later, Malcolm gave the movement its shape, texture, and framework. He did so through his unrelenting pursuit of Black dignity both as a member of the Nation of Islam and as an independent organizer of the Muslim Mosque Incorporated and the Organization of Afro-American Unity.

After Malcolm's February 21, 1965, assassination in New York City, Black Power's visibility grew exponentially. Thousands of Black students, activists, and ordinary citizens drawn to Malcolm's call for political self-determination created study groups, Black student unions, and independent political parties with the goal of achieving citizenship through political power, racial solidarity, and cultural transformation. Historical events accelerated the already-fertile political context. The signing of the Voting Rights Act (VRA) on August 6, 1965, marked the high point of the heroic period of the modern civil rights movement. And yet landmark legislation proved ineffective in the face of the depth and breadth of racial injustice in America. Less than a week after the VRA was signed into law, Watts, Los Angeles, exploded in violence after police assaulted a Black man accused of theft, exposing the face of police brutality, segregation, racial violence, and poverty.

Urban rebellions in major American cities inspired protest, political organizing, and poetry. The Black Arts Repertory Theatre and School (BARTS), founded in 1965 by the activist-poet Amiri Baraka (LeRoi Jones), culled aspects of Malcolm's call for pride, dignity, and self-love into a cultural movement that was determined to reimagine Black history and culture as an antiracist political weapon capable of defeating injustice and nourishing wounded Black souls. The Black Arts movement introduced the world to the brilliant writings of Sonia Sanchez, Nikki Giovanni, Larry Neal, and Haki Madhubuti, extraordinary artists who redefined the contours of Black identity for subsequent generations.

On June 16, 1966, Stokely Carmichael, a community organizer and chairman of the Student Nonviolent Coordinating Committee, emerged as the brash, telegenic face of Black Power. Trinidadian born, raised in the Bronx, and sanctified in the early civil rights struggles that found him celebrating his twentieth birthday on a Mississippi prison farm, Carmichael underwent a remarkable transformation from a civil rights militant who deeply admired King and the social-democratic peace activist Bayard Rustin, into the best-known radical activist of his generation. Following his release from the prison in Greenwood, Mississippi, for trying to put up a tent during a three-week civil rights march through the Magnolia State, Carmichael unleashed the speech that changed his life and the movement. "This is the twenty-seventh time that I've been arrested," Carmichael told a crowd of six hundred. "I ain't going to jail no more. The only way we gonna stop them white men from whuppin' us is to take over. What we gonna start saying now is Black Power!"

Black Power scandalized the nation, with whites interpreting the cry as a call for retribution and Blacks instantly embracing the slogan as an opportunity for political self-determination. Carmichael emerged as a major leader, intellectual, and celebrity: the Black Power movement's rock star. Black Power increased his personal access to, and political disagreements with, Martin Luther King, Jr.

In October 1966, at the University of California in Berkeley, Carmichael linked Black Power, the Vietnam War, and the struggles against white supremacy and imperialism to a larger and global freedom movement that electrified the New Left. He offered a blueprint for Black radicals to internationalize the movement and set the stage for the emergence of some of the era's most important political groups, most notably the Black Panthers. Black Power activists paid a steep cost for openly advocating an antiracist political revolution in America and around the world. Local, state, federal, and international surveillance and police agencies that once stalked Malcolm and Martin now shadowed Stokely and the wider movement, deploying counterintelligence measures that monitored, harassed, imprisoned, and at times led to the deaths of scores of activists.

Malcolm's death, Stokely's rise, and Vietnam radicalized Martin Luther King, Jr. King imbibed aspects of Black Power while rejecting any hints of violence. King's most robust antiwar speeches followed Carmichael's lead at Berkeley, and on April 15, 1967, at the largest antiwar demonstration, at the time, in American history, they shared the stage outside the United Nations. Black Power forced King, the prince of peace, to acknowledge that his own nation was "the biggest purveyor of violence in the world." The sentiment poisoned King's relationship with President Lyndon Johnson and galvanized racist opposition against civil rights and Black Power activism.

The Black Panthers mixed revolutionary Black nationalism, socialism, and Marxism into a daring blend of revolutionary politics that, over time, galvanized millions of activists around the world. The group's ten-point program called for an end to police brutality, poverty, failing schools, and racism. Panther leaders including Kathleen Cleaver, Huey P. Newton, Bobby Seale, and Elaine Brown became icons of an interpretation of Black Power that viewed revolution as based more on class than race. In 1968 Carmichael emerged as the "honorary prime minister" of the Black Panther Party as part of his efforts to help free imprisoned minister of defense Huey P. Newton. The Panther-SNCC alliance proved to be short-lived, riven by political and ideological differences. A little more than a year later, Carmichael resigned his affiliation with the group. By this time, Carmichael had married the South African singer Miriam Makeba and relocated to Conakry, Guinea, where he studied under former Ghanaian prime minister Kwame Nkrumah and Guinea's own Sékou Touré. Always ready for revolution, Carmichael (who would adopt the name Kwame Ture in honor of both political leaders) now considered pan-Africanism to be the highest stage of Black Power and vowed to spread that political message from the continent itself.

By 1969, Black Power had redefined the contours of the Black freedom struggle. Black Power radicalism influenced and helped shape Black Panthers in California and New Haven serving poor Black children free breakfast, welfare rights organizers in New Orleans, college and high school students in New York City, and Black feminists such as Angela Davis, Frances Beal, and members of the Third World Women's Alliance. Mainstream politics noticed: President Richard Nixon supported "Black capitalism" while Black Power and Urban League head Whitney Young belatedly championed the phrase after initially denouncing it. "Say It Loud, I'm Black and I'm Proud!" by soul singer James Brown became a catchphrase that popularized one aspect of a movement that Malcolm X had helped birth only a few years before.

Black Power survived its heyday to be institutionalized in American popular and political culture in the rise of Black elected officials, the development of Black studies programs in higher education, the spread of Black History Month, and the deeply ingrained and globally Black political consciousness that informs contemporary Black-led social movements. Black Power sought universality, however imperfectly, from the lived experiences of Black people. BLM activists have done the same by linking an expansive definition of freedom and global citizenship to movements to end mass incarceration, racial violence, sexism, environmental racism, public school and residential segregation, and inequality in every facet of American life. In doing so, they have built on both Malcolm X's and Martin Luther King, Jr.'s notions of Black dignity and Black citizenship. They have radically expanded these political frameworks by centering the most marginalized Black identities as the beating heart of a new, more inclusive struggle. It is a holistic struggle for human rights that seeks universal justice through the lens of Black people's historic oppression and struggle for self-determination, culminating in the long-overdue quest for Black power.

1969–1974

PROPERTY

KEEANGA-YAMAHTTA TAYLOR

———

THE SUMMER OF 1968 SAW THE MOST FAR-REACHING AND historic changes to housing policy in American history. In the days after the murder of Dr. Martin Luther King, Jr., on April 4, Congress finally passed a federal fair housing law to ban all forms of racist discrimination in the rental or sale of housing. Then in June the Supreme Court ruled in the landmark case *Jones v. Mayer* that all racist discrimination in housing must immediately end.

In a departure from most legal decisions regarding racist discrimination, the Court rooted its actions in the Thirteenth Amendment, which banned slavery, as opposed to the Fourteenth Amendment, which called for equal treatment. It argued that residential segregation was redolent of slavery in its collective exclusion of African Americans from the benefits of freedom, including the right to move about in whichever way they saw fit.

In August 1968, President Lyndon Johnson signed into law one of his last major bills aimed at curing the so-called urban crisis. Many envisioned the Housing and Urban Development Act of 1968 as a tool to produce an unprecedented 26 million units of new and rehabilitated housing within ten years. In addition to the creation of millions of units of housing, the centerpiece of the legislation was a new low-income homeownership program, administered by the Department of Housing and Urban Development (HUD). The legislation did not specify that it was targeting African Americans, but the acute urban housing crisis had been a catalyst for the urban uprisings.

The homeownership program had been partly inspired by an earlier effort in 1967 among life insurance executives who formed a con-
sortium to create a billion-dollar mortgage pool that was intended to
finance Black businesses, apartment developments, and single-family
housing in areas that would, under normal circumstances, have been
redlined. They called their organization the Joint Committee on
Urban Problems. By the fall of 1969, they had pledged another $1 bil-
lion to continue to create more housing opportunities for African
Americans in the "urban core."

The changes in U.S. housing policy during the late 1960s and early
'70s seemed to open to Black Americans the possibility of meaningful
citizenship and real access to the riches of the country's economy. This
historic shift in policy had been made possible by the end of federal
redlining by the Federal Housing Administration (FHA). In the two
decades after World War II, the FHA had become well known for
championing suburban development around the white nuclear family.
Now the FHA was poised to use its power and influence to develop
Black communities within American cities. This shift from exclusion
to inclusion of African Americans also fit with President Richard
Nixon's stated goal to develop Black capitalism in the cities.

Beneath the rosy talk about urban "redevelopment," Black capitalism, and homeownership, however, the commitment to inequality,
exploitation, and residential segregation continued. While new forms
of finance capital were allowed into the cities to fund new initiatives,
African Americans did not have the mobility to leave. Exclusionary
zoning in suburbs and the commitment to racist business practices by
bankers and real estate brokers kept Black buyers and renters confined to urban spaces or to new but still segregated suburban spaces.
The predominant role of real estate and banks in the production of
the new and rehabilitated housing, as well as the low-income homeownership program, invariably tied the racist business practices of
these businesses to federal housing policy.

Where the FHA had once excluded African Americans from participating in the conventional real estate market, it now made Black
buyers vulnerable to new exploitative and predatory practices. These

public-private partnerships provided methods for the extractive relationship between African Americans and capital.

Very quickly, brokers and bankers wielded the new homeownership programs to enrich themselves while leaving poor Black families
homeless with shattered credit. Speculators and real estate brokers
took hold of dilapidated urban properties, performed cosmetic re-
pairs, then flipped the properties to Black families, often headed by
Black women. The terms of the programs had allowed mortgage
bankers to be repaid in full if the owners went into foreclosure, and
because mortgage payments were tied to the income of the owner—
not to the value of the house—appraisers working for the FHA were
easily enticed to take bribes to inflate the value of the city houses.
Mortgage bankers who made their money on originating mortgages
and other fees were quick to foreclose, recoup their investment, and
begin the practice all over again. Everyone got paid except the poor
and working-class Black families who were preyed upon. And within
a few years, nearly seventy thousand homes had fallen into foreclosure and tens of thousands more were in default, meaning they were
only a few payments away from foreclosure.

As news of the fraud and corruption in these programs peaked in
1972, headlines rarely got the story right. The real story was that the
real estate industry and mortgage bankers were fleecing African
Americans with an assist from an utterly passive federal government.
The government's failure to seriously enforce its own fair housing
laws—as demonstrated by the paltry funding appropriated to fight
racist housing discrimination—had left Black buyers and renters vulnerable to the racism of the real estate industry. Instead, members of
Congress, the media, and the private sector itself pinned the crisis in
the programs on the disproportionately Black program participants.
Everyone involved described Black mothers, in particular, as "unso-
phisticated buyers," even as white businessmen, a U.S. senator, and
multiple agents working within the FHA were indicted for conspiracy and fraud.

In 1973 Richard Nixon used the scandal surrounding the HUD
homeownership programs as an excuse to impose a moratorium on all

subsidized housing programs. Nixon dismissed HUD as the nation's "largest slumlord" and argued that HUD's crisis was proof that local government, as opposed to the federal government, should make its own decisions regarding housing. It was an argument fueled on "common sense" that confirmed the suspicion and hostility with which federal programs were held.

Nixon and his replacement, Gerald Ford, used the failures of the 1968 HUD Act to hoist their new approach to low-income housing and urban development: the Housing and Community Development Act (HCDA), passed in August 1974. The HCDA deployed "block grants," instead of direct federal appropriations, to fund federal programs. Block grants were "blocks" of money sent to localities, which would decide how the money was spent. While this fed into the folksy notion that locals knew better, it ignored that for decades African Americans had called on the federal government to protect them from the unchecked, abject racism in local governments.

The legislation also acquiesced to the segregative impulses that had guided much federal decision making regarding housing policies. Ford decided to focus on "existing" housing instead of new building for low-income housing, willfully conceding the status quo. All too often "existing" or used housing was in cities, while new construction was affordable only in outlying and mostly white suburban localities. Six years after the experiment initiated by the HUD Act, the federal approach to housing returned to its roots of local control and segregated housing.

This history is critical to understanding why some communities came to be designated as prime or subprime in the color-blind discourse of 1990s and 2000s. The foreclosures hastened by reckless federal policies unleashed by the 1968 HUD Act, along with a lackadaisical routine to address housing discrimination, legitimized the devaluation of Black homes and Black communities. These became the pretext, in a post–civil rights world, for treating Black housing consumers differently: from higher or adjustable interest rates to higher risk fees to the subprime designation.

The crisis from the 1970s also rehearsed earlier arguments that African Americans lacked sophistication and basic impulse control when it came to purchasing property. Instead, they wanted more than they could handle and nearly crashed the economy as a result. Then as now, it was a deft way of turning the discussion away from the corporate underpinnings of public policy—in this case, housing policy. It was then and it is now a failure to grapple with the central contradiction of public policies that rely on private sector institutions to fulfill them. The reliance on the private sector to address the social provision of housing has resulted in public policies that reflect the racism embedded in the U.S. housing market.

This has continued to hasten housing insecurity within African American communities—from new lows in Black homeownership to the overrepresentation of African Americans among the rent-burdened. The continued American reliance upon the private sector as the main source of housing production has meant a continuation of the inequality that systematically disadvantages African Americans in search of home.

1974-1979

COMBAHEE RIVER COLLECTIVE

BARBARA SMITH

——

IN 1974 THE CITY OF BOSTON WAS IN THE MIDDLE OF A RACE war. A federal judge had ruled that public schools must finally desegregate and establish a busing plan to make it happen. Boston's particular brand of virulent racism was well known to members of the Black community. But across the nation, many were surprised by supposedly liberal white Bostonians' violent opposition to integration, which rivaled anything that had occurred in the Deep South more than a decade earlier.

In the mid-1970s, Black Power and Black Nationalism were dominant political ideologies. Within these movements, roles for Black women were frequently even more circumscribed than they had been during the civil rights era. Since 1969, the Nixon administration had implemented numerous strategies calculated to roll back hard-won gains in civil rights. Organizations were dealing with the repercussions of the FBI's decades of surveillance and its murderous disruption of the Black liberation struggle. During the mid-1970s, the federal government began investigating lesbian feminist communities and impaneled grand juries to locate women radicals who had gone underground to elude capture.

In this atmosphere of racial turmoil and right-wing backlash, a handful of Black women came together in 1974 to form the group that became the Combahee River Collective. We were sick of the violence. We were sick of being voiceless. We were sick of being exploited. We were sick of being told to walk three or seven paces behind. We were sick of being invisible. We were sick of it all. We wanted and needed Black feminism. Since there were few indications that such existed, we decided to build it for ourselves.

The Combahee River Collective was a Black feminist organization that worked in Boston from 1974 through 1980. Originally a chapter of the National Black Feminist Organization, the collective decided in 1975 to become independent. We named ourselves after the Combahee River, where Harriet Tubman led a military raid during the Civil War that freed more than 750 enslaved people. During the second half of the 1970s, the collective engaged in action on multiple fronts including study, political analysis, protests, campaigns, cultural production, and coalition work around a range of issues, all with the objective of defining and building Black feminism.

Combahee was never just about talk. Most of us had been politically active well before Combahee, including in the movement to end the war in Vietnam, the Black Panthers, Black student organizing, the Congress of Racial Equality (CORE), the Institute of the Black World, Marxist Leninist organizing, support for Eritrean independence, and more.

Not long after its founding, Combahee supported campaigns to free Joan Little and Ella Ellison, Black women who had been unfairly prosecuted by the criminal injustice system. When Dr. Kenneth Edelin, a Black physician, was convicted of manslaughter in 1975 for performing a legal abortion at Boston City Hospital, we joined in the effort to get his conviction overturned.

In 1977 Combahee initiated a series of seven political retreats held over three years in locations around the East Coast, where Black feminists who did not live in Boston could meet, strategize, and work together. Among those who regularly participated were the writers Cheryl Clarke, Akasha (Gloria) Hull, and Audre Lorde.

We accomplished all this and much more while going to our day jobs, going to school, and struggling to get by financially. Combahee never had an airy, spacious office. We never had an office at all. We had no executive director or staff. We did not have funders. If we needed money, usually for photocopying, we would take up a collection. What we did have was each other and a vision.

After we stopped meeting at the Cambridge Women's Center, we met in each other's apartments. As serious as we were about the work, our meetings were full of laughter. *Saturday Night Live* premiered in the fall of 1975, and we often began with recaps of the latest episode. We always shared food, most of it homemade. Demita Frazier talked with us about vegetarianism, alternative healing, and spirituality. In the summer, we met by the Charles River and took day trips to local beaches. One of our most memorable outings was to Amandla, a concert held in 1979 to benefit the anti-apartheid struggle in South Africa, featuring Bob Marley and Patti LaBelle.

Most people know about us because of our Combahee River Collective Statement. In 1977 my sister Beverly Smith, Demita Frazier, and I wrote the statement for Zillah Eisenstein's *Capitalist Patriarchy and the Case for Socialist Feminism*. With a clear anticapitalist perspective, the statement captured the voices and concerns of Black women and articulated the concept of simultaneous, interlocking oppressions, laying the groundwork for intersectionality. By explicitly challenging homophobia, the statement was groundbreaking, although some, particularly members of our Black community, viewed it as incendiary.

Few are aware that the widely used and often-maligned concept of "identity politics" originated in the statement. Attacked by both the right and the left, identity politics has been consistently misunderstood. What we meant was that Black women had a right to determine their own political agendas based upon who they were and the multiple systems of oppression that targeted them. Although narrow interpretations of identity politics have been used to justify separatism, Combahee believed in coalitions and was open to working with anyone with whom we shared political values and goals.

On January 29, 1979, the bodies of two teenaged Black women were found dumped in Roxbury. During the next four months, twelve Black women were murdered, all but one in Black neighborhoods. When Combahee began, a race war was raging. Now we faced a war on Black women. The collective's Black feminist analysis and relationships with diverse segments of the community put us in a unique position to provide leadership in a time of crisis.

We produced a pamphlet titled *Six Black Women: Why Did They Die* about the pervasive reality of violence against women and made a particular effort to circulate it in the Black and Latino/a community. The murders were initially framed as racially motivated, despite the fact that all the victims were women and some of them had been raped. The pamphlet insisted that the murders had to be understood in the context of both sexual and racial violence in order to organize effectively and to increase Black women's safety. We eventually distributed forty thousand copies and were a major force in building coalitions among communities that had not previously worked together, especially people of color and antiracist white feminists. The fact that we did this bridge building as out Black lesbians was unprecedented. All that the collective had stood for and built since 1974 culminated in our response to the Roxbury murders.

Almost half a century ago we could not have known that in the twenty-first century, the paradigm-shifting Black Lives Matter movement would arise and use Black feminist analysis to address injustices not primarily rooted in gender or sexuality. We could not know that the Colectiva Feminista en Construcción, which was centrally involved in unseating the governor of Puerto Rico in 2019, would draw inspiration from Combahee.

In many ways, the equivalent of political lightning struck in 1974 to bring together in one improbable place the women who created Combahee. I am grateful to have been there for the creation.

AND THE RECORD REPEATS

CHET'LA SEBREE

───

There's dust, a scratch in a groove,
and here we are repeating
the same two seconds of "Strange Fruit."

It's the same sound from the 78 rpm
to the vintage vinyl to which we listen
in our apartments, where we return

bruised and bloodied and beaten,
unrecognizable in our mothers' arms,
if we find the right path back to them.

All our lives we've cried a rallying cry,
from the river, from the water wanting
baptism, a rebirth to an earth

where it wasn't dangerous to be
young and gifted and us—slinging
school bags over shoulders—where

we could go to church and
little Black girls could remain
little Black girls

not only in memoriam.
Through a liturgy, no,
a litany, we learned to pray.

Warriors taught us
to dance through minefields—
pirouette and grand jeté a revelation

in the face of annihilation,
bouquets blossoming
between cracks in concrete.

In pressed page
and in song
and on stage,

we felt the weight
of sun and rainbows and shade,
patient tenderness and pennilessness,

felt a rhapsody reverberate our ribcages.
The good Lorde told us
we weren't meant to survive,

but we've always been good
at going about our lives
in factories and on our knees

in houses we cleaned
with tables at which
we would never eat.

But still we fell in line,
took to boot, tank, and sky.
In Busan, in Ardennes, in Hue,

young men threw themselves
over booby trap and grenade
never to return to an ostensible parade.

Strangers in a homeland
still no man's—
the barbed lancets of a bee.

But, still, there was honey.
There were arias and
Chisholm-chiseled sightlines

as the tale of our roots writhed.
So we broke step
as we dreamed dreams

deferred again and again,
as we congregated
over hot buttered toast,

took our seats at the table,
called on our mothers
to grease and braid hair of babes,

as we curled close together
in Harlem and Trenton
on nights alight with our injuries.

To the disquieting phrasing
of *Black bodies swinging,*
we still curl close

to loved ones
in different cities,
teach our children

their ABCs and 123s,
how to pas de bourrées
and kick-ball-change,

as we work to lift
our fists, the needle,
put on a new record to play.

PART TEN

1979–1984

THE WAR ON DRUGS

James Forman, Jr.

━━

I N THE SPRING OF 1983, AT A CRUCIAL MOMENT IN THE HIS-
tory of American drug policy, Harlem congressman Charles Rangel
gaveled to order the House Select Committee on Narcotics Abuse
and Control. In Washington, D.C., heroin's resurgence had led residents to deluge city officials with letters demanding relief from the
growing number of addicts congregating on corners and sleeping on
park benches. In Los Angeles, phencyclidine, more commonly known
as angel dust or PCP, seemed to be taking over; the *Los Angeles Sentinel,* the city's leading Black newspaper, complained that the city had
become "the PCP capital of the world." In New York and Miami,
entrepreneurs were discovering that baking powder, cocaine, and a
stove were all they needed to create the inexpensive and potent new
product that would soon come to be called crack.

President Ronald Reagan, for his part, had already seized on illegal drug use as a political issue. "We're making no excuses for drugs—
hard, soft, or otherwise," Reagan said in a radio address to the nation
in October 1982. "Drugs are bad, and we're going after them." Repeating what would become one of his signature phrases, Reagan claimed
that "we've taken down the surrender flag and run up the battle flag.
And we're going to win the war on drugs."

Decades later, we know what that war has helped produce: ruined
lives, hollowed-out communities, and mass incarceration. But could
the war have been fought differently?

Dozens of witnesses appeared before Rangel's committee with an answer to that question. Almost to a person, they agreed: if America was going to meet its drug crisis, it needed to make a robust commitment to drug treatment. According to the head of the National Institute for Drug Abuse, people who participated in adequately funded programs reduced their drug use, committed fewer crimes, and were more likely to find and keep a job.

Treatment didn't always work, of course—some programs weren't very good, while others limped along on shoestring budgets, and even the best ones failed sometimes. Addiction is a terrible disease, witnesses explained, and addicts often needed multiple chances before finding success. But treatment worked better than any of the alternatives and at lower cost. Since you could put eight people in a drug program for the cost of a single prison bed, treatment was what one New York official called "the cheapest game in town."

The biggest problem with drug treatment was that there wasn't enough of it. When a national association surveyed states about their treatment capacity, 94 percent said that they couldn't meet their citizens' needs. In one twenty-four-hour period, nine heroin overdose victims were brought unconscious to Boston City Hospital; emergency personnel saved them all, but because every program in the city was full, officials couldn't offer treatment to any of them.

It was a powerful case. But not for the first—or last—time, politics, ideology, fear, and racism would prove more powerful. Ignoring the call to fund more treatment, research, and prevention, the Reagan administration did the opposite and shifted funds toward law enforcement. Where the Nixon administration had devoted two-thirds of the federal drug budget to treatment and one-third to law enforcement, Reagan reversed that ratio to what it has remained since: two-thirds law enforcement, one-third treatment. A New Jersey official, describing the massive waiting lists for programs in his state, complained to Rangel's committee that this reallocation of funding constituted "simple abandonment by the Federal Government of the prevention and treatment field."

By cutting treatment in the midst of a drug crisis, the Reagan administration established the template that would define drug policy in America for decades to come. The consequences have been grave and lasting. Most immediately, cutting funding for treatment denied help to people in pain. After all, behind every statistic presented in the testimony before Rangel's committee were people, most of them poor, struggling to keep their families and lives together in the face of dependency and addiction.

But drug warriors of the era succeeded in presenting drug users in a different light. Defining addiction as an individual choice and personal failure, they contended that society bore no responsibility for the consequences. If a person became dependent on or addicted to drugs, it was because they were weak, selfish, irresponsible, or depraved. Female drug users were especially frequent targets of denunciation. For example, when asked about the challenge of caring for pregnant women addicted to crack, D.C.'s health commissioner blamed the women. "The response of a rational person would be to come in and find out whether they are pregnant, but we aren't talking about rational people," he said. "We are talking about women who simply do not care. The maternal instinct is being destroyed."

Claims that pregnant users didn't care about their children shifted attention away from the core issue: the fact that the government was failing to treat its neediest citizens. Washington, D.C., for example, had the resources to assist only one in ten of the city's addicts. Just 13 percent of New York City's drug treatment programs accepted pregnant women addicted to cocaine, while the city's residential treatment facilities had space for only 2 percent of its heroin and cocaine addicts.

The refusal to fund drug treatment programs also helped pave the way for an unprecedented experiment in prison building. With drug markets proliferating, overdose deaths rising, and treatment centers closing, the American impulse toward harsh justice found full expression. Almost nothing was out of bounds. Legislators in Delaware contemplated bringing back the whipping post for drug sellers. Federal officials proposed they receive the death penalty.

Though whipping posts never became law, the same vengeful impulse found an outlet in extreme prison sentences. The federal government led the way with the now-infamous hundred-to-one crack-cocaine ratio, under which a person possessing just 5 grams (about 1½ teaspoons) of crack faced the same mandatory sentence as somebody possessing 500 grams (2½ cups) of powder. While racially neutral on its face, the crack/powder distinction combined with discriminatory policing and prosecution strategies to produce flagrant racial disparities in arrest and incarceration rates. Even though most crack users were white, Black people were seven times more likely to go to federal prison for crack offenses.

Prominent voices in the Black community sometimes joined in the calls for more severe penalties for drug sellers. Editors at the *Los Angeles Sentinel* called for drug dealers to be "tarred and feathered, burned at the stake, castrated, and any other horrendous thing which can be imagined." Maxine Waters, then in the California state legislature, led a successful effort to increase penalties for the sale of PCP. Johnnie Cochran, Los Angeles County's first Black assistant district attorney, said that those who sold PCP "should be dealt with swiftly, surely and in those instances where the facts warrant it—harshly."

To be sure, African Americans who fell prey to the punitive impulse often combined their call for tougher penalties with another set of demands—they asked the government to address the underlying inequalities that led to drug use or, at a minimum, provide treatment for addicts and heavy users. Representative Rangel, for example, asked the Reagan administration for "more prosecutors, more judges, more agents, and more prisons," yet he also pressed it to address "the Nation's chronically underfunded treatment and prevention programs." But the strategy of asking for both prisons and treatment proved to be a failure. Instead of both, Rangel—and the Black community—got only the prisons.

Rising levels of abuse, addiction, and drug-related violence should have been a sign that something was wrong with America. It should have led the nation to focus on the myriad ways in which 350 years of white supremacy had produced persistent Black suffering and disadvantage. It should have caused politicians to interrogate the cumulative impact of convict leasing, lynching, redlining, school segregation, and drinking water poisoned with lead. Instead of asking, "What kind of people are *they* that would use and sell drugs?" the nation should have been asking a question that, to this day, demands an answer: "What kind of people are *we* that build prisons while closing treatment centers?"

1984–1989

THE HIP-HOP GENERATION

BAKARI KITWANA

——

I VOTED FOR THE FIRST TIME IN A NATIONAL ELECTION IN 1988. Although I was eligible to vote in 1984, I felt I had no stake in U.S. presidential politics. It was not an uncommon view for young Black men in those days. But something changed for me and many others of my generation between Jesse Jackson's run for president in 1984 and his subsequent campaign in 1988.

In 1986 seventeen-year-old Rakim of the hip-hop duo Eric B and Rakim began "dropping science" in his rhymes, taking the art form to new lyrical heights and depths. He drew inspiration from the teachings of the Five Percent Nation, whose philosophy of Black empowerment resonated with young Black leaders in the New York City region during the early 1980s.

"I found it almost divine the way the Five Percent Nation affected the evolution of hip-hop," Rakim recalls in his memoir, *Sweat the Technique: Revelations on Creativity from the Lyrical Genius*. "We [were] equipped with a language and information intricate to our studies that empowered us. So it was right up our alley to want to express ourselves through rapping. We felt we had something to say that was unique to our time."

Less than a year later, albums would follow from Eric B and Rakim, Public Enemy, and Boogie Down Productions that similarly tapped into core messages of the 1960s and '70s—referencing book titles, honing in on aspects of Black history, and sampling speeches of Black men such as Malcolm X, Louis Farrakhan, Kwame Touré, and the music of James Brown. Collectively, they pioneered the subgenre that would come to be known as "conscious hip-hop," a style of music that, along with Jesse Jackson's campaigns for president, signaled the convergence of civil rights/Black Power–era politics with an emerging hip-hop political voice in a way that made Blackness cool for a new generation.

To be sure, Jackson's presidential campaigns were the culmination of late 1960s and early '70s activism that had led to the Gary, Indiana, Black Political Convention of 1972. The convention ushered in the greatest wave of Black elected officials that the country had seen since Reconstruction, including the historic election of Harold Washington as Chicago's first Black mayor—right in Jackson's backyard.

Part of this was the result of the Voting Rights Act of 1965. However, since Blacks won the right to vote, Black voter participation had remained at essentially the same level for three presidential election cycles until it surged to 55.8 percent during Jackson's historic run in 1984.

A protégé of Dr. Martin Luther King, Jr., Jackson was charismatic and bold, and gave voice to a vision that went far beyond anything U.S. presidential candidates had previously articulated. Jackson demanded the totality of freedom and inclusion that Black leaders had demanded of the United States for generations.

What Jackson advocated for the nation ("America is not a blanket but a quilt") was also in sync with hip-hop's own emerging philosophy (from DJ Kool Herc and Afrika Bambaataa to KRS-one—"peace, love, unity and having fun" and universal humanism).

The early 1980s was also marked by Louis Farrakhan's rise to the leadership of the new Nation of Islam (NOI). In 1985 I was among a group of Black students who chartered a bus to take students to attend Farrakhan's national coming-out in New York City when he was rebuilding the NOI in alignment with what he saw as the original vision of founder Elijah Muhammad. Many young people joined the Nation, including more college students and college graduates than at any point in its history. That October a 25,000-strong audience filled Madison Square Garden to hear a message of Black economic self-sufficiency and empowerment.

Farrakhan had been an avid supporter of Jesse Jackson during the 1984 campaign. To many of us, Farrakhan appealed to the more radical vision of Black political thought that we embraced at the time. When he and Jackson stood together during the campaign, they helped us imagine new possibilities beyond the historic integration versus separation divide.

Other influential voices inspired our search for a new Black political center that made sense for our time. Reaching out from college campuses to the grass roots were individuals like Julian Bond, Maulana Karenga, Sonia Sanchez, Kwame Touré, Naim Akbar, Bobby Seale, Haki Madhubuti, and Nikki Giovanni.

The 1986–87 school year jump-started a series of National Black Student Unity Conferences: the first featured keynotes by Jackson and Farrakhan and topped seven hundred attendees. Conferences would follow in 1987–88 at Howard University and at Columbia University the following school year.

All these developments, including Jackson's presidential campaign, helped shape our political consciousness. But the most significant development that captivated our generation was the emergence on the national scene of hip-hop with conscious messages of resistance.

Hip-hop in those days was not yet fully embraced as mainstream culture. It was still largely an underground phenomenon and a lived folk culture that we saw as our own. Wherever hip-hop showed up, we saw it as the source of our own entry. But even more, this convergence of Black Power generation politics with hip-hop's emerging political impulse gave our generation agency.

In 1987, on the heels of their debut, *Yo! Bum Rush the Show*, Public Enemy sampled Malcolm X's speech "Message to the Grassroots" on their single "Bring the Noise," which would become the lead single for their second album, *It Takes a Nation of Millions to Hold Us Back* (1988). Malcolm's haunting words at the start of the song hung in the air and captured the tone of the moment: "Too Black, too strong."

Similar to *It Takes a Nation of Millions*, KRS-one's *By All Means Necessary* sent Black youth scrambling for books he referenced, such as *Message to the Blackman in America* by Elijah Muhammad, *The Au-*

tobiography of Malcolm X, and *How to Eat to Live,* also by Elijah Muhammad. His album laid the groundwork for the Stop the Violence
movement. 1988 also saw the release of Eric B and Rakim's *Follow the
Leader* on July 25, one week after Jackson's second address to the
Democratic National Convention. Talib Kweli recently called *Follow
the Leader* "the most important hip-hop record ever."

1989 mirrored 1988 as a year of essential conscious hip-hop music.
Few can remember the year 1989 and not recall Chuck D's words
"1989, the year, another summer." Those words capture that singular
moment in time when nearly everyone in hip-hop was fighting the
power: Spike Lee's film *Do the Right Thing; The Cress Theory of Color
Confrontation* reprinted inside the jacket of Public Enemy's *Fear of a
Black Planet;* Queen Latifah's album *All Hail the Queen;* and Reginald
Hudlin's film *House Party* (all of which placed front and center hip-
hop's Afrocentric aesthetic such as crowns, African prints, Africa-
shaped leather medallion necklaces, and African hairstyles epitomized
by Kid and Play).

The hip-hop generation shaped American history for decades to
follow. The Million Man March in 1995, for example, was heavily supported by the hip-hop community. The 2004 National Hip-Hop Political Convention—inspired by the Gary, Indiana, convention of
1972—brought over four thousand young Black people to Newark,
New Jersey. Black youth political participation witnessed a surge during the elections of Barack Obama in 2008 and 2012. These young
Black voters were between the ages of eighteen and twenty-nine. At
the core of each of these moments is what it has meant for the hip-
hop generation to come into its own.

ANITA HILL

Salamishah Tillet

—

E VERY EVENING WHEN MY FAMILY ENTERS OUR COMFORT-able three-bedroom townhouse in downtown Newark, a large, limited-series, fire-truck-red-framed poster greets us. Originally made by the Kitchen Table Women of Color Press, the poster is a reproduction of a full-page ad taken out on November 17, 1991, in eight of our nation's largest newspapers, including *The New York Times*.

On that Sunday morning, the ad headline, "African American Women in Defense of Ourselves," appeared one month after law professor Anita Hill testified before Congress with allegations that Supreme Court nominee Clarence Thomas had sexually harassed her while he was her supervisor at the Department of Education and the Equal Employment Opportunity Commission from 1981 to 1982.

Before I received my own copy as a gift, I'd seen the poster only two other places. The first was in the foyer of Gloria Steinem's home, hanging high like mine, in spaces traditionally reserved for photographs of presidents, prime ministers, or religious symbols. The second time was in the hallway of Spelman College's famed Women's Research and Resource Center, founded by Beverly Guy-Sheftall in 1981. During both visits, I'd lose myself in a trance parsing through and memorizing the names of the more than sixteen hundred Black women who—organized by feminist scholars Barbara Ransby, Deborah King, and Elsa Barkley Brown—made history by declaring their unwavering public support for Hill.

"We were all Anita Hill at that moment," Barbara Ransby told *The Washington Post* in an interview in 2018 about the ad's origins. "Elsa set up a bank account," she recalled. "Someone had a husband who worked at an ad agency in New York. We collected lots and lots of small checks." Combining word of mouth and a 1-800 number, they raised the $50,000 necessary for the ad campaign. "Now we tweet or text," Ransby opined.

I was sixteen years old when I saw Anita Hill for the first time. In my memory, I sat glued to the television, trying to interpolate every detail of Hill's statement into my newly forming Black feminist consciousness. But the truth is, I didn't watch it live. At the actual time of her testimony, I was finishing my senior year at my predominantly white private high school in Livingston, New Jersey, and spent the hours between English class and soccer practice arguing about the merits of her allegations.

I knew many of my white classmates looked at Hill as an oddity because most of the Black women with whom they were in regular contact were their nannies at home or our school's cafeteria staff. In their suburban enclaves, Yale Law School–educated Black women did not exist. That Hill dared to stand before the all-white, all-male Senate Judiciary Committee was even more confounding.

The summer before Anita Hill testified, in her now-iconic teal linen skirt suit, with her left hand slightly hidden behind her back, her right hand held high to be sworn in, I had undergone my own political conversion. I spent the summer in Boston with my dad, first street canvassing for the National Environmental Law Center, then volunteering for the NAACP. But I also read three books that changed my life: Toni Morrison's *The Bluest Eye*, Alice Walker's *The Color Purple,* and *The Autobiography of Malcolm X* as told to Alex Haley. Because of these narratives, I learned to see how my racial and gender identities were interlinked. That if my Blackness overdetermined my past and future opportunities, my experiences as a girl heightened my vulnerability and my likelihood to be a victim of misogyny and violence.

So by the time Hill came forward, I had already had a primer into a debate that had been happening among Black people since slavery.

Reflecting on the impact of the hearings, Toni Morrison would later write, "In matters of race and gender, it is now possible and necessary, as it seemed never to have been before, to speak about these matters without the barriers, the silences, the embarrassing gaps in discourse."

Before Thomas's nomination, Thurgood Marshall was the only African American to be appointed to the Supreme Court. When Marshall announced his plan to retire in June 1991, President George H. W. Bush saw it as an opportunity to increase his support among two disparate, and increasingly dispirited, political blocs: the anti-abortion, anti-affirmative-action white American base of his own Republican Party; and right-leaning, Reagan-voting African Americans. In Clarence Thomas, a forty-three-year-old African American Republican from Pinpoint, Georgia, with only two years of experience as a federal judge, Bush found the ideal candidate to help him appeal to both these constituencies.

The dissent was immediate. The NAACP, the AFL-CIO, and the National Organization for Women (NOW) released statements vowing to fight Thomas's nomination. NOW was concerned with his stance on abortion; the AFL-CIO opposed his conservative positions. But it was the board of directors of the NAACP, the nation's largest racial justice organization, whose position stands out in a 49–1 vote. "While we appreciate the fact that Judge Thomas came up in the school of hard knocks and pulled himself up by his own bootstraps," NAACP chairman William F. Gibson said in a press conference, "our concern is for the millions of blacks who have no access to bootstraps, theirs or others."

Despite this stance, Thomas polled well among African American voters. And more important for Republicans, his nomination initially found little resistance during the Senate Judiciary Committee's confirmation hearings that September. After a few days of testimony, the committee, chaired by Senator Joe Biden (D-Del.), split its vote, moving the process to the Senate floor without a clear majority in Thomas's favor. After learning of Hill's allegations in late August, a small group of Democratic senators led by Edward Kennedy (D-Mass.) urged Biden to take up Hill's case. After weeks of going back and forth with Democratic staffers and senators over how best to protect her privacy, Hill held a press conference on October 7, 1991, and said she was willing to testify.

In those few days leading up to her appearance, we learned a few facts about her. Like Thomas, she was born into a family of Southern farmers, had graduated from Yale Law School, and was a registered Republican. At the time, Republicans erased many of the same aspects of Hill's biography that they extolled as virtues in Thomas's. Framing Thomas as a rural, working-class African American who worked his way into the upper echelon of academia and the federal government, they used his life story to discredit Hill, eventually leading to a wide-scale character assault on her. Arlen Specter (R-Penn.) accused Hill of "flat-out perjury." Republicans drew on centuries of sexist images of women as delusional, and racist ideas of Black women as hypersexual. Conservative John Doggett, a Texas businessman and lawyer, testified that Hill was an erotomaniac who fantasized about dating him.

In response, Hill revealed in great detail the extent of Thomas's harassment. "He talked about pornographic materials depicting individuals with large penises or large breasts, involved in various sex acts," she quietly recounted to the all-white, all-male Senate panel. "On several occasions, Thomas told me graphically of his own sexual prowess."

In trying to refute Hill's claims before the Senate Judiciary Committee, Thomas called the hearing "a high-tech lynching for uppity Blacks." He conjured up one of the most violent acts of America's racial history to shore up his support among white liberals and conservatives alike. Not only was he successful, he also introduced a new racial and gendered trope that was well known among African Americans but less familiar to white Americans: the Black woman as race traitor. "Having made Anita Hill into a villain, he proceeded— wittingly or not—to erase her and return to a simpler and more conventional cast," historian Nell Irvin Painter wrote.

> By the end of his story Anita Hill had lost the only role, that of villain, that his use of stereotype had allowed her. She finally disappeared, as he spun out a drama pitting the lone and per-

secuted figure of Clarence Thomas, the black man, against an army of powerful white assailants. Democratic senators became the lynch mob; Thomas became the innocent lynch victim. As symbol and as actual person, Anita Hill was no longer to be found.

By the mid-twentieth century, the horror of lynching was transformed from a material reality to a political metaphor, one that Thomas not only used to his advantage but also canonized on the national stage. When R. Kelly, Bill Cosby, and Justin Fairfax, the lieutenant governor of Virginia, fended off charges from Black women (and in the case of Cosby, white women, from over several decades as well) who accused them of rape, they compared themselves to lynching victims. It is only now, in this age of #MeToo, that such analogies have started to ring hollow.

In the 1990s, however, the battles were much more internecine. "A conversation, a serious one among black men and women, has begun in a new arena, and the contestants defy the mold," reflected Morrison.

By the end of the hearings, African American support for Thomas was the highest it had been, with 70 percent of African Americans backing his nomination and 50 percent of whites, according to an ABC News–*Washington Post* poll that was conducted the weekend after the hearings closed. The result was that Democrats and Republicans, emboldened by the public response, voted 52–48 to confirm Clarence Thomas as a justice of the Supreme Court.

The morning that the vote was announced, I was late for school. The radio in my family's car, a used beige Jaguar, whose blaring muffler always made me shrink a little out of embarrassment as we climbed the driveway of my school, was turned on. When we reached the front steps, Michael Stipe, the front man for R.E.M., wailed, "It's the End of the World as We Know It," making me pause as I refastened my jacket and looked in the mirror to smooth my hair. Even then, I knew the song was a premonition.

What I didn't know was that a year later, I'd experience this same scene of emotional shock and sartorial realignment as I walked to my dorm room, the morning after a well-respected African American man, three years my senior, sexually assaulted me. The Hill hearings had betrayed a simple and tragic truth: if I were to come forward against this upwardly mobile, Ivy League–educated Black man, most Black people would not believe me.

But I believed Hill. And Hill's words did change the world, bit by bit and for the better. Sexual harassment cases more than doubled, according to Equal Employment Opportunity Commission filings, from 6,127 in 1991 to 15,342 in 1996. During that period, awards to victims under federal laws nearly quadrupled, from $7.7 million to $27.8 million. 1992 was dubbed the "Year of the Woman" in politics because more women ran and won their elections. Five women became U.S. senators, including Carol Mosley Braun, the first African American woman ever elected, and twenty-four women won new seats in the House of Representatives.

The hearings also set in motion a breakup between African American voters and the Republican Party that had been looming since the 1960s. Calling it the "Clarence Thomas Effect," Harvard sociologist Lawrence Bobo suggests that 1992 was the last real moment when African Americans chose racial allegiance over ideology and party. Once Thomas's judicial opinions proved to be as conservative as he had suggested they would be during the hearings, or more so, it became hard for any Black Republican (a notable exception was future secretary of state Colin Powell), much less one running for office, to have significant African American support again.

By 2008, 95 percent of African American voters were voting Democratic in presidential elections. And statewide races didn't look different. Reflecting on his own theory twenty years later, Bobo wrote to me in an email, "One can easily amass a lot of evidence to support [this theory]. A variety of Black republicans who have run for statewide elections don't typically get large and loyal Black following."

In 2018 Anita Hill opened a *Times* op-ed with "There is no way to redo 1991, but there are ways to do better." Two days after Christine Blasey Ford came forward with her allegation that Supreme Court justice nominee Brett Kavanaugh had sexually assaulted her when they both were teenagers, Hill was trying to prevent her history from repeating itself: in her 1991 case, senators had prevented other women from testifying, like Angela Wright, whom Thomas had also allegedly harassed while he was her supervisor. But history did repeat itself. On September 27, Ford appeared alone to testify to the Senate Judiciary Committee, in a navy skirt suit reminiscent of Hill's, despite the fact that other women were also willing to testify against Kavanaugh.

The next week a full-page ad with sixteen hundred names, in a tiny font, appeared in the Sunday *Times* stating, "We believe Anita Hill. We also believe Christine Blasey Ford." This time the signatories were all men, of various races, who were taking up the charge given to them by Black women almost thirty years earlier. They could not redo 1991, but they did better.

THE CRIME BILL

ANGELA Y. DAVIS

—

ON SEPTEMBER 13, 1994, THE VIOLENT CRIME CONTROL AND Law Enforcement Act was signed into law by President Bill Clinton. Ironically, this day marked the twenty-third anniversary of the violent suppression of the Attica Prison rebellion in 1971. On the fifth day of the uprising, New York governor Nelson Rockefeller ordered a force made up of 550 New York state police troopers and some two hundred sheriff's deputies, along with National Guard helicopters, to retake the prison. According to historian Heather Ann Thompson,

> Ultimately, the human cost of the retaking was staggeringly high: 128 men were shot—some of them multiple times. Less than half an hour after the retaking had commenced, nine hostages were dead and at least one additional hostage was close to death. Twenty-nine prisoners had been fatally shot. Many of the deaths in D Yard—both hostages and prisoners—were caused by the scatter of buckshot, and still others resulted from the devastating impact of unjacketed bullets.

The use of unjacketed bullets, banned by the Geneva Conventions, and wide-arc buckshot was undoubtedly designed to produce as many casualties as possible. The New York commissioner of corrections, Russell Oswald, remarked, "I think I have some feeling now of how Truman must have felt when he decided to drop the A-bomb."

Twenty-three years later, the passage of the Crime Bill—although not as explosively violent, and unfolding over the course of many years rather than in the minutes-long catastrophe created by official gunmen on the grounds of Attica Prison—would cause immense devastation in Black, Brown, and poor communities. The Crime Bill became widely recognized as a major accelerator of what came to be known as mass incarceration. On the occasion of signing the bill, Bill Clinton remarked:

> Today the bickering stops, the era of excuses is over, the law-abiding citizens of this country have made their voices heard. Never again should Washington put politics and party above law and order.... Gangs and drugs have taken over our streets and undermined our schools. Every day we read about somebody else who has literally gotten away with murder.

These remarks reflect the expansive reach of the discourse on law and order, which since the 1970s tended to conflate "crime" with civil rights protests in the South and with the widespread turmoil generated by racism in the North. The moral panic produced by this discourse increasingly meant that the "law and order" slogan served as a proxy for more explicit calls to suppress Black movements and ultimately also to criminalize indiscriminately broad swaths of the Black population.

By 1994, the deindustrialization of the U.S. economy, produced by global economic shifts, was having a deleterious impact on working-class Black communities. The massive loss of jobs in the manufacturing sector, especially in cities like Detroit, Philadelphia, Chicago, New York, and Los Angeles, had the result, according to Joe William Trotter, that "the black urban working class nearly disappeared by the early 1990s." Combined with the disestablishment of welfare state benefits, these economic shifts caused vast numbers of Black people to seek other—sometimes "illegal"—means of survival. It is not accidental that the full force of the crack epidemic was felt during the 1980s and early '90s.

During this period there were few signs of governmental effort to address the circumstances responsible for the rapid impoverishment of working-class Black communities, and the 1994 Crime Bill was emblematic of the turn to carceral "solutions" as a response to the impact of forces of global capitalism. As Cedric Robinson has pointed out, capitalism has always been racial capitalism, and the Crime Bill was a formidable indication that Republicans and Democrats in Washington were united in their acceptance of punitive strategies to stave off the effects of Black impoverishment. Originally written by Senator Joe Biden, who would become vice president during the two terms of Barack Obama, the 356 pages of the bill contained provisions for one hundred thousand new police and over $12 billion in funding for state prisons, giving precedence to states that had enacted three-strikes laws and truth-in-sentencing. Moreover, the stipulations of the bill, which terminated Pell Grants for prisoners, led to the disestablishment of degree-granting educational programs in prisons. Recreational facilities began to be increasingly removed from prison settings as well.

The passage of the Crime Bill consolidated a political "law and order" environment, which prompted state legislatures to complement its provisions by passing ever more repressive laws affecting imprisoned people. During the same month that the bill was passed, the Mississippi legislature, which met in a special session to address prison overcrowding, instead focused on passing legislation to revoke prisoner access to amenities. According to *The New York Times,*

> There was talk of restoring fear to prisons, of caning, of making prisoners "smell like a prisoner," of burning and frying, of returning executions to the county seat and of making Mississippi "the capital of capital punishment," as Gov. Kirk Fordice, a Republican, put it.
>
> By the time the Legislature adjourned, reality had come close to the rhetoric. There will be no more private televisions for inmates and no radios, record players, tape or compact disc players, computers or stereos. Weight-lifting equipment, too, will be eliminated.

In sum, prison populations grew increasingly larger and the institutions themselves became more repressive and less likely to encourage people in prison to engage in self-rehabilitative activities—whether studying toward a degree or weight training. This punitive turn was especially apparent in the inclusion of the Violence Against Women Act within the Crime Bill, which proposed criminalization and carceral "solutions" to gender violence and helped to encourage the development of carceral feminism.

In response to this governmental promotion of state violence, antiprison activism intensified throughout the country, and in the fall of 1998 a massive conference drew 3,500 advocates, activists, artists, and scholars under the rubric "Critical Resistance: Beyond the Prison Industrial Complex." The ultimate goal of this gathering was to propose new vocabularies and a new discourse that would help to shift the "law and order" rhetoric to one that acknowledged the role played by the multifaceted criminalization of Black, Brown, and poor communities in consolidating the punitive turn. Emphasizing the danger of authorizing incarceration as the primary response to disrupted social relations—economic disorder, illiteracy, the lack of healthcare, harm, etc.—and as the legitimate and immutable foundation of justice, the conference initiated broad conversations on racism and repression within the prison system. Challenging the reverberations of the 1994 Crime Bill and the political climate defined by "law and order" rhetoric, Critical Resistance inaugurated a movement philosophically anchored by the notion of abolition that would popularize radical analyses of the ways imprisonment and policing mask structural racism.

THE BLACK IMMIGRANT

ESTHER ARMAH

KADIATOU DIALLO. HER PEOPLE CALLED HER KADI. SHE got married at thirteen, to an older man who already had one wife. She didn't want to get married, but for her family in Guinea, a predominantly Muslim nation in West Africa, marriage was her purpose. She was sixteen when her firstborn child came into the world. He started his life's journey in Liberia. His life ended on the steps of a Bronx apartment building on February 4, 1999. His body was riddled with bullets from forty-one shots fired from the guns of four New York Police Department officers. He was twenty-four years old.

His name was Amadou Diallo.

An African immigrant, America-bound in search of a future he could not find in Liberia. His path was purposed with dreams of becoming a teacher. He was proud of his American savings account with $9,000. Happy with his girlfriend. Confident about his promise to his mother, Kadi, that he would enroll in college.

In her 2003 memoir, Kadi describes her son as quiet and soft-spoken, with kind eyes. The NYPD officers believed her kind-eyed son was a serial rapist.

Amadou was part of an African-born population in the United States that from 1980 to 2009 grew from just under 200,000 to almost 1.5 million. In 2019 Africans made up 3.9 percent of 38.5 million immigrants in the United States. The 1965 Immigration and Nationality Act eased entry for Africans desiring to enter the country. Legal journeys reveal little about emotional ones. Yet the emotional journeys are the bedrock of so many millions of African immigrants. And they were also the launchpad from which Kadi waved anxiously as her America-bound firstborn child left a war-torn nation in search of the sweet probability of realized purpose. Amadou Diallo was born in Liberia. And it was from West Africa—nations like Nigeria, Ghana, and Senegal—that Black immigrants poured into the United States after the passage of the 1965 Immigration Act.

Numbers tell only partial stories, however. They are not conveyers of ambition, disappointment, discovery, falling in love, or battling America's racism.

Amadou means "to praise" in Arabic. But he was much more than a name. The killing of this twenty-four-year-old Black man brought a city to its feet, brought New Yorkers to the streets, and incited rage poured into protest, throats hoarse from screaming "41 shots!"

In 1999, the year the NYPD gunned Amadou down, Bill Clinton was the president of the United States. In 2004 George W. Bush was the occupant of 1600 Pennsylvania Avenue. And by 2017, the White House was occupied by a man who described the country Amadou Diallo called home as a "shithole country." In Trump's America, the language of immigration focuses on Brown Spanish-speaking bodies.

Immigrant. The word carries currency. Loaded. Weighed down by a politics of emotionality. Fear reigns and rules. It shrouds policy and reaches into these borders of manufactured fear where the walls are thick with America's rewritten history of immigration, featuring the accents of bigotry and unapologetic open political warfare turning small screens of news shows into horror movies where caged children are vilified and their proponent, America's forty-fifth president, is deified.

Trump leads a Republican Party where politicians invoke floods tossing the sons and daughters of Mexico onto America's shores. The police believed Amadou was a serial rapist. The language of trigger-happy police officers in 1999 would be shared by a president in 2016, when he called border-trampling Mexicans "rapists."

The four police officers who killed Amadou were all acquitted on February 25, 2000. This act would become a pattern, one that would lead to a hashtag, sparking a nationwide and global movement. Ama-

dou's embattled corpse would become bloody fertile ground for later
chants of "Black lives matter!" His life mattered, his accent did not.

The Bronx, where Amadou was killed, is the borough that birthed
hip-hop. In its corners you hear accents from Caribbean islands that
feel like hugs from home and are a welcome respite from a belonging-
free political America where immigrants are fodder to be dashed and
demonized for political capital.

Those forty-one shots did not have an accent. They were immune
to journeys, language, culture, and custom. They did not know Kadi's
path, her worry for her firstborn, or the dreams Amadou carried from
his home in Liberia. There are nations and grandmas and uncles
whose immigrant dreams collide with the American Dream for which
they were neither considered nor included. Amadou's Blackness
merged into the narrative of African American men as sexual preda-
tors and threats, criminalizing his body and justifying the brutality of
each of those forty-one shots.

The Nigerian-British singer Sade sang on her track "Immigrant"
from her 2000 album *Lovers Rock,*

> He didn't know what it was to be Black. . . .
> 'Til they gave him the change, but didn't wanna touch his hand

Amadou's brutal killing was a lesson in Blackness for African immigrants.

Our accents will not protect us. Not from police brutality. Our accents are remixed to the beat of America's racism. They can identify us
and a corner of this continent so many have left or fled but call and
claim as home. They can be a balm from the reality that is the United
States in 2019 and a president for whom speaking the word *immigrant*
constitutes political point-scoring.

In African nations, education was an elevator to status. It required
you to put your head down and keep it there in order to ascend. That
legacy of colonialism fed an illusion of inclusion, a path where your
African exceptionalism, your difference from American-grown
Blackness, would guarantee a different outcome. Some believed they
would thrive. Unlike them. That meant some African immigrants

taste their difference as sweeter, marking them immune to the racism for which they might sometimes blame Black Americans—not simply for challenging or enduring but actually for attracting. The "you" and "them" by African Americans meant sharpened tongues, ugly names—African booty-scratchers—communicating neither desire nor claim to any corner of this continent.

Immigration in the United States today thrives and flounders due to a politics of emotionality. Immigrants are not born of sixteen-year-old mothers with journeys and dreams and futures. Not one of the forty-one shots recognized the love of Amadou's mother, nor the space of Blackness that he occupied. Not one bullet came wrapped in an Ivy League education. Police encounters do not litigate our peculiar and particular Blacknesses. We—African Americans and immigrants of African nations and of island nations—do that. The back-and-forth between the Blackness born and raised in, shaped by, and rejected in America and that of journeying African immigrants was—and continues to be—a landscape of simmering tensions that sometimes explode. Those tensions serve to separate, when what is necessary now are creative collectives and coalitions. There is no comfort from the emotional litigation of our Blacknesses. Confusion yes. Clarity no. This is what a legacy of untreated trauma looks like. What is required is emotional justice.

We have to reimagine a Blackness that is not marked as singular based on the brutality of bullets and America's limitations. We must expand it to honor our accents, cultures, and customs as we navigate rocky paths to build creative coalitions and continue to a freedom where our peculiar and particular Blackness can be and breathe.

Amadou's future was choked out of him with each of the forty-one bullets. His bones are buried where his extended family resides, on his mother's land, in Hollande Bourou in the Fouta Djallon region of Guinea. His blood still stains the streets of the Bronx. He breathed New York City air as an African immigrant. His death taught us that, in the United States, his breath was Black.

HURRICANE KATRINA

Deborah Douglas

—

O N A MIDDLE-SCHOOL FIELD TRIP TO TENNESSEE'S REELFOOT Lake in 1978, a classmate almost made me disappear. We were just up the road from my new home of Covington, a Delta town where Blow Pops were made, thick and swirly vowels rolled off people's tongues, and a bronze Confederate statue greeted visitors at the square. At eleven years old, I was a Chicago-born Detroiter, new and working to fit in, calibrating my ear to accents without sharp angles and other ways of being. I wondered, for example, why the school instantly segregated by race as soon as the first period bell rang. White kids went to higher-level classes, and Black kids went somewhere else. I don't know exactly where because, well, I went with the white kids.

On this occasion, I noticed a group of white students from English huddled together when one of them, a short fella I'll call J., came over. A new friend perhaps? J. proceeded to announce, "Heretell, you think you something." He said it in a dusty drawl, like *suuuuumthin.*

I was perplexed. Was that a question or a statement? Was I supposed to answer? Well, I've always been told I'm a child of God. My activist Detroit teachers, fresh from the revolution, always told me to raise my hand and speak up, which I did. Maybe I *was* something, I didn't know. Who said such a thing, and why would it matter? In my heart, I knew J.'s trouble was *he* thought I was something. Whatever light of intellect, curiosity, and hope emanated from me and Black girls like me needed to be dispatched. This is what I call "depresencing." He was chosen to do it because apparently some people are born to be seen and others are meant to recede, useful only to validate white supremacy.

On that fall day at a place born when the river ran backward, this would not be the first time I would be asked to shrink and be a little less . . . there. The Black women and girls impacted by Hurricane Katrina, which landed near New Orleans on August 29, 2005, know a great deal about a lack of regard that renders their lived experiences invisible.

The idea of Black women and girls being fully present, inhabiting space and exercising their powers of wit, talent, and dexterity, would be a recurring theme. A lexicon has grown to address the tension between who Black women truly are and aspire to be, and the validatory bit part they are repeatedly asked to play, if any at all. Scholars Kimberlé Crenshaw's "intersectionality" and Moya Bailey's "misogynoir" provide a level of validation and language that feels good to not feel, well, crazy.

The devastating weather event that was Hurricane Katrina can best be described as what historian Barbara Ransby calls the "gendered nature of the disaster."

The category-four hurricane made landfall near New Orleans and proceeded to unleash destruction that ravaged the Gulf Coast, including Mississippi, Alabama, Georgia, and Florida. The levee system that had protected New Orleans from the waters of Lake Pontchartrain and Lake Borgne was overwhelmed. About 1.2 million people heeded Mayor Ray Nagin's order to evacuate. Most of the city flooded.

Many residents didn't leave because they could not or would not, or they sought shelter at the New Orleans Convention Center or the Louisiana Superdome. While many possess the privilege of picking up and leaving without much thought, studies show (and folks will tell you) that low-income residents, minorities, the elderly, and the disabled are less likely to evacuate. In New Orleans, impoverished residents didn't have the money, the cars, or the network to relocate. Their homes and communities bore the brunt of the devastation.

Media reports showed desperate people on rooftops begging to be rescued from their flooded communities. Survivors languished at the Superdome and convention center without food, water, and proper sanitary conditions. Residents were further dispossessed when they were referred to as "refugees" rather than "evacuees," a point made by the Reverend Jesse Jackson, among others.

Hurricane Katrina is easily a metaphor for America's attitude toward Black women: rejected, neglected, and never protected. But Black women's persistence and their insistence on survival and restoration are a metaphor for their attitude toward America.

FEMA chief Michael Brown is the poster boy for the way established power approached this natural and man-made disaster. When George W. Bush showered him with praise, saying "Brownie, you're doing a heck of a job," nobody thought like that.

The vacationing Bush embodied this mindset in his own slow response. On his way back to the White House on August 31, he flew over New Orleans, surveying the damage. He didn't land to take stock of the situation because he said it would draw on law enforcement resources. Failure to engage at a most human level hit a nerve, as New Orleans was a majority-Black city where more than a quarter lived in poverty.

When former first lady Barbara Bush broke her characteristic public silence, she diminished the humanity of survivors. In discussing evacuees in Texas, she told the radio program *Marketplace*, "And so many of the people in the arena here, you know, were underprivileged anyway," she said, "so this is working very well for them."

Except it wasn't working, especially for Black women, many of whom were heads of their households. More women than men lived in poverty before Katrina. Women are prone to gender-based violence when they are vulnerable. The disaster response was simply humiliating. In a 2006 article, Ransby recounted that a middle-aged Black woman on CNN who was "dirty, desperate and crying . . . looked into the camera and said to the viewers, 'We do not live like this.' She repeated it over and over again."

City leaders who banked on remaking a demographically different kind of city did Black women no favors, either. They failed to include in recovery planning the Black women who lived in "the Bricks," the Big Four public housing complexes. Public housing was demolished and replaced with mixed-income developments.

The city lost more than half of its population after the hurricane, falling to 230,172 residents in 2006 from 484,674, according to the Data Center. In the metro area, many of these lost residents were African American women and girls, whose numbers dropped to 37 percent from 47 percent, according to a 2010 report by the Institute for Women's Policy Research. Poverty levels fell, but that doesn't prove poverty dropped for Black girls and women who lived there before Katrina.

The disaster response that stranded thousands or made people feel occupied more than protected by police and military failed to take into account the Black women's work of holding themselves together. These women were doing what author and commentator Avis Jones-DeWeever described as easing "the hunger and thirst of babies and toddlers left in their care in the sweltering heat and the inhumane conditions associated with post-disaster survival." In the wake of the storm, women, Black and white, cared for the elderly and infirm, "yet, women's service and suffering were all but invisible as are their continuing struggles to this day."

The lexicon must make room for white patriarchy's specific way of disregarding the humanity of Black women in literal physical spaces like New Orleans during and after Katrina, and in the narratives and policy making that either created a pathway home or left them stranded. Every step of the Katrina response "depresenced" Black women, forced them to bear the weight of natural disaster while carrying the cellular memory of trauma one can imagine will pass through bloodlines like so many others.

Unlike *erasure*, which requires one's presence to be recognized so it can be obliterated, *depresencing* never acknowledges presence at all. When deployed, people just look right through Black women as if they weren't there.

As violent and silent as depresencing is, there's an antidote. The response to Hurricane Katrina was not the first time the U.S. government abandoned Black women, and it would not be the last. Black women resisted by showing up in the story of their lives, by loving, learning, and leading—despite the systemic barriers and humiliations designed to make them small enough to practically disappear. But Black women did not disappear, and they will not disappear because we know something established power does not: we are something.

THE *SHELBY* RULING

KARINE JEAN-PIERRE

———

"**E**VERY TIME I VOTE," OPRAH WINFREY SAID ON A 2004 EPISODE of *The Oprah Winfrey Show* dedicated to voting, "I cast my vote for Otis Moss, Sr., who walked eighteen miles in one day to have the chance to do it. That's why I vote."

Oprah invokes the story of Otis Moss, Sr., frequently when she talks about voting. It's a story she heard in her twenties from his son, Cleveland's Rev. Otis Moss, and one she says she'll never forget. It's one I'll never forget, either.

Otis Moss, Sr., grew up without the right to vote. His family were sharecroppers in the racist Jim Crow era, in a "democracy" that still denied millions of Black and Brown people the right to vote. But one day that changed. The Voting Rights Act passed in 1965, thanks to the civil rights movement, and for the first time ever, Otis by law had the right to vote. And on the day of the first-ever election where he could actually cast a ballot, where he could actually have his voice counted, he put on his best suit and walked six miles to the nearest polling station. He didn't have any other form of transportation. But when he got to the polling station and tried to cast his vote, the people working there told him he couldn't vote at that polling station. He had to go to another one.

Still in his best suit, Otis walked another five or six miles to that other polling station. But by the time he got there, the people working there told him it was too late, the polls had closed. He walked home, another six miles, defeated. In total, Otis Moss, Sr., walked eighteen miles that day, all for the chance to vote. All for the chance to exercise a right that was legally his.

Otis Moss, Sr., died before the next election. In all his years, not once did he get to vote. Not once did the United States of America, a supposed democracy that depends on free and fair elections, allow him to vote. Not once.

That story, a story of Jim Crow and how laws may change but may not change everything, that's the story Oprah takes with her when she votes. I want to quickly tell you another story, a story of a man not unlike Otis Moss, Sr.

Eddie Lee Holloway, Jr., was a fifty-eight-year-old Black man who moved to Wisconsin from Illinois. He was ready to vote: he had his expired Illinois photo ID, his birth certificate, and his Social Security card, so he could get the Wisconsin ID he needed to vote. But when he went to the DMV in Milwaukee, they rejected his application. It turned out that on his birth certificate, due to a clerical error, his name was written as "Eddie Junior Holloway," not "Eddie Holloway Junior."

Eddie didn't give up, however. He made seven more trips to different agencies and offices to try to get his paperwork together, all so he could vote. Like Otis, he was determined. He spent over $200 trying to get everything in order. But even after all these attempts, he still wasn't able to get the identification he needed to be able to vote in Wisconsin. Eventually, Eddie was so dejected he moved back to Illinois. He was never able to vote in Wisconsin.

Both Eddie and Otis were denied the right to vote even though the law said they were entitled to it. Both men were victims of a centuries-long effort in the United States to deny Black people the right to vote. But Eddie, unlike Otis, wasn't a sharecropper living under Jim Crow. Eddie was a Black man trying to vote in Wisconsin in the 2016 presidential election. Not in 1946. Not in 1956. In 2016. Since Otis's attempt to vote, the United States has sent people to the moon, created electric cars, launched the Internet, and elected the first Black president. But if, like Eddie, you're voting as a Black or Brown person, it can sometimes feel like nothing has changed at all.

Eddie was one of hundreds of thousands of predominantly Black and Brown victims that year of a new voter ID law in Wisconsin that, according to one study, successfully suppressed 200,000 votes in 2016. Donald Trump won the state by 22,748 votes.

When I reflect on these two stories, I think of how much more similar they are than different. I think of the fact that, a half century later, Black people in this country are still struggling for the right to vote. I think of the fact that white supremacy and voter suppression, though they look different today, are still very much alive—and flourishing.

In 2013 I was in New York City working in city politics when the *Shelby County v. Holder* decision came down, bringing down with it crucial parts of the Voting Rights Act. I had only recently left the Obama administration. Barack Obama had cobbled together a mighty coalition of people young and old, Black and white. The diversity of the coalition that backed him demonstrated the future he sought, one where people of all backgrounds would come together and push our great nation forward. The power of that thought, the audacity of his imagination to dream of what a better, more inclusive country might look like, frightened many who saw their lives dependent on the continuation of a racial hierarchy.

I think many of us were naïve then. We thought things would only get better, not worse. Many thought of the election of Barack Obama, not as the end of racism, but certainly as a turning point. And it was. But for many, President Obama's election was a turning point in a different direction. It spurred a backlash among white supremacists invested in maintaining the status quo.

It can be no coincidence that the carnage of the Voting Rights Act so central to the *Shelby* decision occurred during the presidency of our first-ever Black president. It is no coincidence that in the decade since Obama's election, voter suppression has gained more momentum, velocity, and animosity than it had in the previous three elections combined. Since *Shelby County v. Holder*, voter suppression has taken on more pervasive and pernicious forms than ever before.

Voter purges are on the rise. Between 2006 and 2008, states removed 4 million voters from their rolls, as they are permitted to do under the Constitution in order to maintain the accuracy of their voter rolls. Between 2014 and 2016, that number jumped to 16 million people. Voter ID laws, like the one that stopped Eddie Holloway, Jr., from voting in the 2016 election, have seeped into state constitutions across the country. Felon disenfranchisement laws and voter access laws run rampant.

It was, technically, a change in the law that spurred these vile additions to voter suppression. But it had much more to do with what had happened five years before *Shelby County v. Holder*, with the election of President Obama. His election signaled that the direction of power in this country was shifting; the growth in voter suppression we've seen over the last decade is a response to that election and to that signal.

Laws alone have never changed this country. The Voting Rights Act would never have happened without the Freedom Rides, the Montgomery Bus Boycott, and the brave souls who sat at that lunch counter at Woolworth's in 1960. The Voting Rights Act, as historic and critical as it was, was not enough to give Otis Moss, Sr., his vote.

At the March on Washington in 1963, John Lewis was just twenty-three years old. Standing on the steps of the Lincoln Memorial, he said:

> To those who have said, "Be patient and wait," we have long said that we cannot be patient. We do not want our freedom gradually, but we want to be free now! We are tired. We are tired of being beaten by policemen. We are tired of seeing our people locked up in jail over and over again. And then you holler, "Be patient." How long can we be patient? We want our freedom and we want it now.... We must say: "Wake up America! Wake up!" For we cannot stop, and we will not and cannot be patient.

When it comes to our democracy, and who we determine to have the right to vote—our most sacred of rights—patience is no virtue. We must never be patient when someone else's rights are in the balance. We cannot wait on laws, or elected officials, or anyone else. The only virtue when it comes to the right to vote is impatience.

BLACK LIVES MATTER

ALICIA GARZA

———

CHANGE DOES NOT OCCUR WITHOUT BACKLASH—AT LEAST, any change worth having—and that backlash is an indicator that the change is so powerful that the opposing forces resist that change with everything they have.

On August 9, 2014, Michael Brown was shot and killed by police officer Darren Wilson in Ferguson, a small suburb outside St. Louis. His body lay in the street for four hours as angry crowds gathered, demanding to know why an eighteen-year-old boy had been shot and killed by police just steps away from his mother's home. After Brown was shot, he reportedly was still alive, and yet he was denied medical attention. Later that afternoon the crowd erupted and began to march to the Ferguson police station a few blocks away.

What unfolded that fateful day is painful and complex. It is a story that the people who joined in that uprising that day and in the days, weeks, months, and years afterward are most fit to tell. Storytelling is often connected to power and influence, and even today the voices of activists in Ferguson, from their own perspectives and viewpoints, are too hard to come by and often eclipsed by those who want to center themselves within a story that is not their own.

Such has been the case with Black Lives Matter, which I started with Patrisse Cullors and Opal Tometi a little more than a year prior to Brown's death, after the acquittal in 2013 of George Zimmerman in the murder of Trayvon Martin, a Black teenager, in Sanford, Florida. Such has been the case with all social movements as we seek to best understand their origins, their impacts, their failures, and their methods and strategies.

There are lessons that can be drawn from this tapestry of stories that point to a simple truth—Black lives still do not matter in American society. Whether it be the murder of Trayvon Martin by a vigilante, the murder of Michael Brown by a local police officer, the murder of Renesha McBride by a private citizen, the murder of Kayla Moore by police officers, the murder of Mia Henderson, or the mysterious death of Sandra Bland, who was found dead in a jail cell she should not have been in after a routine traffic stop—Black lives, be they poor or middle class, transgender or cisgender, disabled, adult or child, are seen as disposable.

The movement addressing this simple yet painful truth has deep historical roots. It has emerged from previous iterations not only to fight back against the state-sanctioned violence occurring against Black people each and every day. The movement has declared that all Black lives are worth fighting for.

This Black Renaissance understands that it is not only cisgender, heterosexual middle-class Black people who deserve to live full and dignified lives, but also Black people who are subject to discrimination, oppression, and marginalization of many types all at once. It was this Black Renaissance that propelled activists to refuse to allow traditional Black church leaders to speak on their behalf, to tell them to go home in the dead of night and be content with allowing the system to run its course as Michael Brown lay dying in the street. It is this Black Renaissance that declares that the lives of Black transgender women must not end in homicide before they are thirty-five years old. It is this Black Renaissance that refuses to make the coffee and the copies while the men do the real work. It is this Black Renaissance that questions the stated role of policing in this country, and that calls attention to the Black disabled people who are killed at eight times the rate of people who are not disabled. This Black Renaissance has dutifully carried on the tradition of resistance that our ancestors gifted us, and it has continued to push for the changes that they did not complete.

There were more protests in one year, 2014, than at any time during the last period of civil rights activism. Black Lives Matter—the hashtag, the organization, and the movement—exploded around the world. Making Black lives matter meant fighting back against the oppression of Black people, which also meant investing in loving Blackness in all its forms.

The explosion of this Black Renaissance came with a swift, strong backlash. Soon after Black Lives Matter began making a cultural and systemic impact, refrains of "All Lives Matter" and "Blue Lives Matter" began to counter it. These Americans denied the existence of racism and branded whoever dared to expose it as people who were "playing the race card," ostensibly for sympathy or to deny culpability in their own oppression. These Americans framed Black Lives Matter activists as domestic terrorists who posed a threat to the lives of law enforcement.

The 2016 presidential election was the platform upon which this backlash against the Black Renaissance took place. Hillary Clinton, the Democratic presidential nominee, expected the allegiance of Black voters and yet became the subject of numerous protests by Black organizers. The Republican presidential nominee, Donald Trump, allayed the fears of white voters, promising to restore law and order to the country, to support law enforcement, and, after the first Black president, to "Make America Great Again."

A few months after Trump was sworn in as the forty-fifth president of the United States—a president who has been accused of groping or otherwise sexually assaulting no fewer than thirty-five women—Harvey Weinstein was accused of sexually assaulting, harassing, or raping over eighty women. Exposure of these allegations prompted a hashtag known as #MeToo, which was the original creation of Tarana Burke more than a decade ago to support survivors of sexual assault to find resilience and hope. Since then, the #MeToo movement has exposed a widespread epidemic of sexual violence, particularly by powerful men like Weinstein, actor Kevin Spacey, and music mogul R. Kelly.

The #MeToo movement has proven to be a radical upheaval of societal norms that degrade, abuse, and devalue women-identified people. It has also amplified the voices of those who are survivors of that harm, and it encourages them to celebrate their resilience in the face of such violence. Harvey Weinstein's career is now over, and he faces multiple lawsuits and court cases, intended to hold him to account for his abusive behavior over decades. Kevin Spacey's career has also effectively ended, and the popular television show that he once starred in has been canceled. R. Kelly was finally charged with abusing underage girls.

And still the backlash has been swift. Not only have those who have come forward with their stories, daring to be resilient after having survived such horrible traumas, been interrogated, ridiculed, and picked apart; even those who dare to provide platforms for such voices have received death threats as a result of their service. Beyond the retaliation against individuals, a powerful countermovement now misrepresents this movement as harmful to men.

Three years into Trump's first term, at the four-hundred-year mark of African American history, white nationalism exploded nationally and globally. Although white nationalism is not a new phenomenon, it had formerly been politically fraught to declare sympathies with white nationalism in public. In 2019 alone, more than 250 people in the United States were killed in mass shootings. The overwhelming majority of the shooters were white nationalists.

Today white nationalists openly serve in the White House and in Congress. Trump's first year in office saw the designation of a new category of terrorist—the Black identity extremist, defined as a Black person who takes pride in their culture and wants to cause harm to law enforcement officials. Though the designation has recently been dropped after being exposed as fiction, the fact still remains that the backlash against the powerful Black Lives Matter movement that rose in 2013 and exploded in 2014 was deemed a threat by the FBI.

Activists valuing and defending the lives of Black people were considered a threat, but not a president who openly bragged about grabbing women "by the pussy," calls immigrants of color to America "foreign invaders," called Haiti a "shithole country," and said that majority-Black Baltimore was a "rat infested city." Trump personified the backlash against all those Americans saying Black lives mattered.

A looming question faces antiracist social movements in the

United States: Will the backlash become a force powerful enough to prevail? Or will our organizing become stronger and sharper in the face of such backlash, assured that its presence alone has already declared our victory?

Only time—and strategic organizing—will tell the next four hundred years of African America.

AMERICAN ABECEDARIAN

Joshua Bennett

—

A IS FOR ATOM BOMB. B IS FOR BLACKS BELTING BLUES BE-fore burial, the blood they let to give the flag its glimmer. C is for cocoon & its cognates. Cocaine, coca-cola, the cacophonous wail of drones filling air with wartime. D is for demagogue. E is for elephants & their semblances, every political animal laboring under some less than human name. F is for foxhole. Firefight. Fears we cathect onto men holding best intentions close to the chest as one might guilt or guns & of course G is for guns, g-men, guillotines draped in flame we dream any hellscape holds if it's up to snuff. H is for Horsepower. I is for *I*. I is for individual drive trumps all concern when it comes to this business of living joyously at the edge of wit, watching half a world drown with your hands tied. J is for jeans. K is for Krispy Kreme. L is for loss. L is for loveliness. L is for lean in the cups of boys in white shirts billowing free in Mississippi towns so small, they are visible only when passing through them, like death. M is for metafiction. N is for next: next wife, next car, next life I would spend the bones in this flesh one by one to touch. O is for opulence. Opportunity. Occasional anguish but nothing compared to what I will reach when I peak & P is for Preakness. Poverty & bodies that flee it. Oh body, like a storm of horses. Oh questions we dare not ask for fear of breaking rank or losing funding. Q is for quarantine. R is for repair, Revolution, other conflicts that lack limit in any definitional sense. S is for stars we adore & reflect. T is for tragedy. U is for upper-middle working class when the survey asks. V is for the viola my mother plays in the 1970s as her hometown collapses without fanfare. W is for Windows 98 in the public school computer lab & every fourth-grader playing Oregon Trail there. X is for xanthan gum, every everyday ingredient you couldn't identify by sight if you tried. Y is for Yellowstone. Y is for the yachts in the docks in our eyes. Z is for zealotry: national pride like an infinite zipline, hyperdrive, the fastest way down.

CONCLUSION

OUR ANCESTORS' WILDEST DREAMS

KEISHA N. BLAIN

T HERE'S A SAYING THAT HAS CIRCULATED IN BLACK COMMU-nities for decades: "I am my ancestors' wildest dreams."

Its origins are unknown. Yet its power is unmistakable. It speaks to all that Black people have overcome that did not seem possible generations before.

I've often wondered what my ancestors dreamed about. I wish my great-great-grandparents who were enslaved somewhere in the Caribbean had left letters detailing all their hopes and dreams for themselves and me. I'll never know for sure their wishes, their desires. But I can say with certainty that they wanted a life of freedom.

When I hear passing stories of my great-grandmother Felicity, a sassy and strong-willed Black woman from Grenada, I imagine that she had a lot of dreams and desires. Did she want to travel abroad? Did she want to obtain an education? Did she want to learn a particular skill?

What were her wildest dreams?

I'll never actually know—no matter how much others might tell me about her.

So I am left to imagine and question. What did a Black woman living in Grenada in the early twentieth century desire? What did

Felicity desire? What did Mary Jane Langdon, the great-grandmother of Malcolm X who lived in Grenada during this period, desire?

Although slavery had been formally abolished in Grenada in 1833, the experiences of Black people on the island were similar to those of Black people who were enslaved in the United States. Black people in the Caribbean could not claim a life of what historian Kim Butler has described as "full freedom." Grenada, much like other Caribbean islands, had been colonized by the British during the eighteenth century (after previously being colonized by the French a century earlier). A Black woman living under colonialism in the Caribbean—much like a Black woman living under slavery in the United States during this period—could certainly dream. No one could have stopped them from imagining a better future, even if they tried.

But they could stand in the way of those dreams becoming a reality. And they certainly did. By design, slavery and colonialism stripped from Black people the right to live their lives as they wanted: on their own terms. They restricted Black people from having access to and control of their own resources. They stripped Black people of their "full freedom" and attempted to chip away at their personhood. They tried to crush their dreams.

The millions of Black people who shaped American history—whether descendants of enslaved people or of colonized people—all had dreams. Some dreamed of "home"—the place they could truly call their own. Some dreamed of the opportunity to explore and travel. Others dreamed of the opportunity to obtain a quality education. Regardless of the diversity of their individual hopes, they all dreamed of freedom. "Full freedom."

Are we our ancestors' wildest dreams? Are Black people in the United States now living the lives our ancestors of the past imagined for us?

I am not so sure.

Today, a little over four hundred years since the arrival of "20 or so odd Negroes" in Jamestown, Virginia, Black people across the nation continue to face many of the same problems our ancestors fought to correct. Despite the many political gains and triumphs over the years, racism and white supremacy persist in all aspects of American life

and culture. As disparities in maternal mortality rates and the dispro-
portionate impact of COVID-19 diagnoses and deaths reveal, Black
Americans experience poorer healthcare access and lower quality of
care than any other racial group. In the educational sector, Black students lag behind their white peers—not for lack of talent and ability
but because decades-long structural inequalities have impeded their
success. From police violence and mass incarceration to voter suppression and unequal access to housing, the social and economic disparities that shape contemporary Black life are all legacies of slavery
and colonialism.

These two distinct yet deeply connected systems of power, oppression, and exploitation sealed the fate of the group of Africans who
arrived in Jamestown in 1619. They influenced centuries of laws and
policies that determined how Black people could live out their lives.
They tried to stifle Black people's dreams, and when they were unsuccessful, their architects and beneficiaries simply set up barriers and
restrictions to make it nearly impossible for them to attain them.

But as the narratives in *Four Hundred Souls* reveal, Black people
have never stopped dreaming, or fighting for those dreams to become
a reality. Elizabeth Keye, for example, fought to secure her freedom in
1656—becoming one of the first Black people in British North America to successfully sue for freedom and win. During the eighteenth
century, American maroons skillfully resisted their enslavement, hiding out in faraway places to maintain some measure of control over
their lives. In Boston during the 1830s, Maria Stewart stood boldly to
demand the rights and freedom of Black people, becoming the first
woman in the United States to speak publicly to a mixed audience of
men and women. These stories and many others, highlighted in *Four
Hundred Souls,* capture the spirit of determination that guided Black
people in the United States—every step of the way.

Together, despite the odds, we have made it this far. The powerful
essays and poetry in *Four Hundred Souls* are a testament to how much
we have overcome, and how we have managed to do it together, despite our differences and diverse perspectives.

Yet I am not convinced we are our ancestors' wildest dreams. At
least not yet.

I'll never know what ran through my great-grandmother Felicity's mind as she rested quietly in the evenings. But I suspect that her wildest dream for herself and for me mirrors my own. In this dream, Black people have "full freedom"—equal access to all the rights and privileges afforded to others. In this dream, Black people, regardless of gender, religion, sexuality, and class, are living their lives uninhibited by the chains of racism and white supremacy that bind us still.

This dream is not yet a reality. We have much work left to do.

While I remain doubtful that we are our ancestors' wildest dreams, I believe we can be. More than four hundred years since the symbolic birthdate of Black America, we still have the unique opportunity to shape our current dreams into future realities.

The task ahead is not an easy one. But we can help chart out a path that leads us all to a better future—the kind of future that will more closely resemble our ancestors' wildest dreams.

ACKNOWLEDGMENTS

I AM ENORMOUSLY GRATEFUL FOR THE KINDNESS OF SO MANY individuals. My husband, Jay, and our son, "Little Jay," have been an unwavering source of love and support. I am also grateful for the other members of my family, especially my mom for her invaluable help and understanding. Many thanks to Ibram for being a wonderful friend and collaborator, and thank you to our amazing editor, Chris, for carefully guiding this project—and enthusiastically supporting our vision. I am grateful to the brilliant writers who entrusted us with their work. Last, but not least, thank you to the research assistants who helped us with this project. I owe a debt of gratitude to Adam, Richard, and Tiana.

—KEISHA N. BLAIN, OCTOBER 2020

I WANT TO FIRST AND FOREMOST ACKNOWLEDGE AND THANK Keisha Blain. When I embarked on this editorial project, I knew I could not do it alone. I knew I should not do it alone. And I'm so glad we came together to co-edit this historic tome. You made the enormity of this project seem manageable. Your exceptional expertise, experience, determination, and insight have been invaluable to everyone involved in putting together *Four Hundred Souls*. I'm thankful we walked this long and winding editorial process together.

This has been a grueling, thrilling, and rewarding process, working closely with Professor Blain to make history and compose history by bringing together ninety Black writers. I want to thank each and every writer and poet for taking some time out of their busy schedules to contribute a piece. Not just any kind of piece. Moving and informative and relevant pieces and poems that were almost meant to be together. I don't see this as my book, or Professor Blain's book, or our book, but your book. The community's book. The book of the community of writers, and the deceased and living community we are writing for. I want to thank you for sharing with the world and with history a sense of this community.

I must thank the incomparable literary agent who loved this book on first sight of the idea. Thank you, Ayesha Pande, for instantly seeing our vision for this book, for paving the way for the dream to once again become a beautiful reality that stands time's test.

And we knew it would take a special editor to seamlessly edit fiction, nonfiction, and poetry—to fuse so many distinctive writing voices into one voice and many voices simultaneously. Editing a single writer is hardly easy. Try editing ninety writers and two editors for a single volume. Try editing a sweeping history of four hundred years. I don't know how Chris Jackson pulled it off, but for history's sake, I'm so glad that he did. Thank you, as always, Chris, for your greatness as an editor.

To the entire team at One World, especially Maria Braeckel, Nicole Counts, Stacey Stein, and Ayelet Gruenspecht, you know I'm forever grateful for your wisdom, your grace, your hard work, your determination to ensure every human being is reading this history, this community history.

To my partner, Sadiqa, and my daughter, Imani, thank you for being the rock and north star and loves of my existence. To my parents, Larry and Carol, and second parents, Nyota and B.T.; to my brother, Akil, and second brother, Macharia—thank you for your love. To all my family and friends, I learn love from you each day, and I strive to love you each day—as I do the Black community, as I do the American community, as I do the human community.

When we were putting the finishing touches on this book in the spring and summer of 2020, the human community, the American community, and especially the Black American community were facing one of the deadliest pandemics humanity has ever known. Between 9 April 2020, when states started releasing racial demographic data of coronavirus patients, and October, Black people have consistently died at more than twice the rate of white people from COVID-19. I want to acknowledge the already forty thousand Black lives lost, many of whom would still be with us if not for racism. You will never be forgotten. Your souls will always be cherished. This book is dedicated to you.

—IBRAM X. KENDI, OCTOBER 2020

NOTES

A COMMUNITY OF SOULS

xiv **"A muster roll"**: Thomas C. Holt, *Children of Fire: A History of African Americans* (New York: Hill and Wang, 2011), 3.

xvi **"a Dutch man"**: John Rolfe to Sir Edwin Sandys, January 1619/1620, *Encyclopedia Virginia*, www.encyclopediavirginia.org.

1619–1624: ARRIVAL

3 **sixty-six grueling days**: "*Mayflower* and *Mayflower* Compact," Plimoth Patuxet, www.plimoth.org/learn/just-kids/homework-help/mayflower -and-mayflower-compact.

3 **its 102 passengers**: Patricia Scott Deetz and James F. Deetz, "Passengers on the *Mayflower:* Ages & Occupations, Origins & Connections," Plymouth Colony Archive Project (2000), www.histarch.illinois.edu/ plymouth/Maysource.html.

3 **We know all their names**: "Find Your *Mayflower* Ancestors," *American Ancestors,* New England Historic Genealogical Society, mayflower .americanancestors.org/pilgrim-database.

3 **"one of the most"**: Rebecca Beatrice Brooks, "History of the *Mayflower* Ship," *History of Massachusetts,* August 12, 2011, historyofmassachusetts .org/the-mayflower/.

4 **"20 and odd"**: Beth Austin, "1619: Virginia's First Africans," *Hampton History Museum,* December 2018, 9.

4 **"No one sensed"**: Lerone Bennett, Jr., *Before the Mayflower: A History of the Negro in America, 1619–1964* (1962; New York: Penguin Books, 1988), 29.

4 **Some 40 percent**: Austin, "1619," 8.

4 **"back alley"**: Bennett, *Before the Mayflower,* 87.

5 **"It is indeed extremely"**: W.E.B. Du Bois, *Black Reconstruction* (1935; New York: Russell & Russell, 1956), 711, 714.

5 **"This, for the purpose"**: Frederick Douglass, "What to the Slave Is the Fourth of July?" July 5, 1852, *Teaching American History,* teachingameri

canhistory.org/library/document/what-to-the-slave-is-the-fourth-of
-july/.

6   **"Your country?":** W.E.B. Du Bois, *The Souls of Black Folk* (1903; Oxford: Oxford University Press, 2007), 128.

7   **"Nations reel and stagger":** Du Bois, *Black Reconstruction*, 714.

1629–1634: WHIPPED FOR LYING WITH A BLACK WOMAN

11   **"abusing himself":** William Waller Hening, ed., *The Statutes at Large: Being a Collection of All the Laws of Virginia, from the First Session of the Legislature in the Year 1619* (New York, 1823), 1:146.

11   **Africans as heathens:** Paul Lovejoy, "The Abolition of the Slave Trade," New York Public Library, abolition.nypl.org/print/us_slave_trade/.

13   **when another white man:** Crandall Shifflett, "The Practise of Slavery," *Virtual Jamestown*, www.virtualjamestown.org/praclink.html.

1634–1639: TOBACCO

16   **a woman running away:** Lerone Bennett, *Before the Mayflower: A History of Black America*, 8th ed. (Chicago: Johnson Publishing Co., 1987), 36.

16   **The lie is that the Africans:** On gender and slavery, see Jennifer L. Morgan, *Laboring Women: Reproduction and Gender in the Making of New World Slavery* (Philadelphia: University of Pennsylvania Press, 2004). For a broad overview of slavery in the United States, see Ira Berlin, *Many Thousands Gone: The First Two Centuries of Slavery in North America* (Cambridge, MA: Belknap Press of Harvard University Press, 1998).

1639–1644: BLACK WOMEN'S LABOR

18   **Neither white nor Indigenous women:** Indigenous female servants above the age of sixteen became tithables in 1658. "Tithables: Everything You Wanted to Know," *Bob's Genealogy Filing Cabinet: Southern and Colonial Genealogies*, genfiles.com/articles/tithables.

20   **many female laborers among them:** Martha McCartney, *A Study of the Africans and African Americans on Jamestown Island and at Green Springs* (Williamsburg, VA: National Parks Service, Colonial Williamsburg Foundation, 2003), 56.

20   **practiced crop rotation:** Gwendolyn Midlo Hall, *Slavery and African Ethnicities in the Americas* (Chapel Hill: University of North Carolina Press, 2005), Kindle loc. 3082–88.

20   **pigs, and other livestock:** John Thornton, "Notes and Documents: The African Experience of the '20 and Odd Negroes' Arriving in Virginia in 1619," *William and Mary Quarterly*, 3rd series, 55, no. 3 (1998): 421–34; James Deetz, *Flowerdew Hundred: The Archaeology of a Virginia Planta-*

tion, 1619–1864 (Charlottesville: University of Virginia Press, 1995), 20–22; T. H. Breen and Stephen Innes, *"Myne Owne Ground": Race and Freedom on Virginia's Eastern Shore* (1980; New York: Oxford University Press, 2005), 71; William Thorndale, "The Virginia Census of 1619," *Magazine of Virginia Genealogy* 33 (1995): 155–70; Linda Heywood and John K. Thornton, "In Search of the 1619 African Arrivals: Enslavement and Middle Passage," *Virginia Magazine of History and Biography* 127, no. 3 (2019): 204–5.

21 **sought-after market item**: Anne Hilton, *The Kingdom of Kongo* (Oxford: Clarendon Press, 1985), 90–103.

21 **"on the advice of our Negroes"**: "Angela, Brought to Virginia 1619," *Jamestown Chronicles*, n.d., www.historyisfun.org/sites/jamestown-chronicles/angela_more1.html.

21 **Archaeological records**: "The Young Woman from Harleigh Knoll: Unearthing Untold Stories," National Museum of Natural History, naturalhistory.si.edu/education/teaching-resources/written-bone/forensic-case-files/young-woman-harleigh-knoll; "Young Woman from Harleigh Knoll," Clippix ETC, etc.usf.edu/clippix/picture/young-woman-from-harleigh-knoll.html.

21 **ten thousand English pounds**: Deetz, *Flowerdew Hundred,* 20, 46.

1649–1654: THE BLACK FAMILY

26 **In 1649 three hundred**: Warren M. Billings, ed., *The Old Dominion in the Seventeenth Century: A Documentary History of Virginia, 1606–1689* (Chapel Hill: University of North Carolina Press, 1975), 148.

26 **New Amsterdam**: Leslie Harris, *In the Shadow of Slavery: African Americans in New York City, 1626–1863* (Chicago: University of Chicago Press, 2003), 15.

26 **Many of them struggled**: Regarding the sale of people in New Netherland and Virginia in this period, see Joyce D. Goodfriend, "Black Families in New Netherland," *Selected Rensselaerswijc Seminar Papers,* 148, www.newnetherlandinstitute.org/files/3513/5067/3660/6.1.pdf; and J. Douglas Deal, *Race and Class in Colonial Virginia: Indians, Englishmen, and Africans on the Eastern Shore During the Seventeenth Century* (New York: Garland, 1993), 168–69, 280–81.

27 **Emmanuel Pietersen**: "Slavery in New Netherland," New Netherland Institute, www.newnetherlandinstitute.org/history-and-heritage/digital-exhibitions/slavery-exhibit/family-and-community.

27 **through baptism or marriage**: Regarding marriage in the Dutch Reformed Church, see Goodfriend, "Black Families in New Netherland," 149.

27   **forty-nine children for baptism**: Graham Russell Hodges, *Root and Branch: African Americans in New York and East Jersey, 1613–1863* (Chapel Hill: University of North Carolina Press, 1999), 16.

28   **By 1656, the Dutch Reformed**: Harris, *In the Shadow of Slavery*, 17; Hodges, *Root and Branch*, 18–24; Goodfriend, "Black Families in New Netherland," 151–52.

28   **"The Negroes occasionally"**: Hodges, *Root and Branch*, 21; Rev. Henricus Selyns to the Classis of Amsterdam, June 9, 1664, in John Franklin Jameson, ed., *Narratives of Early American History*, vol. 8, *Narratives of New Netherland* (New York: Scribner, 1909), 409.

28   **"children that are slaves"**: "An Act Declaring That Baptisme of Slaves Doth Not Exempt Them from Bondage" (September 1667), in William Waller Hening, ed., *The Statutes at Large: Being a Collection of All the Laws of Virginia, from the First Session of the Legislature in the Year 1619* (New York, 1823), 2:260.

29   **"out of the Naturall love"**: Quoted in T. H. Breen and Stephen Innes, *"Myne Owne Ground": Race and Freedom on Virginia's Eastern Shore, 1640–1676* (1980; New York: Oxford University Press, 2005), 85.

29   **racing toward full dependence**: Deal, *Race and Class in Colonial Virginia*, 279–87; Breen and Innes, *"Myne Owne Ground,"* 75–79.

1654–1659: UNFREE LABOR

30   **"the necessary evil upon which"**: Frank E. Lockwood, "Bill by Sen. Tom Cotton Targets Curriculum on Slavery," *Arkansas Democrat Gazette*, July 26, 2020, www.arkansasonline.com/news/2020/jul/26/bill-by-cotton-targets-curriculum-on-slavery/.

31   **fulfilled his indenture contract**: Indentured servitude, the prevalent labor system in the early days of British colonization, required that a person contract to serve a "master" from five to seven years before they gained freedom and land.

31   **"Johnson had kept him"**: "Court Ruling on Anthony Johnson and His Servant (1655)," *Encyclopedia Virginia*, www.encyclopediavirginia.org/court_ruling_on_anthony_johnson_and_his_servant_1655.

31   **"serve his said master"**: "Meeting Minutes July 9, 1640," *Minutes of the Council and General Court of Colonial Virginia* (Richmond, VA: Colonial Press, 1924), 466.

31   **"under pretense that the said"**: "Court Ruling," *Encyclopedia Virginia*.

31   **"corne and leather"**: T. H. Breen and Stephen Innes, *"Myne Owne Ground": Race and Freedom on Virginia's Eastern Shore, 1640–1676* (1980; New York: Oxford University Press, 2005), 14.

31   **"hee had him"**: "Court Ruling," *Encyclopedia Virginia*.

32 **"returne unto the service"**: Ibid.

32 **named the estate Angola**: John K. Thornton and Linda M. Heywood, *Central Africans, Atlantic Creoles, and the Foundation of the Americas, 1585–1660* (New York: Cambridge University Press, 2007), 283.

32 **"never to trouble or molest"**: "York County Deeds, Orders, and Wills, Selected Virginia Records Relating to Slavery," *Virtual Jamestown,* www.virtualjamestown.org/practise.html.

33 **all kinds of labor in the region**: Thelma Wills Foote, *Black and White Manhattan: The History of Racial Formation in Colonial New York City* (New York: Oxford University Press, 2005), 40.

33 **working for themselves**: Ibid., 39.

1659–1664: ELIZABETH KEYE

39 **"1662 Act XII"**: In the nineteenth-century reproduction of the law, the Latin phrase is inserted. "Negro Womens Children to Serve According to the Condition of the Mother" (1662), in William Waller Henig, ed., *The Statutes at Large: Being a Collection of All the Laws of Virginia, from the First Session of the Legislature in the Year 1619* (New York, 1823), 2:170.

40 **"Black Besse"**: Warren M. Billings, "The Cases of Fernando and Elizabeth Key: A Note on the Status of Blacks in Seventeenth-Century Virginia," *William and Mary Quarterly,* 3rd series, 30, no. 3 (1973): 467–74. The last name is variously rendered *Key, Keye,* and *Keyes* in the documents; I have unified the spelling as *Keye.*

40 **at least ten years longer**: Brent Tarter and the Dictionary of Virginia Biography, "Elizabeth Key (fl. 1655–1660)," *Encyclopedia Virginia,* www .encyclopediavirginia.org/Key_Elizabeth_fl_1655-1660.

42 **free of economic and racial violence**: Dorothy Roberts, *Killing the Black Body: Race, Reproduction, and the Meaning of Liberty* (New York: Vintage, 1998); Alys Weinbaum, *The Afterlife of Reproductive Slavery: Biocapitalism and Black Feminism's Philosophy of History* (Durham, NC: Duke University Press, 2019).

1664–1669: THE VIRGINIA LAW ON BAPTISM

43 **most Christian demographic**: David Masci, "Five Facts about the Religious Lives of African Americans," Pew Research Center, February 7, 2018, www.pewresearch.org/fact-tank/2018/02/07/5-facts-about-the-re ligious-lives-of-african-americans/.

43 **"It is enacted and declared"**: "An Act Declaring That Baptisme of Slaves Doth Not Exempt Them from Bondage" (1667), *Encyclopedia Virginia,* www.encyclopediavirginia.org/_An_act_declaring_that_baptisme _of_slaves_doth_not_exempt_them_from_bondage_1667.

43 **could not enslave other Christians**: Rebecca Anne Goetz, *The Baptism of Early Virginia: How Christianity Created Race* (Baltimore: Johns Hopkins University Press, 2012), 17.

43 **"Whereas some doubts have risen"**: "An Act Declaring," *Encyclopedia Virginia*.

44 **To challenge slavery on moral grounds**: Sean Michael Lucas, *For a Continuing Church: The Roots of the Presbyterian Church in America* (Phillipsburg, NJ: P&R Publishing, 2015), 39–45.

1669–1674: THE ROYAL AFRICAN COMPANY

47 **town hall**: Anthony Tibbles, "TextPorts Conference, April 2000," National Museums Liverpool, www.liverpoolmuseums.org.uk/ports-of-transatlantic-slave-trade.

47 **Cunard Building**: "Racism and Resistance," Historic England, historicengland.org.uk/research/inclusive-heritage/another-England/a-brief-history/racism-and-resistance/.

47 **Martins Bank**: "File: Slave relief: Martins Bank Liverpool.jpg," Wikimedia Commons, commons.m.wikimedia.org/wiki/File:Slave_relief_,_Martins_Bank_Liverpool.jpg.

47 **"a reminder that Liverpool"**: David Ward, "Martins Bank and Its Slave Trade Iconography," Liverpool Preservation Trust, February 22, 2011, liverpoolpreservationtrust.blogspot.com/2011/02/martins-bank-and-its-slave-trade.html?m=1.

48 **Royal African Company (RAC)**: William A. Pettigrew, *Freedom's Debt: The Royal African Company and the Politics of the Atlantic Slave Trade, 1672–1752* (Chapel Hill: University of North Carolina Press and Omohundro Institute of Early American History and Culture, 2013), 11.

48 **precursor to British imperialism**: Tahira Ismail, "Royal African Company and Empire," *Janus UMD Undergraduate History Journal*, October 28, 2018, www.umdjanus.com/single-post/2018/10/28/The-Royal-African-Company-and-Empire.

48 **Gambia and Ghana**: Ana Mosioa-Tunya, "The Role of the Royal African Company in Slavery," Global Black History, October 9, 2018, www.globalblackhistory.com/2018/10/the-role-of-the-royal-african-company-in-slavery.html.

48 **granted a monopoly**: Ann M. Carlos and Jamie Brown Kruse, "The Decline of the Royal African Company: Fringe Firms and the Role of the Charter," *Economic History Review*, new series 49, no. 2 (1996): 291.

48 **"had the whole, entire and only trade"**: "Britain and the Trade," National Archives (UK), www.nationalarchives.gov.uk/pathways/blackhistory/africa_caribbean/britain_trade.htm.

49 **joint stock company**: Derek Wilson, "Royal African Company: How the Stuarts Birthed Britain's Slave Trade," History Answers, December 7, 2017, www.historyanswers.co.uk/kings-queens/royal-african-company -how-the-stuarts-birthed-britains-slave-trade/.

49 **stockholders elected**: W. R. Scott, "The Constitution and Finance of the Royal African Company of England from Its Foundation till 1720," *American Historical Review* 8, no. 2 (1903): 245.

49 **monopolized the trade**: Carlos and Kruse, "Decline," 291.

49 **company was authorized**: Kenneth Gordon Davies, *The Royal African Company* (London: Routledge, 1999), 97–99.

49 **crown was entitled**: Scott, "Constitution," 245.

49 **"Negro Servants, Gold, Elephants teeth"**: "Royal Proclamation Regarding the Royal African Company with Signatures, 2 December 1674," Massachusetts Historical Society, www.masshist.org/database/1927.

50 **convict lease system**: Devon Douglas-Bowers, "Slavery by Another Name: The Convict Lease System," Hampton Institute, October 30, 2013, thehamptoninstitute.wordpress.com/2013/10/30/slavery-by-another -name-the-convict-lease-system/.

50 **criminalized minor offenses**: David A. Love and Vijay Das, "Slavery in the U.S. Prison System," Al Jazeera, September 9, 2017, www.aljazeera .com/indepth/opinion/2017/09/slavery-prison-system-1709010825220 72.html.

50 **immigration industrial complex**: Karen Manges Douglas and Rogelio Sáenz, "The Criminalization of Immigrants & the Immigration-Industrial Complex," *Daedalus* 142, no. 3 (2013): 199–227.

1674–1679: BACON'S REBELLION

51 **"a carpenter, formerly"**: "A List of Those That Have Been Executed for the Late Rebellion in Virginia, by Sir William Berkeley, 1676," *Virtual Jamestown*, www.virtualjamestown.org/exist/cocoon/jamestown/fha/J1055.

51 **Irish dockworkers**: Michael C. Connolly, "Black Fades to Green: Irish Labor Replaces African-American Labor Along a Major New England Waterfront, Portland, Maine, in the Mid-Nineteenth Century," *Colby Quarterly* 37, no. 4 (2001): 357–73.

51 **"hate strikes"**: David M. Lewis-Colman, *Race Against Liberalism: Black Workers and the UAW in Detroit* (Champaign: University of Illinois Press, 2008), 15–16.

52 **Bacon's anti-Native fervor**: Erin Blakemore, "Why America's First Colonial Rebels Burned Jamestown to the Ground," History.com, August 8, 2019, www.history.com/news/bacons-rebellion-jamestown-co

lonial-america; James D. Rice, "Bacon's Rebellion (1676–1677)," *Encyclopedia Virginia,* www.encyclopediavirginia.org/Bacon_s_Rebellion _1676-1677.

53 **"English, and other white"**: "An Act for Preventing Negroes Insurrections" (June 1860), in William Waller Hening, ed., *The Statutes at Large: Being a Collection of All the Laws of Virginia, from the First Session of the Legislature in the Year 1619* (New York, 1823), 2:481–82.

53 **any indentured white servant**: "Run-aways" (March 1661–62), ibid., 2:116–17.

53 **"lift[ing] his or her hand"**: "An Act Concerning Servants and Slaves" (October 1705), ibid., 3:447–63.

54 **stopped importing white servants**: Theodore Allen, *Class Struggle and the Origin of Slavery: The Invention of the White Race* (Stony Brook, NY: Center for the Study of Working Class Life, 2006).

1679–1684: THE VIRGINIA LAW THAT FORBADE BEARING ARMS

55 **"happened one law at a time"**: *Africans in America* (documentary), PBS, 1998.

55 **"lift[ed] up his hand"**: "An Act Concerning Servants and Slaves" (October 1705), in William Waller Hening, ed., *The Statutes at Large; Being a Collection of All the Laws of Virginia from the First Session of the Legislature in the Year 1619* (New York, 1823), 3:447–63.

56 **"eighty Guns"**: Philip D. Morgan, *Slave Counterpoint: Black Culture in the Eighteenth-Century Chesapeake and Lowcountry* (Chapel Hill: University of North Carolina Press, 1998), 389–91.

56 **NRA lent its support**: See Thad Morgan, "The NRA Supported Gun Control When the Black Panthers Had the Weapons," History.com, March 22, 2018, www.history.com/news/black-panthers-gun-control -nra-support-mulford-act; Adam Winkler, *Gunfight: The Battle Over the Right to Bear Arms in America* (New York: W. W. Norton, 2013).

1684–1689: THE CODE NOIR

57 **"prohibited the exchange"**: Gad J. Heuman and James Walvin, eds., *The Slavery Reader* (New York: Routledge, 2003), 199.

58 **"one of the most"**: Tyler Stovall, "Race and the Making of the Nation: Blacks in Modern France," in Michael A. Gomez, ed., *Diasporic Africa: A Reader* (New York: NYU Press, 2006), 205.

58 **"the French American"**: William Renwick Riddell, "Le Code Noir," *Journal of Negro History* 10, no. 3 (1925): 321–29.

59 **"salary and a portion"**: Thomas N. Ingersoll, "Free Blacks in a Slave So-

ciety: New Orleans, 1718–1812," *William and Mary Quarterly* 48, no. 2 (1991): 176.

60 **"since girls and women"**: Ibid., 186.

1689–1694: THE GERMANTOWN PETITION AGAINST SLAVERY

63 **"are brought hither"**: "Germantown Friends' Protest Against Slavery 1688" (facsimile), Library of Congress, www.loc.gov/resource/rbpe.14 000200/?st=text.

63 **"one of the first documents"**: Katharine Gerbner, *Christian Slavery: Conversion and Race in the Protestant Atlantic World* (Philadelphia: University of Pennsylvania Press, 2018), 70.

1694–1699: THE MIDDLE PASSAGE

65 **"in human flesh and blood"**: Malyn Newitt, *The Portuguese in West Africa, 1415–1670: A Documentary History* (Cambridge, UK: Cambridge University Press, 2010), 156.

65 **slowly eroded the Portuguese monopoly**: Richard Bean estimates that the Portuguese exported nearly 100,000 sterling worth of gold annually in the late fifteenth and early sixteenth century; see Bean, "A Note of the Relative Importance of Slaves and Gold in West African Exports," *Journal of African History* 15, no. 3 (1974): 351–56. See also Rebecca Shumway, *The Fante and the Transatlantic Slave Trade* (Rochester, NY: University of Rochester Press, 2011), 37–40; and Johannes Postma, *The Dutch in the Atlantic Slave Trade, 1600–1815* (New York: Cambridge University Press, 2008), 87.

65 **number of enslaved people**: The estimated number of enslaved men, women, and children from the Gold Coast rose from 2,429 in 1641–50 to 40,443 in 1691–1700. Voyages: The Trans-Atlantic Slave Trade Database, National Endowment for the Humanities, www.neh.gov/explore/voyages-the-trans-atlantic-slave-trade-database.

66 **the ruler of Ardra**: Carl A. Hanson, *Economy and Society in Baroque Portugal, 1668–1703* (Minneapolis: University of Minnesota Press, 1981), 243; C. R. Boxer, *The Golden Age of Brazil, 1695–1750: Growing Pains of a Colonial Society* (Berkeley: University of California Press, 1962), 153.

66 **"Axim, Ackum"**: Peter C. W. Gutkind, "The Canoemen of the Gold Coast (Ghana): A Survey and an Exploration in Precolonial African Labour History," *Cahiers d'études africaines* 29, nos. 115–16 (1989): 339–76.

66 **"the bigger canoes"**: Duarte Pacheco Pereira, *Esmeraldo de Situ Orbis*, trans. George H. T. Kimble (1506; Farnham, Surrey, UK: Ashgate, 2010), 116, 121, 122, 132.

66 **"the fittest and most experienced"**: Robert Smith, "The Canoe in West African History," *Journal of African History* 11, no. 4 (1970): 517.

67 **"It was customary for Mina fishermen"**: Willem Bosman, *A New and Accurate Description of the Coast of Guinea . . .* (London: James Knapton and Dan. Midwinter, 1705), 344.

1699–1704: *THE SELLING OF JOSEPH*

73 **"October 12. Shipped"**: "Samuel Sewall, Merchant," in *Proceedings of the Massachusetts Historical Society,* vol. 52, *October 1918–June 1919* (Boston: Massachusetts Historical Society, 1919), 335.

73 **"been long and much"**: *Diary of Samuel Sewall, 1674–1729,* vol. 2, *1699–1700–1714* (Boston: Massachusetts Historical Society, 1879), 16.

73 **"these Blackamores"**: Samuel Sewall, *The Selling of Joseph: A Memorial* (Boston, 1700), 2–3.

74 **The opening**: From 1676 to 1708, the enslaved population in Massachusetts more than doubled, from about 200 to approximately 550 enslaved people. An estimated two-thirds of them lived in Boston. Some of this demographic change can be attributed to the British Parliament's revocation of the Royal African Company's monopoly on the transatlantic slave trade, enabling merchants in Massachusetts to engage more freely in the lucrative trade in enslaved Africans.

74 **"There is such"**: Sewall, *Selling of Joseph,* 2.

74 **"sons of Adam"**: Ibid., 1–2.

74 **"for the freeing"**: *Diary of Samuel Sewall,* 16.

74 **"FOR AS MUCH"**: Sewall, *Selling of Joseph,* 1.

75 **"To persist in holding"**: Ibid., 3.

75 **"SEVERAL IRISH MAID SERVANTS"**: *Boston News Letter,* September 13, 1714, in Lorenzo Greene, *The Negro in Colonial New England, 1620–1776* (New York: Columbia University Press, 1942), 41.

75 **"Cowardly and cruel"**: Lawrence W. Towner, "The Sewall-Saffin Dialogue on Slavery," *William and Mary Quarterly* 21, no. 1 (1964): 48.

75 **He had made peace**: By 1715, the enslaved population of Boston had grown to approximately two thousand. The enslaved Africans and African Americans of eighteenth-century Massachusetts would face even stricter regulations than had preceding generations, including restrictions on buying provisions at market, keeping livestock, carrying canes, and being in public areas at night.

76 **his uncle's protest**: *The Selling of Joseph* was reprinted only once in the eighteenth century, by the Quaker abolitionist Benjamin Lay in 1737. It then fell into obscurity and was not reprinted again until 1863.

1709–1714: THE REVOLT IN NEW YORK

82 "gathered in an orchard": Edwin G. Burrows and Mike Wallace, *Gotham—The History of New York City to 1898* (New York: Oxford University Press, 1999), 148.

82 "had resolved to revenge themselves": Ibid.

82 enslaved to British owners: James E. Allen, *The Negro in New York* (Hicksville, NY: Exposition Press, 1964), 15.

82 20,613 enslaved Blacks in New York: Neil Smith and Don Mitchell, eds., *Revolting New York: How 400 Years of Riot, Rebellion, Uprising, and Revolution Shaped a City* (Athens: University of Georgia Press, 2018), 29.

83 "Koramantines and Pawpaws": Ibid., 148.

83 "themselves to secrecy": Herbert Aptheker, *American Negro Slave Revolts* (New York: International Publishers, 1943), 172. Aptheker cites an article found in the *Boston Weekly News-Letter*, April 7–14, 1712.

83 "Several did": Ibid., 148.

83 "Hunted down": Ibid., 149.

84 "The real legacy": Ibid., 149.

1714–1719: THE SLAVE MARKET

85 "socially relevant feature": Stephanie Smallwood, *Saltwater Slavery: A Middle Passage from Africa to American Diaspora* (Cambridge, UK: Cambridge University Press, 2007), 35.

86 "grow likely": Walter Johnson, *Soul by Soul: Life Inside the Antebellum Slave Market* (Cambridge, MA: Harvard University Press, 1999), 21.

86 "possibilities of their wombs": Jennifer L. Morgan, *Laboring Women: Reproduction and Gender in the Making of New World Slavery* (Philadelphia: University of Pennsylvania Press, 2004), 3.

86 chattel principle: Walter Johnson, *The Chattel Principle: Internal Slave Trades in the Americas* (New Haven, CT: Yale University Press, 2004), 1.

86 One enslaved woman: Richard Shannon Moss, *Slavery on Long Island: A Study in Local Institutional and Early African-American Communal Life* (New York: Garland, 1993), 51.

87 between 1715 and 1718: Jeanne Chase, "New York Slave Trade 1698–1741: The Geographic Origins of a Displaced People," *Historie & Measure* 18, no. 2 (2003): 95–112, 98.

87 "undesired testimony": Smallwood, *Saltwater Slavery*, 159–61.

87 Between 1715 and 1763: Moss, *Slavery on Long Island*, 35.

88 plainly visible in their tears: Saidiya V. Hartman, *Scenes of Subjection: Terror, Slavery, and Self-Making in Nineteenth-Century America* (New York: Oxford University Press, 1997), 38–39.

1719–1724: MAROONS AND MARRONAGE

89 **"two good ones"**: Le Page du Pratz, *The History of Louisiana or of the Western Parts of Virginia and Carolina* (London: T. Becket, 1774), 22, 27.

90 **policy of divide and conquer**: E. B. O'Callaghan, ed., *Documents Relative to the Colonial History of the State of New York* (Albany, NY: Weed, Parsons, 1855), 5:674.

90 **"lest [Africans] prove as troublesome"**: "Documents," *American Historical Review* 1 (October 1895–July 1896): 89.

90 **"refuge to the runaway negroes"**: Lt. Governor Bull to Board of Trade, May 8, 1760, in Tom Hatley, *The Dividing Paths: Cherokees and South Carolinians Through the Revolutionary Era* (New York: Oxford University Press, 1995), 74.

90 **"many Times Slaves run away"**: Walter Clark, ed., *The State Records of North Carolina, 1715–1776* (Goldsboro, NC: Nash Brothers, 1904), 23:201.

91 **"safer among the alligators"**: Liverpool *Albion*, February 20, 1858.

91 **Cornelia Carney**: Charles L. Perdue, Jr., and Thomas E. Barden, eds., *Weevils in the Wheat: Interviews with Virginia Ex-Slaves* (Charlottesville: University of Virginia Press, 1976), 66.

91 **Some maroons did not**: Sylviane A. Diouf, *Slavery's Exiles: The Story of the American Maroons* (New York: NYU Press, 2014), 1, 218, 301.

92 **"I taste how it is"**: John George Clinkscales, *On the Old Plantation: Reminiscences of His Childhood* (Spartanburg, SC: Band & White, 1916), 20.

1724–1729: THE SPIRITUALS

93 **"the syncretic Afro-Brazilian"**: Jonathon Grasse, "Calundu's 'Winds of Divination': Music and Back Religiosity in Eighteenth- and Nineteenth-Century Minas Gerais, Brazil," *Yale Journal of Music and Religion* 3, no. 2 (2017): 43.

94 **"The music is everywhere!"**: Eileen Southern, *The Music of Black Americans: A History*, 3rd ed. (1971; New York: W. W. Norton, 1997), xxi.

94 **"Song texts generally"**: Ibid., 16.

94 **"A most striking"**: Guthrie P. Ramsey, Jr., "Cosmopolitan or Provincial?: Ideology in Early Black Music Historiography, 1867–1940," *Black Music Research Journal* 16, no. 1 (1996): 14.

95 **"Afro-American music"**: Dena J. Epstein, "Black Spirituals: Their Emergence into Public Knowledge," *Black Music Research Journal* 10, no. 1 (1990): 59.

1729–1734: AFRICAN IDENTITIES

97 **Samba Bambara's:** Gwendolyn Midlo Hall, *Africans in Colonial Louisiana: The Development of Afro-Creole Culture in the Eighteenth Century* (Baton Rouge: Louisiana State University Press, 1992), 107.

97 **Marie-Joseph Angélique:** Ibid., 100–101; Afua Cooper, *The Hanging of Angélique: The Untold Story of Canadian Slavery and the Burning of Old Montréal* (Athens: University of Georgia Press, 2007), 14–22.

98 **New York had the largest:** Thelma Foote, *Black and White Manhattan: The History of Racial Formation in Colonial New York City* (New York: Oxford University Press, 2004), 69–70; Ira Berlin and Leslie M. Harris, eds., *Slavery in New York* (New York: W. W. Norton, 2005), 8, 60–71.

99 **Among the many ethnolinguistic:** Gwendolyn Midlo Hall, *Slavery and African Ethnicities in the Americas: Restoring the Links* (Chapel Hill: University of North Carolina Press, 2005), 55–79.

99 **"sickly" and "melancholy" "refuse":** Lorena Walsh, *From Calabar to Carter's Grove: The History of a Virginia Slave Community* (Charlottesville, VA: University Press of Virginia, 2001), 76, 79; Douglas Chambers, "'My own Nation': Igbo Exiles in the Diaspora," in David Eltis and David Richardson, eds., *Routes to Slavery: Direction, Ethnicity, and Mortality in the Atlantic Slave Trade* (London: Frank Cass & Co Ltd, 1997), 83–84; Gwendolyn Midlo Hall, "The Clustering of Igbo in the Americas," in Toyin Falola and Raphael Chijioke Njoku, eds., *Igbo in the Atlantic World: African Origins and Diasporic Destinations* (Bloomington: Indiana University Press, 2016), 149–53.

1734–1739: FROM FORT MOSE TO SOUL CITY

102 **"Spanish bureaucrats":** Jane Landers, "Gracia Real de Santa Teresa de Mose: A Free Black Town in Spanish Colonial Florida," in *A Question of Manhood: A Reader in U.S. Black Men's History and Masculinity,* ed. Darlene Clark Hine and Earnestine Jenkins (Bloomington: Indiana University Press, 1999), 1:92.

103 **"organized, governed":** Damien Cave, "In a Town Apart, the Pride and Trials of Black Life," *New York Times,* September 28, 2008.

104 **"Spanish support":** Landers, "Gracia Real," 106.

1739–1744: THE STONO REBELLION

112 **home to a Black majority:** Peter Wood, *Black Majority: Negroes in Colonial South Carolina from 1670 Through the Stono Rebellion* (New York: W. W. Norton, 1974), 131.

112 **"Carolina looks more":** Samuel Dyssli to family in Switzerland, Decem-

ber 3, 1737, in *South Carolina Historical and Genealogical Magazine* 23, no. 3 (1922): 90.

112 **free any enslaved person**: Ira Berlin, *Many Thousands Gone: The First Two Centuries of Slavery in North America* (Cambridge, MA: Belknap Press of Harvard University Press, 1998), 73.

112 **about twenty Black rebels**: Mark M. Smith, *Stono: Documenting and Interpreting a Southern Slave Revolt* (Columbia: University of South Carolina Press, 2005), xiii.

113 **At least twenty-three**: Ibid., 83.

113 **"Having found rum"**: Alexander Hewatt, *An Historical Account of the Rise and Progress of the Colonies of South Carolina and Georgia* (London, 1779), 2:34.

114 **"I sho' does come"**: George P. Rawick, ed., *The American Slave: A Composite Autobiography: Supplement,* series 1, vol. 11, *North Carolina and South Carolina Narratives* (Westport, CT: Greenwood, 1977), 56.

1744–1749: LUCY TERRY PRINCE

115 **"over the Green Mountains"**: Sidney Kaplan and Emma Nogrady Kaplan, *The Black Presence in the Era of the American Revolution,* rev. ed. (Amherst: University of Massachusetts Press, 1989), 241.

115 **alongside Phillis Wheatley**: David R. Proper, "Lucy Terry Prince: 'Singer of History,'" *Contributions in Black Studies* 9, no. 15 (1992).

116 **"King George's War"**: Catherine Adams and Elizabeth H. Pleck, *Love of Freedom: Black Women in Colonial and Revolutionary New England* (Oxford: Oxford University Press, 2010), 64.

116 **"wrote" the poem**: Frances Smith Foster and Kim D. Green, "Ports of Call, Pulpits of Consultation: Rethinking the Origins of African American Literature," in *A Companion to African American Literature,* ed. Gene Andrew Jarrett (Hoboken, NJ: Blackwell, 2010), 50.

116 **Baptized in 1735**: "Lucy Terry," in Margaret Busby, ed., *Daughters of Africa* (London: Jonathan Cape, 1992), 16–17.

116 **"three divisions"**: George Sheldon, *Negro Slavery in Old Deerfield* (Boston, 1893), 56.

116 **"a place of resort"**: Ibid.

116 **"where folks were"**: Ibid., 50.

116 **litigated before the Vermont supreme court**: Barbara M. Wertheimer, *We Were There: The Story of Working Women in America* (New York: Pantheon Books), 35–36.

117 **"in this remarkable woman"**: Quoted in Kaplan and Kaplan, *Black Presence,* 241.

117 **"know-your-place aggression"**: See, for instance, Koritha Mitchell,

"Identifying White Mediocrity and Know-Your-Place Aggression: A Form of Self-Care," *African American Review* 51, no. 4 (2018): 253–62.

117 **bell hooks**: See bell hooks, *Ain't I a Woman: Black Women and Feminism* (Abington-on-Thames, UK: Routledge, 2014).

1749–1754: RACE AND THE ENLIGHTENMENT

119 **race became an object**: Emmanuel Chukwudi Eze, ed., *Race and the Enlightenment: A Reader* (Malden, MA: Blackwell, 1997); Dorothy Roberts, *Fatal Invention: How Science, Politics, and Big Business Re-create Race in the Twenty-First Century* (New York: New Press, 2011), 28–32.

120 **scientists pointed to nature**: Terence Keel, *Divine Variations: How Christian Thought Became Racial Science* (Stanford, CA: Stanford University Press, 2018).

120 **"supernaturalist to scientific"**: Joseph L. Graves, "Great Is Their Sin: Biological Determinism in the Age of Genomics," *Annals of the American Academy of Political and Social Science* 661, no. 1 (2015): 24–50.

120 **Benjamin Franklin, one**: Ibram X. Kendi, *Stamped from the Beginning: The Definitive History of Racist Ideas in America* (New York: Nation Books, 2016), 80.

120 **innately and immutably**: Ibid., 84–85; Roberts, *Fatal Invention*, 30, 83–84.

121 **"the real distinctions"**: Thomas Jefferson, *Notes on the State of Virginia*, ed. David Waldstreicher (New York: Palgrave, 2002), 176–77.

121 **a religious treatise**: Kendi, *Stamped*, 88; John Woolman, *Some Considerations on the Keeping of Negroes. Recommended to the Professor of Christianity of Every Denomination* (Philadelphia: James Chattin, 1754).

121 **He advocated**: Phillips P. Moulton, ed., *The Journal and Major Essays of John Woolman* (Richmond, IN: Friends United Press, 1989).

121 **many Quakers had concluded**: Kendi, *Stamped*, 88; Brian Temple, *Philadelphia Quakers and the Antislavery Movement* (Jefferson, NC: McFarland, 2014).

121 **"Who can now find"**: Benjamin Franklin, *Observations Concerning the Increase of Mankind, Peopling of Countries* (Boston: Kneeland, 1755), 9.

122 **"The number of purely"**: Ibid., 10.

1754–1759: BLACKNESS AND INDIGENEITY

123 **dispossession of millions**: Roxanne Dunbar-Ortiz, *An Indigenous Peoples' History of the United States* (Boston: Beacon Press, 2014), 2.

123 **"British were the conquerors"**: Richard White, *The Middle Ground: Indians, Empires, and Republics in the Great Lakes Region, 1650–1815* (New York: Cambridge University Press, 2011), chap. 5, esp. 256.

123 **to justify taking their land**: For a visualization, see Claudio Saunt's inter-

active map of Indigenous land loss over time: "Invasion of America," usg.maps.arcgis.com/apps/webappviewer/index.html?id=eb6ca76e008 543a89349ff2517db47e6.

123   **central characters**: Jean O'Brien, *Firsting and Lasting: Writing Indians Out of Existence in New England* (Minneapolis: University of Minnesota Press, 2010), xiv.

124   **savagery and civilization**: Michael Witgen, *An Infinity of Nations: How the Native New World Shaped Early North America* (Philadelphia: University of Pennsylvania Press, 2012), 38.

124   **the combined power**: Ira Berlin, *Many Thousands Gone: The First Two Centuries of Slavery in North America* (Cambridge, MA: Belknap Press of Harvard University Press, 1998), 99.

124   **Georgia's enslaved population**: Betty Wood, "Slavery in Colonial Georgia," *New Georgia Encyclopedia*, June 3, 2019, www.georgiaencyclopedia .org/articles/history-archaeology/slavery-colonial-georgia.

124   **"To live in Virginia"**: "Reverend Peter Fontaine's Defense of Slavery in Virginia" (1757), *Africans in America*, www.pbs.org/wgbh/aia/part2/ 2h6t.html.

124   **Paul Cuffe**: Lamont D. Thomas, *Rise to Be a People: A Biography of Paul Cuffe* (Urbana: University of Illinois Press, 1986), 3–9.

1759–1764: ONE BLACK BOY

126   **"a Negroe boy"**: John Porteous Letter Book, 1767–1769, William L. Clements Library, University of Michigan, Ann Arbor. The brackets in this quotation indicate the uncertainty about this officer's last name, which is difficult to decipher in the record. This reference to the African American boy in Porteous's letter book is discussed briefly in Tiya Miles, *The Dawn of Detroit: A Chronicle of Slavery and Freedom in the City of the Straits* (New York: New Press, 2017), 35.

127   **defenders of the land**: I am borrowing the term *defenders* from Lisa Brooks, who consistently uses it instead of the more commonplace and ideologically laden *warriors* to describe Native men and women during King Philip's War. See Lisa Brooks, *Our Beloved Kin: A New History of King Philip's War* (New Haven, CT: Yale University Press, 2018). See also Jon William Parmenter, "Pontiac's War: Forging New Links in the Anglo-Iroquois Covenant Chain, 1758–1766," *Ethnohistory* 44, no. 4 (1997): 617–54, 627–29. For more on Pontiac's War, especially regarding the spiritual aspects of Native resistance and Neolin's role, see Gregory Evans Dowd, *War Under Heaven: Pontiac, the Indian Nations, and the British Empire* (Baltimore: Johns Hopkins University Press, 2002), 3, 86, 90. For a new analysis of gender and the representation of women

413

in histories of Pontiac's War, see Karen L. Marrero, *Detroit's Hidden Channels: The Power of French-Indigenous Families in the Eighteenth Century* (East Lansing: Michigan State University Press, 2020), chap. 6.

127 **a certain "Negroe boy"**: Richard Middleton, *Pontiac's War: Its Causes, Course, and Consequences* (New York: Routledge, 2007), 72.

128 **visible status symbol**: Pontiac sought a Black servant as a status symbol decades before the most prominent Native American slaveholders in the South—the Cherokees and Choctaws—installed Black servants in their homes and adopted plantation agriculture in part to display "civilizational" status and wealth. For more on Black slavery in southern Indian nations, see Celia Naylor, *African Cherokees in Indian Territory* (Chapel Hill: University of North Carolina Press, 2008); Fay A. Yarbrough, *Race and the Cherokee Nation: Sovereignty in the Nineteenth Century* (Philadelphia: University of Pennsylvania Press, 2008); Barbara Krauthamer, *Black Slaves, Indian Masters: Slavery, Emancipation, and Citizenship in the Native American South* (Chapel Hill: University of North Carolina Press, 2013); Tiya Miles, *Ties That Bind: The Story of an Afro-Cherokee Family in Slavery and Freedom* (2005; reprint, Berkeley: University of California Press, 2010); and Christina Snyder, *Great Crossings: Indians, Settlers, and Slaves in the Age of Jackson* (New York: Oxford University Press, 2017).

128 **approximately sixty-five others**: Donna Valley Russell, ed., *Michigan Censuses 1710–1830: Under the French, British, and Americans* (Detroit: Detroit Society for Genealogical Research, 1982), 121. The 1762 British census of Detroit counted five enslaved people with no designation of race. The 1865 census did not include numbers for enslaved people.

128 **network of merchant elites**: Norman McRae, "Blacks in Detroit, 1736–1833: The Search for Freedom and Community and Its Implications for Educators" (PhD diss., University of Michigan, 1982), 55; James Sterling Letter Book, 1761–1765, William L. Clements Library, University of Michigan, Ann Arbor; Miles, *Dawn of Detroit*, 30–31; Marrero, *Detroit's Hidden Channels*, 150–55.

128 **state prison in Jackson**: "Jackson: Prison System," Michigan History, michiganhistory.leadr.msu.edu/jackson-an-introduction/jackson -prisonsystem; Michigan State Industries, "History of Michigan Industries," www.michigan.gov/msi/0,9277,7-383-89195---,00.html; "Michigan's Prison Museum at the State Prison of Southern Michigan," Cell Block 7, www.cellblock7.org/; Howard B. Gill, "The Prison Labor Problem," *American Academy of Political and Social Science* 157, no. 1 (1931): 83–101, 84, 93; Blake McKelvey, "Prison Labor Problem: 1875–1900," *Journal of Criminal Law and Criminology* 25, no. 2 (1934): 254–70.

129 **largest incarcerated group**: "Michigan Profile," Prison Policy Initiative, www.prisonpolicy.org/profiles/MI.html (based on 2010 data).

129 **Racialized sentencing policies**: Melanca Clark, "How Michigan Can Reduce Its Prison Population," *Detroit Free Press*, August 31, 2018. Clark's figures are supported by "Michigan Profile," Prison Policy Initiative.

129 **expansion of convict labor**: Heather Thompson and Matthew Lassiter to author, July 17 and August 3, 2019; Heather Ann Thompson, "Unmaking the Motor City in the Age of Mass Incarceration," *Journal of Law and Society* 15 (2013): 41–61, esp. 47, 48, 49, 50 ("vicious cycle"), 54, 55; and Elizabeth Hinton, *From the War on Poverty to the War on Crime: The Making of Mass Incarceration in America* (Cambridge, MA: Harvard University Press, 2016), 191–202.

129 **"carceral landscape"**: Walter Johnson, *River of Dark Dreams: Slavery and Empire in the Cotton Kingdom* (Cambridge, MA: Harvard University Press, 2013), 209.

1764–1769: PHILLIS WHEATLEY

130 **The date Phillis**: Phillis Wheatley's first published poem, "On Messers Hussey and Coffin," and the accompanying note, were published in the *Newport Mercury* on December 21, 1767.

130 **"the difficult miracle"**: June Jordan, "The Difficult Miracle of Black Poetry in America," Poetry Foundation, August 15, 2006.

132 **"extraterrestrial and the supernatural"**: James Levernier, "Style as Protest in the Poetry of Phillis Wheatley," *Style* 27, no. 2 (1993): 172–93.

1769–1774: DAVID GEORGE

135 **"had not the fear of God"**: David George, "An Account of the Life of Mr. David George from Sierra Leone, Africa, Given by Himself," in Woody Holton, ed., *Black Americans in the Revolutionary Era: A Brief History with Documents* (New York: St. Martin's Press, 2009), 112.

135 **first Black Baptist church**: Sidney Kaplan and Emma Nogrady Kaplan, *The Black Presence in the Era of the American Revolution* (Amherst: University of Massachusetts Press, 1989), 91.

135 **shared religious life and culture**: Sylvia R. Frey, *Water from the Rock: Black Resistance in a Revolutionary Age* (Princeton: Princeton University Press, 1991), 37.

137 **any religious tradition**: See the Pew Research Center's surveys of the "religiously unaffiliated," www.pewresearch.org/topics/religiously-unaffiliated/.

1774–1779: THE AMERICAN REVOLUTION

139 **"All men are born"**: *Constitution or Frame of Government, Agreed upon by the Delegates of the People of the State of Massachusetts Bay* (Boston: Benjamin Edes & Sons, 1780).

139 **These same rights**: Emily Blanck, "Seventeen Eighty-Three: The Turning Point in the Law of Slavery and Freedom in Massachusetts," *New England Quarterly* 75, no. 1 (2002): 24–51; Arthur Zilversmit, "Quok Walker, Mumbet, and the Abolition of Slavery in Massachusetts," *William and Mary Quarterly* 25, no. 4 (1968): 614–24; and Christopher Cameron, "The Puritan Origins of Black Abolitionism in Massachusetts," *Historical Journal of Massachusetts* 39, no. 1–2 (2011): 78–107.

140 **Mumbet's political education**: Richard D. Brown, *Revolutionary Politics in Massachusetts: The Boston Committee of Correspondence and the Towns, 1772–1774* (Cambridge, MA: Harvard University Press, 1970).

140 **"all indentured servants"**: John Murray, "Printed copy of John Dunmore's Proclamation . . . , November 7, 1775," National Archives, Kew (UK).

140 **carried into subsequent conflicts**: Douglas R. Egerton, *Death or Liberty: African Americans and Revolutionary America* (New York: Oxford University Press, 2009).

141 **characterized the founding texts**: George William Van Cleve, *We Have Not a Government: The Articles of Confederation and the Road to the Constitution* (Chicago: University of Chicago Press, 2017).

141 **"Brom & Bett"**: *"Brom & Bett vs. J. Ashley, 1781,"* in Catherine M. Lewis and J. Richard Lewis, eds., *Women and Slavery in America: A Documentary History* (Fayetteville: University of Arkansas Press, 2011), 150–52.

142 **incomplete and misleading monument**: Blanck, "Seventeen Eighty-Three"; Zilversmit, "Quok Walker, Mumbet"; Cameron, "Puritan Origins of Black Abolitionism"; and Catharine Maria Sedgwick, "Slavery in New England," *Bentley's Miscellany* (1853): 417–24.

1779–1784: SAVANNAH, GEORGIA

149 **"were expected to become"**: Walter J. Fraser, Jr., "James Edward Oglethorpe and the Georgia Plan," in Leslie Harris and Daina Ramey Berry, eds., *Slavery and Freedom in Savannah* (Athens: University of Georgia Press, 2014), 2–3. For a general overview of the history, see Harris and Berry, *Slavery and Freedom;* and Whittington B. Johnson, *Black Savannah, 1788–1864* (Fayetteville: University of Arkansas Press, 1996).

149 **"built around central squares"**: Buddy Sullivan, "Savannah," *New Geor-*

gia Encyclopedia, www.georgiaencyclopedia.org/articles/counties-cities
-neighborhoods/savannah.

150   **about four hundred enslaved people**: James A. McMillin, "The Slave
Trade Comes to Georgia," in Harris and Berry, *Slavery and Freedom*, 9.

150   **oldest Black church**: "The Oldest Black Church in North America,"
First African Baptist Church, August 10, 2019, www.firstafricanbc.com/
history.php.

150   **Reverend Andrew Bryan**: Sandy D. Martin, "Andrew Bryan (1737–1812),"
New Georgia Encyclopedia, www.georgiaencyclopedia.org/articles/arts
-culture/andrew-bryan-1737–1812.

151   **"twelve negroes"**: Benjamin Quarles, *The Negro in the American Revolution* (Chapel Hill: University of North Carolina Press, 1961), 154.

151   **"were instrumental in the defense"**: Ibid., 148.

151   **1,094 of these soldiers**: Ibid., 82.

1784–1789: THE U.S. CONSTITUTION

153   **two enslavers**: "Richard Allen: Apostle of Freedom," Historical Society
of Pennsylvania, hsp.org/history-online/exhibits/richard-allen-apostle
-of-freedom/allenenslaved.

153   **didn't know hard work**: "The Life, Experience, and Gospel Labours of
the Rt. Rev. Richard Allen . . . ," Documenting the American South,
docsouth.unc.edu/neh/allen/allen.html.

154   **hard just to live**: Richard S. Newman, *Freedom's Prophet: Bishop Richard
Allen, the AME Church, and the Black Founding Fathers* (New York:
NYU Press, 2008), 198.

154   **"A nation, without"**: Federalist Papers, No. 85, Avalon Project, avalon
.law.yale.edu/18th_century/fed85.asp.

154   **"do good" to those**: Newman, *Freedom's Prophet*, 206.

155   **The abuse and affront**: "Life, Experience, and Gospel Labours."

155   **"this mode of alluding to slaves"**: Abraham Lincoln's Cooper Union Address, February 27, 1860, www.nytimes.com/2004/05/02/nyregion/full
-text-abraham-lincolns-cooper-union-address.html.

156   **Free African Society (FAS)**: "The Free African Society," Historical
Society of Pennsylvania, hsp.org/history-online/exhibits/richard-allen
-apostle-of-freedom/the-free-african-society; "Free African Society,"
Encyclopædia Britannica, www.britannica.com/topic/Free-African-So
ciety.

156   **1,849 freed men**: "Organizing the Community," Black Founders: The
Free Black Community in the Early Republic, librarycompany.org/
blackfounders/section6.htm.

156 turned the first shovel: "Life, Experience, and Gospel Labours."

156 African Methodist Episcopal Church: "Our History," African Methodist Episcopal Church, www.ame-church.com/our-church/our-history.

1789–1794: SALLY HEMINGS

158 "careful Negro woman": Thomas Jefferson to Francis Eppes, August 30, 1785, quoted in Annette Gordon-Reed, *The Hemingses of Monticello: An American Family* (New York: W. W. Norton and Company, 2008), 191.

159 "Mr. Jefferson's concubine": Annette Gordon-Reed, *Thomas Jefferson and Sally Hemings: An American Controversy* (Charlottesville: University of Virginia Press, 1997), 246.

1794–1799: THE FUGITIVE SLAVE ACT

163 "And be it further enacted": Fugitive Slave Act of 1793, www.ushistory .org/presidentshouse/history/slaveact1793.php.

163 Ona Judge: See Erica Armstrong Dunbar, *Never Caught: The Washingtons' Relentless Pursuit of Their Runaway Slave, Ona Judge* (New York: 37 Ink, 2018).

164 Black people in Haiti: For a more detailed discussion of tactical violence and Black abolitionism, see Kellie Carter Jackson, *Force and Freedom: Black Abolitionists and the Politics of Violence* (Philadelphia: University of Pennsylvania Press, 2019).

164 In Pointe Coupée, Louisiana: Gwendolyn Midlo Hall, "The 1795 Slave Conspiracy in Pointe Coupée: Impact of the French Revolution," in *Proceedings of the Meeting of the French Colonial Historical Society* 15 (1992): 130–41.

1799–1804: HIGHER EDUCATION

166 Francisco de Miranda: John S. Ezell, ed., *The New Democracy in America: Travels of Francisco de Miranda in the United States, 1783–84,* Judson P. Wood, trans. (Norman: University of Oklahoma Press, 1963), 70–71.

166 Moreau de Saint-Méry: Kenneth Roberts and Anna M. Roberts, trans. and ed., *Moreau de St. Méry's American Journey [1793–1798]* (Garden City, NY: Doubleday, 1947), 103–09.

166 Isaac Weld: Isaac Weld, Jr., *Travels Through the States of North America, and the Provinces of Upper and Lower Canada, during the Years, 1795, 1796, and 1797* (London: John Stockdale, 1807), I: 259–60.

167 "wasted & destroyed": Craig Steven Wilder, "'Sons from the Southward & Some from the West Indies': Slavery and the Academy in Revolutionary America," in Leslie M. Harris, James T. Campbell, and

Alfred L. Brophy, eds., *Slavery and the University: Histories and Legacies* (Athens: University of Georgia Press, 2019); John H. Livingston, "To the Honourable, the Legislative Council and General Assembly of the State of New Jersey," Box 1, Folder 12, MC 089, Elizabeth R. Boyd Historical Collection, Special Collections and University Archives, Alexander Library, Rutgers University.

167   **close their schools or relocate**: Craig Steven Wilder, "'Sons from the Southward.'"

167   **tripled the number**: Ibid.

168   **Transylvania College**: Donald G. Tewksbury, *The Founding of American Colleges and Universities before the Civil War with Particular Reference to the Religious Influences Bearing upon the College Movement* (New York: Teachers College, 1932), 32–35.

168   **church with national reach**: Craig Steven Wilder, "War and Priests: Catholic Colleges and Slavery in the Age of Revolution," in *Slavery's Capitalism: A New History of American Economic Development,* eds. Sven Beckert and Seth Rockman (Philadelphia: University of Pennsylvania Press, 2016), 227–42.

168   **Father Patrick Smyth**: Patrick Smyth, *The Present State of the Catholic Missions Conducted by the Ex-Jesuits in North America* (Dublin: P. Byrne, 1788), esp. 17–19; *American Catholic Historical Researches* (July 1905), 193–206; Jennifer Oast, *Institutional Slavery: Slaveholding Churches, Schools, Colleges, and Businesses in Virginia, 1680–1860* (New York: Cambridge University Press, 2016), introduction.

168   **"keeping harems of Negro women"**: J. P. Brissot de Warville, *New Travels in the United States of America, 1788* (Cambridge, MA: Harvard University Press, 1964), 346.

1809–1814: THE LOUISIANA REBELLION

173   **Charles Deslondes**: Daniel Rasmussen, *American Uprising: The Untold Story of America's Largest Slave Revolt* (New York: HarperCollins, 2018).

174   **"At present I am"**: Governor William C. C. Claiborne to James Madison, New Orleans, July 12, 1804, in Elizabeth Donnan, ed., Documents Illustrative of the History of the Slave Trade to America (Washington, DC: Carnegie Institution, 1935), 4:663.

175   **They wielded clubs**: Leon A. Waters, "Jan 8, 1811: Louisiana's Heroic Slave Revolt," Zinn Education Project, n.d., www.zinnedproject.org/news/tdih/louisianas-slave-revolt/.

175   **"They were brung here"**: Rasmussen, *American Uprising,* 148.

176   **"Had not the most prompt"**: Ibid., 148–49.

1814–1819: QUEER SEXUALITY

177–178 **"African homosexuality"**: Stephen O. Murray and Will Roscoe, eds., *Boy-Wives and Female Husbands: Studies of African Homosexualities* (New York: St. Martin's Press, 1998), xv.

178 **"the range of emotional"**: Daina Ramey Berry and Leslie M. Harris, eds., *Sexuality and Slavery: Reclaiming Intimate Histories in the Americas* (Athens: University of Georgia Press, 2018), 1.

178 **"evade capture and to subvert"**: Ibid.

179 **"transcend their laboring"**: Sharon Block, *Colonial Complexions: Race and Bodies in Eighteenth-Century America* (Philadelphia: University of Pennsylvania Press, 2018), 123.

179 **"One of the unfortunate things"**: Jessica Marie Johnson, interview by author, February 21, 2019.

179 **"I have been in the practice"**: Jonathan Ned Katz, *Love Stories: Sex between Men before Homosexuality* (Chicago: University of Chicago Press, 2013).

1819–1824: DENMARK VESEY

187 **Rapper Kanye West**: Harmeet Kaur, "Kanye West Just Said 400 Years of Slavery Was a Choice," CNN, May 4, 2018, www.cnn.com/2018/05/01/entertainment/kanye-west-slavery-choice-trnd/index.html.

187 **he rented or owned**: David Robertson, *Denmark Vesey: The Buried Story of America's Largest Slave Rebellion and the Man Who Led It* (New York: Vintage Books, 1999), 42.

187 **over 77 percent**: Ibid., 34.

187 **It seems that**: Thomas Jefferson, *Notes on the State of Virginia*, ed. William Harwood Peden (1955; Chapel Hill: University of North Carolina Press, 1996).

188 **The Haitian Revolution**: Robert Jones, Jr., "The Wretched Refuse of Your Teeming Shore," *Medium*, theprophets.medium.com/the-wretched-refuse-of-your-teeming-shore-9a3396556be6.

188 **Smartly, he had faked**: Douglas R. Egerton, "Before Charleston's Church Shooting, a Long History of Church Attacks," in *Charleston Syllabus: Readings on Race, Racism, and Racial Violence*, eds. Chad Louis Williams, Kidada E. Williams, and Keisha N. Blain (Athens: University of Georgia Press, 2016), 26.

188 **he joined the new**: Robertson, *Denmark Vesey*, 42.

188 **the Work House**: Ibid., 35.

188 **Dylann Storm Roof**: Rachel Kaadzi Ghansah, "A Most American Ter-

rorist: The Making of Dylann Roof," *GQ*, August 21, 2017, www.gq
.com/story/dylann-roof-making-of-an-american-terrorist.

188   **recruited as many**: Robertson, *Denmark Vesey*, 4, 42.

189   **What motivated**: Ibid., 70–71, 80–81.

189   **All transcripts**: Ibid., 17.

189   **threatened with arrest**: Ibid., 10.

1824–1829: *FREEDOM'S JOURNAL*

191   **"We wish to plead our"**: "John Brown Russwurm (Bowdoin Class of
1826)," Africana Studies Resources, library.bowdoin.edu/arch/subject
-guides/africana-resources/john-brown-russwurm/index.shtml.

193   **number of Black journalists**: Table O, "Employees by Minority Group,"
News Leaders Association, www.asne.org/content.asp?contentid=147.

193   **2019 annual survey**: "People of Color in TV News," RTDNA/Hofstra
University Newsroom Survey 2019, www.rtdna.org/uploads/images/
RTDNA-Hofstra%202019%20TV%20news%20diversity%20among
%20non%20Spanish%20language%20stations.png and "2019 Research:
Local Newsroom Diversity," RTDNA, June 13, 2019, www.rtdna.org/
article/2019_research_local_newsroom_diversity#TVPOC.

193   **circulation of leading newspapers**: Pamela Newkirk, *Within the Veil:
Black Journalists, White Media* (New York: NYU Press, 2000), 65.

193   *Essence:* It's worth noting that Richelieu Dennis, the owner of *Essence,*
was born in Liberia, where Russwurm relocated as a leader of the colonization movement. There he established the *Liberia Herald.*

194   *Hollywood Diversity Report:* Darnell Hunt and Ana-Christina Ramon,
Hollywood Diversity Report: A Tale of Two Hollywoods (UCLA College
of Social Sciences, 2019), 3, socialsciences.ucla.edu/wp-content/up
loads/2020/02/UCLA-Hollywood-Diversity-Report-2020-Film-2-6
-2020.pdf.

1829–1834: MARIA STEWART

195   **prominent speaker and writer**: Valerie Cooper, *Word, Like Fire: Maria
Stewart, the Bible, and the Rights of African Americans* (Charlottesville:
University of Virginia Press, 2011), 120. See also James Oliver Horton,
Free People of Color: Inside the African American Community (Washing-
ton, DC: Smithsonian Institution Press, 1993).

196   **first woman in the United States**: Paula Giddings, *When and Where I
Enter: The Impact of Black Women on Race and Sex in America* (New
York: HarperCollins, 1984); Marilyn Richardson, ed., *Maria W. Stewart, America's First Black Political Writer: Essays and Speeches* (Bloomington: Indiana University Press, 1987); and Carole B. Conaway and

Kristin Waters, *Black Women's Intellectual Traditions: Speaking Their Minds* (Burlington: University of Vermont Press, 2007).

196 **"women did not speak"**: Giddings, *When and Where*, 49.

196 **"promiscuous" audience**: Richardson, *Maria Stewart*, xiii.

196 **"Her original synthesis"**: Ibid.

196 **several of Stewart's writings**: In addition to these essays, Richardson's edited collection of Stewart's political essays and speeches includes Stewart's later writings, letters, and biographical sketches.

197 **gain economic independence**: Stewart asked, "How long shall a set of men flatter us with their smiles, and enrich themselves with our hard earnings, their wives' fingers sparkling with rings, and they themselves laughing at our folly?" She replied, "Until we begin to promote and patronize each other." Richardson, *Maria Stewart*, 38.

197 **"possess the spirit"**: Ibid.

197 **called out racial prejudice**: Ibid., 48.

197 **"Farewell Address to"**: Ibid., 68–69. Richardson has identified the full source of Stewart's citations as John Adams, *Woman: Sketches of the History, Genius, Disposition, Accomplishments, Employments, Customs and Importance of the Fair Sex in All Parts of the World Interspersed with Many Singular and Entertaining Anecdotes by a Friend of the Sex* (London, 1790).

197 **"talk, without effort"**: Richardson, *Maria Stewart*, 58.

1839–1844: RACIAL PASSING

201 **George Latimer and his pregnant wife**: Asa J. Davis, "The George Latimer Case: A Benchmark in the Struggle for Freedom," Rutgers, edison.rutgers.edu/latimer/glatcase.htm.

201 **"travelled as a gentleman"**: Ibid.

202 **"beaten and whipped"**: Ibid.

202 **"We all know"**: Nell Irvin Painter, *Southern History Across the Color Line* (Chapel Hill: University of North Carolina Press, 2002), 15, 18.

202 **federal legislation**: Maeve Glass, "Citizens of the State," *University of Chicago Law Review* (June 2018): 870.

203 **"No, never"**: Davis, "Latimer Case."

203 **"RANAWAY from the subscriber"**: Ibid.

204 **"women—whether slave"**: Painter, *Southern History*, 91.

204 **"Can this flesh"**: Davis, "Latimer Case."

1844–1849: JAMES MCCUNE SMITH, M.D.

205 **valedictorian of the medical school**: Simon Newman, "180th Anniversary for Former Slave James McCune Smith," University of Glasgow,

April 27, 2017, www.gla.ac.uk/news/archiveofnews/2017/may/headline
_523751_en.html.

205 **university scholarships**: "Description: James McCune Smith Scholarship," University of Glasgow Scholarships and Funding, www.gla.ac
.uk/scholarships/jamesmccunesmithscholarship/.

205 **formal medical degree**: Harriet A. Washington, "The Invisible Man: African Americans in Biomedical Research," unpublished manuscript,
July 2006.

206 **Glasgow Emancipation Society**: Bob Davern, "Surgeon and Abolitionist
James McCune Smith: An African American Pioneer," *Readex*, April 17,
2012, tinyurl.com/y5o65qqc.

206 **profits from enslavement**: No more than eighty slaves are thought to
have lived in Scotland before it banned chattel enslavement in 1778,
and the nation utterly abolished slavery the year after McCune Smith
arrived. However, the university, like the nation, profited handsomely
from the imperial slave trade. See Annie Brown, "Scotland and Slavery," *Black History Month* (August 19, 2015), www.blackhistorymonth
.org.uk/article/section/history-of-slavery/scotland-and-slavery; "Slavery, Freedom or Perpetual Servitude? The Joseph Knight Case," National Records of Scotland, www.nrscotland.gov.uk/research/learning/
slavery; "Slavery and the Slave Trade," National Records of Scotland,
webarchive.nrscotland.gov.uk/20170203095547/https://www.nrscot
land.gov.uk/research/guides/slavery-and-the-slave-trade; Iain Whyte,
Scotland and the Abolition of Black Slavery, 1756–1838 (Edinburgh: Edinburgh University Press, 2006).

206 **against American enslavement**: Davern, "Surgeon and Abolitionist."

206 **Samuel Cartwright**: Samuel Adolphus Cartwright, "Report on the Dis-
eases and Physical Peculiarities of the Negro Race," *New Orleans Medical and Surgical Journal* 7 (1851): 691–715.

206 **Josiah Nott**: J. C. Nott, "The Mulatto a Hybrid—Probable Extermi-
nation of the Two Races If the Whites and Blacks Are Allowed to
Intermarry," *American Journal of the Medical Sciences* 6 (July 1843):
252–56.

207 **"free" and "enslaved"**: U.S. State Department, "Compilation of the Enu-
meration of the Inhabitants and Statistics of the United States, as Obtained at the Department of State, from the Returns of the Sixth
Census" (1841).

207 **particularly mental health**: Albert Deutsch, "The First U.S. Census of
the Insane (1840) and Its Use as Pro Slavery Propaganda," *Bulletin of
the History of Medicine* 15 (1944): 469–82; Louis Dublin, "The Problem
of Negro Health as Revealed by Vital Statistics," *Journal of Negro Edu-*

cation 6 (1937): 268–75; and Clayton E. Cramer, *Black Demographic Data, 1790–1860: A Sourcebook* (Westport, CT: Greenwood, 2003).

207 **freedom could prove fatal**: Thomas Mays, "Human Slavery as a Prevention of Pulmonary Consumption," *Transactions of the American Climatological Association* 20 (1904): 192–97; and Clovis Semmes, *Racism, Health, and Post-Industrialism: A Theory of African-American Health* (Greenwood, CT: Praeger, 1996), 49–88.

207 **detailed report**: James McCune Smith, M.D., "The Memorial of 1844 to the U.S. Senate" (1844), in Herbert Morais, *The History of the Afro-American in Medicine* (Cornwells Heights, PA: Publishers Agency, 1976), 212–13.

207 **never formally corrected**: Robert W. Wood, *Memorial of Edward Jarvis, M.D.* (Boston: T. R. Martin & Sons, 1885), 12, 13. See also "Startling Facts from the Census," *The American Journal of Insanity* 8 (October 1851): 153–55; ajp.psychiatryonline.org/doi/abs/10.1176/ajp.8.2.15.

207 **posthumous acceptance**: "New York Academy of Medicine Awards a Posthumous Fellowship to Dr. James McCune Smith 171 Years After It Was Withheld," New York Academy of Medicine, November 5, 2018, nyam.org/news/article/academy-awards-posthumous-fellowship-dr-james-mccune-smith/.

207 **orphans' asylum was burned**: Jeffrey Kraus, "The Burning of the Colored Orphanage Asylum, NYC," *Antique Photographics*, April 24, 2012, antiquephotographics.com/the-colored-orphan-asylum-nyc.

207 **his 1865 death**: "Descendants of First Black US Doctor Mark NYC Grave," African America, September 26, 2010, www.africanamerica.org/topic/descendants-of-1st-black-us-doctor-mark-nyc-grave.

1849–1854: OREGON

212 **"dangerous subjects"**: Gregory R. Nokes, "Dangerous Subjects," *Oregon Humanities Magazine*, August 9, 2013.

212 **2016 statistics**: "Data Profiles," American Community Survey, 2016, www.census.gov/acs/www/data/data-tables-and-tools/data-profiles/2016/.

1854–1859: DRED SCOTT

214 **"a point of illumination"**: Don E. Fehrenbacher, *The Dred Scott Case: Its Significance in American Law and Politics* (New York: Oxford University Press, 1978), 7.

1859–1864: FREDERICK DOUGLASS

225 **The formerly enslaved**: Frederick Douglass, *Narrative of the Life of Frederick Douglass* (Boston, 1845).

225 **he fled to Britain**: David W. Blight, *Frederick Douglass: Prophet of Freedom* (New York: Simon & Schuster, 2018), 305.

225 **"was about to rivet"**: Frederick Douglass, *Life and Times of Frederick Douglass* (Hartford, CT: 1892), 390.

225 **"I knew if my enemies"**: Ibid., 396.

226 **Douglass had quietly**: Blight, *Douglass,* 319.

226 **"shall not brand"**: Frederick Douglass, "The Mission of the War," address delivered at Cooper Institute, New York City, January 13, 1864, in *New York Tribune,* January 14, 1864.

226 **"The republic was"**: Blight, *Douglass,* 388.

226 **severely restricted**: Manisha Sinha, *The Slave's Cause: A History of Abolition* (New Haven, CT: Yale University Press, 2016), Kindle loc. 6882.

226 **Abolitionists faced murder**: Ibid., Kindle loc. 5184.

227 **"We stand in our place"**: Douglass, "Mission of the War."

227 **"The recruitment of black"**: James M. McPherson, *Battle Cry of Freedom* (New York: Oxford University Press, 1988), 621.

227 **"It came to be"**: Douglass, *Life and Times,* 405.

227 **"as to giving the"**: Frederick Douglass, "The Reasons for Our Troubles," speech delivered in National Hall, Philadelphia, January 14, 1862, in *Douglass' Monthly,* February 1862.

228 **"abolition, though now"**: Douglass, "Mission of the War."

228 **"a mightier work"**: "Our Work Is Not Done," speech delivered at the annual meeting of the American Anti-Slavery Society, Philadelphia, December 3–4, 1863.

228 **"They dreaded the clamor"**: Douglass, *Life and Times,* 471–72.

228 **"Patrick, Sambo"**: Faye E. Dudden, *Fighting Chance: The Struggle over Woman Suffrage and Black Suffrage in Reconstruction America* (New York: Oxford University Press, 2011), 169.

228 **so-called Redeemers**: Eric Foner, *Reconstruction: America's Unfinished Revolution, 1863–1877* (New York: HarperCollins, 1988), Kindle loc. 11087.

229 **useless to the emancipated**: Lawrence Goldstone, *Inherently Unequal: The Betrayal of Civil Rights by the Supreme Court, 1865–1903* (New York: Walker & Co., 2011), Kindle loc. 239.

229 **"The Reconstruction amendments"**: Eric Foner, *The Second Founding: How the Civil War and Reconstruction Remade the Constitution* (New York: W. W. Norton, 2019), xxi.

229 **"Men talk of"**: Quoted in Blight, *Douglass,* 737.

1864–1869: THE CIVIL WAR

230 **won themselves freedom**: Steven Hahn, *A Nation Under Our Feet: Black Political Struggles in the Rural South from Slavery to the Great Migra-*

tion (Cambridge, MA: Belknap Press of Harvard University Press, 2003), 82.

230 **U.S. Colored Troops**: www.afroamcivilwar.org/about-us/usct-history
.html.

230 **"300 reliable colored"**: William A. Doback, *Freedom by the Sword: The U.S. Colored Troops, 1862–1867* (Washington, DC: Center of Military History, 2011), 6.

230 **tried to organize**: James M. McPherson, *Battle Cry of Freedom* (New York: Oxford University Press, 1988), 563.

231 **Emancipation Proclamation**: Doback, *Freedom by the Sword*, 9. It is significant that the Emancipation Proclamation did not extend to enslaved people in border states (Kentucky, Missouri, Delaware, and Maryland).

231 **thousands of Black Americans**: Doback, *Freedom by the Sword*, 10.

231 **"Once let the black"**: McPherson, *Battle Cry of Freedom*, 620.

231 **"If they stake"**: Ibid.

231 **"apostles of black"**: Eric Foner, *Reconstruction: America's Unfinished Revolution, 1863–1877* (New York: HarperCollins, 1988), 71.

232 **"old army uniforms"**: Hahn, *Nation Under Our Feet*, 174.

232 **"protect, strengthen"**: Ibid., 177.

232 **Union Leagues**: Ibid., 186.

233 **"several republican clubs"**: Douglas R. Egerton, *The Wars of Reconstruction: The Brief, Violent History of America's Most Progressive Era* (New York: Bloomsbury, 2014), 241.

233 **"double victory"**: Matthew Delmont, "Why African-American Soldiers Saw World War II as a Two-Front Battle," *Smithsonian*, August 24, 2017, www.smithsonianmag.com/history/why-african-american
-soldiers-saw-world-war-ii-two-front-battle-180964616/.

1869–1874: RECONSTRUCTION

235 **could possibly outweigh**: David J. Hacker, "A Census-Based Count of the Civil War Dead," *Civil War History* 57, no. 4 (2011): 307–48.

235 **more than 700,000 Black people**: U.S. Commission on Civil Rights, *Political Participation* (1968), www2.law.umaryland.edu/marshall/usccr/documents/cr12p753.pdf.

236 **"there is no existing"**: *White v. Clements*, 39 Ga. 232 (1869).

237 **"waited upon"**: Ku-Klux-Klan, *The Ku-Klux Reign of Terror. Synopsis of a Portion of the Testimony Taken by the Congressional Investigating Committee* (broadside), no. 5., n.p. (1872), Library of Congress, www.loc.gov/item/rbpe.23700800.

238 **A military report**: Charles Lane, *The Day Freedom Died: The Colfax Mas-*

sacre, the Supreme Court, and the Betrayal of Reconstruction (New York: Henry Holt, 2008), 265–66.

238 **McEnery and Penn**: Dorothea Lange, "Battle of Liberty Place Monument" (photograph), Washington, DC, c.1936, Library of Congress, hdl.loc.gov/loc.pnp/pp.print.

1874–1879: ATLANTA

239 **writing an article for *Harper's*:** Ernest Ingersoll, "The City of Atlanta," *Harper's Magazine* 60 (December 1879): 30–43.

239 **"feature of the city"**: Ibid., 42.

239 **"random collection"**: Ibid., 43.

241 **"drainage is therefore"**: Ibid., 40. On African American life and labor in Shermantown, see Tera W. Hunter, *To 'Joy My Freedom: Southern Black Women's Lives and Labors After the Civil War* (Cambridge, MA: Harvard University Press, 1997).

241 **"There are certain features"**: Ingersoll, "City of Atlanta," 33–34.

1879–1884: JOHN WAYNE NILES

244 **Callie House's National Ex-Slave**: Mary Frances Berry, *My Face Is True Is Black: Callie House and the Struggle for Ex-Slave Reparations* (New York: Random House, 2006).

244 **"a burly and muscular"**: "Niles Nailed: The Chief of the 'Indemnity Party,' A Colored Rogue and Swindler, Placed in the Penitentiary," *Daily Arkansas Gazette*, June 3, 1882; "The Seat of Government: Agitating the Establishment of a Colored Man's Territory," *St. Louis Globe-Democrat*, September 3, 1883; "Negro Niles: A Further Account of the Man Who Is Raising the Indemnity Party," *St. Louis Globe-Democrat*, June 6, 1882.

245 **"more illiterate of his own race"**: "Negro Niles: A Further Account," *St. Louis Globe-Democrat*.

245 **In 1869, in Tennessee**: Charlotte Hinger, "John Wayne Niles (1842–?)," *Black Past*, July 29, 2014, www.blackpast.org/vignette_aahw/niles-john-wayne-1842.

245 **the Exodusters movement**: Nell Painter, *Exodusters: Black Migration to Kansas After Reconstruction* (1976; New York: W. W. Norton, 1986).

245 **Nicodemus, Kansas, colony project**: Kevin Marvin Hamilton, "The Settlement of Nicodemus: Its Origins and Early Promotion," *Promised Land on the Solomon: Black Settlement at Nicodemus, Kansas*, National Park Service of the U.S. Department of the Interior (Kansas State Historical Society, Entourage Inc., 1984).

246 **"The judge who criticized"**: Ibid., 10.

246 **W. H. Smith, president**: "The Fraudulent Niles," *Daily Rocky Mountain* (Denver), April 11, 1878.

246 **Indemnity Party**: "Negro Niles: A Further Account," *St. Louis Globe-Democrat.*

247 **he was convicted again**: "Niles Nailed," *Daily Arkansas Gazette.*

247 **It would constitute**: "The Seat of Government," *St. Louis Globe-Democrat;* "Niles of Arkansas: The Colored Fomenter of Discord," *Daily Arkansas Gazette,* October 17, 1883; "Republicanism and the Negroes," *Fayetteville Observer* (North Carolina), October 4, 1883; "Mr. J. W. Niles of Arkansas Thinks That the Colored People of the South Should Take Themselves Up Bag and Baggage and Flee to Some Community Where There Are No White Men," *New York Globe,* October 27, 1883; "Negro Colonies: Proposed Separation of the Blacks from the Whites," *Daily Evening Bulletin* (San Francisco), November 9, 1883.

247 **"declare war against"**: "Republicanism and the Negroes," *Fayetteville Observer.*

247 **Respectable voices in the Black community**: "Mr. J. W. Niles of Arkansas," *New York Globe.*

247 **it was America's officialdom**: "On Motion by Mr. Ingalls," *Journal of the Senate of the United States,* Serial Set, vol. 2260 (1885), 178.

247 **deflected the Indemnity Party's**: "Niles of Arkansas: That Colored Fomenter of Discord," *Daily Arkansas Gazette,* October 20, 1883.

1884–1889: PHILADELPHIA

249 **"lead the masses"**: V. P. Franklin, "'Voice of the Black Community': *The Philadelphia Tribune,* 1921–1941," in *Pennsylvania History: A Journal of Mid-Atlantic Studies* 51, no. 4 (1984): 261, 262. The earliest archived issues of the *Tribune* begin in 1912.

249 **country's first penitentiary**: *Patrolman's Manual: Bureau of Police, City of Philadelphia* (Philadelphia: Department of Public Safety, 1913), 62; Leslie Patrick-Stamp, "Numbers That Are Not New: African Americans in the Country's First Prison, 1790–1835," in *Pennsylvania Magazine of History & Biography* 119, no. 1–2 (1995): 96, 98–100.

250 **arrested for murder**: Kali Nicole Gross, *Hannah Mary Tabbs and the Disembodied Torso: A Tale of Race, Sex, and Violence in America* (New York: Oxford University Press, 2016), 30–31.

250 **followed him from Newport**: "A Woman to Hang: Annie E. Cutler Sentenced to Death for Murder," *Philadelphia Inquirer,* October 17, 1885. For Mettler Bros., see *Gopsill's Philadelphia City Directory for 1884; Eastern State Penitentiary, Convict Description Docket,* #A3013, October 16, 1885.

250   **in front of several witnesses**: "Murdered in the Street," *New York Times*, April 22, 1885.

251   **"He did not look at me"**: "Annie Cutler Committed," *Philadelphia Inquirer*, April 25, 1885.

251   **to her mother**: Kali N. Gross, *Colored Amazons: Crime, Violence, and Black Women in the City of Brotherly Love, 1880–1910* (Durham, NC: Duke University Press, 2006), 90–93.

251   **sentence be postponed**: "Annie E. Cutler Pleads Not Guilty," *Philadelphia Inquirer*, May 8, 1885; "Murder in the First Degree," *New York Times*, May 23, 1885; and "The First Degree: Annie Cutler Declared a Deliberate Murderess," *Philadelphia Inquirer*, May 23, 1885.

252   **"The sentence of the law"**: "The First Degree," *Philadelphia Inquirer;* "A Woman to Hang," *Philadelphia Inquirer*.

252   **board of pardons**: "Annie Cutler to Be Hanged," *New York Times*, October 17, 1885; and "She Must Be Saved," *Philadelphia Inquirer*, October 19, 1885.

252   **signed petitions**: "Local Summary," *Philadelphia Inquirer*, October 29, 1885. Also "George D. McCreary, James S. Wright, Drs. Morton and Caspar Wister and Others, Are Interesting Themselves to Save the Poor Girl's Life, and It Is Likely That They Will Succeed," *Philadelphia Inquirer*, October 31, 1885; "About Town," *Philadelphia Inquirer*, November 7, 1885. Clergy from Newport, Rhode Island, signed and sent a petition for commutation for Annie; see "Case of Annie Cutler," *Philadelphia Inquirer*, November 17, 1885.

252   **"directly connected"**: "Woman's Rights: A Member of the Citizens' Suffrage Association Resigns on Account of a Discussion," *Philadelphia Inquirer*, June 3, 1885.

252   **seemed like a win**: "Annie Cutler," *Philadelphia Inquirer*, December 8, 1885; "Annie Cutler's Defense," *Philadelphia Inquirer*, December 17, 1885; Gross, *Colored Amazons*, 141.

1889–1894: LYNCHING

254   **"I found that in order"**: Ida B. Wells, *Crusade for Justice: The Autobiography of Ida B. Wells* (Chicago: University of Chicago Press, 1970), 71.

254   **"that most frightful crime"**: Philip Alexander Bruce, *The Plantation Negro as a Freeman* (1889; Nabu Press, 2012), 83, 84.

255   **"nobody in this section"**: *Free Speech* (May 21, 1892).

255   **In exile from Memphis**: Ida B. Wells, *Southern Horrors* (1892), *A Red Record* (1895), and *Mob Rule in New Orleans* (1900), published in *On Lynchings* (New Hampshire: Ayer, 1991). For other Wells publications, see "How Enfranchisement Stops Lynchings," *Original Rights Magazine*

(June 1910); "Lynch Law in America," *Arena* (January 1900); "Lynching and the Excuse for It," *Independent* (May 16, 1901); and "Our Country's Lynching Record," *Survey* (February 1, 1913).

256 **"To justify their own barbarism"**: Ida B. Wells-Barnett, *The Red Record* (1895), www.gutenberg.org/files/14977/14977-h/14977-h.htm.

256 **"Suspected, Innocent and Lynched"**: Ibid.

257 **white men's sexual assault**: Wells recounted the rape of black women in *Southern Horrors* under the heading "The Black and White of It," 16–27. When she described the brutal lynching of Eph. Grizzard, who was accused of raping a white woman in Tennessee, she pointed out that a white man who raped an eight-year-old Black girl was in the same cell with Grizzard when the mob took him. Wells once again highlighted the double standard in the rape-lynch discourse when she declared, "The outrage upon helpless childhood needed no avenging in this case; she was black."

257 **"Color Line Justice"**: Wells, *Red Record,* 148. A similar quote, in which she identified the young woman as Mrs. Camphor, appeared in *Southern Horrors,* 25.

1894–1899: *PLESSY V. FERGUSON*

258 **Citizens' Committee**: "Report of the Proceedings of the Citizens' Committee" contained names of all that had donated to support the case, listing local and South-wide support for their efforts. *Plessy v. Ferguson* Records, Amistad Research Center, Tulane University.

259 **had portraits**: For more on the roots of Black photography and portraiture, see Maurice O. Wallace and Shawn Michelle Smith, eds., *Pictures and Progress: Early Photography and the Making of African American Identity* (Durham, NC: Duke University Press, 2012).

259 **"the Committee engaged"**: Rodolphe Lucien Desdunes, *Our People and Our History: Fifty Creole Portraits,* trans. and ed. Dorothea Olga McCants (Baton Rouge: Louisiana State University Press, 1973), 144; Albion W. Tourgée Papers, 1801–1924, Kent State University.

260 **purchase her freedom**: The family discovery of the story of Agnes Mathieu is detailed in Michael Nolden Henderson, *Got Proof!: My Genealogical Journey* (Suwanee, GA: Right Image, 2013).

260 **legacy of activism**: For more on Victor Dupart's role in Homer Plessy's upbringing, see Keith Weldon Medley, *We as Freemen:* Plessy v. Ferguson (Gretna, LA: Pelican, 2012), 27.

260 **French side of Canal Street**: Arthe A. Anthony, "The Negro Creole Community in New Orleans, 1880–1920: An Oral History" (PhD diss., University of California, Irvine, 1978); Keith Weldon Medley, "The Sad Story

of How 'Separate but Equal' Was Born," *Smithsonian* 24, no. 11 (1994): 106–7; *Soard's City Directory, New Orleans, 1900*, Williams Research Center, New Orleans; Keith Weldon Medley, "The Life and Times of Homer Plessy and John Ferguson," *Times-Picayune*, May 18, 1996.

260 **New Orleans schools**: Medley, *We as Freemen*, 31–32.

261 **Highway 10**: Laine Kaplan-Levenson, "'The Monster': Claiborne Avenue before and after the Interstate," WWNO, New Orleans Public Radio, May 5, 2016, www.wwno.org/post/monster-claiborne-avenue -and-after-interstate.

1899–1904: BOOKER T. WASHINGTON

267 **"Negro problem"**: Gunnar Myrdal, *An American Dilemma: The Negro Problem and Modern Democracy* (1944; New Brunswick, NJ: Transaction, 1996), 1:lxxvii–xci; and George M. Fredrickson, *The Black Image in the White Mind: The Debates of Afro-American Character and Destiny, 1817–1914* (New York: Harper & Row, 1971). For an example of a racist assessment, see N. S. Shaler, "The Negro Problem," *Atlantic*, November 1884, www.theatlantic.com/magazine/archive/1884/11/the-negro-prob lem/531366/.

268 **"age of Booker T."**: August Meier, *Negro Thought in America, 1880–1915: Racial Ideologies in the Age of Booker T. Washington* (Ann Arbor: University of Michigan Press, 1963). See also Louis R. Harlan, *Booker T. Washington: The Making of a Black Leader* (New York: Oxford University Press, 1972).

268 **"at the top instead"**: Booker T. Washington, "The Atlanta Exposition Address, 1895," in *Afro-American Primary Sources*, ed. Thomas R. Frazier (New York: Harcourt, Brace & World, 1970), 216–20.

268 **"'Cast down your bucket'"**: Ibid.

268 **"agriculture, mechanics"**: Ibid., 218.

269 **"The wisest among"**: Ibid., 219.

269 **541 African Americans**: "Lynchings: By Year and Race," Archives at Tuskegee Institute, University of Missouri, Kansas City, law2.umkc .edu/faculty/projects/ftrials/shipp/lynchingyear.html.

269 **the story is even more**: Ishmael Reed, "Introduction: Booker vs. Negro Saxons," in Booker T. Washington, *Up from Slavery* (1901; New York: Signet Classics, 2010), xxii.

269 **"would be about"**: Washington, *Up from Slavery*, 5.

269 **valuable lessons**: Ibid., 33, 37–39.

270 **chastised Black people**: Ibram X. Kendi, *Stamped from the Beginning: The Definitive History of Racist Ideas in America* (New York: Nation Books, 2016), 283–84; Washington, *Up from Slavery*, 84–85, 120–23.

270 **"Within the last fortnight"**: Booker T. Washington, in *Birmingham Age-Herald*, February 29, 1904.

270 **a distinction**: Fitzhugh Brundage, "Reconsidering Booker T. Washington and *Up from Slavery*," in *Booker T. Washington and Black Progress: Up from Slavery 100 Years Later*, ed. W. Fitzhugh Brundage (Gainesville: University Press of Florida, 2003), 1.

1904–1909: JACK JOHNSON

272 **"But one thing remains"**: Jack London, *New York Herald*, December 27, 1908.

1909-1914: THE BLACK PUBLIC INTELLECTUAL

274 This chapter draws on Guy-Sheftall's work in her "Foreword" to *Convergences: Black Feminism and Continental Philosophy*, Maria del Guadalupe Davidson, Kathryn T. Gines, Donna-Dale L. Marcano, eds. (Albany: State University of New York Press, 2010).

1914–1919: THE GREAT MIGRATION

278 **"They left as though"**: Emmett Jay Scott, *Negro Migration During the War* (New York: Oxford University Press, 1920), 44.

278 **"their fate was"**: David L. Cohn, *God Shakes Creation* (New York: Harper & Bros., 1936).

281 **"I went to the station"**: Quoted in Scott, *Negro Migration*, 41.

282 **"folk movement of"**: Neil R. McMillen, *Dark Journey: Black Mississippians in the Age of Jim Crow* (Urbana: University of Illinois Press, 1990), 263.

1919–1924: RED SUMMER

284 **1919 Race Riot**: Chicago Commission on Race Relations, *The Negro in Chicago: A Study of Race Relations and a Race Riot* (Chicago: University of Chicago Press, 1922), 595–651.

284 **increased by 148 percent**: National Register Nomination for Chicago's Black Metropolis, National Park Service, 1986.

284 **Black Belt**: "Black Belt," *Encyclopedia of Chicago*, Chicago Historical Society, 2005, encyclopedia.chicagohistory.org/pages/140.html.

284 **Black veterans were not**: Darlene Clark Hine, William C. Hine, and Stanley Harrold, *African Americans: A Concise History* (New York: Pearson, 2012), 383–87.

285 **diverse population**: "Chicago, IL," DataUSA, datausa.io/profile/geo/chicago-il/.

285 **buried in snow**: Whet Moser, "Snowpocalypse Then: How the Blizzard

of 1979 Cost the Election for Michael Bilandic," *Chicago Magazine*, February 2, 2011.

285   **"Vrdolyak 29"**: "Council Wars," *Encyclopedia of Chicago*.

286   **closed more than fifty schools**: Valerie Strauss, "Chicago Promised That Closing Nearly 50 Schools Would Help Kids in 2013: A New Report Says It Didn't," *Washington Post*, May 24, 2018; Miles Kampf-Lassin, "Rahm Emanuel Will Be Remembered as Chicago's 'Murder Mayor,'" *Nation*, September 5, 2018.

286   **highly segregated neighborhoods**: Noreen Nasir, "Segregation Among Issues Chicago Faces 100 Years After Riots," Associated Press, July 24, 2019; Curtis Black, "In Final Act, Emanuel Cements Legacy of Tolerating Corruption, Promoting Segregation," *Chicago Reporter*, March 7, 2019.

286   **discrepancy in life expectancy**: Lisa Schencker, "Chicago's Lifespan Gap: Streeterville Residents Live to 90. Englewood Residents Die at 60. Study Finds It's the Largest Divide in the U.S.," *Chicago Tribune*, June 6, 2019.

286   **disparities are evident**: Alana Semuels, "Chicago's Awful Divide," *Atlantic*, March 28, 2018; "New Report Details Chicago's Racial, Ethnic Disparities," *UIC Today*, May 15, 2017.

1924–1929: THE HARLEM RENAISSANCE

287   **"the first act"**: David Levering Lewis, *W.E.B. Du Bois, 1919–1963: The Fight for Equality and the American Century* (New York: Henry Holt, 2000), 153.

289   **"certify the existence"**: Arnold Rampersad, *The Life of Langston Hughes*, vol. 1, *1902–1941: I, Too, Sing America* (1986; New York: Oxford, 2002), 105.

290   **"mystery woman"**: Mary Helen Washington, "Nella Larsen: Mystery Woman of the Harlem Renaissance," *Ms.*, December 1980, 44–50.

291   **"all tired and worn"**: Hurston to Lawrence Jordan, May 31, 1930, in *Zora Neale Hurston: A Life in Letters*, ed. Carla Kaplan (New York: Anchor Books, 2003), 190.

1929–1934: THE GREAT DEPRESSION

292   **"The Fascist racketeers"**: Angelo Herndon, *Let Me Live* (1937; Ann Arbor: University of Michigan Press, 2007), 166.

293   **anticipated fascism**: Cedric Robinson, "Fascism and the Intersections of Capitalism, Racialism, and Historical Consciousness," *Humanities in Society* 3, no. 1 (1983): 325.

293   **"a symbol of the clash"**: Herndon, *Let Me Live*, 317. Other scholars have

elaborated on the links between Herndon's case, the Communist Party's antilynching and racial justice campaigns, and Black antifascism, most notably Glenda Elizabeth Gilmore, *Defying Dixie: The Radical Roots of Civil Rights, 1919–1950* (New York: W. W. Norton, 2008), chap. 4; Mark Solomon, *Their Cry Was Unity: Communists and African Americans, 1917–1936* (Jackson: University Press of Mississippi, 1998); and Clayton Vaughn-Roberson, "Fascism with a Jim Crow Face: The National Negro Congress and the Global Popular Front" (PhD diss., Carnegie Mellon University, 2019).

293 **mainly in Alabama**: Herndon's memoir tells a different story, but I am relying on the census data, which not only registers Alabama as the birthplace of all of Harriet's children but situates her in Union Church by 1920 with her seven children. Angelo is listed as five, which would push his birth year up to 1914, which is very likely since the 1930 Census lists him (as Eugene Braxton) as age fifteen. U.S. Census 1900, Population Schedule: Union Church, E.D. no. 40; U.S. Census 1920, Population Schedule: Union Church, E.D. nos. 43 and 44.

293 **Sallie Herndon**: Sallie married Harriet's brother Alex (or Aleck) and lived in Union Church with their six children for several years. She moved to Birmingham in the mid- to late 1920s. Alex is not listed as a member of the household, although she is listed as "married." See U.S. Census 1910, Population Schedule: Union Church, E.D. no 44; U.S. Census 1930, Population Schedule: Birmingham, E.D. no. 37-2.

293 **"some kind of a secret"**: Herndon, *Let Me Live*, 72.

293 **Impressed with the Communists**: See Robin D. G. Kelley, *Hammer and Hoe: Alabama Communists During the Great Depression* (Chapel Hill: University of North Carolina Press, 1990), 38.

294 **Atlanta Six**: The best account of the Atlanta Six case is Maryan Soliman, "Inciting Free Speech and Racial Equality: The Communist Party and Georgia's Insurrection Statute in the 1930s" (PhD diss., University of Pennsylvania, 2014).

294 **"back to the cotton fields"**: Ibid., 135.

295 **denying Black Shirts**: Ibid., 132–37; see also Charles Martin, "White Supremacy and Black Workers: Georgia's 'Black Shirts' Combat the Great Depression," *Labor History* 18 (1977): 366–81.

295 **The ILD retained**: On Angelo Herndon's case and the campaign surrounding it, see Charles H. Martin, *Angelo Herndon and Southern Justice* (Baton Rouge: Louisiana State University Press, 1976); Tomiko Brown-Nagin, *Courage to Dissent: Atlanta and the Long History of the Civil Rights Movement* (New York: Oxford University Press, 2011); Gilmore, *Defying Dixie*, chap. 4; Rebecca Hill, *Men, Mobs, and Law:*

Anti-Lynching and Labor Defense in U.S. Radical History (Durham, NC: Duke University Press, 2009); James J. Lorence, *A Hard Journey: The Life of Don West* (Urbana: University of Illinois Press, 2007); and Dennis Childs, "'An Insinuating Voice': Angelo Herndon and the Invisible Genesis of the Radical Prison Slave's Neo-Slave Narrative," *Callaloo* 40, no. 4 (2017): 30–56.

295 **"lynching is insurrection"**: See Gilmore, *Defying Dixie;* Benjamin Davis, Jr., *Communist Councilman from Harlem: Autobiographical Notes Written in a Federal Penitentiary* (New York: International Publishers, 1969), 54–60.

295 **"Today, when the world"**: Herndon, *Let Me Live,* 406.

296 **"Yesterday, Ethiopia"**: Langston Hughes, "Milt Herndon Died Trying to Rescue Wounded Pal," *Baltimore Afro-American,* January 1, 1938; quoted in Vaughn-Roberson, "Fascism with a Jim Crow Face," 90.

1934–1939: ZORA NEALE HURSTON

298 **"*Jonah's Gourd Vine* can be called"**: Margaret Wallace, "Real Negro People," *New York Times,* May 6, 1934.

299 **"had been dammed up"**: Zora Heale Hurston, *Dust Tracks on a Road* (1942; New York: HarperPerennial, 1996), 175.

299 **"Her dialogue manages"**: Richard Wright, "Between Laughter and Tears," *New Masses,* October 5, 1937.

300 **"It is a pity"**: Reece Stuart, Jr., "Author Calls Voodoo Harmless in a Study of Haiti and Jamaica," *Des Moines Register,* November 13, 1938.

300 **"Hurston's poorest book"**: Robert E. Hemenway, *Zora Neale Hurston: A Literary Biography* (Urbana: University of Illinois Press, 1977), 248.

300 **"so grim that"**: Zora Neale Hurston, "Stories of Conflict," *Saturday Review of Literature,* April 2, 1938.

1939–1944: THE BLACK SOLDIER

307 **Isaac Woodard wanted**: Richard Gergel, *Unexampled Courage: The Blinding of Sgt. Isaac Woodard and the Awakening of President Harry S. Truman and Judge J. Waties Waring* (New York: Farrar, Straus and Giroux, 2019).

307 **Black World War I veterans**: On the experience of Black soldiers in World War I, see Chad L. Williams, *Torchbearers of Democracy: African American Soldiers in the World War I Era* (Chapel Hill: University of North Carolina Press, 2011).

308 **victory against racism**: Kimberley L. Phillips, *War! What Is It Good For? Black Freedom Struggles and the U.S. Military from World War II to Iraq* (Chapel Hill: University of North Carolina Press, 2012).

308 **clashed with local whites**: Gail L. Buckley, *American Patriots: The Story of Blacks in the Military from the Revolution to Desert Storm* (New York: Random House, 2001); and Bernard C. Nalty, *Strength for the Fight: A History of Blacks in the Military* (New York: Free Press, 1986).

309 **court-martialed fifty men**: Robert L. Allen, *The Port Chicago Mutiny* (New York: Warner Books, 1989).

309 **on the European front**: On the presence of Black servicemen in D-Day, see Linda Hervieux, *Forgotten: The Untold Story of D-Day's Black Heroes, at Home and at War* (New York: Harper, 2015).

309 **New Guinea campaign**: Robert F. Jefferson, *Fighting for Hope: African American Troops of the 93rd Infantry Division in World War II and Postwar America* (Baltimore: Johns Hopkins University Press, 2008).

309 **served as a longshoreman**: For firsthand accounts of the experiences of Black soldiers in the army, see Phillip McGuire, *Taps for a Jim Crow Army: Letters from Black Soldiers in World War II* (Santa Barbara, CA: ABC-Clio, 1983).

309 **761st Tank Battalion**: Kareem Abdul-Jabbar and Anthony Walton, *Brothers in Arms: The Epic Story of the 761st Tank Battalion, WWII's Forgotten Heroes* (New York: Broadway Books, 2004).

309 **first Black officers**: Richard E. Miller, *The Messman Chronicles: African Americans in the U.S. Navy, 1932–1943* (Annapolis, MD: Naval Institute Press, 2004).

309 **Montford Point**: Melton A. McLaurin, *The Marines of Montford Point: America's First Black Marines* (Chapel Hill: University of North Carolina Press, 2009).

310 **fighters of the 332nd**: J. Todd Moye, *Freedom Flyers: The Tuskegee Airmen of World War II* (New York: Oxford University Press, 2010).

310 **Charity Adams Earley**: Charity Adams Earley, *One Woman's Army: A Black Officer Remembers the WAC* (College Station: Texas A&M University Press, 1989).

311 **permanently blind**: Gergel, *Unexampled Courage.*

311 **abolished segregation**: Jon E. Taylor, *Freedom to Serve: Truman, Civil Rights, and Executive Order 9981* (New York: Routledge, 2012).

311 **Black veterans**: Christopher S. Parker, *Fighting for Democracy: Black Veterans and the Struggle Against White Supremacy in the Postwar South* (Princeton: Princeton University Press, 2009).

1944–1949: THE BLACK LEFT

312 **manifestos of the day**: Gerald Horne, *Black & Red: W.E.B. Du Bois and the Afro-American Response to the Cold War, 1944–1963* (Albany: State

University of New York Press, 1996); Carol Anderson, *Eyes Off the Prize: The United Nations and the African American Struggle for Human Rights, 1944–1955* (New York: Cambridge University Press, 2003), 128–50; and Carole Boyce Davies, *Left of Karl Marx: The Political Life of Black Communist Claudia Jones* (Durham, NC: Duke University Press, 2007), 37–40.

313   **"subversives"**: Glenda Elizabeth Gilmore, *Defying Dixie: The Radical Roots of Civil Rights, 1919–1950* (New York: W. W. Norton, 2008), 400–44.

313   **everything the far right despised**: Martin Duberman, *Paul Robeson: A Biography* (New York: New Press, 1989), 296–380; Gerald Horne, *Paul Robeson: The Artist as Revolutionary* (London: Pluto Press, 2016), 59–124.

313   **full democracy at home**: Martha Biondi, *To Stand and Fight: The Struggle for Civil Rights in Postwar New York City* (Cambridge, MA: Harvard University Press, 2003).

314   **African American exodus**: Manning Marable, *Race, Reform & Rebellion: The Second Reconstruction and Beyond in Black America, 1945–2006* (Jackson: University Press of Mississippi, 2007), 12–37.

314   **other "colored" populations**: Penny M. Von Eschen, *Race Against Empire: Black Americans and Anticolonialism, 1937–1957* (Ithaca, NY: Cornell University Press, 1997).

314   **aspirations might be realized**: Harvard Sitkoff, *The Struggle for Black Equality, 1954–1992* (New York: Hill and Wang, 2003), 13–18; Adam Fairclough, *Better Day Coming: Blacks and Equality, 1890–2000* (New York: Penguin Books, 2001), 203–15; and Raymond Arsenault, *Freedom Riders: 1961 and the Struggle for Racial Justice* (New York: Oxford University Press, 2006), 20–33.

314   **enraged ultranationalists and bigots**: John Egerton, *Speak Now Against the Day: The Generation before the Civil Rights Movement in the South* (New York: Knopf, 1995); and Dayo F. Gore, *Radicalism at the Crossroads: African American Women Activists in the Cold War* (New York: NYU Press, 2011), 74–99.

315   **upcoming recital**: Westchester Committee for a Fair Inquiry into the Peekskill Violence, *Eyewitness: Peekskill, USA—Aug. 27; Sept. 4, 1949* (White Plains, NY: Author, 1949), 2; Duberman, *Paul Robeson*, 341–54, 364.

315   **day of the concert**: Howard Fast, *Peekskill, USA: A Personal Experience* (New York: Civil Rights Congress, 1951), 20–45; Duberman, *Paul Robeson*, 364–65.

315   **"Wake up, America!"**: Fast, *Peekskill, USA,* 61–65, 69–91; Duberman, *Paul Robeson,* 367–75; Horne, *Paul Robeson,* 124–25.

1949–1954: THE ROAD TO *BROWN V. BOARD OF EDUCATION*

318   **"separate educational facilities"**: 347 U.S. 483 (1954).

319   **"these buildings were sawed"**: "NAACP Sets Stage to Enter Hearne Suit," *Informer,* September 27, 1947.

319   ***Sweatt* is widely regarded**: *Sweatt v. Painter,* 339 U.S. 629 (1950).

320   **Prince Edward County**: Robinson and Hill correctly gauged the level of resistance they would find in Prince Edward County. From 1959 to 1964, the county closed the public schools rather than comply with orders to desegregate. Schools opened only after the LDF successfully challenged the school closure in the U.S. Supreme Court. *Griffin v. County School Board of Prince Edward County, Va.,* 377 U.S. 218 (1964), supreme.justia.com/cases/federal/us/377/218/.

320   **the four *Brown* cases**: The *Hearne* case received new attention thanks to Rachel Devlin's excellent book *A Girl Stands at the Door,* which explores the courage and sacrifice of Black girls like Doris Raye and Doris Faye Jennings in *Hearne,* who were often the very deliberately selected "integrators" of Southern schools. *Jennings* did not directly challenge segregation. Black parents wanted a safe and properly constructed and resourced school for their children. Describing the remedy sought in the case, LDF reported, in its docket report to its board in 1948, that the discrimination "must be remedied either by admitting Negro students to the white high school or by providing Negro students with a new, modern and safe high school": that is, separate and truly equal education, or admission to the white school.

1959–1964: THE CIVIL RIGHTS MOVEMENT

327   **"You have begun something"**: Ella Baker, "Bigger than a Hamburger," *Southern Patriot* 18 (June 1960).

327   **"In government service"**: Ella Baker, "Developing Community Leadership," in *Black Women in White America: A Documentary History,* ed. Gerda Lerner (New York: Vintage, 1973), 351.

1964–1969: BLACK POWER

332   **"This is the twenty-seventh"**: Peniel E. Joseph, *Waiting 'Til the Midnight Hour: A Narrative History of Black Power in America* (New York: Henry Holt, 2006), 142.

333   **"the biggest purveyor"**: Martin Luther King, Jr., "Beyond Vietnam" (speech), April 4, 1967, kinginstitute.stanford.edu/king-papers/docu ments/beyond-vietnam.

1974–1979: COMBAHEE RIVER COLLECTIVE

340   **Since 1969, the Nixon administration**: Keeanga-Yamahtta Taylor, *From #BlackLivesMatter to Black Liberation* (Chicago: Haymarket Books, 2016), 55–72.

340   **underground to elude capture**: Barbara Ruth, "When Susan Got Busted, Philadelphia 1975," barkingsycamores.wordpress.com/2016/09/15/when -susan-got-busted-philadelphia-1975-barbara-ruth/.

341   **Joan Little and Ella Ellison**: "This Day in History, Aug. 15: 1975: Joan Little Acquitted," Zinn Education Project, www.zinnedproject.org/ news/tdih/joan-little-acquitted.

341   **Dr. Kenneth Edelin**: Robert D. McFadden, "Kenneth C. Edelin, Doctor at Center of Landmark Abortion Case, Dies at 74," *New York Times*, December 30, 2013.

342   **I wrote the statement**: Zillah R. Eisenstein, *Capitalist Patriarchy and the Case for Socialist Feminism* (New York: Monthly Review Press, 1979).

342   **groundwork for intersectionality**: Terrion L. Williamson, "Why Did They Die? On Combahee and the Serialization of Black Death," *Souls: A Critical Journal of Black Politics, Culture, and Society* 19, no. 3 (2017): 328–41.

343   **Black Lives Matter movement**: Barbara Ransby, *Making All Black Lives Matter: Reimagining Freedom in the 21st Century* (Oakland: University of California Press, 2018), 2–3.

343   **Colectiva Feminista**: Ed Morales, "Feminists and LGBTQ Activists Are Leading the Insurrection in Puerto Rico," *Nation*, August 2, 2019.

1979–1984: THE WAR ON DRUGS

351   **heroin's resurgence**: James Forman, Jr., *Locking Up Our Own: Crime and Punishment in Black America* (New York: Farrar, Straus and Giroux, 2017), 147–48.

351   **"the PCP capital of the world"**: Ibid., 135.

351   **come to be called crack**: David Farber, *Crack: Rock Cocaine, Street Capitalism, and the Decade of Greed* (New York: Cambridge University Press, 2019), 38–43.

351   **"We're making no excuses"**: "Text of President and Mrs. Reagan's Saturday Radio Address," UPI, October 2, 1982.

352 **people who participated**: Select Committee on Narcotics Abuse and Control, H.R. Rep. No. 98-598, at 59 (1983).

352 **"the cheapest game in town"**: Ibid., 41.

352 **national association surveyed**: Ibid., 65.

352 **one twenty-four-hour period**: Ibid., 69.

352 **Reagan reversed that ratio**: Grischa Metlay, "Federalizing Medical Campaigns Against Alcoholism and Drug Abuse," *Milbank Quarterly* 91, no. 1 (2013): 154.

352 **"simple abandonment"**: H.R. Rep. No. 98-598, at 115.

353 **"The response of a rational person"**: Editorial, "Dead and Dying Infants," *Washington Post*, October 4, 1989.

353 **resources to assist**: Forman, *Locking Up Our Own*, 147.

353 **Just 13 percent**: Michael Massing, *The Fix* (Berkeley: University of California Press, 2000), 53.

353 **Legislators in Delaware**: Tom Troy, "Lawmaker Recommends Whipping Post for Drug Traffickers," UPI, January 26, 1989.

354 **most crack users**: Shannon Mullen et al., "Crack vs. Heroin: An Unfair System Arrested Millions of Blacks, Urged Compassion for Whites," *Asbury Park Press* (December 2, 2019), www.app.com/in-depth/news/local/public-safety/2019/12/02/crack-heroin-race-arrests-blacks-whites/2524961002.

354 **"tarred and feathered"**: Editorial, "An Open Letter to PCP Dealers & Other Dogs!" *Los Angeles Sentinel*, September 25, 1980.

354 **Maxine Waters**: Forman, *Locking Up Our Own*, 134.

354 **"should be dealt with"**: Ibid., 137.

354 **"more prosecutors, more judges"**: Farber, *Crack*, 135; H.R. Rep. No. 98-598, at 41.

1984–1989: THE HIP-HOP GENERATION

355 **"I found it almost"**: Rakim, *Sweat the Technique: Revelations on Creativity from the Lyrical Genius* (New York: HarperCollins, 2019), 124–25.

358 **"most important hip-hop"**: Rakim, Talib Kweli, and Chuck D, "Sweat the Technique: The Politics and Poetics of Hip-Hop," a discussion of Rakim's *Sweat* at the California African American Museum, March 11, 2020, youtube.com/watch?v=8kmaT4KVGf8.

1989–1994: ANITA HILL

360 **"We were all Anita"**: DeNeen L. Brown, "The Scathing Ad 1,600 Black Women Bought to Oppose Clarence Thomas," *Washington Post*, September 20, 2018.

361 **"In matters of race"**: Toni Morrison, "Introduction: Friday on the Po-
tomac," in *Race-ing Justice, En-gendering Power: Essays on Anita Hill,
Clarence Thomas, and the Construction of Social Reality*, ed. Toni Morrison (New York: Pantheon, 1992), xxx.

361 **In Clarence Thomas**: Ron Elving, "Anita Hill's Challenge to Clarence
Thomas: A Tale of 2 Lives and 3 Elections," NPR, September 20, 2018.

361 **"While we appreciate"**: William J. Eaton and Douglas Jehl, "NAACP
Vows to Fight Thomas' Confirmation," *Los Angeles Times*, August 1,
1991.

362 **"He talked about pornographic"**: *Hearing before the Committee on the Judiciary, U.S. Senate, Nomination of Judge Clarence Thomas to Be an Associate Justice of the Supreme Court of the United States*, 102nd Congress, first
sess. (Washington, DC: Government Printing Office, 1991).

362 **"Having made Anita Hill"**: Nell Irvin Painter, "Hill, Thomas, and the
Use of Racial Stereotype," in Morrison, *Race-ing Justice*, 205.

363 **"A conversation"**: Morrison, "Introduction," in *Race-ing Justice*, xxx.

363 **70 percent of African Americans**: "Black Support for Nominee Rises,"
Chicago Tribune, October 15, 1991.

364 **Sexual harassment cases**: U.S. Equal Employment Opportunity Commission Enforcement Guidance, *Vicarious Employer Liability for Filing a Charge of Discrimination Unlawful Harassment by Supervisors*,
www.eeoc.gov/employees/charge.cfm; www.eeoc.gov/eeoc/publications/
index.cfm.

364 **"Clarence Thomas Effect"**: Lawrence Bobo to author, September 13,
2019.

364 **"One can easily amass a lot"**: Ibid.

364 **"There is no way"**: Anita Hill, "How to Get the Kavanaugh Hearings
Right," *New York Times*, September 18, 2018.

365 **"We believe Anita Hill"**: "We believe Anita Hill. We also believe Christine Blasey Ford" (advertisement), *New York Times*, September 26, 2018.
See Alexandria Symonds and Katie Van Syckle, "Your Beliefs Here: A
Look at Advocacy Advertising in *The Times*," *New York Times*, September 28, 2018.

1994–1999: THE CRIME BILL

366 **"Ultimately, the human cost"**: Heather Ann Thompson, *Blood in the
Water: The Attica Prison Uprising of 1971 and Its Legacy* (New York: Vintage, 2017), 187–88.

366 **"I think I have"**: Quoted ibid., 193.

367 **"Today the bickering"**: Bill Clinton, "Remarks on Signing the Violent

Crime Control and Law Enforcement Act of 1994," September 13, 1994, *Public Papers of the Presidents of the United States: William J. Clinton* (Washington, DC: Government Printing Office, 1994), 2:1539–41.

367 **moral panic:** See Stuart Hall et al., *Policing the Crisis: Mugging, the State, and Law and Order,* 2nd ed. (New York: Palgrave Macmillan, 2013), for a discussion of the complicated process of racism and criminalization in the UK.

367 **"the black urban working":** Joe William Trotter, Jr., *Workers on Arrival: Black Labor in the Making of America* (Berkeley: University of California Press, 2019), 162.

368 **capitalism has always:** Cedric J. Robinson, *Black Marxism: The Making of the Black Radical Tradition* (Chapel Hill: University of North Carolina Press, 1983).

368 **"There was talk of":** Adam Nossiter, "Making Hard Time Harder, States Cut Jail TV and Sports," *New York Times,* September 17, 1994.

1999–2004: THE BLACK IMMIGRANT

370 **quiet and soft-spoken:** Kadiatou Diallo and Craig Wolff, *My Heart Will Cross This Ocean: My Story, My Son, Amadou* (New York: Random House, 2003).

2004–2009: HURRICANE KATRINA

375 **"gendered nature":** Barbara Ransby, "Katrina, Black Women, and the Deadly Discourse on Black Poverty in America," *Du Bois Review: Social Science Research on Race* 3, no. 1 (2006): 215–22.

376 **"And so many of":** "Bar: Astrodome 'Working Well' for Evacuees," UPI, September 5, 2005.

376 **"dirty, desperate":** Ransby, "Katrina, Black Women."

376 **"the Bricks":** Jane Henrici, Chandra Childers, and Elyse Shaw, *Get to the Bricks: The Experiences of Black Women from New Orleans Public Housing After Hurricane Katrina,* Institute for Women's Policy Research, August 25, 2015, iwpr.org/iwpr-issues/race-ethnicity-gender -and-economy/get-to-the-bricks-the-experiences-of-black-women -from-new-orleans-public-housing-after-hurricane-katrina/.

377 **falling to 230,172 residents:** Allison Plyer, *Facts for Features: Katrina Impact,* August 26, 2016, www.datacenterresearch.org/data-resources/ katrina/facts-for-impact/.

377 **37 percent:** "Study: Less Black Women in Post-Katrina New Orleans," Institute for Women's Policy Research, November 3, 2010, iwpr .org/media/press-hits/study-less-black-women-in-post-katrina-new -orleans/.

377   **"the hunger and thirst"**: Avis Jones-DeWeever, *Women in the Wake of the Storm: Examining the Post-Katrina Realities of the Women of New Orleans and the Gulf Coast,* Institute for Women's Policy Research, April 2008, 1, vawnet.org/sites/default/files/materials/files/2016-08/D481.pdf.

2009–2014: THE *SHELBY* RULING

380   **a new voter ID law**: "Wisconsin's Voter-ID Law Suppressed 200,000 Votes in 2016 (Trump Won by 22,748)," *Nation,* May 9, 2017.

380   **voter suppression has taken**: Carol Anderson, *One Person, No Vote: How Voter Suppression Is Destroying Our Democracy* (New York: Bloomsbury, 2018).

381   **16 million people**: "Purges: A Growing Threat to the Right to Vote," Brennan Center for Justice, July 20, 2018, www.brennancenter.org/our -work/research-reports/purges-growing-threat-right-vote.

CONCLUSION

390   **"full freedom"**: Kim D. Butler, *Freedoms Given, Freedoms Won: Afro-Brazilians in Post-Abolition São Paulo and Salvador* (New Brunswick, NJ: Rutgers University Press, 1998), 210–11.

CONTRIBUTORS

———

DERRICK ALRIDGE is the Philip J. Gibson Professor of Education and an affiliate faculty member in the Carter G. Woodson Institute for African-American and African Studies at the University of Virginia. An educational and intellectual historian, Alridge is the author of *The Educational Thought of W.E.B. Du Bois: An Intellectual History* (2008) and co-editor of *Message in the Music: Hip-Hop, History, and Pedagogy* (2011) and *The Black Intellectual Tradition: African American Thought in the Twentieth Century* (forthcoming in 2021).

ESTHER ARMAH is an internationally award-winning journalist, radio host, writer, public speaker, and playwright, who has lived and worked in New York, London, and Accra. She is executive director of the Armah Institute of Emotional Justice. Her life's work is Emotional Justice, a framework she created, for which she won a Community Healer Award at the 2016 Valuing Black Lives Global Emotional Emancipation Summit in Washington, D.C. Her Emotional Justice essays have been featured by *WARSCAPES, Ebony, AlterNet, Essence, Gawker,* and the Jay Z *4:44 Syllabus,* and in books *Charleston Syllabus: Readings on Race, Racism, & Racial Violence* (2016) and *Love with Accountability: Digging Up the Roots of Child Sexual Abuse* (2019), which won a 2020 Lambda Literary Award. She has written five Emotional Justice plays that have been produced and performed in New York, Chicago, and Ghana. She was named Most Valuable New York Radio Host in *The Nation*'s 2012 Progressive Honors List for her work on *Wake-Up Call* on Pacifica's WBAI. She was named one of Africa's 30 Women Leaders in 2019 by CMO Asia and the Africa Leadership Academy.

MOLEFI KETE ASANTE is professor and chair of the Department of Africology at Temple University. He is the co-founder of Afrocentricity International and president of the Molefi Kete Asante Institute for Afrocentric Studies, as well as the founding and current editor of *Journal of Black Studies.* Asante, often called the most prolific African American scholar, has published ninety-two books; among them are *Radical Insurgencies* (2020), *The History of Africa* (3rd edition,

2019), *The African American People: A Global History* (2011), *Erasing Racism: The Survival of the American Nation* (2009), *Revolutionary Pedagogy* (2017), *African American History: A Journey of Liberation* (1995), *African Pyramids of Knowledge* (2015), *Facing South to Africa* (2014), and the memoir *As I Run Toward Africa* (2011). Asante has published more than five hundred articles and is one of the most quoted living African authors as well as one of the most distinguished thinkers in the African world. At Temple University, he created the first PhD program in African American Studies in 1988. He has directed more than 135 PhD dissertations, making him the top producer of doctorates among African American scholars. He created the theory of Afrocentricity.

WILLIAM J. BARBER II is senior pastor of the Greenleaf Christian Church (Disciples of Christ), president and senior lecturer at Repairers of the Breach, and co-chair of the Poor People's Campaign: A National Call for Moral Revival. A 2018 recipient of the MacArthur Foundation's "genius award," he is the author of *The Third Reconstruction* (2016), *Revive Us Again* (2018), and *We Are Called to Become a Movement* (2020).

KATHRYN SOPHIA BELLE is an associate professor of philosophy and is affiliated with African American studies and women's, gender, and sexuality studies at Pennsylvania State University. Her areas of specialization include African American/Africana philosophy, Black feminist philosophy, continental philosophy (existentialism), and critical philosophy of race. Major figures she engages include Hannah Arendt, Simone de Beauvoir, Anna Julia Cooper, Frantz Fanon, Audre Lorde, Jean-Paul Sartre, Maria W. Stewart, and Richard Wright. She has published on race, feminism, intersectionality, and sex/sexuality. Under the name Kathryn T. Gines, she co-edited *Convergences: Black Feminism and Continental Philosophy* (2010) and wrote *Hannah Arendt and the Negro Question* (2014). She is founding director of the Collegium of Black Women Philosophers, founding co-editor of the journal *Critical Philosophy of Race,* and founder of La Belle Vie Coaching, offering initiatives for high achievers, the happily unmarried, and erotic empowerment.

JOSHUA BENNETT is the Mellon Assistant Professor of English and Creative Writing at Dartmouth. He is the author of three books of poetry and criticism: *The Sobbing School* (2016)—winner of the National Poetry Series and a finalist for an NAACP Image Award—*Being Property Once Myself* (2020), and *Owed* (2020). Bennett earned his PhD in English from Princeton University and an MA in theatre and performance studies from the University of Warwick, where he was a Marshall Scholar. Dr. Bennett's writing has been published in *Best American Poetry, The New York Times, The Paris Review, Poetry,* and elsewhere. He has received fellowships from the National Endowment for the Arts, the Ford Foundation, MIT, and the Society of Fellows at Harvard University. His first work of narrative nonfiction, *Spoken Word: A Cultural History,* is forthcoming from Knopf.

DAINA RAMEY BERRY is the Oliver H. Radkey Regents Professor of History and chair of the history department at the University of Texas at Austin. She is the award-winning author and editor of six books, including *The Price for Their Pound of Flesh: The Value of the Enslaved, from Womb to Grave, in the Building of a Nation* (2017), which received three book awards. Her most recent book, *A Black Women's History of the United States* (2020), co-authored by Kali N. Gross, has received starred reviews from *Kirkus Review* and *Library Journal.* In February 2020, it was listed as one of the top ten books to read by *The Washington Post,* and it is on the longlist for the Brooklyn Public Library's Literary Prize.

Based in Charlottesville, Virginia, and Washington, D.C., JAMELLE BOUIE is a columnist for *The New York Times* and a political analyst for CBS News. He covers campaigns, elections, national affairs, and culture. Prior to his work for the *Times,* Bouie was chief political correspondent for *Slate* magazine and a staff writer at *The Daily Beast* and he held fellowships at *The American Prospect* and *The Nation.* He attended the University of Virginia, where he graduated with a degree in political and social thought, and government. Bouie is also a photographer, documenting his surroundings using digital and analog tools.

HERB BOYD is an award-winning author and journalist who has published a number of books and countless articles for national magazines and newspapers, including the *Amsterdam News.* His most recent book is *Harlem Renaissance Redux* (2019). *Black Detroit: A People's History of Self-Determination* (2017) received several awards and was named a finalist for an NAACP Image Award. Among his other books are *The Diary of Malcolm X* (2013), co-edited with Malcolm's daughter Ilyasah Shabazz, and *By Any Means Necessary—Malcolm X: Real, Not Reinvented* (2012), co-edited with Haki Madhubuti, Ron Daniels, and Maulana Karenga. *Brotherman: The Odyssey of Black Men in America—An Anthology* (1995), co-edited with Robert Allen of the journal *Black Scholar,* won the American Book Award for nonfiction. He teaches African American history and culture at the City College of New York in Harlem, where he also lives.

DONNA BRAZILE is a veteran political strategist, a Fox News contributor, an adjunct professor at Georgetown University, and the King Endowed Chair in Public Policy at Howard University. She previously served as interim chair of the Democratic National Committee and of the DNC's Voting Rights Institute. She managed the Al Gore presidential campaign in 2000 and has lectured at more than 225 colleges and universities on race, diversity, women, leadership, and restoring civility in politics. Brazile is the author of several books, including *Hacks: The Inside Story of the Break-ins and Breakdowns That Put Donald Trump in the White House* (2017).

JERICHO BROWN is the author of *The Tradition* (2019), for which he won the Pulitzer Prize. He is the recipient of fellowships from the Guggenheim Foundation, the Radcliffe Institute for Advanced Study at Harvard, and the National Endowment for the Arts, and the winner of the Whiting Award. Brown's first book, *Please* (2008), won the American Book Award. His second book, *The New Testament* (2014), won the Anisfield-Wolf Book Award. His third collection, *The Tradition*, won the Paterson Poetry Prize and was a finalist for the National Book Award and the National Book Critics Circle Award. His poems have appeared in *The Bennington Review, BuzzFeed, Fence, jubilat, The New Republic, The New York Times, The New Yorker, The Paris Review, TIME*, and several volumes of *The Best American Poetry*. He is the director of the Creative Writing Program and a professor at Emory University.

MAHOGANY L. BROWNE is a writer, organizer, and educator, as well as executive director of Bowery Poetry Club, artistic director of Urban Word NYC, and poetry coordinator at St. Francis College. Browne has received fellowships from Agnes Gund, Air Serenbe, Cave Canem, Poets House, Mellon Research, and the Rauschenberg Foundation. She is the author of *Woke: A Young Poet's Call to Justice* (2020), *Woke Baby* (2018), *Black Girl Magic* (2018), *Kissing Caskets* (2017), and *Dear Twitter* (2010). She is also the founder of the Woke Baby Book Fair (a nationwide diverse literature campaign) and, as an Arts for Justice grantee, is excited to release her first YA novel, *Chlorine Sky*, in January 2021. She lives in Brooklyn, New York.

HOWARD BRYANT is the author of nine books—*Full Dissidence: Notes from an Uneven Playing Field* (2020), *The Heritage: Black Athletes, a Divided America, and the Politics of Patriotism* (2018), *The Last Hero: A Life of Henry Aaron* (2010), *Juicing the Game: Drugs, Power, and the Fight for the Soul of Major League Baseball* (2005), *Shut Out: A Story of Race and Baseball in Boston* (2002), the three-book Legends sports series for middle-grade readers, and *Sisters and Champions: The True Story of Venus and Serena Williams* (2018)—and has contributed essays to fourteen others. He is a two-time Casey Award winner, in 2003 and 2011, for best baseball book of the year, and a 2003 finalist for the Society for American Baseball Research Seymour Medal. *The Heritage* received the 2019 Nonfiction Award from the American Library Association's Black Caucus and the Harry Shaw and Katrina Hazard Donald Award for Outstanding Work in African American Studies. He has been senior writer for ESPN since 2007 and has served as the sports correspondent for NPR's *Weekend Edition Saturday* since 2006. He has won numerous awards, was a finalist for the National Magazine Award for commentary in 2016 and 2018, and earned the 2016 Salute to Excellence Award from the National Association of Black Journalists. In addition, Bryant has appeared in several documentaries, including *Baseball: The Tenth Inning* and *Jackie Robinson,* both directed by Ken Burns, and *Major League Legends: Hank Aaron,* produced by the Smithsonian and Major League Baseball. In 2017 he served as the guest editor for the *Best American Sports Writing* anthology.

Brandon R. Byrd is a scholar of Black intellectual and social history and an assistant professor of history at Vanderbilt University. He is the author of *The Black Republic: African Americans and the Fate of Haiti* (2020). His current research projects include a grassroots and transnational history of the postslavery United States, tentatively titled *Prophets, Vagabonds, and Princes: A History of Emancipation.*

Charles E. ("Charlie") Cobb, Jr., is a veteran of SNCC who served as a field secretary for the organization in Mississippi in 1962–67. He is the author of several books about the civil rights struggle, most recently *This Nonviolent Stuff'll Get You Killed: How Guns Made the Civil Rights Movement Possible* (2014). He is a board member of the SNCC Legacy Project, which in collaboration with Duke University in 2017 launched a digital gateway into SNCC and its work (snccdigital.org). As a journalist, Cobb has worked for NPR and *Frontline.* He was the first Black staff writer for *National Geographic* magazine, in 1985–97. He is a co-founder of the National Association of Black Journalists. In June 2018, he received a Carnegie Fellowship for his latest book project, describing and analyzing the young Movement for Black Lives.

William A. ("Sandy") Darity, Jr., is the Samuel DuBois Cook Professor of Public Policy, African and African American Studies, Economics, and Business at Duke University. He is the founding director of the Samuel DuBois Cook Center on Social Equity, and he has served as chair of Duke's department of African and African American studies. Darity's research focuses on inequality by race, class, and ethnicity; stratification economics; schooling and the racial achievement gap; North-South theories of trade and development; skin shade and labor market outcomes; the economics of reparations; the Atlantic slave trade, the Industrial Revolution, and the history of economics; and the social-psychological effects of exposure to unemployment. In 2017 he was named to the *Politico* 50 list of the most influential policy thinkers over the course of the previous year, and he was honored by the Center for Global Policy Solutions with an award recognizing his work in the development of the effort to study and reverse racial wealth disparities in the United States. He holds a PhD in economics from MIT and has published or edited thirteen books and more than 300 articles in professional journals. His most recent book, co-authored with Kirsten Mullen, is *From Here to Equality: Reparations for Black Americans in the 21st Century* (2020).

Through her activism and scholarship over many decades, **ANGELA Y. DAVIS** has been deeply involved in movements for social justice around the world. Her work as an educator—both at the university level and in the larger public sphere—has always emphasized the importance of building communities of struggle for economic, racial, and gender justice. She is the author of ten books, including *Women, Race and Class* (1981), *Blues Legacies and Black Feminisms: Gertrude "Ma" Rainey, Bessie Smith, and Billie Holiday* (1998), *Are Prisons Obsolete?* (2003), *The Meaning of Freedom and Other Difficult Dialogues* (2003), and most recently, *Freedom Is a Constant Struggle: Ferguson, Palestine, and the Foundations of a Movement* (2015). She draws upon her own experiences in the early seventies as a person who spent eighteen months in jail and on trial after being placed on the FBI's Ten Most Wanted List. Having helped to popularize the notion of a "prison industrial complex," she now urges her audiences to think seriously about the future possibility of a world without carceral systems and to help forge a twenty-first-century abolitionist movement.

SYLVIANE A. DIOUF, a visiting scholar at the Center for the Study of Slavery and Justice at Brown University, is an award-winning historian and curator of the African diaspora. She has authored and edited thirteen acclaimed books, including *Slavery's Exiles: The Story of the American Maroons* (2014), *Servants of Allah: African Muslims Enslaved in the Americas* (1998), and *Dreams of Africa in Alabama: The Slave Ship "Clotilda" and the Story of the Last Africans Brought to America* (2007). She has curated twelve exhibitions. Dr. Diouf has received the Rosa Parks Award, the Pen and Brush Achievement Award, and the Dr. Betty Shabazz Achievement Award; has appeared in several documentaries; and gave a keynote speech to the UN General Assembly on the International Day of Remembrance of the Victims of Slavery and the Transatlantic Slave Trade. She was the inaugural director of the Lapidus Center for the Historical Analysis of Transatlantic Slavery at the Schomburg Center for Research in Black Culture.

DEBORAH DOUGLAS is the Eugene S. Pulliam Distinguished Visiting Professor of Journalism at DePauw University and a senior leader with the OpEd Project, leading fellowships and programs at organizations that include the University of Texas at Austin, Dartmouth College, Columbia University, Urgent Action Fund in South Africa and Kenya, and Youth Narrating Our World. While teaching at her alma mater, Northwestern University's Medill School, she created a graduate investigative journalism capstone on the Civil Rights Act of 1964 and taught best practices in Karachi, Pakistan. An award-winning journalist and the first managing editor of *MLK50: Justice Through Journalism,* Douglas is author of *U.S. Civil Rights Trail: A Traveler's Guide to the People, Places, and Events That Made the Movement* (2021).

MICHELLE DUSTER is a writer, speaker, professor, and advocate for racial and gender equity in public history. She has initiated and supported dozens of local, state, and national initiatives for street names, markers, murals, and monuments to honor her paternal great-grandmother, Ida B. Wells-Barnett, and other African American female historic figures. She has worked on PBS documentary films and organized several film festivals. She has written articles for *The North Star, HuffPost,* and other publications, and she has authored, edited, or contributed to sixteen books, including *Ida B. the Queen* (2021), *Michelle Obama's Impact on African American Women and Girls* (2018), *Ida from Abroad* (2010), and *Ida in Her Own Words* (2008). Born and raised on the South Side of Chicago, she has received numerous awards, including the 2019 Martin Luther King Jr. Social Justice Award from Dartmouth College and the Multi-Generational Activist Award from the Illinois Human Rights Commission.

CRYSTAL N. FEIMSTER is an associate professor in the department of African American Studies, the American studies program, and the history department at Yale University. She earned her PhD in history from Princeton University and her BA in history and women's studies from the University of North Carolina at Chapel Hill. She is the author of *Southern Horrors: Women and the Politics of Rape and Lynching* (2009). She is currently completing a manuscript, *Truth Be Told: Rape and Mutiny in Civil War Louisiana.*

JAMES FORMAN, JR., is the J. Skelly Wright Professor of Law at Yale Law School. He attended public schools in Detroit and New York City before graduating from the Atlanta public schools. After attending Brown University and Yale Law School, he worked as a law clerk for Justice Sandra Day O'Connor of the U.S. Supreme Court. After clerking, he took a job at the Public Defender Service in Washington, D.C., where he represented juveniles and adults in felony and misdemeanor cases. In 1997 he co-founded the Maya Angelou Public Charter School, an alternative school for youth who have struggled in school, dropped out, or been arrested. The school recently celebrated its twentieth anniversary. His first book, *Locking Up Our Own: Crime and Punishment in Black America* (2017), was awarded the Pulitzer Prize for General Nonfiction.

ALICIA GARZA is an organizer, political strategist, and cheeseburger enthusiast. She is the principal at the Black Futures Lab and the Black to the Future Action Fund; the co-creator of #BlackLivesMatter and the Black Lives Matter Global Network; strategy and partnerships director for the National Domestic Workers Alliance; and host of the podcast *Lady Don't Take No.* Her first book was *The Purpose of Power: How We Come Together When We Fall Apart* (2020).

ANNETTE GORDON-REED is the Carl M. Loeb University Professor at Harvard. Gordon-Reed won sixteen book prizes, including the Pulitzer Prize in History in 2009 and the National Book Award in 2008, for *The Hemingses of Monticello: An American Family* (2008). In addition to articles and reviews, her other works include *Thomas Jefferson and Sally Hemings: An American Controversy* (1997); *Vernon Can Read! A Memoir,* a collaboration with Vernon Jordan (2001); *Race on Trial: Law and Justice in American History* (2002); a volume of essays that she edited, *Andrew Johnson* (2010); and, most recently, with Peter S. Onuf, *"Most Blessed of the Patriarchs": Thomas Jefferson and the Empire of the Imagination* (2016). Gordon-Reed was the Vyvyan Harmsworth Visiting Professor of American History at the University of Oxford (Queen's College) in 2014–15. Between 2010 and 2015, she was the Carol K. Pforzheimer Professor at the Radcliffe Institute for Advanced Study at Harvard University. She was the 2018–19 president of the Society for Historians of the Early American Republic and she is the current president of the Ames Foundation. A selected list of her honors includes a fellowship from the Dorothy and Lewis B. Cullman Center for Scholars and Writers at the New York Public Library, a Guggenheim Fellowship in the humanities, a MacArthur Fellowship, the National Humanities Medal, the National Book Award, the Frederick Douglass Book Prize, the George Washington Book Prize, and the Anisfield-Wolf Book Prize. Gordon-Reed was elected a fellow of the American Academy of Arts and Sciences in

2011 and was a member of the Academy's Commission on the Humanities and Social Sciences. In 2019 she was elected as a member of the American Philosophical Society.

FARAH JASMINE GRIFFIN is the inaugural chair of the African American and African diaspora studies department at Columbia University. She is also the William B. Ransford Professor of English and Comparative Literature. She received her BA from Harvard and her PhD in American studies from Yale. She is the author of *Who Set You Flowin?: The African American Migration Narrative* (1995), *Beloved Sisters and Loving Friends: Letters from Rebecca Primus of Royal Oak, Maryland, and Addie Brown of Hartford Connecticut, 1854–1868* (1999), *If You Can't Be Free, Be a Mystery: In Search of Billie Holiday* (2001), and *Harlem Nocturne: Women Artists and Progressive Politics During World War II* (2013). She is the co-author, with Salim Washington, of *Clawing at the Limits of Cool: Miles Davis, John Coltrane, and the Greatest Jazz Collaboration Ever* (2008).

KALI NICOLE GROSS is the Martin Luther King, Jr. Professor of History at Rutgers University in New Brunswick. Her research explores Black women's experiences in the U.S. criminal justice system. Her opinion pieces have been published by BBC News, *HuffPost,* and *The Washington Post,* and she has appeared on NPR and C-SPAN. She has authored two award-winning books: *Colored Amazons: Crime, Violence, and Black Women in the City of Brotherly Love, 1880–1910* (2006) and *Hannah Mary Tabbs and the Disembodied Torso: A Tale of Race, Sex, and Violence in America* (2016). Her latest book, co-authored with Daina Ramey Berry, is *A Black Women's History of the United States* (2020).

ALEXIS PAULINE GUMBS portrayed Phillis Wheatley in first grade in the Black History Month play at her all-white private school. She wrote her first literary essay, on June Jordan's "The Difficult Miracle of Black Poetry in America: Something Like a Sonnet for Phillis Wheatley," while in her first year at Barnard College, which is also June Jordan's alma mater. Gumbs is the author of *Spill: Scenes of Black Feminist Fugitivity* (2016), *M Archive: After the End of the World* (2018), and *Dub: Finding Ceremony* (2020), and is co-editor of *Revolutionary Mothering: Love on the Front Lines* (2016). She is the founder of Brilliance Remastered, creative writing editor for *Feminist Studies,* and celebrant in residence at NorthStar Church of the Arts in Durham, North Carolina, where she and her partner, Sangodare, are creating an intergenerational living library of Black Queer Brilliance.

BEVERLY GUY-SHEFTALL is the founding director of the Women's Research and Resource Center (1981) and Anna Julia Cooper Professor of Women's Studies at Spelman College. She has published a number of texts in African American and women's studies that have been noted as important works by other scholars, including the first anthology on Black women's literature, *Sturdy Black Bridges: Visions of Black Women in Literature* (1979), which she co-edited with Roseann P. Bell and Bettye Parker Smith; her dissertation, *Daughters of Sorrow: Attitudes Toward Black Women, 1880–1920* (1990); and *Words of Fire: An Anthology of African American Feminist Thought* (1995). Her most recent publication is an anthology co-edited with Johnnetta B. Cole, *Who Should Be First?: Feminists Speak Out on the 2008 Presidential Campaign* (2010). In 1983 she became founding co-editor of *Sage: A Scholarly Journal of Black Women,* devoted exclusively to the experiences of women of African descent. She is the past president of the National Women's Studies Association and was recently elected to the American Academy of Arts and Sciences (2017).

NIKOLE HANNAH-JONES is a Pulitzer Prize–winning reporter covering racial injustice for *The New York Times Magazine* and creator of the landmark *1619 Project.* In 2017 she received a MacArthur Foundation Fellowship, known as the Genius Grant, for her work on educational inequality. She has also won a Peabody Award, two George Polk Awards, three National Magazine Awards, and the 2018 John Chancellor Award for Excellence in Journalism from Columbia University. In 2016 she co-founded the Ida B. Wells Society for Investigative Reporting, a training and mentorship organization geared toward increasing the numbers of investigative reporters of color.

MICHAEL HARRIOT is an award-winning journalist with *The Root,* where he covers the intersection of race, politics, and culture. He earned degrees in mass communications and history from Auburn University and a master's in international business and macroeconomics from Florida State University. He was a 2018 fellow at the John Jay College of Criminal Justice Center on Media, Crime, and Justice and created the curriculum for the course "Race as an Economic Construct." He is also a heralded spoken word poet and won the National Association of Black Journalists Award for television newswriting and digital commentary. A native of Hartsville, South Carolina, he currently resides in Birmingham, Alabama.

MARY E. HICKS is an assistant professor of Black studies and history at Amherst College. She has served as a Mamolen Fellow at Harvard University, as well as a

Ford Fellow and Jefferson Fellow. Her research examines the maritime dimensions of the African diaspora, with a particular focus on eighteenth- and early-nineteenth-century colonial Brazil. She is the author of "Financing the Luso-Atlantic Slave Trade: Collective Investment Practices from Portugal to Brazil, 1500–1840" and "Transatlantic Threads of Meaning: West African Textile Entrepreneurship in Salvador da Bahia, 1770–1870," both published in the journal *Slavery & Abolition*. Her forthcoming book is *Captive Cosmopolitans: Black Mariners and the World of South Atlantic Slavery, 1721–1835*.

DaMaris B. Hill is the author of *A Bound Woman Is a Dangerous Thing: The Incarceration of African American Women from Harriet Tubman to Sandra Bland* (2020), which was nominated for the NAACP Image Award for Outstanding Literary Work in Poetry, *The Fluid Boundaries of Suffrage and Jim Crow: Staking Claims in the American Heartland* (2016), and *\Vi-zə-bəl\ \Teks-chərs\ (Visible Textures)* (2015). She has a keen interest in the work of Toni Morrison and theories regarding "rememory" as a philosophy and aesthetic practice. Similar to her creative process, Hill's scholarly research is interdisciplinary. Hill is an associate professor of English, creative writing, and African American studies at the University of Kentucky.

Allyson Hobbs is an associate professor of American history, the director of African and African American studies, and the Kleinheinz Family University Fellow in Undergraduate Education at Stanford University. She is a contributing writer to *The New Yorker*. Her work has been published in *The New York Times, The New York Times Book Review,* and *The Washington Post*. She has appeared on C-SPAN, MSNBC, and NPR. Her first book, *A Chosen Exile: A History of Racial Passing in American Life* (2014), won the Organization of American Historians' Frederick Jackson Turner Prize for best first book in American history, and the Lawrence Levine Prize for best book in American cultural history. The book was selected as a *New York Times Book Review* Editors' Choice and a *San Francisco Chronicle* Best Book, and it was listed by *The Root* as one of the Best 15 Nonfiction Books by Black Authors.

Tera W. Hunter is the Edwards Professor of American History and a professor of African American studies at Princeton University. She is a scholar of labor, gender, race, and Southern history. Her most recent book is *Bound in Wedlock: Slave and Free Black Marriage in the Nineteenth Century* (2017), which won the Stone Book Award, Museum of African American History; the Mary Nickliss Prize, Organization of American Historians; the Joan Kelly Memorial Prize and the Littleton-Griswold Prize, American Historical Association; the Willie Lee Rose Book Award, Southern Association of Women's Historians; and the Deep South Book Prize, Frances S. Sumersell Center for the Study of the South. It was also a finalist for the Lincoln Prize, Gettysburg College, and the Gilder Lehrman Institute. *To 'Joy My Freedom: Southern Black Women's Lives and Labors After the Civil War* (1997) also won multiple awards. She co-edited *Dialogues of Dispersal: Gender, Sexuality and African Diasporas* (2004) with Sandra Gunning and Michele Mitchell and *African American Urban Studies: Perspectives from the Colonial Period to the Present* (2004) with Joe W. Trotter and Earl Lewis. She has been a fellow at the National Humanities Center and the Radcliffe Institute for Advanced Study at Harvard University. A native of Miami, Florida, she received a BA from Duke University and a PhD from Yale University.

SHERRILYN IFILL is the president and director-counsel of the NAACP Legal Defense and Educational Fund (LDF), the nation's premier civil rights law organization fighting for racial justice and equality. LDF was founded in 1940 by legendary civil rights lawyer (and later Supreme Court justice) Thurgood Marshall, and became a separate organization from the NAACP in 1957. The lawyers at LDF developed and executed the legal strategy that led to the Supreme Court's decision in *Brown v. Board of Education*, widely regarded as the most transformative and monumental legal decision of the twentieth century. Ifill is the second woman to lead the organization.

KELLIE CARTER JACKSON is the Knafel Assistant Professor of the Humanities in the department of Africana studies at Wellesley College. Her book *Force and Freedom: Black Abolitionists and the Politics of Violence* (2019) won the James H. Broussard Best First Book Prize, was a finalist for the Stone Book Award at the Museum of African American History, and was named among thirteen books to read on African American history by *The Washington Post*. She is co-editor of *Reconsidering Roots: Race, Politics, and Memory*. Her essays have been featured in *The Washington Post*, *The Atlantic*, the *Los Angeles Times*, NPR, *TIME*, *Transition*, *The Conversation*, *Black Perspectives*, and *Quartz*. She has also been interviewed for her expertise by MSNBC, SkyNews (UK), *The New York Times*, PBS, *Vox*, *HuffPost*, C-SPAN, the BBC, Boston Public Radio, Al Jazeera International, and *Slate*. She has been featured in a host of documentaries on history and race in the United States.

MITCHELL S. JACKSON's debut novel, *The Residue Years* (2013), received wide critical praise and won a Whiting Award as well as the Ernest J. Gaines Prize for

Literary Excellence. His honors include fellowships from the New York Public Library's Cullman Center, the Lannan Foundation, the Ford Foundation, PEN America, TED, the New York Foundation for the Arts, and the Center for Fiction. His writing has appeared in *The New Yorker, Harper's, The New York Times Book Review, The Paris Review, The Guardian, TIME, Esquire,* and elsewhere. The author of the nonfiction book *Survival Math: Notes on an All-American Family* (2019), he teaches creative writing at the University of Chicago.

KARINE JEAN-PIERRE is a seasoned political operative whose professional experience includes running presidential campaigns, leading grassroots activism, and working in the Obama White House. During the 2020 campaign cycle, Jean-Pierre drove strategy and executed major initiatives for the Biden-Harris presidential campaign as senior adviser to the campaign and chief of staff to the vice presidential nominee, Senator Kamala Harris. Prior to this, she served as the chief public affairs officer for MoveOn, one of the nation's largest grassroots progressive organizations, and as a political analyst for NBC and MSNBC. Jean-Pierre is a veteran of electoral and advocacy campaigns on a local, state, and national level. She served as the deputy campaign manager for Martin O'Malley for President in 2016, and she led the ACLU's Reproductive Freedom Initiative as campaign manager. In 2013 she managed Tish James's successful campaign for New York City Public Advocate. Jean-Pierre is proud to be an alumna of the Obama White House and both the 2008 and 2012 presidential campaigns. In 2011 Jean-Pierre served as deputy battleground states director for President Obama's reelection campaign, managing the president's political engagement in key states while leading the delegate selection and ballot access process. Before joining the 2012 campaign, she served as the regional political director for the White House Office of Political Affairs. She was the Southeast regional political director on the Obama for America campaign in 2008, and served the John Edwards for President campaign in the same capacity earlier in the 2008 election cycle.

MARTHA S. JONES is a legal and cultural historian whose work examines how Black Americans have shaped the history of democracy. She is the award-winning author of *Vanguard: How Black Women Broke Barriers, Won the Vote, and Insisted on Equality for All* (2020), *Birthright Citizens: A History of Race and Rights in Antebellum America* (2008), and *"All Bound Up Together": The Woman Question in African-American Public Culture, 1830–1900* (2007). Her work has been featured in *The New York Times, The Washington Post, The Atlantic, USA Today, TIME,* and *The Chronicle of Higher Education.* She lives in Baltimore, where she is the Society of Black Alumni Presidential Professor and a professor of history at the SNF Agora Institute at Johns Hopkins University.

ROBERT JONES, JR., is the author of the novel *The Prophets* (2021). Born and raised in New York City, he has written for numerous publications, including *The New York Times, Essence,* and *The Paris Review*. He is the creator of the social justice social-media community Son of Baldwin, which can be found on Facebook, Instagram, and Twitter.

PENIEL JOSEPH holds a joint professorship appointment at the Lyndon B. Johnson School of Public Affairs and in the history department in the College of Liberal Arts at the University of Texas at Austin. He is the founding director of the LBJ School's Center for the Study of Race and Democracy. In addition to being a frequent commentator on issues of race, democracy, and civil rights, Joseph wrote the award-winning books *Waiting 'Til the Midnight Hour: A Narrative History of Black Power in America* (2006) and *Dark Days, Bright Nights: From Black Power to Barack Obama* (2010). His most recent book, *Stokely: A Life* (2014), has been called the definitive biography of Stokely Carmichael, the man who popularized the phrase "Black Power." He edited *The Black Power Movement: Rethinking the Civil Rights–Black Power Era* (2006) and *Neighborhood Rebels: Black Power at the Local Level* (2010).

BLAIR L. M. KELLEY is assistant dean for interdisciplinary studies and international programs in the College of Humanities and Social Sciences and associate professor of history at North Carolina State University. She is the author of *Right to Ride: Streetcar Boycotts and African American Citizenship in the Era of Plessy v. Ferguson* (2010), which won the prestigious Letitia Woods Brown Memorial Book Award from the Association of Black Women Historians. Kelley is currently at work on *Black Folk: The Promise of the Black Working Class,* which will be published by Liveright, an imprint of W. W. Norton.

ROBIN D. G. KELLEY is a professor of history at UCLA. His books include *Thelonious Monk: The Life and Times of an American Original* (2009), *Freedom Dreams: The Black Radical Imagination* (2002), and *Hammer and Hoe: Alabama Communists During the Great Depression* (1990).

DONIKA KELLY is the author of the chapbook *Aviarium* (2017) and the full-length collections *The Renunciations* (forthcoming) and *Bestiary* (2016), winner of the Cave Canem Poetry Prize, a Hurston/Wright Legacy Award for Poetry, and the Kate Tufts Discovery Award. She is a Cave Canem graduate fellow and member of the collective Poets at the End of the World. She currently lives in Iowa City and is an assistant professor at the University of Iowa, where she teaches creative writing.

BAKARI KITWANA is an internationally known cultural critic, journalist, activist, and thought leader in the area of hip-hop and Black youth political engagement. In 2020 he co-founded the Hip-Hop Political Education Coalition, which convened a major virtual summit on the ways the coronavirus pandemic has exacerbated voter suppression efforts in Black and Brown communities. That convening builds on Kitwana's work as executive director of Rap Sessions, which for the last fifteen years has conducted more than a hundred town hall meetings around the nation on difficult dialogues facing the hip-hop and millennial generations. Kitwana has been editor in chief of *The Source,* editorial director of Third World Press, and the co-founder of the 2004 National Hip-Hop Political Convention, and he served on the organizing committee for the 2013 Black Youth Project convening that launched the millennial Black activist group BYP100. The author of the groundbreaking book *The Hip-Hop Generation* (2002), Kitwana is also the author of *Why White Kids Love Hip-Hop* (2005), collaborating writer for pioneering hip-hop artist Rakim's memoir *Sweat the Technique: Revelations on Creativity from the Lyrical Genius* (2019), and co-editor of the anthology *Democracy Unchained: How to Rebuild Government for the People* (2020). As the 2019–20 Nasir Jones Hiphop Fellow at the Hutchins Center for African and African American Research at Harvard University, he curated the Hiphop and Presidential Elections Video Archive, a collection of more thirty national town hall meetings with hip-hop artists, activists, and scholars during the 2008, 2012, and 2016 presidential elections.

KIESE LAYMON is a Black Southern writer from Jackson, Mississippi. His bestselling memoir *Heavy: An American Memoir* (2018) won the 2019 Andrew Carnegie Medal for Excellence in Nonfiction, the 2018 Christopher Isherwood Prize for Autobiographical Prose, and the Austen Riggs Erikson Prize for Excellence in Mental Health Media, and was named one of the 50 Best Memoirs of the Past 50 Years by *The New York Times.* Laymon is a contributing editor at *Vanity Fair* and *Oxford American.*

CHRISTOPHER J. LEBRON is an associate professor of philosophy at Johns Hopkins University. He specializes in political philosophy, social theory, philosophy of race, and democratic ethics. His first book, *The Color of Our Shame: Race and*

Justice in Our Time (2013), won the American Political Science Association's Foundations of Political Theory Best First Book Award. His second book, *The Making of Black Lives Matter: A Brief History of an Idea* (2017), offers a brief intellectual history of the Black Lives Matter movement. He is the winner of the 2018 Hiett Prize in the Humanities, which recognizes a "career devoted to the humanities and a candidate whose work shows extraordinary promise to have a significant impact on contemporary culture." In addition to his scholarly publications, he is an active public intellectual, writing frequently for *The New York Times*'s philosophy column "The Stone," *Boston Review, The Nation, The Atlantic,* and *Billboard*.

DAVID A. LOVE is a writer, journalist, and commentator based in Philadelphia. He is a contributor to CNN Opinion, *Al Jazeera, The Grio,* and *Atlanta Black Star,* among other publications. He has taught journalism and media studies as an adjunct professor at Rutgers University and Temple University. Previously, he served as executive director of the Pennsylvania Legislative Black Caucus, executive director of Witness to Innocence, and a law clerk to two federal judges. Love received a BA in East Asian studies from Harvard University, a JD from the University of Pennsylvania Law School, and a certificate in international human rights law from the University of Oxford.

WESLEY LOWERY is a Pulitzer Prize–winning journalist and the author of *They Can't Kill Us All: Ferguson, Baltimore, and a New Era in America's Racial Justice Movement* (2016).

KYLE T. MAYS (Black/Saginaw Anishinaabe) is an assistant professor in the department of African American studies, the American Indian Studies Center, and the department of history at the University of California, Los Angeles. He is a transdisciplinary scholar of Afro-Indigenous studies, urban studies, and contemporary popular culture. He is the author of *Hip Hop Beats, Indigenous Rhymes: Modernity and Hip Hop in Indigenous North America* (2018). He has two forthcoming books: *City of Dispossessions: African Americans, Indigenous Peoples, and the Creation of Modern Detroit* and *An Afro-Indigenous History of the United States*.

BERNICE L. McFADDEN is the author of *Praise Song for the Butterflies* (2018), which was long-listed for the Women's Prize for Fiction, and *The Book of Harlan* (2016), winner of the American Book Award and the NAACP Image Award for Outstanding Literary Work. Her eight other critically acclaimed novels include

Sugar (2001), *Loving Donovan* (2003), *Gathering of Waters* (a *New York Times* Editors' Choice and one of the 100 Notable Books of 2012), and *Glorious* (2010), which was featured in *O: The Oprah Magazine* and was a finalist for the NAACP Image Award. She is a four-time Hurston/Wright Legacy Award finalist, as well as the recipient of four awards from the Black Caucus American Library Association.

HEATHER C. McGHEE advances solutions to racial and economic inequality in the United States. During her tenure as president of the inequality-focused think tank Demos (2014–18), she drafted legislation, testified before Congress, and became a regular contributor on NBC's *Meet the Press.* She led Demos's racial equity organizational transformation, resulting in a doubling of its racial diversity and growth across all measures of organizational impact. She was a leader in passing key provisions of the Dodd-Frank Wall Street Reform and Consumer Protection Act in 2010 as well as landmark consumer protections that have saved consumers over $50 billion in credit card fees. She is the chair of the board of Color of Change, the nation's largest online racial justice organization. Her first book, *The Sum of Us: What Racism Costs Everyone and How We Can Prosper Together* (2021), is forthcoming from One World.

TIYA MILES is the author of three multiple-prize-winning histories, most recently *The Dawn of Detroit: A Chronicle of Slavery and Freedom in the City of the Straits* (2017). She has published historical fiction, a study of haunted Southern sites, and academic articles and chapters, as well as op-eds in various venues. Her work has been supported by the MacArthur Foundation, the Mellon Foundation, and the National Endowment for the Humanities. Her forthcoming book, which will be released by Random House, is titled *All That She Carried: The Journey of Ashley's Sack, a Black Family Keepsake.* Miles is currently a professor of history and Radcliffe Alumnae Professor at Harvard University.

BRENTIN MOCK is a writer and editor for Bloomberg CityLab in Pittsburgh, focused on issues of racial, economic, and environmental justice.

JENNIFER L. MORGAN is a professor of history in the department of social and cultural analysis at New York University, which she also serves as chair. She is the author of *Laboring Women: Reproduction and Gender in the Making of New World Slavery* (2004) and the co-editor of *Connexions: Histories of Race and Sex in North America* (2016). Her research examines the intersections of gender and race in the Black Atlantic world. Her recent journal articles include "Partus Sequitur Ventrem: Law, Race, and Reproduction in Colonial Slavery" in *Small Axe* (2018), "Accounting for 'The Most Excruciating Torment': Trans-Atlantic Passages" in *History of the Present* (2016), and "Archives and Histories of Racial Capitalism" in *Social Text* (2015). In addition to her archival work as a historian, Morgan has published a range of essays on race, gender, and the process of "doing history," most notably "Experiencing Black Feminism" in Deborah Gray White's edited volume *Telling Histories: Black Women Historians in the Ivory Tower* (2007). Her newest work, *Reckoning with Slavery: Gender, Kinship, and Capitalism in the Early Black Atlantic*, considers colonial numeracy, racism, and the rise of the transatlantic slave trade in the seventeenth-century English Atlantic world, and will be published by Duke University Press in spring 2021.

PAMELA NEWKIRK is a professor of journalism at New York University and the author of *Diversity Inc.: The Failed Promise of a Billion-Dollar Business* (2019), *Spectacle: The Astonishing Life of Ota Benga* (2016), and *Within the Veil: Black Journalists, White Media* (2000). She is the editor of *Letters from Black America* (2011).

IJEOMA OLUO is the author of the #1 *New York Times* bestseller *So You Want to Talk About Race* (2018) and *Mediocre: The Dangerous Legacy of White Male America* (2020). Her work on race has been featured in *The New York Times* and *The Washington Post*, among many others. She has twice been named to the Root 100, and she received the 2018 Feminist Humanist Award and the 2020 Harvard Humanist of the Year Award from the American Humanist Association. She lives in Seattle, Washington.

DEIRDRE COOPER OWENS is the Linda and Charles Wilson Professor in the History of Medicine and director of the Humanities in Medicine program at the University of Nebraska, Lincoln. She is an Organization of American Historians' distinguished lecturer and a past American College of Obstetricians and Gynecologists research fellow, and has won a number of prestigious honors for her scholarly and advocacy work in reproductive and birthing justice. A popular public speaker, Dr. Cooper Owens has spoken widely across the United States and Europe. She has published articles, essays, book chapters, and think pieces on a number of issues that concern African American experiences and reproductive justice. Her first book, *Medical Bondage: Race, Gender, and the Origins of American Gynecology* (2017), won the 2018 Darlene Clark Hine Book Award from the Organization of American Historians as the best book on African American women's and gender history.

MORGAN PARKER is a poet, essayist, and novelist. She is the author of the California Book Award–nominated young adult novel *Who Put This Song On?* (2019) and the poetry collections *Other People's Comfort Keeps Me Up at Night* (2015), *There Are More Beautiful Things Than Beyoncé* (2017), and *Magical Negro* (2019), which won the 2019 National Book Critics Circle Award and California Book Award. Her debut book of nonfiction is forthcoming from One World. Parker's work has appeared in such publications as *The Paris Review, The New York Times, The New York Review of Books, TIME, Best American Poetry,* and *Playbill.* She is the recipient of a National Endowment for the Arts Literature Fellowship, the winner of a Pushcart Prize, and a Cave Canem graduate fellow. She lives in Los Angeles.

NAKIA D. PARKER is a College of Social Science dean's research associate in the Department of History at Michigan State University. Her research and teaching interests include slavery, migration, African American history, and Native American history. Her current book manuscript, *Trails of Tears and Freedom: Black Life in Indian Slave Country, 1830–1866,* examines the forced migrations, labor practices, kinship networks, and resistance strategies of people of African and Afro-Native descent in Choctaw and Chickasaw slaveholding communities. In addition to her academic articles, her research has been featured on several public history websites and television, including The History Channel, *Teaching Hard History,* and *15 Minute History.*

IMANI PERRY currently serves as the Hughes-Rogers Professor of African American Studies at Princeton University. She joined the faculty at Princeton in 2009, after seven years as a professor at Rutgers School of Law, where she taught constitutional law, contracts, and U.S. legal history. She is the author of six books, including *Prophets of the Hood: Politics and Poetics in Hip Hop* (2004), *More Beautiful and More Terrible: The Embrace and Transcendence of Racial Inequality in the United States* (2011), *Vexy Thing: On Gender and Liberation* (2018), and *May We Forever Stand: A History of the Black National Anthem* (2018). Her next book, *South to America: A Journey,* will be published in summer 2021 by Ecco. This book is a travel narrative in the tradition of Albert Murray's *South to a Very Old Place* and V. S. Naipaul's *A Turn in the South.*

JOHN A. POWELL is director of the Othering and Belonging Institute and professor of law, African American studies, and ethnic studies at the University of California, Berkeley. He was previously the executive director at the Kirwan Institute for the Study of Race and Ethnicity at the Ohio State University, and prior to that, the founder and director of the Institute for Race and Poverty at the University of Minnesota. powell formerly served as the national legal director of the American Civil Liberties Union. He is a co-founder of the Poverty & Race Research Action Council and serves on the boards of several national and international organizations. powell led the development of an "opportunity-based" model that connects affordable housing to education, health, healthcare, and employment and is well known for his work developing the frameworks of "targeted universalism" and "othering and belonging" to effect equity-based interventions. He has taught at numerous law schools, including those at Harvard and Columbia universities. His latest book is *Racing to Justice: Transforming Our Concepts of Self and Other to Build an Inclusive Society* (2012).

LAURENCE RALPH is a professor of anthropology at Princeton University, and before that was a professor at Harvard University for nearly a decade. His research explores how police abuse, mass incarceration, and the drug trade make disease, disability, and premature death seem natural for urban residents of color, who are often seen as disposable. Ralph's first book, *Renegade Dreams* (2014), received the C. Wright Mills Award, one of the most prestigious honors in the social sciences. His second book, *The Torture Letters* (2020), explores a decades-long scandal related to hundreds of Black men who were tortured in police custody. He has been awarded a number of prestigious fellowships for his research, including grants from the National Science Foundation, the Wenner Gren Foundation, the Carnegie Corporation of New York, and the National Research Council of the National Academies. He earned his PhD and master's degrees in anthropology from the University of Chicago, and a bachelor of science degree from Georgia Institute of Technology, where he majored in history, technology, and society. Ralph's writing has been featured in *The Paris Review, The New York Times, The New York Review of Books, The Nation, The Chicago Review of Books, Boston Review,* and *Foreign Affairs,* to name a few.

ISHMAEL REED is the author of novels, plays, poetry, and nonfiction, and has received prizes in every category. His novel *Mumbo Jumbo* has been cited by Harold Bloom as one of five hundred great books of the Western canon. He has received the MacArthur Fellowship and is one of a handful of authors to be nominated for two National Book Awards within the same year. He is also a songwriter whose songs have been recorded by Gregory Porter, Cassandra Wilson, Macy Gray, Taj Mahal, and Bobby Womack. His poem "Just Rollin' Along," about the 1934 encounter between Bonnie and Clyde and Oakland Blues artist L. C. Good Rockin' Robinson was chosen for *The Best American Poetry 2019.* It is also included in *Why the Black Hole Sings the Blues: Poems 2007–2019* (2020). Also published in 2020, from Archway Books, is Reed's ninth and newest play, *The Haunting of Lin-Manuel Miranda*, which premiered at the Nuyorican Poets Cafe in May 2019. His audio book *Malcolm and Me* (2020) is available from Audible. *The Terrible Fours*, the third novel in his "Terrible" series, will be published by Baraka Books in spring 2021. His online literary magazine, *Konch*, can be found at www.ishmaelreedpub.com.

JUSTIN PHILLIP REED is an American writer and amateur bass guitarist whose preoccupations include horror cinema, poetic form, morphological transgressions, and uses of the grotesque. He is the author of two poetry collections, *The Malevolent Volume* (2020) and *Indecency* (2018), both published by Coffee House Press. Born and raised in South Carolina, he participates in vague spirituality and alternative rock music cultures and enjoys smelling like outside.

RUSSELL RICKFORD, an associate professor of history at Cornell University, specializes in the Black radical tradition and African American political culture after World War II. His most recent book, *We Are an African People: Independent Education, Black Power, and the Radical Imagination* (2019), received the Liberty Legacy Award from the Organization of American Historians. He is currently working on a book about Guyana and African American radical politics in the 1970s. His scholarly articles have appeared in the *Journal of American History, Journal of African American History, Souls, New Labor Review,* and other publications. His popular writing has appeared in *In These Times, Truthout, The Washington Post,* and *CounterPunch*.

DOROTHY E. ROBERTS is the fourteenth Penn Integrates Knowledge Professor and George A. Weiss University Professor at University of Pennsylvania, with joint appointments in the departments of Africana studies and sociology and at the Law School, where she is the inaugural Raymond Pace and Sadie Tanner Mossell Alexander Professor of Civil Rights. She is also founding director of the Penn Program on Race, Science, and Society. Internationally recognized for her work on racism in science, medicine, and legal institutions, Roberts is author of *Killing the Black Body: Race, Reproduction, and the Meaning of Liberty* (1998), *Shattered Bonds: The Color of Child Welfare* (2003), *Fatal Invention: How Science, Politics, and Big Business Re-create Race in the Twenty-First Century* (2012), and more than one hundred scholarly articles and book chapters, as well as co-editor of six books. Her honors include election to the National Academy of Medicine and receiving the Society of Family Planning Lifetime Achievement Award.

WALTER C. RUCKER is a professor of African American studies and history at Emory University. He is a specialist in early Atlantic African diaspora and African American history; his teaching and research focus on the generative nexus between slave resistance and culture in the formation of neo-African ethnic groups in the western hemisphere. His books include *Gold Coast Diasporas: Identity, Culture, and Power* (2015), *The River Flows On: Black Resistance, Culture, and Identity Formation in Early America* (2005), a co-edited two-volume work entitled *The Encyclopedia of American Race Riots* (2006), and a co-edited three-volume work entitled *The Encyclopedia of African American History* (2010). In addition, he has published a range of book chapters and articles appearing in the *Journal of Negro History, The Journal of Black Studies,* and *The Black Scholar.*

MAURICE CARLOS RUFFIN is the author of *We Cast a Shadow* (2019), published by One World. The novel was a finalist for the PEN/Faulkner Award. It was long-listed for the PEN America Open Book Prize, the Center for Fiction Prize, and the Aspen Words Literary Prize, and was also a *New York Times* Editor's Choice. Ruffin is the winner of several literary prizes, including the Iowa Review Award in fiction and the William Faulkner–William Wisdom Creative Writing Competition Award for Novel-in-Progress. His work has appeared in *The New York Times*, the *Los Angeles Times*, the *Oxford American, Garden & Gun*, and *Kenyon Review*. A New Orleans native, Ruffin is a professor of creative writing at Louisiana State University, and the 2020–21 John and Renee Grisham Writer-in-Residence at the University of Mississippi. His next book, *The Ones Who Don't Say They Love You*, will be published by One World in 2021.

EUGENE SCOTT joined *The Washington Post* in September 2017 to report on the politics of identity in the Trump era. He previously worked at CNN Politics, where he covered the 2016 presidential election and was a senior reporter on the website's breaking news team. He is a regular on-air contributor, providing analysis on MSNBC, CBS, and NPR. Before receiving his master's from Harvard University's Kennedy School of Government, where he was a researcher for *TIME*, he spent nearly a decade writing for the *USA Today* network in Phoenix. He is on the board of advisers at UNC's Hussman School of Journalism and Media and was recently a fellow at the Georgetown University Institute of Politics.

CHET'LA SEBREE is the author of the forthcoming *Field Study* (2021), winner of the 2020 James Laughlin Award from the Academy of American Poets, and *Mistress* (2019), winner of the 2018 New Issues Poetry Prize and nominated for a

2020 NAACP Image Award. She is an assistant professor of English and the director of the Stadler Center for Poetry & Literary Arts at Bucknell University.

ADAM SERWER is a staff writer at *The Atlantic*. In 2019 he won the Sidney Hillman award for commentary.

BARBARA SMITH is an author, activist, and independent scholar who has played a groundbreaking role in opening up a national cultural and political dialogue about the intersections of race, class, sexuality, and gender. She was among the first to define an African American women's literary tradition and to build Black women's studies and Black feminism in the United States. She has been politically active in many movements for social justice since the 1960s. *Ain't Gonna Let Nobody Turn Me Around: Forty Years of Movement Building with Barbara Smith* was published in 2014 by SUNY Press. A biography of Smith by Joseph R. Fitzgerald is forthcoming.

CLINT SMITH is a staff writer at *The Atlantic* and author of the poetry collection *Counting Descent* (2016), which won the award for best poetry collection from the Black Caucus of the American Library Association and was a finalist for an NAACP Image Award. He is also the author of the forthcoming narrative nonfiction book *How the Word Is Passed* (2021). His writing has been published in *The New Yorker*, *The New York Times Magazine*, *Poetry Magazine*, *The Paris Review*, and elsewhere. Smith received his BA from Davidson College and a PhD in education from Harvard University.

PATRICIA SMITH is the author of eight books of poetry, including *Incendiary Art* (2017), winner of the 2018 Kingsley Tufts Award, the 2017 Los Angeles Times Book Prize, and the 2018 NAACP Image Award and finalist for the 2018 Pulitzer Prize; *Shoulda Been Jimi Savannah* (2012), winner of the Lenore Marshall Prize from the Academy of American Poets; and *Blood Dazzler* (2008), a National Book Award finalist. She is a Guggenheim fellow; an NEA grant recipient; a former fellow at Civitella Ranieri, Yaddo, and MacDowell; a Cave Canem faculty member; professor in the MFA program at Sierra Nevada University; and a distinguished professor for the City University of New York.

BRENDA E. STEVENSON is the Nickoll Family Endowed Chair and a professor of history and African American studies at UCLA. Her book-length publications include *The Journals of Charlotte Forten Grimké* (1988), *Life in Black and White* (1997), *Underground Railroad* (1998), *The Contested Murder of Latasha Harlins*

(2015), and *What Is Slavery?* (2015). Her publications have garnered the Organization of American Historians' James A. Rawley Prize, the Ida B. Wells Award, and the Gustavus Meyer Outstanding Book Prize. Support for her research has come from the John Simon Guggenheim Memorial Foundation, the Ford Foundation, the Mellon Foundation, the American Association of University Women, Stanford's Center for Advanced Study of the Behavioral Sciences, the National Humanities Center, and the American Academy in Berlin. She is the recipient of the UCLA Gold Shield Award, the John Blassingame Award from the Southern Historical Society, and the Carter G. Woodson Medallion from the Association for the Study of African American Life and History.

Keeanga-Yamahtta Taylor is an assistant professor of African American studies at Princeton University. She is the author of *Race for Profit: How Banks and the Real Estate Industry Undermined Black Homeownership* (2019), which was long-listed for a National Book Award for nonfiction and a finalist for the 2020 Pulitzer Prize in History. Taylor's book *From #BlackLivesMatter to Black Liberation* (2016) won the Lannan Cultural Freedom Prize for an Especially Notable Book. She is also the editor of *How We Get Free: Black Feminism and the Combahee River Collective* (2017), which won the Lambda Literary Award for LGBTQ nonfiction. The Organization of American Historians appointed her a distinguished lecturer. Taylor is a contributing writer and columnist for *The New Yorker*.

Nafissa Thompson-Spires is an assistant professor of creative writing at Cornell University. Born and raised in Southern California, she earned a PhD in English from Vanderbilt University and an MFA in creative writing from the University of Illinois. She is the author of *Heads of the Colored People* (2018), which was long-listed for the National Book Award for fiction and was a Kirkus Prize finalist. Her work has appeared or is forthcoming in *The White Review, Los Angeles Review of Books Quarterly, StoryQuarterly, Lunch Ticket,* and *The Feminist Wire,* among other publications. She was a 2016 participant in the Callaloo Creative Writing Workshop and the 2017 Tin House Workshop, as well as a 2017 Sewanee Writers' Conference Stanley Elkin Scholar.

Salamishah Tillet is the Henry Rutgers Professor of African American and African Studies and Creative Writing at Rutgers University, Newark. She earned a BA in English and African American Studies from the University of Pennsylvania, graduating Phi Beta Kappa and magna cum laude, and received an MAT in English from Brown University and both an MA in English and a PhD in American Studies from Harvard. She is the director of New Arts Justice at Express Newark and the co-founder of A Long Walk Home, an arts organization that empowers young people to end violence against girls and women. A contributing critic at large for *The New York Times*, she is the author of *Sites of Slavery: Citizenship and Racial Democracy in the Post–Civil Rights Imagination* (2012) and *In Search of "The Color Purple": The Story of Alice Walker's Masterpiece* (2021). In 2020 Tillet received a Whiting Creative Nonfiction Grant to complete the cultural biography *All the Rage: Mississippi Goddam and the World Nina Simone Made*, forthcoming from Ecco.

JEMAR TISBY is CEO of The Witness Inc., an organization dedicated to Black uplift from a Christian perspective. He is co-host of *Pass the Mic*, a podcast that amplifies dynamic voices for a diverse church. His writing has been featured by *The Washington Post*, CNN, *The Atlantic*, and *The New York Times*. He has spoken nationwide at conferences on racial justice, U.S. history, and Christianity, and is the author of the *New York Times* bestselling *The Color of Compromise: The Truth about the American Church's Complicity in Racism* (2019) and *How to Fight Racism: Courageous Christianity and the Journey Toward Racial Justice* (2020). He studies race, religion, and social movements in the twentieth century as a PhD candidate in history at the University of Mississippi.

SASHA TURNER is an associate professor of history at Johns Hopkins University. She is the author of *Contested Bodies: Pregnancy, Childrearing, and Slavery in Jamaica* (2017), which won the Julia Cherry Spruill Book Prize from the Southern Association of Women Historians and the Berkshire Conference of Women Historians Book Prize. It received honorable mention for the Murdo J. McLeod Book Prize from the Latin American and Caribbean Section of the Southern Historical Association. She is currently working on a book on slavery and emotions. Her article "The Nameless and the Forgotten: Maternal Grief, Sacred Protection, and the Archive of Slavery," published in *Slavery and Abolition* (2017), has won awards from the African American Intellectual History Society, the Association of Black Women Historians, the Southern Association of Women Historians, the North American Conference on British Studies, and the Latin American and Caribbean Section of the Southern Historical Association.

COREY D. B. WALKER is the Wake Forest Professor of the Humanities and is jointly appointed in the department of English and the Interdisciplinary Humanities Program at Wake Forest University. He has published broadly in the areas of Africana studies; critical theory and cultural studies; and religion, ethics, and public life. Professor Walker has held faculty and academic leadership positions at Brown University, the University of Virginia, Winston-Salem State University, and Virginia Union University, and he has had visiting faculty appointments at Friedrich-Schiller Universität Jena, Union Presbyterian Seminary, and the University of Richmond.

HARRIET A. WASHINGTON's books include the forthcoming *Carte Blanche: The Erosion of Medical Consent* (2021) and *Medical Apartheid: The Dark History of Experimentation on Black Americans from Colonial Times to the Present* (2008), which won the National Book Critics Circle Award, a PEN/Oakland Award, and the American Library Association Black Caucus Nonfiction Award. She is a writing fellow in Bioethics at Harvard Medical School and a lecturer in bioethics at Columbia University, and has been a Miriam Shearing Fellow at the University of Nevada's Black Mountain Institute, a Research Fellow in Medical Ethics at Harvard Medical School, a visiting fellow at the Harvard T. H. Chan School of Public Health, a visiting scholar at DePaul University College of Law, and a senior research scholar at the National Center for Bioethics at Tuskegee University. She has also held fellowships at Stanford University and in 2016 was elected a fellow of the New York Academy of Medicine.

CRAIG STEVEN WILDER is the Barton L. Weller Professor of History at MIT and a senior fellow at the Bard Prison Initiative. His most recent book is *Ebony & Ivy: Race, Slavery, and the Troubled History of America's Universities* (2013). He is the author of *A Covenant with Color: Race and Social Power in Brooklyn* (2000) and *In the Company of Black Men: The African Influence on African American Culture in New York City* (2001). He has taught at Columbia University, Dartmouth College, and Williams College and has been a visiting professor at the New School and University College London.

ISABEL WILKERSON, winner of the Pulitzer Prize and the National Humanities Medal, has become a leading figure in narrative nonfiction, an interpreter of the human condition, and an impassioned voice for demonstrating how history can help us understand ourselves, our country, and our current era of upheaval. Through her writing, Wilkerson brings the invisible and the marginalized into the light and into our hearts. Through her lectures, she explores with authority the need to reconcile America's karmic inheritance and the origins of both our divisions and our shared commonality. Her debut work, *The Warmth of Other Suns* (2010), won the National Book Critics Circle Award, the Heartland Prize for Nonfiction, the Anisfield-Wolf Award for Nonfiction, the Lynton History Prize from Harvard and Columbia universities, and the Stephen Ambrose Oral History Prize, and was short-listed for both the Pen-Galbraith Literary Award and the Dayton Literary Peace Prize. She is a native of Washington, D.C., and a daughter of the Great Migration, the mass movement that she would go on to write about. She won the Pulitzer Prize for Feature Writing in 1994, as Chicago bureau chief for *The New York Times,* making her the first African American woman to win a Pulitzer Prize in journalism. She then devoted fifteen years and interviewed more than 1,200 people to tell the story of the 6 million people, among them her parents, who defected from the Jim Crow South. Of her new book, *Caste: The Origins of Our Discontents* (2020), the venerable UK bookseller Waterstones says it is an "expansive, lyrical and stirring account of the unspoken system of divisions that govern our world."

CHAD WILLIAMS is the Samuel J. and Augusta Spector Professor of History and African and African American Studies at Brandeis University. He is author of *Torchbearers of Democracy: African American Soldiers in the World War I Era* (2011), which received the Liberty Legacy Award from the Organization of American Historians and the Distinguished Book Award from the Society for Military History. He is co-editor of *Charleston Syllabus: Readings on Race, Racism, and Racial Violence* (2016) and *Major Problems in African American History,* second edition (2017). He has received fellowships from the Schomburg Center for Research in Black Culture, the Radcliffe Institute for Advanced Study at Harvard University, the Ford Foundation, and the Woodrow Wilson Foundation. He is currently completing a study of W.E.B. Du Bois and World War I, to be published by Farrar, Straus, and Giroux.

HEATHER ANDREA WILLIAMS is Geraldine R. Segal Professor of American Social Thought and a professor of Africana studies at the University of Pennsylvania. She was previously a professor of history at the University of North Carolina at Chapel Hill. She is the author of *Self-Taught: African American Education in Slavery and Freedom* (2005), *Help Me to Find My People: The African American Search for Family Lost in Slavery* (2012), and *American Slavery: A Very Short Introduction* (2014). She has received fellowships from the Ford Foundation, the Spencer Foundation, the Woodrow Wilson Foundation, and the Andrew W. Mellon Foundation. She is currently editing a documentary film about Jamaicans who migrated to the United States in the 1950s and '60s and is writing a book about violence in the antebellum South. She teaches courses on African American history with an emphasis on slavery and the aftermath of the American Civil War.

PHILLIP B. WILLIAMS was born in Chicago, Illinois, and is the author of the poetry collection *Thief in the Interior* (2016), winner of the Kate Tufts Discovery Award and the Lambda Literary Award. He is a recipient of a 2017 Whiting Award and a 2020 Radcliffe Fellowship. He currently teaches at Bennington College and Randolph College's low-residency MFA.

RAQUEL WILLIS is a Black transgender activist, award-winning writer, and media strategist dedicated to elevating the dignity of marginalized people, particularly Black transgender people. She is the director of communications for the Ms. Foundation, the former executive editor of *Out* magazine, and a former national organizer for Transgender Law Center (TLC). In 2018 she founded Black Trans Circles, a project of TLC focused on developing the leadership of Black trans women in the South and Midwest by creating healing justice spaces to work through oppression-based trauma and by incubating community organizing efforts to address anti-trans murder and violence. During her time at *Out*, she published the Trans Obituaries Project to highlight the epidemic of violence against trans women of color and developed a community-sourced thirteen-point framework to end the epidemic. This project won a GLAAD Media Award. Willis is a thought leader on gender, race, and intersectionality. She's experienced in online publications, organizing marginalized communities for social change, and nonprofit media strategy and public speaking while using digital activism as a major tool of resistance and liberation. She will be releasing *The Risk It Takes to Bloom,* her debut essay collection about her coming of identity and activism, with St. Martin's Press in 2021.

KAI WRIGHT is host and managing editor of WNYC's Narrative Unit. He hosts the podcast *The United States of Anxiety,* and is the former host of *There Goes the Neighborhood* (2017–19), *The Stakes* (2019), and the Dupont Award–winning *Caught: The Lives of Juvenile Justice* (2018). Before joining WNYC, Wright was an editor and columnist for *The Nation,* editorial director of *Colorlines,* and a long-time fellow of *Type Investigations.* He is the author, most recently, of *Drifting toward Love: Black, Brown, Gay, and Coming of Age on the Streets of New York* (2008).

CONTRIBUTOR CREDITS

———

INDEX

ROBERT JONES, JR. ★ PAMELA N
EUGENE SCOTT ★ ALLYSON HC
MITCHELL S. JACKSON ★ JOH
ADAM SERWER ★ JAMELLE
TERA W. HUNTER ★ WILLIAM A. D
CRYSTAL N. FEIMSTER ★ BLAIR L. M
DERRICK ALRIDGE ★ HOWARD I
ISABEL WILKERSON ★ MICHELLE I
ROBIN D. G. KELLEY ★ BERNICE
CHAD WILLIAMS ★ RUSSELL
IMANI PERRY ★ CHARLES E.
KEEANGA-YAMAHTTA T/
CHET'LA SEBREE ★ JAMES FOI
SALAMISHAH TILLET ★ ANGE
DEBORAH DOUGLAS
ALICIA GARZA ★